Corporate Fraud Handbook

Corporate Fraud Handbook

Prevention and Detection
Third Edition

Joseph T. Wells

JOHN WILEY & SONS, INC.

To my loving wife,
Judy Gregor Wells

Published by John Wiley & Sons, Inc., Hoboken, New Jersey.

Published simultaneously in Canada.

For general information on our other products and services or for technical support, please contact our Customer Care Department within the United States at (800) 762-2974, outside the United States at (317) 572-3993 or fax (317) 572-4002.

Wiley also publishes its books in a variety of electronic formats. Some content that appears in print may not be available in electronic books. For more information about Wiley products, visit our web site at www.wiley.com.

Library of Congress Cataloging-in-Publication Data:
Wells, Joseph T.
  Corporate fraud handbook : prevention and detection / Joseph T. Wells. – 3rd ed.
     p. cm.
  Includes bibliographical references and index.
  ISBN 978-0-470-63878-1 (cloth); 978-1-118-04451-3 (ebk); 978-1-118-04452-0 (ebk); 978-1-118-04453-7 (ebk)
  1. Fraud. 2. Corporations–Corrupt practices. 3. Fraud investigation. 4. Fraud–Prevention. I. Title.
  HV6691.W45 2011
  658.4'73–dc22   2010050383

Printed in the United States of America

10 9 8 7 6 5 4 3

Contents

Contents

Preface

As I wrote in my fifth book, *Occupational Fraud and Abuse*, few people begin their careers with the goal of becoming liars, cheats, and thieves. Yet that turns out to be the destiny of all too many. Corporate fraud and abuse—as we have seen in such headline-grabbing cases as Enron, WorldCom, Parmalat, and Tyco—costs organizations billions and billions annually. The losses in human terms are incalculable.

The Corporate Fraud Handbook: Prevention and Detection is for those whose job it is to reduce these losses: fraud examiners, auditors, investigators, loss prevention specialists, managers and business owners, criminologists, human resources personnel, academicians, and law enforcement professionals, among others.

There are four broad objectives of this work:

1. To detail a classification system to explain the various schemes used by executives, owners, managers, and employees to commit these offenses
2. To quantify the losses from these schemes
3. To illustrate the human factors in fraud
4. To provide guidance in preventing and detecting occupational fraud and abuse

How this book came about is a story in itself. As improbable as it seems looking back, I am well into my fourth decade in the field of fraud detection and deterrence. Like many of you, my career path did not start where it ended up. In the third grade, I distinctly remember pledging to be an astronomer. But by college, quantum physics had proved my undoing. Just a few credits shy of a math/physics degree, I switched to business school and majored in accounting.

After two years toiling in the ledgers of one of the large international auditing firms, I decided I could not stand it anymore; my life had to have more excitement. So I became a real-life, gun-toting FBI agent. Thankfully, I did not have to use my pistol too many times to track down heinous robbers. And I learned in a hurry that the expensive crimes were not the bank robberies, anyhow—they were the bank embezzlements. For the next nine years, I specialized exclusively in investigating a wide range of white-collar crimes in which the federal government was a party at interest. The cases ran the gamut, from nickel-and-dime con artists to Watergate.

My second decade was with Wells & Associates, a group of consulting criminologists concentrating on white-collar crime prevention, detection, and education. That eventually led to the formation of a professional organization, the Association of Certified Fraud Examiners. For 23 years, I have been chairman of the Board of Directors. I hope to spend the remainder of my professional career with what I have discovered to be my secret love: writing.

The Corporate Fraud Handbook: Prevention and Detection has its genesis in *Occupational Fraud and Abuse*. At the time, I was intrigued by the definition of "fraud" as classically set forth in *Black's Law Dictionary*:

> *All multifarious means which human ingenuity can devise, and which are resorted to by one individual to get an advantage over another by false suggestions or suppression of the truth. It includes all surprise, trick, cunning or dissembling, and any unfair way by which another is cheated.*

This definition implied to me that there was an almost unlimited number of ways people could think up to cheat one another. But my experience told me something else: After investigating and researching literally thousands of frauds, they seemed to fall into definite patterns. If we could somehow determine what those patterns were and in what frequency they occurred, it would aid greatly in understanding and ultimately preventing fraud. And since so much fraud occurs in the workplace, this particular area would be the starting point.

So I began a research project with the aid of over 2,000 certified fraud examiners (CFEs). They typically work for organizations in which they are responsible for aspects of fraud detection and deterrence. Each CFE provided details on exactly how their organizations were being victimized from within. That information subsequently was summarized in a document for public consumption, the *1996 Report to the Nation on Occupational Fraud and Abuse*. Since that time, the report has been published on five occasions, the latest being in 2010.

Although the reports provide a basic framework, this book is intended for a different audience—those of you who need to know all the details. You will discover that while fraud may outwardly seem complex, it rarely is. You do not need an accounting degree—just an understanding of fundamental business procedures and terminology. As the saying could go, fraud ain't rocket science.

Rather than an unlimited number of schemes, this book suggests that occupational fraud and abuse can be divided into three main categories: asset misappropriation, corruption, and fraudulent statements. From the three main categories, there are several distinct schemes identified and classified, and they are covered in detail herein.

The book begins with an overview of the complex social factors that go into creating an occupational offender. People do things for a reason, and understanding why employees engage in this behavior is the key to creating ways to prevent it. You will therefore find these pages rich in personal detail.

Following the introduction, the book is divided into chapters devoted to the specific occupational fraud and abuse schemes. Each of the chapters is organized similarly. First, a case study provides insights. Next, the scheme itself is flowcharted and the scheme variations are scheduled, along with statistics for each method. Finally, observations and conclusions on each chapter will help in devising prevention and detection strategies.

A project such as this is not a solo venture, even though I accept final responsibility for every word, right or wrong. I must first gratefully acknowledge the thousands of CFEs who provided the case examples. I am especially appreciative of the efforts of John Warren and Dawn Taylor, who did much of the detailed research. Jim Ratley, Jeanette LeVie, John Gill, Andi McNeal, and Nancy Bradford merit special recognition. Mary-Jo Kranacher provided invaluable guidance in Chapters 12 and 13. Several writers assisted in preparing case studies: Michael C. Burton, Sean Guerrero, Brett Holloway-Reeves, Katherine McLane, Suzy Spencer, and Denise Worhach.

Special thanks go to the CFEs and other professionals who furnished details of their cases: Bradley Brekke, CFE; Anthony J. Carriuolo, Esq.; H. Craig Christiansen, CFE, CPA; Harvey Creem, CFE, CPA; Jim Crowe, CFE; Harry D'Arcy, CFE; Marvin Doyal, CFE, CPA; Tonya L. DiGiuseppe, CFE, CPA; Harold Dore, CFE, CIA; Stephen Gaskell, CFE; Gerald L. Giles, Jr., CFE, CPA; Paul Granetto; James Hansen, CFE; Paul Hayes, CFE; Charles Intriago, Esq.; Terry Isbell, CFE, CIA; Douglas LeClaire, CFE; Barry Masuda, CFE; Terrence McGrane, CFE, CIA; David McGuckin, CFE; David Mensel, CFE, CPA; Dick Polhemus, CFE; Trudy Riester, CFE; Lee Roberts, CFE; Peter Roman, CFE; James Sell, CFE, CPA; Harry J. Smith III, CFE, CPA; and Donald Stine, CFE, CPA.

Finally, I must thank the one person without whom these pages would not have been written. My wife, Judy, has endured countless weekends and early mornings alone while I sat at this keyboard. She has become accustomed to me jumping up in the middle of dinner to write down a new thought on a scrap of paper. And she has done every bit of it by cheering me on, never complaining. First to Judy Gregor Wells—then to those of you trying to make a better world by reducing fraud—this book is dedicated.

Joseph T. Wells
Austin, Texas
April 2011

About the ACFE

The Association of Certified Fraud Examiners (ACFE) is the world's largest antifraud organization and premier provider of anti-fraud training and education. Together with nearly 55,000 members, the ACFE is reducing business fraud worldwide and inspiring public confidence in the integrity and objectivity within the profession.

Established in 1988, with headquarters in Austin, Texas, the ACFE supports the profession by providing expert instruction, practical tools, and innovative resources in the fight against fraud. The ACFE hosts conferences and seminars year-round while offering informative books and self-study courses written by leading practitioners to help members learn how and why fraud occurs and to build the skills needed to fight it effectively. Members of the ACFE also have the ability to expand their antifraud knowledge and assert themselves in the antifraud community by obtaining the certified fraud examiner (CFE) credential. This globally preferred certification indicates expertise in fraud prevention, deterrence, detection, and investigation.

The ACFE oversees the CFE credential by setting standards for admission, administering the Uniform CFE Examination, and maintaining and enforcing the ACFE Code of Professional Ethics. CFEs on six continents have collectively investigated more than one million suspected cases of civil and criminal fraud.

The ACFE is also committed to providing educational resources to the academic community and has established the Anti-Fraud Education Partnership to address the unprecedented need for fraud examination education at the university level. In pursuit of this objective, the ACFE has provided free training and educational materials to institutions of higher learning throughout the world.

Criminologist and former FBI agent Dr. Joseph T. Wells, CFE, CPA, is chairman and founder of the ACFE as well as an advisory member of the Board of Regents. Dr. Wells writes, researches, and lectures to business and professional groups on fraud-related issues. He has won top writing awards from both the *Internal Auditor* and the *Journal of Accounting* magazines, and he is a winner of the Innovation in Accounting Education Award presented by the American Accounting Association. He was named to *Accounting Today* magazine's annual list of the "Top 100 Most Influential People" in accounting nine times. In 2010, for his contributions to the antifraud field, he was honored as a Doctor of Commercial Science by York College of the City University of New York.

Labeled "the premier financial sleuthing organization" by the *Wall Street Journal*, the ACFE has also been cited for its efforts against fraud by media outlets such as *U.S. News & World Report*, the *New York Times*, CNN, CNBC, *Fortune*, ABC-TV's *Nightline* and *20/20*, and CBS News' *60 Minutes*.

Further information about the ACFE is available at www.acfe.com, or (800) 245-3321.

CHAPTER 1

Introduction

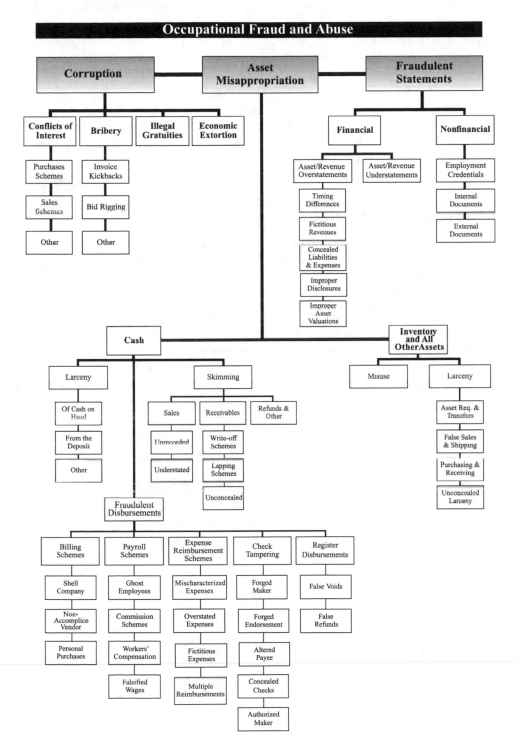

In the world of commerce, organizations incur costs to produce and sell their products or services. These costs run the gamut: labor, taxes, advertising, occupancy, raw materials, research and development—and, yes, fraud and abuse. The latter cost, however, is fundamentally different from the former: The true expense of fraud and abuse is hidden, even if it is reflected in the profit and loss figures.

For example, suppose the advertising expense of a company is $1.2 million. But unknown to the company, its marketing manager is in collusion with an outside ad agency and has accepted $300,000 in kickbacks to steer business to that firm. That means the true advertising expense is overstated by at least the amount of the kickback—if not more. The result, of course, is that $300,000 comes directly off the bottom line, out of the pockets of the investors and the workforce.

DEFINING "OCCUPATIONAL FRAUD AND ABUSE"

The example just given is clear-cut, but much about occupational fraud and abuse is not so well defined, as we will see. Indeed, there is widespread disagreement on what exactly constitutes these offenses.

For purposes of this book, "occupational fraud and abuse" is defined as "the use of one's occupation for personal enrichment through the deliberate misuse or misapplication of the employing organization's resources or assets."[1]

This definition's breadth means that it involves a wide variety of conduct by executives, employees, managers, and principals of organizations, ranging from sophisticated investment swindles to petty theft. Common violations include asset misappropriation, fraudulent statements, corruption, pilferage and petty theft, false overtime, use of company property for personal benefit, and payroll and sick time abuses. As the first *Report to the Nation on Occupational Fraud and Abuse*, from 1996, states: "The key is that the activity (1) is clandestine, (2) violates the employee's fiduciary duties to the organization, (3) is committed for the purpose of direct or indirect financial benefit to the employee, and (4) costs the employing organization assets, revenues, or reserves."[2]

An "employee," in the context of this definition, is any person who receives regular and periodic compensation from an organization for his or her labor. The term is not restricted to the rank and file but specifically includes corporate executives, company presidents, top and middle managers, and other workers.

Defining "Fraud"

In the broadest sense, fraud can encompass any crime for gain that uses deception as its principal modus operandi. Of the three ways to illegally relieve a victim of money—force, trickery, or larceny—all offenses that employ trickery are frauds. Since deception is the linchpin of fraud, we will include *Merriam-Webster's* synonyms: " 'Deceive' implies imposing a false idea or belief that causes ignorance, bewilderment, or helplessness; 'mislead' implies a leading astray that may or may not be intentional; 'delude' implies deceiving so thoroughly as to obscure the truth; 'beguile' stresses the use of charm and persuasion in deceiving."

Although all frauds involve some form of deception, not all deceptions are necessarily frauds. Under common law, four general elements must be present for a fraud to exist:

1. A material false statement
2. Knowledge that the statement was false when it was uttered
3. Reliance on the false statement by the victim
4. Damages as a result

The legal definition is the same whether the offense is criminal or civil; the difference is that criminal cases must meet a higher burden of proof.

Let us assume an employee did not deceive anyone but stole valuable computer chips while no one was looking and resold them to a competitor. Has he committed fraud? Has he committed theft? The answer, of course, is that it depends. Employees have a recognized fiduciary relationship with their employers under the law.

The term "fiduciary," according to *Black's Law Dictionary*, is of Roman origin and means

> *a person holding a character analogous to a trustee, in respect to the trust and confidence involved in it and the scrupulous good faith and candor which it requires. A person is said to act in a "fiduciary capacity" when the business which he transacts, or the money or property which he handles, is not for his own benefit, but for another person, as to whom he stands in a relation implying and necessitating great confidence and trust on the one part and a high degree of good faith on the other part.*[3]

So, in our example, the employee has not only stolen the chips—in so doing, he has violated his fiduciary capacity. That makes him an embezzler.

> *To "embezzle" means willfully to take, or convert to one's own use, another's money or property of which the wrongdoer acquired possession lawfully, by reason of some office or employment or position of trust. The elements of "embezzlement" are that there must be a relationship such as that of employment or agency between the owner of the money and the defendant, the money alluded to have been embezzled must have come into the possession of defendant by virtue of that relationship and there must be an intentional and fraudulent appropriation or conversion of the money.*[4]

In other words, embezzlement is a special type of fraud.

"Conversion," in the legal sense, is

> *an unauthorized assumption and exercise of the right of ownership over goods or personal chattels belonging to another, to the alteration of their condition or the exclusion of the owner's rights. An unauthorized act which deprives an owner of his property permanently or for an indefinite time. Unauthorized and wrongful exercise of dominion and control over another's personal property, to the exclusion of or inconsistent with the rights of owner.*[5]

So by stealing the chips, the employee also engages in conversion of the company's property.

The legal term for stealing is "larceny," which is

felonious stealing, taking and carrying, leading, riding, or driving away with another's personal property, with the intent to convert it or to deprive the owner thereof. The unlawful taking and carrying away of property of another with the intent to appropriate it to a use inconsistent with the latter's rights. The essential elements of a "larceny" are an actual or constructive taking away of the goods or property of another without the consent and against the will of the owner and with a felonious intent. Obtaining possession of property by fraud, trick or device with preconceived design or intent to appropriate, convert, or steal is "larceny."[6]

As a matter of law, the employee in question could be charged with a wide range of criminal and civil conduct: fraud, embezzlement, obtaining money under false pretenses, or larceny. As a practical matter, he probably will be charged with only one offense, commonly larceny.

"Larceny by fraud or deception" means that

a person has purposely obtained the property of another by deception. A person deceives if he purposely: (1) creates or reinforces a false impression, including false impressions as to law, value, intention or other state of mind; but deception as to a person's intention from the act alone that he did not subsequently perform the promise; or (2) prevents another from acquiring information which would affect his judgment of a transaction; or (3) fails to correct a false impression which the deceiver previously created or reinforced, or which the deceiver knows to be influencing another to whom he stands in a fiduciary or confidential relationship; or (4) fails to disclose a known lien, adverse claim, or other legal impediment to the enjoyment of property which he transfers or encumbers in consideration for the property obtained, whether such impediment is or is not valid, or is or is not a matter of official record.[7]

The fraudulent aspect of occupational frauds, then, deals with the employee's fiduciary duties to the organization. If those duties are violated, that action may be considered fraud in one of its many forms. Under the definition of occupational fraud and abuse in this book, the activity must be clandestine. *Black's* defines "clandestine" as "secret, hidden, concealed; usually for some illegal or illicit purpose."[8]

Defining "Abuse"

A litany of abusive practices plagues organizations. Here are a few of the more common examples of how employees "cost" their employers. As any employer knows, it is hardly out of the ordinary for employees to:

- Use employee discounts to purchase goods for friends and relatives.
- Take products belonging to the organization.
- Get paid for more hours than worked.

- Collect more money than due on expense reimbursements.
- Take a long lunch or break without approval.
- Come to work late or leave early.
- Use sick leave when not sick.
- Do slow or sloppy work.
- Work under the influence of alcohol or drugs.

The term "abuse" has taken on a largely amorphous meaning over the years, frequently being used to describe any misconduct that does not fall into a clearly defined category of wrongdoing. *Merriam-Webster's* states that the word "abuse" comes from the Latin word *abusus*—to consume—and that it means "1. A corrupt practice or custom; 2. Improper or excessive use or treatment: misuse; 3. A deceitful act: deception."[9]

Given the commonality of the language describing both fraud and abuse, what are the key differences? An example illustrates: Suppose a teller was employed by a bank and stole $100 from her cash drawer. We would define that broadly as fraud. But if the teller earns $500 a week and falsely calls in sick one day, we might call that abuse—even though each has the exact same economic impact to the company—in this case, $100.

And, of course, each offense requires a dishonest intent on the part of the employee to victimize the company. Look at the way each typically is handled within an organization, though: In the case of the embezzlement, the employee gets fired; there is also the remotest of probabilities that he will be prosecuted. In the case in which the employee misuses sick time, she *perhaps* gets reprimanded, or her pay is docked for the day.

But we also can change the "abuse" example slightly. Let us say the employee works for a governmental agency instead of in the private sector. Sick leave abuse—in its strictest interpretation—could be a fraud against the government. After all, the employee has made a false statement for financial gain (to keep from getting docked). Government agencies can and have prosecuted flagrant instances. Misuse of public money—in any form—can end up being a serious matter, and the prosecutive thresholds can be surprisingly low.

Here is one real example. In 1972, I was a rookie FBI agent assigned to El Paso, Texas. That division covered the Fort Bliss military reservation, a sprawling desert complex. There were rumors that civilian employees of the military commissary were stealing inventory and selling it out the back door. The rumors turned out to be true, albeit slightly overstated. But we did not know that at the time.

So around Thanksgiving, the FBI spent a day surveying the commissary's back entrance. We had made provisions for all contingencies—lots of personnel, secret vans, long-range cameras—the works. But the day produced only one measly illegal sale out the back door: several frozen turkeys and a large bag of yams. The purchaser of the stolen goods tipped his buddy $10 for merchandise valued at about $60. The offense occurred late in the day. We were bored and irritated, and we pounced on the purchaser as he exited the base, following him out the gate in a caravan of unmarked cars with red lights. The poor guy was shaking so badly that he wet his pants. I guess he knew better than we did what was at stake.

Because he was in the wrong place at the wrong time and did the wrong thing, our criminal paid dearly: He pled guilty to a charge of petty theft. So did his buddy at the commissary. The employee was fired. But the purchaser, it turned out, was a retired military colonel with a civilian job on the base—a person commonly known as a double dipper. He was let go from a high-paying civilian job and now has a criminal record. But most expensively, I heard he lost several hundred thousand dollars in potential government retirement benefits. Would the same person be prosecuted for petty theft today? It depends entirely on the circumstances. But it could, and does, happen.

The point here is that the term "abuse" often is used to describe a variety of petty crimes and other counterproductive behavior that have become common, even silently condoned in the workplace. The reasons employees engage in these abuses are varied and highly complex. Do abusive employees eventually turn into out-and-out thieves and criminals? In some instances, yes. We will describe that later.

RESEARCH IN OCCUPATIONAL FRAUD AND ABUSE

Edwin H. Sutherland

Considering its enormous impact, relatively little research has been done on the subject of occupational fraud and abuse. Much of the current literature is based on the early works of Edwin H. Sutherland (1883–1950), a criminologist at Indiana University. Sutherland was particularly interested in fraud committed by the elite upper-world business executive, whether against shareholders or against the public. As renowned criminologist Gilbert Geis noted, Sutherland said, "General Motors does not have an inferiority complex, United States Steel does not suffer from an unresolved Oedipus problem, and the DuPonts do not desire to return to the womb. The assumption that an offender may have such pathological distortion of the intellect or the emotions seems to me absurd, and if it is absurd regarding the crimes of businessmen, it is equally absurd regarding the crimes of persons in the economic lower classes."[10]

For the uninitiated, Sutherland is to the world of white-collar criminality what Freud is to psychology. Indeed, it was Sutherland who coined the term "white-collar crime" in 1939. He intended the definition to mean criminal acts of corporations and individuals acting in their corporate capacity, but since that time the term has come to mean almost any financial or economic crime, from the mailroom to the boardroom.

Many criminologists, myself included, believe that Sutherland's most important contribution to criminal literature lay elsewhere. Later in his career, Sutherland developed the "theory of differential association," which is now the most widely accepted theory of criminal behavior. Until Sutherland's landmark work in the 1930s, most criminologists and sociologists held the view that crime was genetically based; that criminals beget criminal offspring.

Although this argument may seem naive today, it was based largely on the observation of non–white-collar offenders—the murderers, rapists, sadists, and hooligans who plagued society. Numerous subsequent studies have indeed established a genetic base for "street" crime, which must be tempered by environmental considerations. (For a thorough explanation of the genetic base for criminality, see *Crime & Human Nature: The Definitive Study of the Causes of Crime* by Wilson and Herrnstein.[11]) Sutherland was able to explain crime's environmental considerations through the theory of differential association. The theory's basic tenet is that crime is learned, much as are math, English, and guitar playing.[12]

Sutherland believed that learning of criminal behavior occurred with other persons in a process of communication. Therefore, he reasoned, criminality cannot occur without the assistance of other people. Sutherland further theorized that the learning of criminal activity usually occurred within intimate personal groups. In his view, this explains how a dysfunctional parent is more likely to produce dysfunctional offspring. Sutherland believed that the learning process involved two specific areas: the techniques for committing crime; and the attitudes, drives, rationalizations, and motive of the criminal mind. You can see how Sutherland's differential association theory fits with occupational offenders: Dishonest employees will eventually infect a portion of honest ones, but honest employees will also eventually have an influence on some dishonest ones.

Donald R. Cressey

One of Sutherland's brightest students at Indiana University during the 1940s was Donald R. Cressey (1919–1987). Although much of Sutherland's research concentrated on upper-world criminality, Cressey took his own studies in a different direction. Working on his doctorate in criminology, he decided to concentrate on embezzlers. Accordingly, Cressey arranged the necessary permission at prisons in the Midwest and eventually interviewed about 200 incarcerated inmates.

Cressey's Hypothesis

Cressey was intrigued by embezzlers, whom he called "trust violators." He was especially interested in the circumstances that led them to be overcome by temptation. For that reason, he excluded from his research those employees who took their jobs for the purpose of stealing—a relatively minor number of offenders at that time. Upon completion of his interviews, he developed what still remains the classic model for the occupational offender. His research was published in *Other People's Money: A Study in the Social Psychology of Embezzlement.*[13]

Cressey's final hypothesis was:

> *Trusted persons become trust violators when they conceive of themselves as having a financial problem which is nonsharable, are aware this problem can be secretly resolved by violation of the position of financial trust, and are able to apply to their own conduct in that situation verbalizations which enable them to adjust their conceptions of themselves as trusted persons with their conceptions of themselves as users of the entrusted funds or property.*[14]

Over the years, the hypothesis has become better known as the fraud triangle. (See Exhibit 1.1.) The first leg of the triangle represents a *perceived nonsharable financial need,* the second leg represents *perceived opportunity,* and the third leg stands for *rationalization.* As Cressey said:

> *When the trust violators were asked to explain why they refrained from violation of other positions of trust they might have held at previous times, or why they had not violated the*

Exhibit 1.1   The Fraud Triangle

subject position at an earlier time, those who had an opinion expressed the equivalent of one or more of the following quotations: (a) "There was no need for it like there was this time." (b) "The idea never entered my head." (c) "I thought it was dishonest then, but this time it did not seem dishonest at first."[15]

"In all cases of trust violation encountered, the violator considered that a financial problem which confronted him could not be shared with persons who, from a more objective point of view, probably could have aided in the solution of the problem."[16]

Nonsharable Problems

What, of course, is considered nonsharable is wholly in the eyes of the potential occupational offender, Cressey noted:

Thus a man could lose considerable money at the race track daily but the loss, even if it construed a problem for the individual, might not constitute a nonsharable problem for him. Another man might define the problem as one which must be kept secret and private, that is, as one which is nonsharable. Similarly, a failing bank or business might be considered by one person as presenting problems which must be shared with business associates and members of the community, while another person might conceive these problems as nonsharable.[17]

Cressey divided these "nonsharable" problems into six basic subtypes:

1. Violation of ascribed obligations
2. Problems resulting from personal failure
3. Business reversals
4. Physical isolation
5. Status gaining
6. Employer–employee relations

Violation of Ascribed Obligations

Violation of ascribed obligations—the specter of being unable to pay one's debts—has historically proved a strong motivator.

> *Financial problems incurred through non-financial violations of positions of trust often are considered as nonsharable by trusted persons since they represent a threat to the status which holding the position entails. Most individuals in positions of financial trust, and most employers of such individuals, consider that incumbency in such a position necessarily implies that, in addition to being honest, they should behave in certain ways and should refrain from participation in some other kinds of behavior.*[18]

In other words, the mere fact that a person has a trusted position brings with it the implication that he or she can and does properly manage money.

> *When persons incur debts or in some other way become financially obligated as a result of violation of the obligations ascribed to the role of trusted person, they frequently consider that these debts must be kept secret, and that meeting them becomes a nonsharable financial problem. In many instances, the insurance of such debts is also considered incompatible with the duties and obligations of other roles which the person might be enacting, such as those of a husband or father, but the concern here is with such debts only as they represent conflict with the person's role as a trusted person.*[19]

Cressey describes a situation we can all appreciate—not being able to pay one's debts—and then having to admit it to one's employer, family, or friends.

Problems Resulting from Personal Failure

Problems resulting from personal failures, Cressey writes, can be of several different types.

> *While some pressing financial problems may be considered as having resulted from "economic conditions" . . . others are considered to have been created by the misguided or poorly planned activities of the individual trusted person. Because he fears a loss of status, the individual is afraid to admit to anyone who could alleviate the situation the fact that he has a problem which is a consequence of his "own bad judgment" or "own fault" or "own stupidity."*[20]

In short, pride goeth before the fall. If the potential offender has a choice between covering poor investment choices through a violation of trust and admitting to be an unsophisticated investor, it is easy to see how some prideful people's judgment could be clouded.

Business Reversals

Business reversals were the third area Cressey detailed as a part of the nonsharable problem. He saw these as different from personal failures, since many businesspeople consider their financial reverses as coming from conditions beyond their control: inflation, high interest rates, raising capital, and borrowing money. Cressey quoted the remarks of one businessman who borrowed money from a bank using fictitious collateral.

> *Case 36. There are very few people who are able to walk away from a failing business. When the bridge is falling, almost everyone will run for a piece of timber. In business there is this eternal optimism that things will get better tomorrow. We get to working on the business, keeping it going, and we almost get mesmerized by it. . . . Most of us don't know when to quit, when to say, "This one has me licked. Here's one for the opposition."*[21]

Physical Isolation

The fourth category of nonsharable problems Cressey described is physical isolation, in which the person in financial straits is isolated from the people who can help him.

Status Gaining

The fifth category consists of problems relating to status gaining. Although these are easily passed off as living beyond one's means or spending money lavishly, Cressey was interested more in their behavioral implications. He noted:

> *The structuring of status ambitions as being nonsharable is not uncommon in our culture, and it again must be emphasized that the structuring of a situation as nonsharable is not alone the cause of trust violation. More specifically, in this type of case a problem appears when the individual realizes that he does not have the financial means necessary for continued association with persons on a desired status level, and this problem becomes nonsharable when he feels that he can neither renounce his aspirations for membership in the desired group nor obtain prestige symbols necessary to such membership.*[22]

He observed, then, that many occupational offenders are afflicted with the "Keeping Up with the Joneses" syndrome.

Employer–Employee Relations

Finally, Cressey described problems resulting from employer–employee relationships. The most common situation, he stated, was that of an employed person who resents his status within the organization in which he is trusted. The resentment can come from perceived economic inequities, such as pay, or from the feeling of being overworked or underappreciated. Cressey said this problem becomes nonsharable when the individual believes that making suggestions to alleviate perceived maltreatment will possibly threaten his or her status in the organization. There is also a strong motivator for the perceived employee to want to "get even" when he or she feels ill treated.

A Personal Experience

One of my best-remembered examples involves a personal experience, and not a pleasant one. Most people—if they admit the truth—will have stolen on the job at some time in their careers. Some of the thefts are major, some minor. Some are uncovered; many never are. With this preamble (and the fact that the statute of limitations has long expired!), I will tell you the story of one employee thief: me.

The incident occurred during college. Like many of you, I did not work my way through the university just for experience; it was a necessity. One of my part-time jobs was as a salesperson in a men's clothing store, a place I'll call Mr. Zac's. It seems that Mr. Zac had the imagination to name the store after himself, which may give you a clue as to the kind of person he was.

My first day on the job, it became clear by talking to the other employees that they strongly disliked Mr. Zac. It did not take long to figure out why: He was cheap beyond all reason; he was sore-tempered, paranoid, and seemed to strongly resent having to pay the employees who were generating his sales. Mr. Zac was especially suspicious of the help stealing. He always eyed the employees warily when they left in the evening, I assume because he thought their clothing and bags were stuffed with his merchandise. So his employees figured out novel ways to steal for no other reason than to get back at Mr. Zac. I was above all that, or so I thought. But then Mr. Zac did something to me personally, and my attitude changed completely.

One day I was upstairs in the storeroom getting merchandise off the top shelf. Since the high reach had pulled my shirttail out, I was standing there tucking it in when Mr. Zac walked by. He didn't say a word. I went back downstairs to work and thought no more of it. But ten minutes later Mr. Zac called me into his small, cubbyhole office, closed the door, and asked, "What were you tucking in your pants upstairs?" Just my shirt, I replied. "I don't believe you," Mr. Zac said. "Unless you unzip your pants right now and show me, you're fired." At first, of course, it did not register that he was serious. When it finally did, I was faced with a dilemma: Unzip my pants for the boss, or be late on the rent and face eviction. I chose the former, but as I stood there letting my pants fall down around my knees, my face burned with anger and embarrassment. Never before had I been placed in a position like this—having to undress to prove my innocence.

After seeing for himself that I didn't have any of his precious merchandise on my person, Mr. Zac sent me back to the sales floor. I was a different person, though. No longer was I interested in selling merchandise and being a good employee. I was interested in getting even, and that's what I did. Over the next few months I tried my best to steal him blind—clothing, underwear, outerwear, neckties—you name it. With the help of some of the other employees, we even stole a large display case. He never caught on, and eventually I quit the job. Was I justified in stealing from Mr. Zac? Absolutely not. At this age, given the same circumstances, would I do it again? No. But at that particular time, I was young, idealistic, very headstrong, and totally fearless. Criminologists have documented that the reason so many young people lack fear is because they do not yet realize actions can have serious consequences; it never occurred to me that I could have gone to jail for stealing from Mr. Zac.

The impact of job loyalty—or, like Mr. Zac's employees, the lack of it—is an important consideration in the occupational fraud and abuse formula. With changes in the American workforce, we may or may not experience more fraud-related problems. Much has been written recently concerning the downsizing, outsourcing, and increased employee turnover in business. If the employee of the future is largely a contract worker, much of the incentive of loyalty toward organizations could be lost. Such a trend seems to be under way, but its real fraud impact has not been determined. However, fraud is only one cost of doing business. If the outsourcing of corporate America does indeed cause more occupational fraud and abuse, the benefits of restructuring may be seen as outweighing the cost of more crime, at least in the short term. In the long run, it is difficult to justify how employees stealing from organizations can be beneficial to anyone. That was Cressey's theory too.

Sociological Factors

Since Cressey's study was done in the early 1950s, the workforce was obviously different from today's. But the employee faced with an immediate, nonsharable financial need has not changed much over the years. Cressey pointed out that for the trust violator, it is necessary that he believe his financial situation can be resolved in secret. Cressey said:

> In all cases [in the study] there was a distinct feeling that, because of activity prior to the defalcation, the approval of groups important to the trusted person had been lost, or a distinct feeling that present group approval would be lost if certain activity were revealed [the nonsharable financial problem], with the result that the trusted person was effectively isolated from persons who could assist him in solving problems arising from that activity.
>
> Although the clear conception of a financial problem as nonsharable does not invariably result in trust violation, it does establish in trusted persons a desire for a specific kind of solution to their problems. The results desired in the cases encountered were uniform: the solution or partial solution of the problem by the use of funds which can be obtained in an independent, relatively secret, safe, and sure method in keeping with the "rationalizations" available to the person at the time.[23]

Cressey pointed out that many of his subjects in the study mentioned the importance of resolving the problem secretly.

Cressey also discovered, by talking to his trust violators, that they did not see their positions as a point of possible abuse until after they were confronted with the nonsharable financial problem. They used words such as "it occurred to me" or "it dawned on me" that the entrusted monies could be used to cure their vexing situations. In Cressey's view, the trust violator must have two prerequisites: general information and technical skill. With respect to general information, the fiduciary capacity of an employee in and of itself implies that, since it is a position of trust (read: no one is checking), it can be violated.

Cressey said that in addition to general information, the trust violator must have the technical skills required to pull off the fraud in secret. He observed:

> It is the next step which is significant to violation: the application of the general information to the specific situation, and conjointly, the perception of the fact that in addition to having general possibilities for violation, a specific position of trust can be used for the specific purpose of solving a nonsharable problem. . . . The statement that trusted persons must be cognizant of the fact that the entrusted funds can be used secretly to solve the nonsharable problem is based upon observations of such applications of general information to specific situations.[24]

Cressey believed that based on observations, it was difficult to distinguish which came first: the need for the funds, or the realization that they could be secretly used. In other words, did the person have a "legitimate" need for the funds before figuring out how to get his or her hands on them secretly? Or did the person see secret access to funds and find a justification to use them?

Next, Cressey delved into the inner workings of the offenders' minds: How were they able to convince themselves that stealing was okay? He found they were able to excuse their actions to themselves by viewing their crimes in one of three ways:

1. As noncriminal
2. As justified
3. As part of a situation that the offenders do not control

These methods he generalized as "rationalizations." In his studies, Cressey discovered that "in cases of trust violation encountered, significant rationalizations were always present before the criminal act took place, or at least at the time it took place, and, in fact, after the act had taken place the rationalization often was abandoned."[25] That is, of course, because of the nature of us all: The first time we do something contrary to our morals, it bothers us. As we repeat the act, it becomes easier. One hallmark of occupational fraud and abuse offenders is that once the line is crossed, the illegal acts become more or less continuous.

One of the simplest ways to justify unacceptable conduct and avoid guilt feelings is to invent a good reason for embezzling—one sanctioned in the social group as a greater good. Thus, the trust violator's self-image, should she be discovered, must be explainable to herself and others around her.

Offender Types

For further analysis, Cressey divided the subjects into three groups:

1. Independent businessmen
2. Long-term violators
3. Absconders

He discovered that each group had its own types of rationalizations.

Independent Businessmen

Businessmen, for example, used one of two common excuses: (1) They were "borrowing" the money that they converted, or (2) the funds entrusted to them were really theirs—you cannot steal from yourself. Cressey found the "borrowing" rationalization was the most frequently used. Many independent businessmen also expressed the belief that their practices were the rule of the day for other businesses. Nearly universally, the business owners felt that their illegal actions were predicated by an "unusual situation" that Cressey perceived to actually be a nonshareable financial problem.

13

LONG-TERM VIOLATORS

The long-term violators Cressey studied also generally preferred the "borrowing" rationalization. He also described other rationalizations of long-term violators:

1. They were embezzling to keep their families from shame, disgrace, or poverty.
2. Theirs was a case of "necessity"; their employers were cheating them financially.
3. Their employers were dishonest toward others and deserved to be fleeced.

Some even pointed out that it was more difficult to return the funds than to steal them in the first place and claimed that they did not pay back their "borrowings" out of fear of detection. A few in the study actually kept track of their thefts, but most did so only at the outset. Later, as the embezzlements escalate, it is assumed that offenders would rather not know the extent of their "borrowings." All the long-term violators in the study expressed a feeling that they would like to eventually "clean the slate" and repay their debt.

Cressey noted that many of the offenders finally realized they were "in too deep." This realization forces violators to think of the possible consequences of their actions. Cressey said the fear generated from being in over one's head is not caused by the thought of going to jail—after all, offenders do not generally consider their conduct illegal. As Cressey observed, "The trust violator cannot fear the treatment usually accorded criminals until he comes to look upon himself as a criminal."[26]

But at some point, Cressey noted, the offenders start becoming apprehensive about the possible social connotations and, later, the criminal possibilities. A number of offenders described themselves as extremely nervous and upset, tense, and unhappy. Cressey felt that without the rationalization that they are borrowing, long-term offenders in the study found it difficult to reconcile converting money with at the same time seeing themselves as honest and trustworthy. If this is the situation, Cressey says that "as a result, [the offender] either (a) readopts the attitudes of the groups with which he identified before he violated the trust, or (b) he adopts the attitudes of the new category of persons (offenders) with whom he now identifies."[27]

ABSCONDERS

The third group of offenders Cressey discussed was "absconders"—people who take the money and run. He was able to work this group into his theory of a nonsharable financial need by describing their behavior as "isolated." He observed:

> While among persons who abscond with entrusted funds, as among other violators, almost any problem situation may be defined as nonsharable, the problems which are nonsharable for absconders are almost always of that nature, at least in part because the person is physically isolated from other persons with whom he can share his problems. Individuals who abscond with the funds or goods entrusted to them usually are unmarried or separated from their spouses, live in hotels or rooming houses, have few primary group associations of any sort, and own little property. Only one of the absconders interviewed had held a higher status position of trust, such as an accountant, business executive, or bookkeeper.[28]

Cressey says that although absconders recognize their behavior as criminal, they justify their actions by claiming that the behavior is caused by outside influences beyond their control. Absconders also frequently express an apathetic attitude. Moreover, they are more likely to claim that their own personal "defects" led to their criminality.

In the 1950s, when Cressey gathered this data, embezzlers were considered

> *persons of higher socioeconomic status who took money over periods of time . . . while "thieves" are persons of lower status who take whatever funds are at hand. Since most absconders identify with the lower status group, they look upon themselves as belonging to a special class of thieves rather than trust violators. Just as long-term violators and independent businessmen do not at first consider the possibility of absconding with the funds, absconders do not consider the possibility of taking relatively small amounts of money over a period of time.*[29]

One of the most fundamental observations of the Cressey study was that it took all three elements perceived motive, perceived opportunity, and the ability to rationalize—for the trust violation to occur.

Cressey concluded that

> *[a] trust violation takes place when the position of trust is viewed by the trusted person according to culturally provided knowledge about and rationalizations for using the entrusted funds for solving a nonsharable problem, and that the absence of any of these events will preclude violation. The three events make up the conditions under which trust violation occurs and the term "cause" may be applied to their conjecture since trust violation is dependent on that conjecture. Whenever the conjecture of events occurs, trust violation results, and if the conjecture does not take place there is no trust violation.*[30]

Conclusion

Cressey's classic fraud triangle helps explain the nature of many—but not all— occupational offenders. For example, although academicians have tested his model, it has still not fully found its way into practice in terms of developing fraud prevention programs. Our sense tells us that one model—even Cressey's—will not fit all situations. Furthermore, the study is over half a century old; there has been considerable social change during the interim. Now many antifraud professionals believe there is a new breed of occupational offender—one who simply lacks a conscience sufficient to overcome temptation.

Even Cressey saw the trend later in his life. After doing this landmark study in embezzlement, Cressey went on to a distinguished academic career, eventually writing 13 books as well as nearly 300 articles on criminology matters. He rose to the position of Professor Emeritus in Criminology at the University of California, Santa Barbara.

I was honored to know Cressey personally. Indeed, he and I collaborated extensively before he died in 1987, and his influence on my own antifraud theories has been significant. Our families are acquainted; we stayed in each other's homes; we traveled together—he was my friend. In a way, we made the odd couple; he the academic, me the businessman; he the theoretical, me the practical.

I met him as the result of an assignment, in about 1983, when a Fortune 500 company hired me on an investigative and consulting matter. It had a rather messy case of a high-level vice president who was put in charge of a large construction project for a new company plant. But the $75 million budget for which he was responsible proved too much of a temptation. Construction companies wined and dined the vice president and eventually provided him with tempting and illegal bait: drugs and women. He bit.

From there the vice president succumbed to full kickbacks. By the time the dust settled, he had secretly pocketed about $3.5 million. After completing the internal investigation for the company, assembling documentation and interviews, I worked with prosecutors, at the company's request, to put the perpetrator in prison. Then the company came to me with a very simple question: "Why did he do it?" As a former FBI agent with hundreds of fraud cases under my belt, I must admit I had not thought much about the motives of occupational offenders. To my mind, they committed these crimes simply because they were crooks. But the company—certainly progressive on the anti-fraud front for the time—wanted me to invest the resources required to find out why and how employees go bad, so that it could do something to prevent it. This quest took me to the vast libraries of the University of Texas at Austin, which led me to Cressey's early research. After reading Cressey's book, I realized that he had described to a T the embezzlers I had encountered. I wanted to meet him.

Finding Cressey was easy enough. I made two phone calls and found that he was still alive, well, and teaching in Santa Barbara. He was in the telephone book—I called him. He agreed to meet me the next time I came to California. That began what became a very close relationship between us which lasted until his untimely death in 1987. It was he who recognized the real value of combining the theorist with the practitioner; he used to proclaim that he learned as much from me as I from him. And in addition to Cressey's brilliance, he was one of the most gracious people I have ever met. Although we worked together professionally for only four years, we covered a lot of ground. Cressey was convinced there was a need for an organization devoted exclusively to fraud detection and deterrence. The Association of Certified Fraud Examiners, started about a year after his death, is in existence in large measure because of his vision. Moreover, although he did not know it at the time, he created the concept of what eventually became the certified fraud examiner.

It happened like this. Don, his wife, Elaine, my wife, Judy, and I were returning from a fraud conference in Australia when we stopped over in Fiji for two days. As he and I were sitting on the beach talking, Cressey theorized that it was time for a new type of "corporate cop"—one trained in detecting and deterring the crime of the future: fraud. Cressey pointed out that the traditional policeman was ill-equipped to deal with sophisticated financial crimes, as were the traditional accountants. It was just one of many ideas he had discussed that day, but that one stuck.

Dr. W. Steve Albrecht

Not too long thereafter, I met another pioneer researcher in occupational fraud and abuse, Dr. Steve Albrecht of Brigham Young University. Unlike Cressey, Albrecht was educated as an accountant. We discussed, among other things, Cressey's vision. Albrecht agreed with Cressey's vision: Traditional accountants, he said, were ill-equipped to deal with complex financial crimes. Eventually my colleagues and I decided that this new kind of "corporate cop" would have training in four disciplines:

accounting, law, investigation, and fraud prevention and deterrence. And that new corporate cop is now the certified fraud examiner (CFE).

Albrecht Study

Steve was helpful in commencing the CFE program, and his research contributions in fraud have been enormous. He and two of his colleagues, Keith Howe and Marshall Romney, conducted an analysis of 212 frauds in the early 1980s under a grant from The Institute of Internal Auditors Research Foundation, leading to their book *Deterring Fraud: The Internal Auditor's Perspective.* The study's methodology involved obtaining demographics and background information on the frauds through the extensive use of questionnaires. The participants in the survey were internal auditors of companies that had experienced frauds.

The study covered several areas, one of the most interesting of which concentrated on the motivations of the perpetrators of occupational frauds and abuses. They classified these motivators as one of nine different types:

1. Living beyond their means
2. An overwhelming desire for personal gain
3. High personal debt
4. A close association with customers
5. Feeling pay was not commensurate with responsibility
6. A wheeler-dealer attitude
7. Strong challenge to beat the system
8. Excessive gambling habits
9. Undue family or peer pressure[31]

As can be seen from the list, these motivators are very similar to the nonsharable financial problems Cressey discussed. The study by Albrecht and associates also disclosed several interesting relationships between the perpetrators and the frauds they committed. For example, perpetrators of large frauds used the proceeds to purchase new homes and expensive automobiles, recreational property, and expensive vacations; to support extramarital relationships; and to make speculative investments. Those committing small frauds did not.

There were other observations: Perpetrators who were interested primarily in "beating the system" committed larger frauds. However, perpetrators who believed their pay was not adequate committed primarily small frauds. Lack of segregation of responsibilities, placing undeserved trust in key employees, imposing unrealistic goals, and operating on a crisis basis were all pressures or weaknesses associated with large frauds. College graduates were less likely to spend the proceeds of their loot to take extravagant vacations, purchase recreational property, support extramarital relationships, and buy expensive automobiles. Finally, those with lower salaries were more likely to have a prior criminal record.[32]

Like Cressey's study, the Albrecht study suggests there are three factors involved in occupational frauds:

a situational pressure (nonsharable financial pressure), a perceived opportunity to commit and conceal the dishonest act (a way to secretly resolve the dishonest act or the lack of deterrence by management), and some way to rationalize (verbalize) the act as either being inconsistent with one's personal level of integrity or justifiable.

Fraud Scale

To illustrate this concept, Albrecht developed the "Fraud Scale," shown in Exhibit 1.2, which included the components of situational pressures, perceived opportunities, and personal integrity.[33] When situational pressures and perceived opportunities are high and personal integrity is low, occupational fraud is much more likely to occur than when the opposite is true.[34]

The authors describe situational pressures as "the immediate problems individuals experience within their environments, the most overwhelming of which are probably high personal debts or financial losses."[35] Opportunities to commit fraud, Albrecht and coauthors say, may be created by deficient or missing internal controls—those of the employee or the company. Personal integrity "refers to the personal code of ethical behavior each person adopts. While this factor appears to be a straightforward determination of whether the person is honest or dishonest, moral development research indicates that the issue is more complex."[36]

Albrecht and his colleagues believed that, taken as a group, occupational fraud perpetrators are hard to profile and that fraud is difficult to predict. His research examined comprehensive data sources to assemble a complete list of pressure, opportunity, and integrity variables, resulting in a collection of 82 possible red flags or indicators of

Exhibit 1.2   Fraud Scale

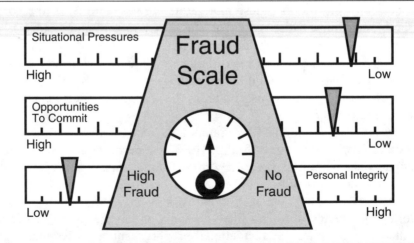

Source: Steve Albrecht, Keith Howe, and Marshall Romney, *Deterring Fraud: The Internal Auditor's Perspective* (Altamonte Springs, FL: Institute of Internal Auditors Research Foundation, 1983), p. 6.

occupational fraud and abuse. The red flags ranged from unusually high personal debts, to belief that one's job is in jeopardy; from no separation of asset custodial procedures, to not adequately checking the potential employee's background.[37]

Although such red flags may be present in many occupational fraud cases, Albrecht and associates caution that the perpetrators are hard to profile and fraud is difficult to predict. To underscore this point, their research does not address—and no current research has been done to determine—if nonoffenders have many of the same characteristics. If so, then the list may not be discriminating enough to be useful. In short, while potential red flags should be noted, they should not receive undue attention absent more compelling circumstances.

Richard C. Hollinger

Hollinger-Clark Study

In 1983, Richard C. Hollinger of Purdue University and John P. Clark of the University of Minnesota published federally funded research involving surveys of nearly 10,000 American workers. Their book, *Theft by Employees*, reached a different conclusion from that of Cressey. They concluded that employees steal primarily as a result of workplace conditions and that the true costs of the problem are vastly understated. "In sum, when we take into consideration the incalculable social costs . . . the grand total paid for theft in the workplace is no doubt grossly underestimated by the available financial estimates."[38]

Hypotheses of Employee Theft

In reviewing the literature on employee theft, Hollinger and Clark concluded that experts had developed five separate but interrelated sets of hypotheses of employee theft. The first was external economic pressures, such as the "nonshareable [sic] financial problem" that Cressey described. The second hypothesis was that contemporary employees, specifically young ones, are not as hardworking and honest as those in past generations. The third theory, advocated primarily by those with years of experience in the security and investigative industry, was that every employee can be tempted to steal from an employer. This theory assumes that people are greedy and dishonest by nature. The fourth theory was that job dissatisfaction is the primary cause of employee theft, and the fifth, that theft occurs because of the broadly shared formal and informal structure of organizations; that is, over time, the group norms—good or bad—become the standard of conduct. The sum of Hollinger and Clark's research led them to conclude that the fourth hypothesis was correct: Employee deviance is primarily caused by job dissatisfaction.

Employee Deviance

Employee theft is at one extreme of employee deviance, which can be defined as conduct detrimental to the organization and to the employee. At the other extreme is counterproductive employee behavior such as goldbricking, industrial sabotage, and even wildcat strikes. Hollinger and Clark define two basic categories of deviant behavior by employees: (1) acts by employees against property and (2) violations of the norms regulating acceptable levels of production. The former includes misuse and theft of company property, such as of cash or inventory; the latter involves acts of employee deviance that affect productivity.

During the three-year duration of the study, Hollinger and Clark developed a written questionnaire that was sent to employees in three different sectors: retail, hospital, and manufacturing. They eventually received 9,175 valid employee questionnaires, representing about 54 percent of those sampled. The results of the questionnaires are discussed next. Exhibit 1.3 represents property deviance only.[39]

Exhibit 1.3   Hollinger-Clark Property Deviance

Combined Phase I and Phase II Property Deviance
Items and Percentage of Reported Involvement, by Sector

	Involvement				
Items	Almost Daily	About Once a Week	4 to 12 Times a Year	1 to 3 Times a Year	Total
Retail Sector (N = 3,567)					
Misuse the discount privilege	0.6	2.4	11	14.9	28.9
Take store merchandise	0.2	0.5	1.3	4.6	6.6
Get paid for more hours than were worked	0.2	0.4	1.2	4	5.8
Purposely underring a purchase	0.1	0.3	1.1	1.7	3.2
Borrow or take money from employer without approval	0.1	0.1	0.5	2	2.7
Be reimbursed for more money than spent on business expenses	0.1	0.2	0.5	1.3	2.1
Damage merchandise to buy it on discount	0	0.1	0.2	1	1.3
Total involved in property deviance					35.1
Hospital Sector (N = 4,111)					
Take hospital supplies (e.g., linens, bandages)	0.2	0.8	8.4	17.9	27.3
Take or use medication intended for patients	0.1	0.3	1.9	5.5	7.8
Get paid for more hours than were worked	0.2	0.5	1.6	3.8	6.1
Take hospital equipment or tools	0.1	0.1	0.4	4.1	4.7
Be reimbursed for more money than spent on business expenses	0.1	0	0.2	0.8	1.1
Total involved in property deviance					33.3
Manufacturing Sector (N = 1,497)					
Take raw materials used in production	0.1	0.3	3.5	10.4	14.3
Get paid for more hours than were worked	0.2	0.5	2.9	5.6	9.2
Take company tools or equipment	0	0.1	1.1	7.5	8.7
Be reimbursed for more money than spent on business expenses	0.1	0.6	1.4	5.6	7.7
Take finished products	0	0	0.4	2.7	3.1
Take precious metals (e.g., platinum, gold)	0.1	0.1	0.5	1.1	1.8
Total involved in property deviance					28.4

Source: Adapted from Richard C. Hollinger and John P. Clark, *Theft by Employees* (Lexington, KY: Lexington Books, 1983), p. 42.

In order to empirically test whether economics had an effect on the level of theft, the researchers also sorted the data by household income, under the theory that the lower the level of income, the greater the degree of thefts. However, they were unable to confirm such a statistical relationship. This would tend to indicate—at least in this study—that absolute income is not a predictor of employee theft. But they were able to confirm that there was a statistical relationship between a person's "concern" over his or her financial situation and the level of theft.

Exhibit 1.4 provides a summary of the Hollinger and Clark research with respect to production deviance. Not surprisingly, the most common violations were taking too long for lunch or breaks, with more than half of the employees involved in this activity.[40]

Exhibit 1.4   Hollinger-Clark Production Deviance

**Combined Phase I and Phase II Production Deviance
Items and Percentage of Reported Involvement, by Sector**

| | Involvement | | | | |
Items	Almost Daily	About Once a Week	4 to 12 Times a Year	1 to 3 Times a Year	Total
Retail Sector (N = 3,567)					
Take a long lunch or break without approval	6.9	13.3	15.5	20.3	56
Come to work late or leave early	0.9	3.4	10.8	17.2	32.3
Use sick leave when not sick	0.1	0.1	3.5	13.4	17.1
Do slow or sloppy work	0.3	1.5	4.1	9.8	15.7
Work under the influence of alcohol or drugs	0.5	0.8	1.6	4.6	7.5
Total involved in production deviance					65.4
Hospital Sector (N = 4,111)					
Take a long lunch or break without approval	8.5	13.5	17.4	17.8	57.2
Come to work late or leave early	1	3.5	9.6	14.9	29
Use sick leave when not sick	0	0.2	5.7	26.9	32.8
Do slow or sloppy work	0.2	0.8	4.1	5.9	11
Work under the influence of alcohol or drugs	0.1	0.3	0.6	2.2	3.2
Total involved in production deviance					69.2
Manufacturing Sector (N = 1,497)					
Take a long lunch or break without approval	18	23.5	22	8.5	72
Come to work late or leave early	1.9	9	19.4	13.8	44.1
Use sick leave when not sick	0	0.2	9.6	28.6	38.4
Do slow or sloppy work	0.5	1.3	5.7	5	12.5
Work under the influence of alcohol or drugs	1.1	1.3	3.1	7.3	12.8
Total involved in production deviance					82.2

Source: Adapted from Richard C. Hollinger and John P. Clark, *Theft by Employees* (Lexington, KY: Lexington Books, 1983), p. 45.

Hollinger and Clark presented the employees with a list of eight major concerns, from personal health, to education issues, to financial problems.

Being concerned about finances and being under financial pressure are not necessarily the same. However, if a respondent considered his or her finances as one of the most important issues, that concern could be partially due to "nonshareable economic problems," or it could also be that current realities are not matching one's financial aspirations regardless of the income presently being realized.[41]

The study concluded that "in each industry, the results are significant, with higher theft individuals more likely to be concerned about their finances, particularly those who ranked finances as the first or second most important issue."[42] The researchers were unable to confirm any connection between community pressures and the level of theft.

Age and Theft

Hollinger and Clark believe there is a direct correlation between age and the level of theft, stating: "Few other variables . . . have exhibited such a strong relationship to theft as the age of the employee."[43] The reason, they concluded, was that younger employees had less tenure with the organization and therefore lower levels of commitment to it. "By definition," they say, "these employees are more likely to be younger workers."[44] In addition, there is a long history of connection between many levels of crime and youths. Sociologists have suggested that the central process of control is determined by a person's "commitment to conformity." Under this model—assuming employees are all subject to the same deviant motives and opportunities—the probability of deviant involvement depends on the stakes that one has in conformity.

The researchers suggest that the policy implications from the commitment to conformity theory are that rather than subject employees to draconian security measures,

companies should afford younger workers many of the same rights, fringes, and privileges of the tenured, older employees. In fact, by signaling to the younger employee that he or she is temporary or expendable, the organization inadvertently may be encouraging its own victimization by the very group of employees that is already least committed to the expressed goals and objectives of the owners and managers.[45]

Hollinger and Clark were able to confirm a direct relationship between an employee's position and the level of the theft, with those levels of theft highest in jobs with almost unrestricted access to the things of value in the work organization. Although they saw obvious connections between opportunity and theft (e.g., retail cashiers with daily access to cash had the highest incidence), the researchers believed opportunity to be "only a secondary factor that constrains the manner in which the deviance is manifested."[46]

Job Satisfaction and Deviance

The research of Hollinger and Clark strongly suggests that all age groups of employees who are dissatisfied with their jobs, but especially younger workers, are the most likely to seek redress through counterproductive or illegal behavior in order to right the perceived "inequity." Other writers, notably anthropologist Gerald Mars and researcher David Altheide, have commented on this connection. You can probably remember your own instances of "getting back" at the organization for its perceived shortcomings, as I did with Mr. Zac.

As another example, I heard a legendary story when I was in the FBI about an agent we will call Willis. Stories such as this one have a way of taking on a life of their own, and I therefore cannot vouch for its complete accuracy. At any rate, Willis was apparently attempting to arrest a fugitive when his suit was ripped to shreds. On his next expense voucher, Willis claimed $200 for the suit. But a clerk in charge of paying the voucher for the FBI called him. "Willis," the clerk said, "there is no way the government is going to pay you for ripping your suit—forget it." Willis reasoned this was extremely unfair. After all, he would now have to go out of pocket for a new suit. This would not have been necessary were it not for his job, Willis rationalized. The clerk, however, was unimpressed.

The following month the clerk received the FBI agent's next expense voucher and examined it with a fine-tooth comb to make sure Willis did not try again. Convinced the voucher was satisfactory, the clerk called Willis. "I'm glad to see you didn't try to claim the cost of that suit again," the clerk said. Willis reputedly replied, "That's where you're wrong. The cost of that suit is in the voucher. All you have to do is find it."

This story illustrates the same concept that Mars observed consistently among hotel dining room employees and dock workers. The employees believed that pilferage was not theft; it was "seen as a morally justified addition to wages; indeed, as an entitlement due from exploiting employers."[47] Altheide also documented that theft is often perceived by employees as a "way of getting back at the boss or supervisor."[48] From my own experience with Mr. Zac, I can verify this sentiment. Criminologist Jason Ditton documented a pattern in U.S. industries called "wages in kind," in which employees "situated in structurally disadvantaged parts [of the organization] receive large segments of their wages invisibly."[49]

Organizational Controls and Deviance

Try as they might, Hollinger and Clark were unable to document a strong relationship between control and deviance. They examined five different control mechanisms: company policy, selection of personnel, inventory control, security, and punishment.

Company policy can be an effective control. Hollinger and Clark pointed out that companies with a strong policy against absenteeism have a lesser problem with it. As a result, they would expect policies governing employee theft to have the same impact. Similarly, they believed that employee education as an organizational policy has a deterrent effect. Control through selection of personnel is exerted by hiring persons who will conform to organizational expectations. Inventory control is required not only for theft but for procedures to detect errors, avoid waste, and ensure that a proper amount of inventory is maintained. Security controls involve proactive and reactive measures, surveillance, internal investigations, and others. Control through punishment is designed to deter the specific individual as well as others who might be tempted to act illegally.

Hollinger and Clark interviewed numerous employees in an attempt to determine their attitudes toward control. With respect to policy, they concluded:

> *The issue of theft by employees is a sensitive one in organizations and must be handled with some discretion. A concern for theft must be expressed without creating an atmosphere of distrust and paranoia. If an organization places too much stress on the topic, honest employees may feel unfairly suspected, resulting in lowered morale and higher turnover.*[50]

Employees in the study also perceived, in general, that computerized inventory records added security and made theft more difficult. With respect to security control, the researchers discovered that employees regarded the purpose of a security division as taking care of outside—rather than inside—security. Few employees were aware that security departments investigate employee theft, and most such departments had a poor image among the workers. With respect to punishment, the employees who were interviewed felt that theft would result in job termination in a worst-case scenario. They perceived that minor thefts would be handled only by reprimands.

Hollinger and Clark conclude that formal organizational controls provide both good and bad news.

> *The good news is that employee theft does seem to be susceptible to control efforts. . . . Our data also indicate, however, that the impact of organizational controls is neither uniform nor very strong. In sum, formal organizational controls do negatively influence theft prevalence, but these effects must be understood in combination with the other factors influencing this phenomenon.*[51]

Employee Perception of Control

The researchers examined the perception—not necessarily the reality—of employees who believed that they would be caught if they committed theft: "We find that perceived certainty of detection is inversely related to employee theft for respondents in all three industry sectors—that is, the stronger the perception that theft would be detected, the less the likelihood that the employee would engage in deviant behavior."[52]

Social control in the workplace, according to Hollinger and Clark, consists of both formal and informal social controls. The former control can be described as the internalization by the employee of the group norms of the organization; the latter, external pressures through both positive and negative sanctions. These researchers, along with a host of others, have concluded that, as a general proposition, informal social controls provide the best deterrent. "These data clearly indicate that the loss of respect among one's acquaintances was the single most effective variable in predicting future deviant involvement." Furthermore, "in general, the probability of suffering informal sanction is far more important than fear of formal sanctions in deterring deviant activity."[53]

Conclusion

Hollinger and Clark reached five other conclusions based on their work. First, they believe that "substantially increasing the internal security presence does not seem to be appropriate, given the prevalence of the problem. In fact, doing so may make things worse.''[54] Second, they conclude that the same kinds of employees who engage in other workplace deviance are also principally the ones who engage in employee theft. They found persuasive evidence that slow or sloppy workmanship, sick-leave abuses, long coffee breaks, alcohol and drug use at work, late arrival, and early departure were more likely to be present in the employee-thief.

Third, the researchers hypothesize that if efforts are made to reduce employee theft without reducing its underlying causes (e.g., employee dissatisfaction, lack of ethics), the result could create a ''hydraulic effect,'' whereby tightening controls over property deviance may create more detrimental acts affecting the productivity of the organization—for example, pushing down employee theft may push up goldbricking. Fourth, they agreed that increased management sensitivity to its employees will reduce all forms of workplace deviance. Fifth, they concluded that special attention should be afforded young employees, as these are the ones statistically the most likely to steal. However, although the incidence of theft is higher among younger employees, the losses are typically lower than those of more senior employees with financial authority.

Hollinger and Clark believe management must pay attention to four aspects of policy development:

1. Clearly understanding theft behavior
2. Continuously disseminating positive information reflective of the company's policies
3. Enforcing sanctions
4. Publicizing sanctions

The researchers sum up their observations by saying

perhaps the most important overall policy implication that can be drawn . . . is that theft and workplace deviance are in large part a reflection of how management at all levels of the organization is perceived by the employee. Specifically, if the employee is permitted to conclude that his or her contribution to the workplace is not appreciated or that the organization does not seem to care about the theft of its property, we expect to find greater involvement. In conclusion, a lowered prevalence of employee theft may be one valuable consequence of a management team that is responsive to the current perceptions and attitudes of its workforce.[55]

2010 REPORT TO THE NATIONS ON OCCUPATIONAL FRAUD AND ABUSE

In 1993, the Association of Certified Fraud Examiners (ACFE) began a major study of occupational fraud cases with the goal of classifying occupational frauds and abuses by the methods used to commit them. There were other objectives too. One was to get an idea of how the professionals—the certified fraud examiners—view the fraud problems faced by their own companies. After all, they deal with fraud and abuse on a daily basis. Another goal was to gather demographics on the perpetrators: How old are they? How well educated? What percentage of offenders are men? Were there any correlations that we could identify with respect to the offenders? What about the victim companies: How large were they? What industries did they cover? For good measure, the ACFE also decided to ask the CFEs to take an educated guess—based on their experience—of the extent of fraud and abuse within their own organizations.

Beginning in 1993, the ACFE distributed a detailed four-page questionnaire to about 10,000 CFEs, asking them to report the details of one fraud case they had investigated. By early 1995, 2,608 surveys had been returned for analysis, including 1,509 usable cases of occupational fraud. Although the survey design was not perfect, the sheer number of responses made it—to the ACFE's knowledge—the largest such study on this subject at the time. Of the cases analyzed, the total loss caused by fraud was about $15 billion, ranging from a low of $22 to a high of $2.5 billion. From that survey, the ACFE developed in 1996 the first *Report to the Nation on Occupational Fraud and Abuse*. Association president Gil Geis decided that the name *Report to the Nation on Occupational Fraud and Abuse* was a bit long, so he alternatively titled it *The Wells Report*.

Since 1996, the ACFE has released five updated editions of the *Report*—in 2002, 2004, 2006, 2008, and the most recent version in 2010. Each edition has been based on detailed case information provided by CFEs and has built on the findings of its predecessors.

The ACFE's most recent survey was conducted in late 2009 and resulted in the *2010 Report to the Nations on Occupational Fraud and Abuse*, the first ACFE *Report* to include cases from countries outside the United States. The current edition of the *Report* is based on 1,843 actual cases of occupational fraud that were investigated worldwide between January 2008 and December 2009. The CFEs who participated were asked to provide information on the single largest case they investigated during this time period; from this information, researchers were able to observe trends in and draw conclusions about how fraud is committed, how it can be classified, and how it affects business across the globe.

The majority of statistical data pertaining to the ACFE's research on occupational fraud that is cited in this book is derived from the results of the *2009 Global Fraud Survey*, as reported in the *2010 Report to the Nations on Occupational Fraud and Abuse*.

Measuring the Costs of Occupational Fraud

Participants in the *2009 Global Fraud Survey* were asked what percent of gross revenues they believe—based on their personal experience and general knowledge—the typical organization loses to fraud and abuse. The median response was 5 percent, a slight decrease from the 6 and 7 percent estimates provided by respondents in previous editions of the survey. Optimistically, this reduction could be viewed as progress in the war against fraud.

However, because the responses provided were only estimates, the data should not be read as a literal representation of the true rate of fraud in organizations throughout the world. Nevertheless, even at a rate of 5 percent, this estimate of the cost of fraud is astounding. Applying this figure to the gross world product—which, for 2009, was estimated to be $58.07 trillion[56]—results in a projected total global fraud loss of $2.9 trillion annually. It is a staggering sum, to say the least.

But what does the figure really mean? It is simply the collective opinions of those who work in the antifraud field. Unfortunately, finding the actual cost of fraud may not be possible by any method. One obvious approach would be to take a scientific poll of the workforce and ask the tough questions: Have you stolen or committed fraud against your organization? If so, how? And how much was the value of the fraud or abuse you committed? But the unlikelihood of people answering such questions candidly would make any results obtained by this method unreliable at best.

Another approach to finding the cost of fraud would be to do a scientific poll of a representative sample of organizations. Even assuming that respondents answered the poll correctly, there would still be an obvious flaw in the data: Organizations typically do not know when they are being victimized. And of course, there is the definitional issue that plagues all the methods: Where do we draw the line on what constitutes occupational fraud and abuse? So asking the experts—the approach used here—may be as reliable as anything else. But the reader must be cautioned that, by any method of estimation, the numbers on fraud and abuse are soft and subject to various interpretations.

Whatever the actual costs, organizations are unwittingly paying them already as a part of their total operating expenses. Such is the insidious nature of fraud, and what can we do about it? How can we possibly detect something we do not know about in the first place? It is as if a secret "fraud tax" has been levied on organizations. And interestingly, many organizations may silently condone fraud and abuse, which is committed from the top down. Indeed, some sociologists see abuse as an informal employment benefit and have even suggested that chronic pilferage and certain other abuses might actually have a positive effect on morale and therefore increase productivity.

Losses Reported in the *2009 Global Fraud Survey*

As was stated earlier, the *2009 Global Fraud Survey* yielded 1,843 usable cases of occupational fraud for our study. Among those cases, the median loss experienced by the victim organizations was $160,000. The chart in Exhibit 1.5 illustrates the distribution of all losses. Note that nearly one-fourth of the cases in the study (23.7 percent) caused losses of $1 million or more.

Exhibit 1.5 *2009 Global Fraud Survey*: **Distribution of Losses**

Exhibit 1.6 *2009 Global Fraud Survey*: **Percent of Cases by Position**

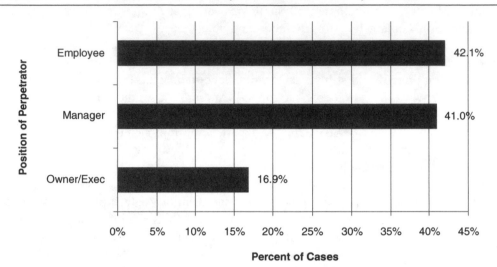

Perpetrators of Fraud

By definition, the perpetrators of occupational fraud are employed by the organization they defraud. Participants in the 2009 survey provided information on the perpetrators' position, gender, age, education, department, tenure, and criminal histories. In cases where there was more than one perpetrator, respondents were asked to provide data on the *principal perpetrator*, which was defined as the person who worked for the victim organization and who was the primary culprit.

Effect of the Perpetrator's Position

Personal data gathered about the perpetrators indicated that most of the frauds in this study were committed by either employees (42.1 percent) or managers (41 percent). Owner/executives made up less than one-fifth of the perpetrators. (See Exhibit 1.6.)

Although the highest percentage of schemes was committed by employees, these frauds had the lowest median loss, at $80,000 per incident. Frauds committed by managers caused median losses of $200,000 per incident, while the median loss in schemes committed by owner/executives was $723,000. This figure is more than nine times higher than the typical loss in employee schemes. The differences in the loss amounts were most likely a result of the degree of financial control exercised at each level: Those with the highest positions also have the greatest access to company funds and assets. (See Exhibit 1.7.)

Effect of Gender

The results of the *2009 Global Fraud Survey* showed that male employees caused median losses more than twice as large as those of female employees; the median loss in a scheme caused by a male employee was $232,000 while the median loss caused by a female employee was $100,000. The most logical explanation for this disparity seems

Exhibit 1.7   *2009 Global Fraud Survey*: **Median Loss by Position**

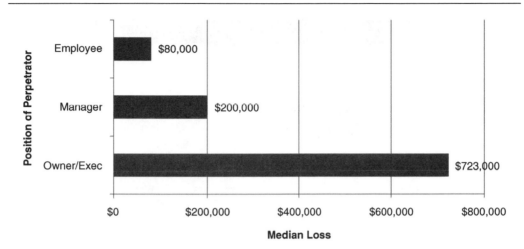

to be the ''glass ceiling'' phenomenon; generally, men occupy higher-paying positions than their female counterparts, and, as we have seen, there is a direct correlation between median loss and position.

According to our survey data, males are also the principal perpetrator in a majority of cases, accounting for 67 percent of frauds in our study versus the 33 percent in which a female was the primary culprit. (See Exhibits 1.8 and 1.9.)

Effect of Age

The ACFE *Reports* continually reveal a direct and linear correlation between the perpetrator's age and median loss. The reason for the trend, we believe, is that those in an organization who are older generally tend to occupy higher-ranking positions with greater access to revenues, assets, and resources. In other words, we believe age to be only a secondary factor to that of position as a predictor of relative fraud losses.

Exhibit 1.8   *2009 Global Fraud Survey*: **Median Loss by Gender**

Exhibit 1.9 *2009 Global Fraud Survey*: **Percent of Cases by Gender**

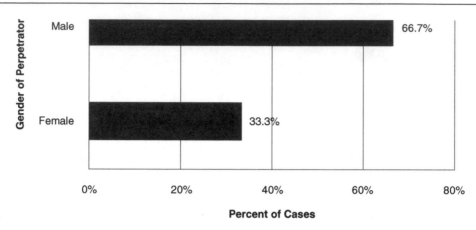

Those in the oldest age group were responsible for median losses almost 65 times higher than the youngest perpetrators. Furthermore, although some studies, including those of Hollinger and Clark, have suggested that younger employees are more likely to commit occupational crime, only 5 percent of the frauds in our study were committed by individuals below the age of 26, while nearly half the frauds were committed by persons over the age of 40. (See Exhibits 1.10 and 1.11.)

Exhibit 1.10 *2009 Global Fraud Survey*: **Median Loss by Age**

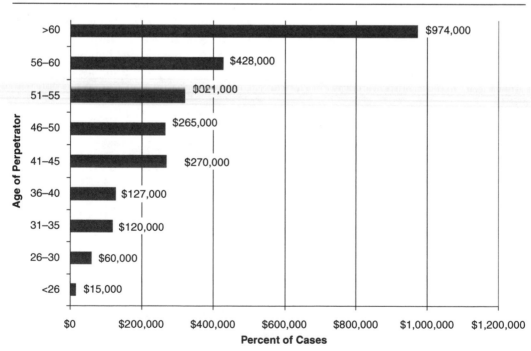

Exhibit 1.11   *2009 Global Fraud Survey*: **Percent of Cases by Age**

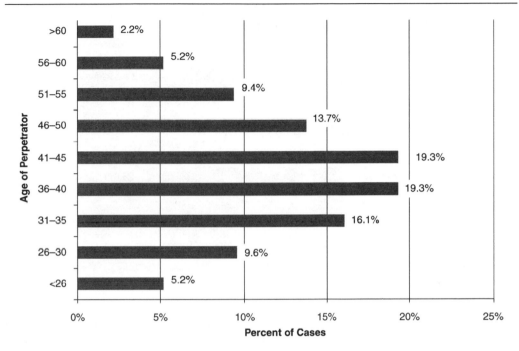

Effect of Education

In general, those with higher education levels would be expected to occupy higher positions in an organization and to have greater access to organizational assets. Therefore, we expected a fairly linear correlation between education and median loss. Fraudsters with only a high school education caused median losses of $100,000, but that figure more than doubled for perpetrators who had a college degree. The median loss caused by those with postgraduate degrees (14 percent of fraudsters) was $300,000. (See Exhibits 1.12 and 1.13.)

Exhibit 1.12   *2009 Global Fraud Survey*: **Median Loss by Education**

Exhibit 1.13   *2009 Global Fraud Survey*: **Percent of Cases by Education**

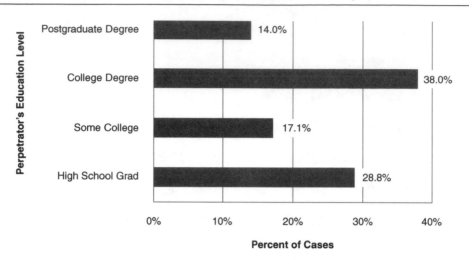

Effect of Collusion

It was not surprising to see that in cases involving more than one perpetrator, fraud losses rose substantially. The majority of survey cases (57 percent) only involved a single perpetrator, but when two or more persons conspired, the median loss more than tripled. (See Exhibits 1.14 and 1.15.)

Perpetrator's Department

Of the fraud cases studied, 22 percent were perpetrated by an employee in the accounting department. Further, 80 percent of all the frauds were committed by employees in

Exhibit 1.14   *2009 Global Fraud Survey*: **Percent of Cases by Number of Perpetrators**

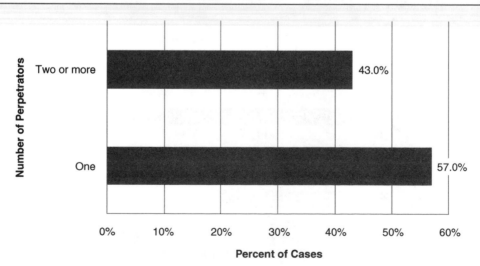

Exhibit 1.15 *2009 Global Fraud Survey*: Median Loss by Number of Perpetrators

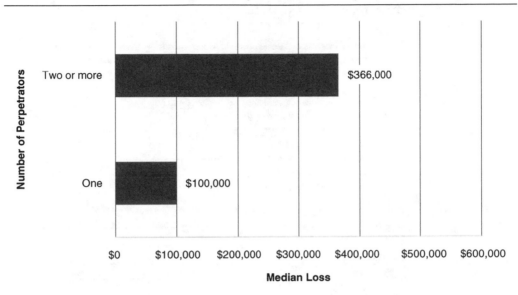

six departments: accounting, operations, sales, executive/upper management, customer service, and purchasing. (See Exhibit 1.16.) The perpetrators holding the highest levels of autonomy and authority within the organization—those in executive/upper management roles and those on the board—caused the greatest losses to the victim organizations, at $829,000 and $800,000, respectively. (See Exhibit 1.17.)

Exhibit 1.16 *2009 Global Fraud Survey*: Percent of Cases by Department of Perpetrator

Exhibit 1.17 *2009 Global Fraud Survey*: **Median Loss by Department of Perpetrator**

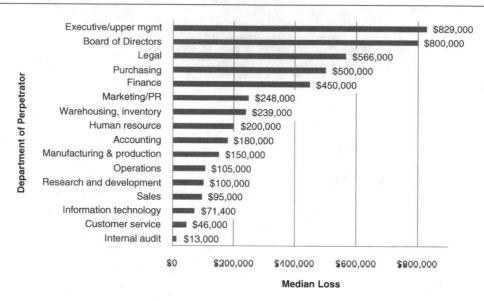

Effect of Tenure

The results of the 2009 survey revealed a direct correlation between the length of time an employee had been employed by a victim organization and the size of the loss in the case. Employees who had been with the victim for ten years or more caused median losses of $289,000, whereas employees who had been with their employers for one year or less caused median losses of $47,000. Additionally, employees with tenure of one to five years were involved in the greatest percentage of fraud cases. (See Exhibits 1.18 and 1.19.)

Exhibit 1.18 *2009 Global Fraud Survey*: **Median Loss by Years of Tenure**

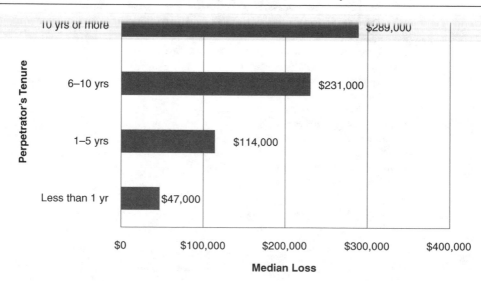

Exhibit 1.19 *2009 Global Fraud Survey*: Percent of Cases by Years of Tenure

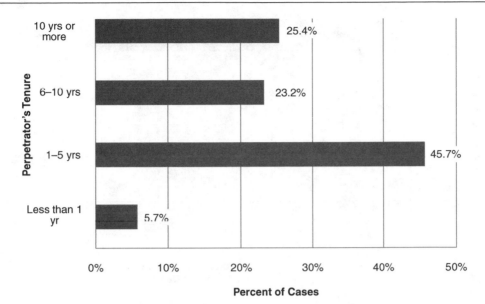

Criminal History of the Perpetrators

Only approximately 7 percent of the perpetrators identified in the 2009 study were known to have been convicted of a previous fraud-related offense. Another 8 percent of the perpetrators had previously been charged but never convicted. These figures are consistent with other studies that have shown most people who commit occupational fraud are first-time offenders. The findings are also consistent with Cressey's model, in which occupational offenders do not perceive themselves as lawbreakers. (See Exhibit 1.20.)

Victims

The victims of occupational fraud are organizations who are defrauded by those they employ. Our 2009 survey asked respondents to provide information on, among other things, the size and type of organizations that were victimized and the antifraud measures those organizations had in place at the time of the frauds.

Type of the Victim Organization

Most of the cases reported in the *2009 Global Fraud Survey* involved victims that were privately held companies (42 percent), whereas not-for-profit organizations had the lowest representation (10 percent). It should be noted that we made no effort to obtain a random sample of business organizations. The *Report* was based on a survey of CFEs throughout the world; consequently, the demographics of the victim organizations in the study depended in large measure on the organizations that retain CFEs. (See Exhibit 1.21.)

Exhibit 1.20   *2009 Global Fraud Survey*: Percent of Cases by Criminal History

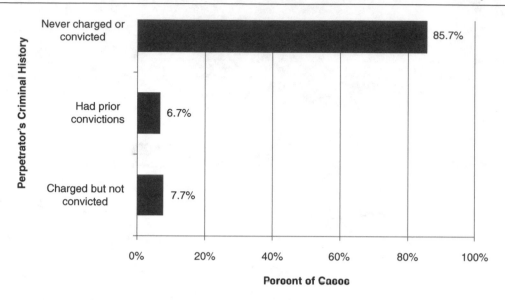

Our study revealed that privately held and publicly traded companies were not only the most heavily represented organization types; they also suffered the largest losses, at $231,000 and $200,000 respectively. In comparison, losses in government ($100,000) and not-for-profit organizations ($90,000) were about half as much. (See Exhibit 1.22.)

Size of the Victim Organization

The cases in our 2009 study were fairly evenly distributed among organizations of all sizes, with the smallest entities experiencing the greatest percentage of frauds by a

Exhibit 1.21   *2009 Global Fraud Survey*: Percent of Cases by Organization Type

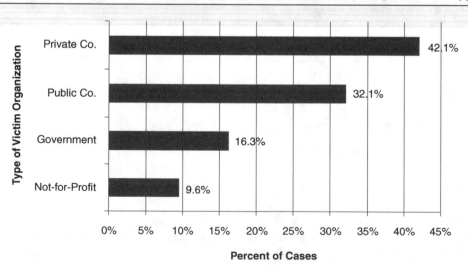

Exhibit 1.22 *2009 Global Fraud Survey*: Median Loss by Organization Type

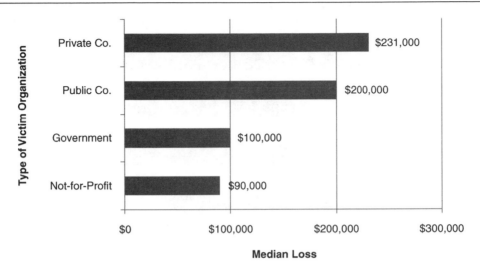

small margin. Over 30 percent of the cases occurred in small organizations—those with fewer than 100 employees.

Organizations with 100 to 999 employees experienced the largest median loss ($200,000), whereas organizations employing 1,000 to 9,999 had the lowest median loss ($139,000). Interestingly, the organizations on either end of the size spectrum—those with fewer than 100 employees and those with 10,000 or more employees—had losses in the middle, at $155,000 and $164,000 respectively. Although the smallest organizations did not experience the largest median loss in absolute terms, the relative size of the median loss for small companies indicates that these entities are disproportionately vulnerable to occupational fraud and abuse. Put more simply, absorbing a $155,000 loss is typically a much bigger burden on a small company than absorbing a $164,000 loss is on an organization with 10,000 or more employees.

We theorize that the disproportionate nature of fraud losses at small companies exists for two reasons. First, smaller businesses have fewer divisions of responsibility, meaning that fewer people must perform more functions. One of the most common types of fraud encountered in our studies involved small business operations that had a one-person accounting department—that employee writes checks, reconciles the accounts, and posts the books. An entry-level accounting student could spot the internal control deficiencies in that scenario, but apparently many small business owners cannot or do not.

Which brings up the second reason we believe losses are so high in small organizations: There is a greater degree of trust inherent in a situation where everyone knows each other by name and face. Who of us would like to think our coworkers would or do commit these offenses? As a result, our defenses are naturally relaxed. There again is the dichotomy of fraud: It cannot occur without trust, but neither can commerce. Trust is an essential ingredient at all levels of business—we can and do make handshake deals every day. Transactions in capitalism simply cannot occur without trust. The key is seeking the right balance between too much and too little. (See Exhibits 1.23 and 1.24.)

Exhibit 1.23 *2009 Global Fraud Survey*: Percent of Cases by Number of Employees

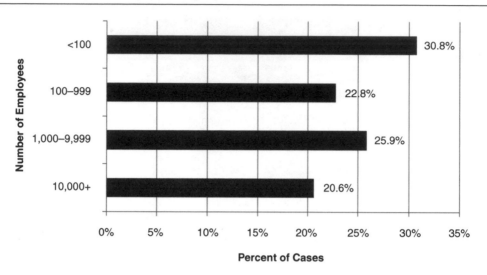

Antifraud Measures at the Victim Organization

CFEs who participated in our *2009 Global Fraud Survey* were asked to identify which, if any, of 15 common antifraud measures were utilized by the victim organizations at the time the reported frauds occurred. More than three-quarters of the victim organizations had their financial statements audited by external auditors, whereas two-thirds had dedicated internal audit or fraud examination departments, and almost 60 percent had independent audits of their internal controls over financial reporting. Additionally, nearly

Exhibit 1.24 *2009 Global Fraud Survey*: Median Loss by Number of Employees

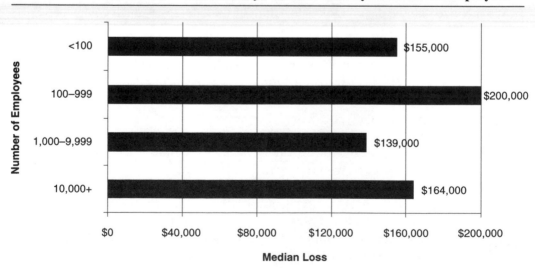

Exhibit 1.25   *2009 Global Fraud Survey*: **Frequency of Antifraud Controls**

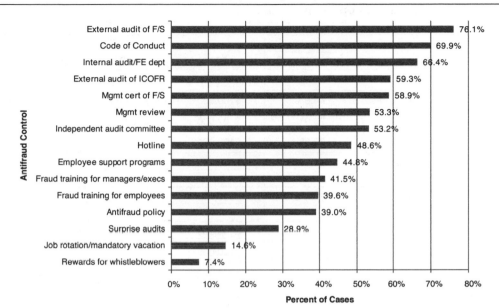

70 percent of the organizations had a formal code of conduct in place at the time of the fraud, although only 39 percent extended that to include a formal antifraud policy.

To examine the effectiveness of these common antifraud controls, researchers also compared by those organizations that had a particular antifraud control in place against the median loss for those organizations without that control at the time of the fraud (excluding all other factors). The results indicate that hotlines, employee support programs, and surprise audits were the mechanisms most associated with a reduced cost of fraud. Organizations without these mechanisms in place reported frauds that cost more than twice as much as those in organizations that had any one of these mechanisms in place at the time of the fraud. Conversely, external audits—the most common antifraud measure utilized by victim organizations—showed the second lowest impact on median losses in our study. (See Exhibits 1.25 and 1.26.)

Detecting and Preventing Occupational Fraud

Initial Detection of Frauds

The obvious question in a study of occupational fraud is: What can be done about it? Given that our study was based on actual fraud cases that had been investigated, we thought it would be instructional to ask how these frauds were initially detected by the victim organizations. Perhaps by studying how the victim organizations had uncovered fraud, we would be able to provide guidance to other organizations on how to tailor their fraud-detection efforts. Respondents were given a list of common detection methods and were asked how the frauds they investigated were detected initially. As these results show, the frauds in our study were most commonly detected by tip (40.2 percent).

Exhibit 1.26   *2009 Global Fraud Survey*: Impact of Antifraud Measures on Median Loss

Control	% of cases implemented	Yes	No	% Reduction
Hotline	48.6%	$100,000	$245,000	59.2%
Employee support programs	44.8%	$100,000	$244,000	59.0%
Surprise audits	28.9%	$ 97,000	$200,000	51.5%
Fraud training for employees	39.6%	$100,000	$200,000	50.0%
Fraud training for managers/execs	41.5%	$100,000	$200,000	50.0%
Job rotation/mandatory vacation	14.6%	$100,000	$188,000	46.8%
Code of conduct	69.9%	$140,000	$262,000	46.6%
Antifraud policy	39.0%	$120,000	$200,000	40.0%
Mgmt review	53.3%	$120,000	$200,000	40.0%
External audit of ICOFR	59.3%	$140,000	$215,000	34.9%
Internal audit/FE dept	66.4%	$145,000	$209,000	30.6%
Independent audit committee	53.2%	$140,000	$200,000	30.0%
Mgmt cert of F/S	58.9%	$150,000	$200,000	25.0%
External audit of F/S	76.1%	$150,000	$200,000	25.0%
Rewards for whistleblowers	7.4%	$119,000	$155,000	23.2%

Unfortunately, as shown previously, the majority of fraud victims did not have established reporting structures in place at the time they were defrauded. It is also interesting—and rather disconcerting—to note that accident was the fourth-most-common detection method, accounting for 8.3 percent of the fraud cases in the survey, while external audits detected less than 5 percent of the reported frauds. (See Exhibit 1.27.)

Methods

The principal goal of the first *Report to the Nation* was to classify occupational frauds and abuses by the methods used to commit them. As a result of the 1996 study, we were able to develop a classification system known informally as the fraud tree that accounts for most, if not all, of the most common occupational fraud and abuse schemes. We tested the structure of the fraud tree against the cases in all of our subsequent studies to make sure that our classification system accounted for every scheme that was reported. Among the six studies, we have applied the fraud tree classification system to well over 6,400 cases of fraud and have found that it has covered them all.

Exhibit 1.27   *2009 Global Fraud Survey*: **Initial Detection of Frauds**

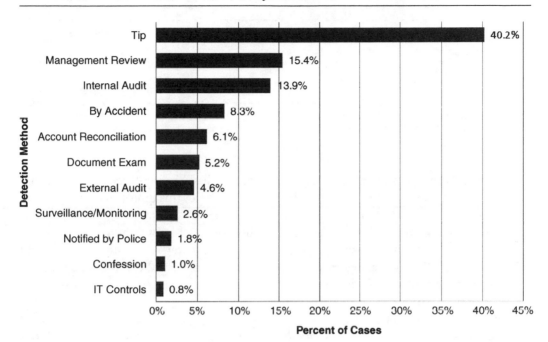

By classifying and categorizing occupational frauds, we are able to study these crimes in more detail. Instead of lumping every case under the general heading of "fraud," we observe discrete groups of frauds with similar characteristics in order to learn what methods are most commonly used to commit occupational fraud and what schemes tend to cause the biggest losses. Also, by comparing schemes in well-defined categories, we can identify common methods used by the perpetrators as well as common vulnerabilities in the victim organizations that allow such frauds to succeed. This in turn should help in the development of better, more efficient antifraud tools.

According to the fraud tree, there are three major categories of occupational fraud:

1. *Asset misappropriations*, which involve the theft or misuse of an organization's assets. (Common examples include skimming revenues, stealing inventory, and payroll fraud.)

2. *Corruption*, in which fraudsters wrongfully use their influence in a business transaction in order to procure some benefit for themselves or another person, contrary to their duty to their employer or the rights of another. (Common examples include accepting kickbacks and entering into conflicts of interest.)

3. *Fraudulent statements*, which involve purposeful misreporting of financial information about the organization with the Intent to mislead those who rely on it. (Common examples include overstating revenues and understating liabilities or expenses.)

Exhibit 1.28 *2009 Global Fraud Survey*: **Major Occupational Fraud Categories**

Scheme Type	Pct. Cases[1]	Median Cost
Asset Misappropriations	86.3	$135,000
Corruption Schemes	32.8	$250,000
Fraudulent Statements	4.8	$4,100,000

[1]The sum of percentages listed in this column exceeds 100% because some cases involved multiple fraud schemes that fell into more than one category. The same is true for every scheme classification chart in this book based on the *2009 Global Fraud Survey*.

The data from our study on frequency and median loss for the three major occupational fraud categories are presented in Exhibit 1.28. Asset misappropriations made up more than 85 percent of the cases encountered but were by far the least costly in terms of median loss. Meanwhile, fraudulent statements were the least common, accounting for less than 5 percent of cases, but they caused far greater harm, on average, than schemes in the other two categories. Corruption schemes were the "middle children" of the study; they were more common than fraudulent statements and more costly than asset misappropriations.

Within each of the three major categories, there are several subcategories of fraud scheme types. In coming chapters we address each of these subcategories in turn, looking at research on their costs and effects, identifying how the schemes are committed, and discussing how organizations can defend against them.

NOTES

1. Association of Certified Fraud Examiners, *The Report to the Nation on Occupational Fraud and Abuse* (Austin, TX: Author, 1996), p. 4.
2. Ibid., p. 9.
3. Henry Campbell Black, *Black's Law Dictionary*, 5th ed. (St. Paul, MN: West, 1979), p.563.
4. Ibid, p. 468.
5. Ibid., p. 300.
6. Ibid., p. 792.
7. Ibid., p. 793.
8. Ibid., p. 225.
9. *Merriam-Webster's Collegiate Dictionary*, 11th ed. (Springfield, MA: Merriam-Webster, 2008), p. 321.
10. Gilbert Geis, *On White Collar Crime* (Lexington, KY: Lexington Books, 1982).
11. James Q. Wilson and Richard J. Herrnstein, *Crime & Human Nature: The Definitive Study of the Causes of Crime* (New York: The Free Press, 1985).
12. Larry J. Siegel, *Criminology*, 3rd ed. (New York: West, 1989), p. 193.
13. Donald R. Cressey, *Other People's Money* (Montclair, NJ: Patterson Smith, 1973).
14. Ibid., p. 30.
15. Ibid., p. 33.

16. Ibid., p. 34.
17. Ibid., p. 34.
18. Ibid., p. 36.
19. Ibid., p. 38.
20. Ibid., p. 42.
21. Ibid., p. 47.
22. Ibid., p. 54.
23. Ibid., pp. 66–67.
24. Ibid., p. 86.
25. Ibid., p. 94.
26. Ibid., p. 121.
27. Ibid., p. 122.
28. Ibid., p. 128.
29. Ibid., p. 133.
30. Ibid., p. 139.
31. W. Steve Albrecht, Keith R. Howe, and Marshall B. Romney, *Deterring Fraud: The Internal Auditor's Perspective* (Altamonte Springs, FL: The Institute of Internal Auditor's Research Foundation, 1984), p. xiv.
32. Ibid., p. xv.
33. Ibid., p. 6.
34. Ibid., p. 5.
35. Ibid., p. 6.
36. Ibid., p. 6.
37. Ibid., pp. 12–13.
38. Richard C. Hollinger and John P. Clark, *Theft by Employees* (Lexington, KY: Lexington Books, 1983), p. 6.
39. Ibid., p. 42.
40. Ibid., p. 57.
41. Ibid.
42. Ibid.
43. Ibid., p. 63.
44. Ibid., p. 67.
45. Ibid., p. 68.
46. Ibid., p. 77.
47. Ibid., p. 86.
48. Ibid.
49. Ibid.
50. Ibid., p. 106.
51. Ibid., p. 117.
52. Ibid., p. 120.
53. Ibid., p. 121.
54. Ibid., p. 144.
55. Ibid., p. 146.
56. United States Central Intelligence Agency, *The World Factbook*, www.cia.gov/library/publications/the-world-factbook/geos/xx.html.

PART I
ASSET MISAPPROPRIATIONS

CHAPTER 2

Introduction to Asset Misappropriations

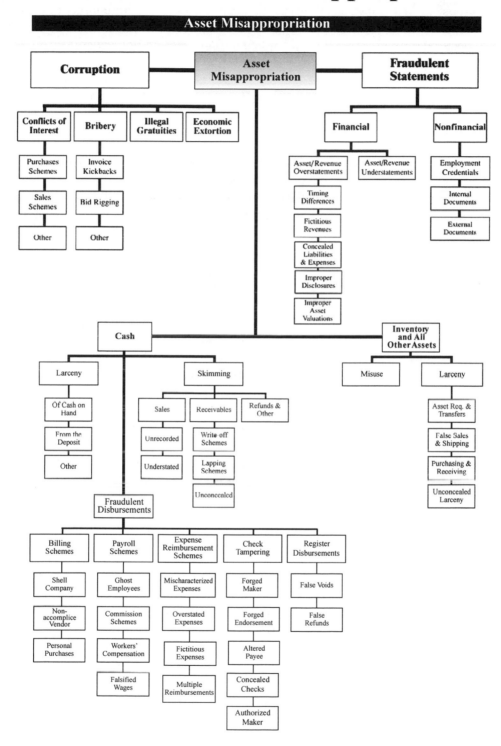

OVERVIEW

The purpose of this chapter is to provide an overview of the favorite target of occupational fraud offenders: the organization's assets. Before defining assets, let us first learn what constitutes misappropriation. According to *Black's Law Dictionary*,

> *misappropriation [is] the act of misappropriating or turning to a wrong purpose; wrong appropriation, a term that does not necessarily mean peculation, although it may mean that. The term may also embrace the taking and using of another's property for sole purpose of capitalizing unfairly on good will and reputation of property owner.*[1]

The definition in *Webster's* is a little more pointed: "to appropriate wrongly (as by theft or embezzlement)."[2] For our purposes, misappropriation includes more than theft or embezzlement. It involves the misuse of any company asset for personal gain. Therefore, employees using a company computer after hours for their own side business have not stolen an asset, but they have misappropriated it for their own benefit.

DEFINITION OF "ASSETS"

In commerce, the purpose of assets is to produce income. If a business produces oil, the rigs, trucks, and even the land are all assets. Should the business sell clothing, its merchandise and display cases are assets. According to Marshall and McManus, "Assets are probable future economic benefits obtained or controlled by a particular entity as a result of past transactions or events. In brief, assets represent the amount of resources owned by the entity."[3]

Because of the breadth of this accounting definition, exactly what constitutes an asset can become very esoteric to the nonaccountant. For example, the logo of the Coca-Cola Company is recognized worldwide. For many people, all they need to know about a soft drink is its logo before they buy. As a result, the trademarked logo of Coke is worth millions, perhaps billions. Just exactly how much it is worth cannot be determined accurately unless Coke decides to sell the logo itself—an unlikely event. The logo alone is called an intangible asset, one of the two types of assets in commerce.

Intangible Assets

According to Marshall and McManus,

> *intangible assets [are] long-lived assets that differ from property, plant, and equipment that has been purchased outright or acquired under a capital lease—either because the asset is represented by a contractual right, or because the asset results from a purchase transaction but is not physically identifiable. Examples of the first type of intangible assets are leaseholds, patents, and trademarks; the second type of asset is known as goodwill.*[4]

Intangible assets are difficult to misappropriate because they are not "physically identifiable."

Tangible Assets

Webster's defines "tangible" as "(1a) capable of being perceived, especially by the sense of touch: palatable; (b) substantially real: material; (2) capable of being precisely identified or realized by the mind; (3) capable of being appraised at an actual or approximate value, e.g., assets."[5] If we cannot see it, feel it, or smell it, chances are the asset is not tangible. Tangible assets of a business or organization, for accounting purposes, are classified on the entity's books as one of five principal types: cash, accounts receivable, inventory, plant and equipment, or investments. And, of course, it is invariably one or more of these types of assets that are misappropriated by employees.

But some of the assets subject to misappropriation within an organization are not necessarily classified as such in the books. For example, included in our specific definition of assets are the two categories of supplies and information. Supplies normally are carried on an organization's books as expenses because they tend to be consumed by the organization within a year of purchase. And information does not find its way directly to the entity's books. Instead, it is recognized when the information is sold at a later time. But any organization would tell you that information is one of its most valuable resources; employees who engage in industrial spying and sabotage for a competing organization are becoming increasingly common and expensive.

HOW ASSET MISAPPROPRIATIONS AFFECT BOOKS OF ACCOUNT

You do not need to know much accounting to understand how asset misappropriations affect the organization's books. And this book assumes that you do not know anything about accounting. Readers with an accounting background will find the following material elementary, perhaps even amusing. But the discussion will be a good refresher in light of possible fraud.

Let us assume you own a small business of restoring and selling electric guitars. And let us say your assets are $225,000, but you owe $75,000 on the business. Your equity in the business is then $150,000, the difference. One of your employees steals a rare 1954 Fender Telecaster, for which you paid $3,000, excluding $500 in parts, labor, and other costs to restore it. You were going to sell the restored guitar for $6,000.

So to the question: How does this theft affect your books? Did you lose $3,000, $3,500, or $6,000? Under what are called generally accepted accounting principles (GAAP), your loss is $3,500—what you paid for the guitar plus the repairs. But why is the loss not what you would have gotten when you sold the guitar? Because the GAAP of conservatism requires us to keep our books to reflect the cost of the product, not the amount for which it sells. A more complete discussion of accounting concepts can be found in Chapter 12.

The accounting profession prefers companies to keep their books so that the value of all the assets is at least what is reflected on the financial statements. If the value is more, then so be it. We will recognize the value of that rare guitar when it is finally sold. In that particular transaction, we will effectively trade one asset (the restored Fender Telecaster) for another asset: $6,000 in cash. The difference is called our gross profit.

So when the guitar is stolen by an employee, how do we record that loss on our books, and what effect does it have on you, the owner of the guitar shop? That accounting transaction is quite simple: The stolen asset comes directly out of your equity in the business. You had a beginning equity of $150,000. Now you must bear the entire $3,500 loss yourself. So your total assets are now $221,500, and your total equity is $146,500.

The fact that you might owe money on the guitar is irrelevant to the amount you lost—you still must pay your bills. There is, then, a dollar-for-dollar set-off to your equity when someone steals an asset. You cannot claim the $6,000 for which the guitar would have sold; this $2,500 you would have made is called a lost profit. The reason you cannot claim it is because you did not have the guitar to sell—it has been stolen; your potential profit is moot, even though it is a real loss to you.

Accounting Equation

The last example is actually an illustration of the accounting equation, which is:

$$\text{Assets} = \text{Liabilities} + \text{Owner's Equity}$$

This equation is self-balancing. That is, increases or decreases on one side of the equation will always be reflected on the other side as increases or decreases. Liabilities are "probable future sacrifices of economic benefits arising from present obligations of a particular entity to transfer assets or provide services to other entities in the future as a result of past transactions of events. In brief, liabilities are amounts owed to other entities."[6]

As stated, asset misappropriations have no effect whatsoever on the liabilities of the organization. And of course, no one misappropriates liabilities. But if you would like to steal some of my bills and pay them, help yourself. Although asset misappropriations have no effect on the liabilities, they do have a direct effect on the equity account. You can consider the equity account for what it is: simply the difference between the assets and liabilities. But how does that difference arise? It arises in one of two basic ways. First, if you put your own money into the guitar shop, it goes directly to the equity account. So do the profits and losses your guitar shop makes. The profits will increase your equity, and the losses will decrease it.

In the guitar shop illustration, our equity before the misappropriation was $150,000. Suppose that you put $10,000 in the business when it was started. Then the remaining $140,000 consists of profits you have not taken out of the business. If, for example, you had, over a period of several years, accumulated $200,000 in profits, but you had taken out $60,000 for yourself, your earned equity portion of the $150,000 is $140,000. The remainder is called contributed capital.

Balance Sheet and Income Statement

Commercial enterprises keep financial records in order to produce two key statements: the balance sheet and the income statement. The balance sheet uses the exact formula of the accounting equation: Assets = Liabilities + Owner's Equity. The purpose of the balance sheet is to allow the owner, investors, creditors, and others with an interest to know the approximate book worth of the business at a particular date. The book worth of the business and its actual value are not the same. The net worth for purposes of the books should always be lower. Its actual value cannot be determined precisely until the business is sold. If the business has been profitable historically, a potential purchaser will determine the value of the business primarily by what it earns. But whatever the real value of the business, asset misappropriations affect the balance sheet dollar for dollar. They are difficult to detect at the balance sheet level itself, however, unless the misappropriation is quite large. The way asset misappropriations affect the balance sheet through the equity account is via the income statement, which sometimes is called the statement of profit and loss.

Where the formula for the balance sheet is Assets = Liabilities + Owner's Equity, the formula for the income statement is

$$\text{Revenue} - \text{Expenses} = \text{Profit or (Loss)}$$

Revenue results from selling a product or service; expenses result from those costs incurred—both direct and indirect—to sell the product or service. And while the balance sheet takes a "picture" of the business at a particular date, the income statement is historical, covering a specified period of time, most commonly a year. The two statements tie together through the equity account. Remember, profits increase the equity account while losses decrease it.

In the guitar example, we said that the theft of the $3,500 guitar is a dollar-for-dollar set-off to the equity account. That set-off is accomplished by recognizing the theft of the $3,500 guitar as an expense called cost of goods sold, listed on the income statement. The income statement is closed to profit and loss, which is then transferred to the equity account. So as we said much earlier, occupational fraud and abuse is an expense of doing business, in much the same way that we pay expenses for electricity, taxes, and wages.

The big difference, though, is that we always know what we are paying for electricity. We know what we pay for fraud only when it is discovered, as in the example of the stolen guitar. If the theft of the guitar went undetected because you failed to inventory your merchandise one year, you may never recognize that theft. But it still cost $3,500—you just do not know it yet. And you may never know it.

Several concepts used in accounting for income and expense have application in asset misappropriations; however, keep your eye on the ball: People steal assets, not income or expenses.

Cash versus Accrual Accounting

Businesses have an option to keep their books on the cash basis or the accrual basis, whichever provides the more accurate and conservative picture of the business. On the cash basis, income is recognized when it is collected, and expenses are incurred when they are paid. But if you stop and think, that method usually does not properly reflect what you have made in a year—only what you have collected and paid out. The accrual basis tries to match that income and those expenses year by year. Most businesses keep their books on an accrual basis, even though their tax returns may be filed on a cash basis.

Accountants use the matching concept to tie the balance sheet and the income statement together in accrual basis accounting. The logical idea is that the expenses used to produce income—all of them—should be matched in a consistent manner against that income. Since, for example, you are in the guitar business and want to match all expenses in the years they produced income, what do you do about having to purchase brand-new woodworking equipment every three years? Since your statement of profit and loss is kept by the year, the matching concept would require you to write off one-third of the value of that equipment each year as an expense.

This write-off is called *depreciation*, and it has no application to asset misappropriations, except to help determine the amount of book value write-off to be taken if that equipment is misappropriated. And often what the equipment is valued at on the books and what it actually will bring if sold are two different numbers. The third number is replacement cost. Let us take again the example of the woodworking equipment.

If you paid $9,000 for it and the equipment was stolen at the end of the first year, the amount valued on your books would be $6,000. But perhaps the equipment would have brought only $2,000 if sold in an emergency. And perhaps the $9,000 equipment would cost $11,000 to replace. Still, GAAP would necessitate the loss to be written off against profit, and equity would be $6,000.

Depreciation is especially applicable when companies try to overvalue their assets and net worth; the lower their depreciation expense, the higher the company's profits. That topic and many other accounting concepts used to do the same thing are discussed in Part III of this book.

Another accounting term that has no bearing on asset misappropriations is "accruals." Under the matching concept, we need to make sure that any expenses incurred but not paid by the end of the year are counted in our records of profit and loss. For example, if our guitar shop paid its insurance premiums every September but kept its books on a calendar-year basis, then one-fourth of the premium should be shown as an expense for this year and three-fourths for next year, no matter when it is actually paid. These are called *accrued expenses*, and accountants figure out how much these expenses total, so they can be included in the correct year. After making all the necessary adjustments to a company's books to match the income with the expenses, a final profit is determined for the company. Remember, the profit figure the company shows and the amount of cash it collected will not be the same under accrual basis accounting.

Organization of Financial Records

The way financial records are organized varies somewhat by entity. For example, some companies computerize their entire record-keeping process while others use the pen-and-ink system that has been around for centuries. Regardless, the applications are largely the same. Books are organized by "accounts," which are individual captions in the financial statements. For each item of income, expense, asset, liability, and equity, a separate account is created to keep track of their changes.

The heart of the bookkeeping system is the checkbook. All enterprises—no matter what they do—collect revenue and pay out expenses. But the checkbook is inadequate for bookkeeping purposes. Again, the amount of profit a company makes and its receipts over disbursements (the balance in the checkbook at a particular date) will be different. To help keep track of the differences, companies keep journals.

Books of Account

There are two types of books of account: journals and ledgers. The term "journal" is "(derived from the French word *jour,* meaning day) [and] is a day-by-day, or chronological, record of transactions."[7] Financial information is taken from source documents and recorded in the journals. Most businesses typically have at least four journals: a cash receipts and disbursements journal; a sales or accounts receivable journal, in which all sales made on credit or cash are listed; a purchases (or accounts payable) journal, which records all acquisitions of merchandise or services purchased on credit; and a general journal, which reflects transactions not covered by other journals. The general journal also is the one used to adjust the books.

The journals are kept and summarized, usually monthly, in a ledger. This process is called *posting*. In a manual bookkeeping system, a ledger usually is a loose-leaf notebook, with entries made only once per month. At the end of the year, the net of these ledger accounts is carried directly to the financial statements. In other words, the financial statements are a summary of the account balances carried in the ledger.

For example, in order to prepare financial statements, the bookkeeper for your guitar shop would go through your checkbook regularly. For each item of deposit, he would record its source in a journal—in this case, the cash receipts and disbursements journal. And for every check, he also would record what that disbursement paid. In a simple illustration, assume the bookkeeper noticed that one deposit in the checkbook contained two items: sales of merchandise amounting to $500 and a bank loan of $7,500, for a total deposit of $8,000.

In order to keep your books accurately, the bookkeeper must separate the item of income, which determines your profit or loss, from the item of the loan, which is not income; it must be repaid. In the cash receipts and disbursements journal, your bookkeeper would "spread," or code, these two transactions, recording one in the journal's income column and one in the liability column. And the bookkeeper would record the checks you wrote during the month for labor, parts, electricity, repayment of bank loans, and other expenses in the expense portion of the journal, with an account for each item of expense. In order for the bookkeeper to make sure he has accounts for all your transactions, he will prepare a chart of accounts. Most of the time, this is simply a sheet of paper with numbers on it for each account. The bookkeeper would record in the checkbook the number of the account (instead of its name) to which he posted the transaction.

Once your bookkeeper has recorded all the transactions, he can create *journal entries* to record transactions that were not recorded in the checkbook. For example, each month the bank deducts a service charge from your bank account. That is an item for which a check has not been written. If, over a period of a year, the bank charged you $100 in service charges, your books must be adjusted downward by that amount, or the balance in your checking account will not agree with what is on your books by that $100. Your bookkeeper or accountant, then, will make a journal entry lowering your bank balance by $100, which is offset against your profit as an expense in the same amount. Now your books agree with what is in the bank. The bookkeeper keeps a written record of all the journal entries made during a year. Each journal entry should contain an explanation as to why it was made.

Double-entry bookkeeping, invented in the fourteenth century, is an extension of the accounting equation, Assets = Liabilities + Equity. Since this equation is always in balance, both sides of any transaction are recorded. The asset side is known also as the debit side or the charge side, and it is reflected on the left. The right-hand side of the equation is also known as the credit side. Each transaction, then, is both a debit and a credit. Here is how debits and credits affect the financial accounts:

Debits: Increase assets and expenses and/or decrease liabilities and/or equity.

Credits: Decrease assets and expenses, and/or increase liabilities and/or equity.

The normal balances of the accounts are:

Asset or expenses   Debits

Income, equity, or liability   Credits

This produces the next formula for the balance sheet:

$$\text{Debits (Assets)} = \text{Credits (Liabilities} + \text{Equity)}$$

which in turn produces the next formula for the income statement:

$$\text{Credits (Income)} = \text{Debits (Expenses} + \text{Profit [Loss])}$$

The excess credits (or debits) on the income statement are used to increase (or decrease) the equity account. Journal entries and transactions from the journals are used to adjust the ledgers to the proper amount through debits and credits.

Let us again return to the guitar example. Since the guitar valued at $3,500 was stolen, that transaction is not reflected in the books until we make an adjustment—by hand if you will—to show it. After all, the theft did not go through the checkbook, and it was not posted to a journal. Since we already have discussed the fact that the theft of the guitar is an expense, which offsets directly against our equity, the bookkeeper will make the next journal entry in the form of debits and credits:

Journal Entry #1

	Debit (Dr.)	Credit (Cr.)
Cost of Goods Sold (an expense account)	$3,500	
Inventory (an asset account)		$3,500

To record the theft of 1954 Fender Telecaster Guitar by employee

As a result of this transaction, our books are now in balance again. The debits equal the credits. By debiting an expense account, we ultimately reduce our equity by the same amount when our books are closed and the loss is tallied. By crediting the inventory account, we are reducing our assets—inventory—to reflect the fact that the guitar is missing and now cannot be sold. Again, we get to claim nothing on our books for the profit we would have made as a result of the ultimate sale of the guitar.

Concealing Asset Misappropriations

Asset misappropriations generally are concealed in the books of account as either false debits or omitted credits. However, many misappropriations are not concealed at all, and they will be reflected in the books as an out-of-balance condition.

Out-of-Balance Conditions

By removing a tangible asset from the business (a debit), the books will be out of balance by the exact amount of the tangible asset misappropriated. Therefore, if all tangible assets were counted after a theft, the debits and credits would not equal. Of course, tangible assets are rarely counted in their entirety. As a result, the out-of-balance condition may not be known.

Let us take an absurdly simple example. Wendall works at McDonald's as a cashier. One day you go to Mickey D's and order a Big Mac, large order of fries, soft drink, and one of those hot apple pies that seem to come out of the oven at about 3,000 degrees. You give Wendall the exact change, in this case, $4.22. Rather than ringing the sale on the register, Wendall simply puts the money in his pocket. He has now appropriated an asset: $4.22 in currency. If we could stop the business right after the theft and close our books, we would find that the credits exceed the debits by $3.51, the cost to McDonald's for the Big Mac, large order of fries, soft drink, and hot apple pie. The 71-cent difference is the gross profit on the sale, which Wendall also stole. But McDonald's will not account for that loss until it determines its profits at the end of the year.

Out-of-balance conditions occur during larcenies, when thieves make no attempt to conceal the fact that the debits and credits do not match. Of course, the perpetrator is counting on the fact that McDonald's will not close immediately after the theft and count debits and credits, and therefore the scheme will not be detected. That alone is the perpetrator's ''concealment method''—the thefts are lost in the shuffle.

False Debits

Let us carry the example further and assume that McDonald's would be dumb enough (it is not) to let Wendall not only be a cashier but keep the books too. Now Wendall controls both the money and how it is counted. Since he knows the credits really exceed the debits by $3.51, he decides to do some creative accounting to take care of the difference. He creates a journal entry and debits ''miscellaneous expense'' on the books for $3.51; and he credits the food inventory account for $3.51. His books are now in balance. The debit to miscellaneous expense in this case is false and designed to replace the cash Wendall stole. Wendall had his choice of false debits: to expenses or to assets.

Expenses

Smart perpetrators like Wendall who have chosen to cover their trails will invariably select an expense account over an asset account to create a false debit. The fictitious entry to an expense account accomplishes two different but interrelated objectives. First, many expense items are not represented by ''hard'' merchandise, which can be counted and inventoried. Second, on an annual basis, expense accounts are closed to a zero balance and the remainders are transferred to the profit and loss account. Once the expense account is closed, it becomes a historical item and probably will never be reviewed again. If the false debit is not detected in the expense account by the time the books are closed, it is gone forever, as my colleague Steve Albrecht once observed.

Forced Balances

A variation to the out-of-balance condition is a forced balance. Those using this technique invariably have access to the books and records. In this method, an incorrect total is carried from the journal to the ledger or from the ledger to the financial statements. Let us return for a moment to the example of Wendall as a bookkeeper for McDonald's. The only indication we have in our books that Wendall skimmed $4.22 is the fact that our inventory is short by its cost, $3.51. Let us assume that Wendall wanted to cover that loss in McDonald's books. He can do so by forcing his inventory balance. Rather than making a journal entry reducing the inventory account, he can purposely add incorrectly when he is totaling up the inventory.

For example, if inventory of food at McDonald's was counted and totaled $4,680.44, then this amount should be reflected in the inventory or purchases journal. But Wendall adds $3.51 to that figure and makes the total of the numbers $4,683.95. When the balance of the inventory is transferred from the journal to the ledger, the latter will be overstated by $3.51. When the ledgers are used to prepare the financial statements, inventory will be overstated by $3.51 and expenses by the same amount. But the only way to detect the forced balance is to go back and add the original column of figures in the inventory account, which will be off by the $3.51.

Assets

Wendall also could have created his fictitious journal entry to debit an asset. It matters not what the asset is, although he probably would not chose a fictitious debit to the cash account, because the asset of cash is watched closely and accounted for to the penny. Since McDonald's does not have charge accounts, Wendall probably would not show his debit as accounts receivable. But he could add it to any fixed asset account—furniture and fixtures, investments, plant and equipment, or a host of others. The point is that the false debit to an asset account is much easier to detect. And the false asset debit stays on the books until some action is taken to remove it.

Omitted Credits

Omitted credits are used to conceal revenue skimmed from the organization. In Wendall's case, he failed to ring up a sale on the cash register. The credit he omitted was to sales, and he stole the debit portion—$4.22 in cash. The books are therefore technically in balance, but merchandise is missing. The principal way to detect omitted credits from books of account is through trend analysis—a form of indirect proof. That is because of the method Wendall chose to commit his theft. Because he did not ring the sale on the cash register, McDonald's never knew a sale occurred. But, as stated, if the company stopped and added its debits and credits, the credits would exceed the debits by $3.51, the amount of the missing merchandise. All we know from that scenario, though, is that merchandise—the burger, fries, soft drink, and pie—is missing. We do not know where it is, who took it, or whether it was stolen at all. It could have been thrown away accidentally, spoiled, or even eaten by a hungry employee.

Let us take a separate illustration of omitted credits, one much more difficult to detect. Say Wendall worked for a dry cleaning establishment and did exactly the same thing: took $4.22 from a customer for laundry, pocketed the money, and failed to ring up the sale. Remember, our books are still in balance—Wendall omitted the credit (the sale) and stole the debit ($4.22 in currency). Since we are not missing merchandise, the indirect proof will be that our profits are lower by the cost of the service we provided. If our direct costs to launder the clothing amount to $3.51, then our profits suffer by the same amount. The remaining 71 cents is lost revenue, which will not be reflected in the books at all. Detecting thefts such as this one requires sophisticated revenue and expense analysis on a line-by-line basis. And, of course, if the thefts are at a level where they leave no obvious trends, the odds of detecting such a loss from the dry cleaner's books of account are small. If, for example, Wendall confined his thefts to that one transaction, it would hardly be noticeable in an operation that grossed several hundred thousand dollars a year.

But we know from examining thousands of occupational fraud cases that the single, individual theft is exceedingly rare. The basic trend seems to be for such frauds to start off small but grow larger as time progresses. Of course, that makes sense—if Wendall is not detected the first time, why should he stop? And by the time he has gotten away with the theft ten times, he starts feeling invincible, and escalates the frequency and the amounts he steals. If he were smart, he would determine a threshold amount he could steal without arousing suspicion. There is no way of knowing how many such smart people there are, since we certainly are not catching them. The cases in this book show a consistent trend of excess by the perpetrators. Some might assume such people secretly want to be caught. Although that is certainly possible, those cases are far outweighed by people who simply lose sight of the amount of money they are stealing—they either do not know or do not want to know.

In fraud classes I have taught over the years, a common question asked is "What is the most effective technique to catch employees stealing?" Only partially in jest, I reply, "Time is the most effective detection technique. Left unchecked, many occupational frauds will finally surface when there is nothing left for the employee to steal and the company goes broke." Such a comment underscores a key element of occupational fraud and abuse—its repetitive nature feeds on itself. It is not just a good idea to control fraud and abuse; it is an economic necessity.

NOTES

1. Henry Campbell Black, *Black's Law Dictionary*, 5th ed. (St. Paul, MN: West, 1979), p. 901.w.
2. *Webster's Dictionary* (Boston: Houghton Mifflin, 1996), p. 472.
3. David H. Marshall and Wayne W. McManus, *Accounting: What the Numbers Mean*, 3rd ed. (Chicago: Irwin, 1981), p. 32.
4. Ibid., p. 217.
5. *Webster's*, p. 1205.
6. Marshall and McManus, *Accounting*, p. 32.
7. Ibid., p. 107.

CHAPTER 3

Skimming

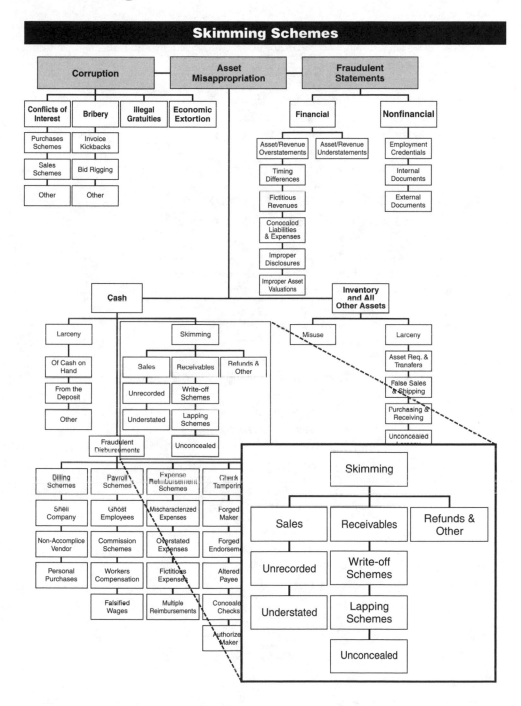

Case Study: Shy Doc Gave Good Face

Brian Lee* excelled as a plastic surgeon. His patients touted Lee's skill and artistry when privately confiding the secret of their improved appearance to their closest friends. Exuding a serious, gentle manner, the 42-year-old bachelor took quiet pride in his beautification efforts—mainly nose jobs, face lifts, tummy tucks, and breast enhancements.

Lee practiced out of a large physician-owned clinic of assorted specialties, housed in several facilities scattered throughout a growing suburb in the Southwest. As its top producer, Lee billed more than $1 million annually and took home $300,000 to $800,000 a year in salary and bonus. But during one four-year stretch, Lee also kept his own secret stash of unaccounted revenue—possibly hundreds of thousands of dollars.

Once Lee's dishonesty came to light, the clinic's board of directors (made up of fellow physician-shareholders) demanded an exact accounting. The clinic's big-city law firm hired Doug Leclaire, a certified fraud examiner (CFE) based in Flower Mound, Texas, who had worked well with the lawyers earlier that year on an unrelated case, to conduct a private investigation.

"The doctors wanted an independent person to root around and document how much money was missing," recalled Leclaire. "They also wanted to see how deep this scam ran. As far as I could determine, no one else was involved." Lee's secretary and nurse knew that Lee was performing the surgeries, but they were unaware that the doctor was withholding patient payments from the clinic. Leclaire marveled at the simplicity of the fraud. He said Lee's ill-gotten gains came easily, given the discreet nature of his business.

Leclaire first familiarized himself with both clinic and office policies. (Doctors ran their offices as autonomous units.) During a confidential, free consultation, Lee would examine the patient and explain various options, the expected results, and his total fee. The doctor or his secretary would then discuss payment requirements.

According to Leclaire, "If the patient planned on filing an insurance claim for covered procedures—such as nonemergency, reconstructive surgery for a car crash victim whose nose smashed into a windshield—the patient must pay the deductible beforehand." For pure cosmetic surgery such as liposuction, which is not covered by insurance, patients had to pay the entire amount by cash or check prior to the procedure. Like many plastic surgeons, Lee accepted no credit cards, presumably to guard against economic reprisals from "buyer's remorse." The one-time payment included all postop visits as well.

Once a patient decided to go under the knife, Lee or his secretary would schedule another appointment or review the doctor's master surgery log to schedule a mutually agreeable date and time. Lee performed the surgeries at the clinic or an affiliated hospital. In theory, a patient would check in at the reception area for a scheduled procedure and pay the secretary, who would immediately attach the

---

*Several names and details have been changed to preserve anonymity.

payment along with an accompanying receipt to the appropriate procedure form and record the transaction on a daily report. The secretary kept all payments, receipts, and forms in a small lockbox for temporary safekeeping.

"At the end of the day, the doctor, his nurse, or his receptionist would submit all paperwork and payments—easily totaling tens of thousands of dollars—to the clinic cashier across the hall," explained Leclaire. "If it was late in the day, the doctor would sometimes lock the box in his desk drawer until the following day." For procedures performed at an affiliated hospital, the patient paid in advance, and the clinic relied on someone from the doctor's office to submit the completed paperwork to the head cashier, allowing the clinic to declare its cut.

But even the best-laid plans often fail in their execution, noted Leclaire. The case that finally nailed the plastic surgeon was that of Rita Mae Givens, a rhinoplasty patient. The clinic offices were arranged so that when patients stepped off the elevator, they could turn right and enter the clinic's main reception area or turn left and walk down the hall to enter Lee's office reception area. Getting off the elevator on the fifth floor, Givens proceeded to her left as Lee had instructed earlier. Givens gained admittance via Lee's private office door, bypassing the clinic secretary and receptionist down the hall on the right. As planned, the unsuspecting clinic staff never knew that Lee made the appointment with Givens, nor that he performed surgery to correct her deviated septum and trim her proboscis. Givens had paid the doctor by check.

During her recovery, Givens reviewed her insurance policy, which stated that rhinoplasty may be covered under certain circumstances, or at least may count toward meeting the yearly deductible. She decided to file an insurance claim. But Givens realized she had never received a billing statement to attach to her claim form, which was mandated by her carrier. So Givens made an unplanned call to the clinic's office to request a copy of her bill, which then set off a series of spontaneous reactions. Lee's clinic's cashier located the patient's file, but it showed no charges for the procedure performed. The cashier thought this quite odd. Givens assured the cashier that the procedure had been performed and that she had paid for the surgery with a personal check.

The cashier in turn checked with the office manager of the clinic for the corresponding record of Givens's payment. Of course the office manager failed to find the record and called the clinic administrator in on the search. Knowing that doctors sometimes forgot to reconcile procedures performed at other facilities immediately, the clinic administrator suggested they look at the doctor's surgery log, under the time and date that Givens had provided, for any clues. Meanwhile, the office manager asked the patient to provide a copy of her canceled check, which they later discovered had been endorsed and deposited in the doctor's personal bank account.

The clinic administrator verified that Lee had performed the surgery but had never submitted the payment to the head cashier. When confronted, the doctor admitted his wrongdoing. The administrator alerted the board, which then hired Leclaire to investigate.

The private eye interviewed Lee several times over the course of the investigation. Leclaire described Lee as very apologetic and helpful in reviewing his misdeeds. The doctor only stole payments from elective surgery patients, he explained, so as not to alert any insurance providers that may have requested additional documentation from the clinic. Sometimes Lee helped himself to payments in his secretary's lockbox before turning it in to the head cashier. Sometimes he swiped a payment directly from a patient with a surreptitious appointment. He preferred cash but often took checks made payable to "Dr. Lee." The doctor often held checks in his desk drawer for a few weeks before depositing them into his personal bank account or cashing them. Lee simply destroyed the receipts that were to accompany payments, he told Leclaire. Out of a sense of professional duty, Lee scrupulously maintained all patient medical files, though.

Because the perpetrator cooperated so fully, Leclaire called this case "fun and easy." The doctor kept meticulous records of all his actions, whether they were legitimate or not. With Lee's help, Leclaire compared the doctor's detailed Day Timer personal organizer against the clinic's records and readily identified the missing payments. Lee even turned over his bank statements so Leclaire could match the deposits to the booty. Lee also opened up his investment portfolio to Leclaire to quash any doubts over additional unreported revenue.

"The doctor didn't try to hide anything," said Leclaire, who has spent 20 years conducting criminal investigations. "I was able to document everything." In all his talks with the doctor, "Everything he told us was pretty much on the up-and-up."

After spending so much time with the doctor, Leclaire finally asked Lee the one question that everyone puzzled over: Why? Greed, he said. With all his money, he still craved more. Driven like his father and brother, who are also successful, Lee had little time to enjoy sports and recreation. Wealth was the family obsession, one-upmanship the family game. "It grew to be a serious competition," said Leclaire. "Who could amass the most? Who had the best car?"

To win the game, Lee resorted to grand larceny, which carried an enormous risk of punishment should the fraud be detected. "I kind of felt sorry for the doctor. A guy in that position could have lost everything," Leclaire said.

After weeks of work, the law firm and its private investigator brought their findings to the board and made recommendations as requested. Leclaire prefaced his report with lessons that were learned from this case. "Weak internal controls tempt all employees, even those earning over $100,000. If given the opportunity, means, and a very slim chance for detection, there are employees who will justify the commission of a fraud in their own minds."

Leclaire suggested they revamp their entire payment system, setting up a central billing area, posting signs to educate the patients, and assigning and spreading out distinct tasks to several office workers during the payment process. "They had no oversight," said the investigator. He told them they needed to reconcile all steps along the way and perform routine internal audits.

This fraud escaped detection for more than four years, Leclaire told his attentive audience. The bottom line? By his audit, Lee had embezzled about $200,000.

Much discussion and a question-and-answer period followed. Some board members insisted Lee be terminated immediately. ''Others showed real sympathy for one of their brethren,'' said Leclaire.

''Their biggest concern was the clinic's income tax liability.'' Leclaire, who had been a special agent with the Internal Revenue Service's criminal investigations department for nine years, assured them the clinic held no liability for uncollected income. No one wanted an IRS audit, given the clinic's history of scant oversight and the doctors' uncertainty over their own culpability, said Leclaire. They feared federal agents would snoop around and perhaps find other instances of unreported income or questionable activity. He warned that taxes would definitely be due upon restitution, however.

''The doctors had worked out an agreement among themselves.'' They decided not to prosecute or terminate Lee. Of course the doctors expected Lee to make immediate and full restitution of $200,000, plus interest. (For the first installment, Leclaire picked up $15,000 in cash the doctor had lying around his modest abode.) They also insisted that Lee place another $200,000 in escrow to cover any contingencies. And naturally, the doctor would foot the bill for both the lawyers and the private investigator involved in the case.

His fellow physicians agreed to let their top moneymaker continue to practice at the clinic, provided Lee went for professional counseling to correct his aberration. They would help him any way they could, they said. Encouraged to show Lee there were other things in life besides work, from then on the doctors invited him along on their fishing and hunting trips. On the advice of his psychiatrist, Lee eagerly accepted. The reformed loner even enjoyed himself.

To curb temptations, the clinic immediately instituted new policies on payment procedures. Good thing, said Leclaire: the good doctor later told him that if given a chance, ''I would probably do it again.''

OVERVIEW

Skimming, as illustrated in the previous case, is the removal of cash from a victim entity prior to its entry in an accounting system.[1] Employees who skim from their companies steal sales or receivables before they are recorded in the company books. Because of this aspect of the nature of skimming schemes, they are known as off-book frauds; they leave no direct audit trail. The fact that the funds have not yet been recorded means that the victim company may not be aware that the cash was received. Consequently, it may be very difficult to detect that the money has been stolen. This is the prime advantage of a skimming scheme to the fraudster.

Skimming can occur at any point where funds enter a business, so almost anyone who processes cash receipts may be in a position to skim money. This includes salespeople, tellers, waitstaff, and others who receive cash directly from customers. In addition, many skimming schemes are perpetrated by employees whose duties include receiving and logging payments made by customers through the mail. These employees are able to slip checks out of the incoming mail for their own use rather than posting them to the proper revenue or customer accounts. Those who deal directly with customers or who handle customer payments are obviously the most likely candidates to skim funds. Skimming schemes generally fall into one of four categories:

1. Unrecorded sales
2. Understated sales and receivables
3. Theft of checks through the mail
4. Short-term skimming

SKIMMING DATA FROM ACFE *2009 GLOBAL FRAUD SURVEY*

Frequency and Cost

In Chapter 1, we learned that there are three major categories of occupational fraud: asset misappropriations, corruption, and fraudulent statements. We further learned asset misappropriation schemes are the most common of these categories; of the 1,843 cases in our study, 1,590, or over 85 percent, involved some form of asset misappropriation

As the fraud tree illustrates, asset misappropriations can in turn be subdivided into two categories: cash schemes and noncash schemes. Exhibit 3.1 shows the percentage of asset misappropriation cases and median losses for each of these two subcategories. As we see, cash schemes were much more common than noncash schemes in the ACFE's *2009 Global Fraud Survey* and also had a higher median cost.

It is important to note that fraudsters often utilize a variety of tactics to pilfer the victim's money; thus, many fraud schemes involve multiple methods of fraud. Therefore, in contrast to our previous studies, we asked survey respondents to identify both the total loss caused by the fraud and the amount of the loss directly attributable to each specific type of asset misappropriation scheme. This subdivision provides us with a more accurate picture of the effects of asset misappropriation schemes than we had previously obtained. Consequently, the median loss amounts reported throughout this text reflect just that portion of the fraud loss attributable to the specific scheme being discussed.

Again returning to the fraud tree, we see that cash schemes are subdivided into three distinct categories: skimming, cash larceny, and fraudulent disbursements. Among these subcategories, fraudulent disbursement schemes were the most common, occurring in more than two-thirds of the cash misappropriation cases included in our study.

Exhibit 3.1 *2009 Global Fraud Survey*: **Cash versus Noncash Schemes**

Scheme Type	Percent of Asset Misappropriation Cases[1]	Median Loss
Cash Misappropriations (1,361 cases)	85.6%	$120,000
Non-Cash Misappropriations (322 cases)	20.3%	$90,000

[1]As was stated in Chapter 1, the sum of percentages in this exhibit, as in several tables and charts throughout this book, exceed 100% because some cases involved multiple fraud schemes that fell into more than one category.

Exhibit 3.2   *2009 Global Fraud Survey*: Frequency of Cash Misappropriations

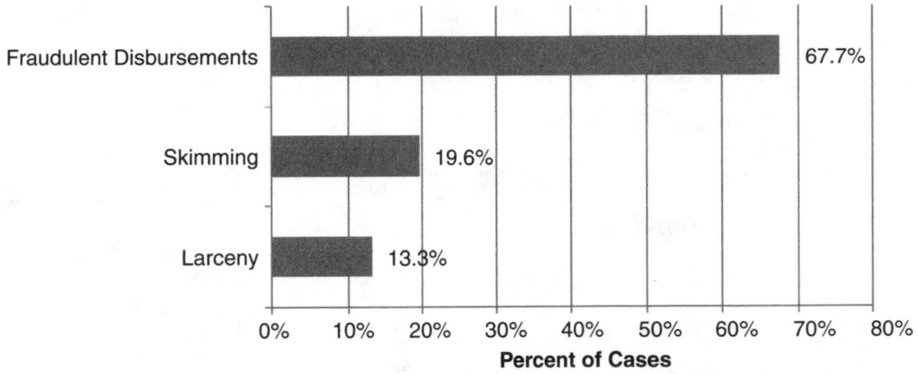

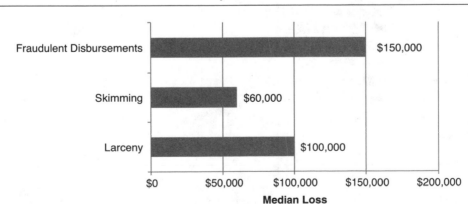

These schemes also caused the highest median loss ($150,000) of the three cash scheme categories (see Exhibits 3.2 and 3.3). In contrast, skimming schemes were a part of 20 percent of the cash misappropriation cases and caused the lowest median loss of the three categories ($60,000).

Exhibit 3.4 shows the distribution of dollar losses among the 197 skimming cases for which a loss amount was provided, compared with the dollar loss distribution for all cases in the survey. As this chart shows, more than half of the skimming cases studied caused a loss of less than $100,000.

Detection of Skimming Schemes

The most common way skimming schemes were detected in our 2009 study was through *tips,* which was cited in 42.1 percent of the 259 cases in which a detection method was identified.

The most significant deviation from the distribution of all cases involved detection *by accident.* Skimming cases were more likely to be detected by accident than occupational frauds in general. Skimming schemes, however, were slightly less likely to be

Exhibit 3.3   *2009 Global Fraud Survey*: Median Loss of Cash Misappropriations

Exhibit 3.4   *2009 Global Fraud Survey*: Dollar Loss Distribution for Skimming Schemes

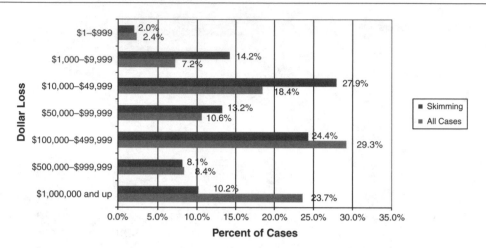

detected by management review or internal audit than other forms of occupational fraud. (See Exhibit 3.5.)

Perpetrators of Skimming Schemes

Of the 267 skimming cases in our study, we received 243 responses in which the position of the principal perpetrator was identified. Over 48 percent of those who committed skimming schemes were identified as employees; approximately 34.6 percent were identified as employees, and 17.3 percent were owner/executives. (See Exhibit 3.6.)

Consistent with other data on occupational fraud, the median losses for skimming schemes were higher among managers than employees and were highest among owner/executives. While the median loss for all skimming schemes was $60,000, when we

Exhibit 3.5   *2009 Global Fraud Survey*: Detection of Skimming Schemes

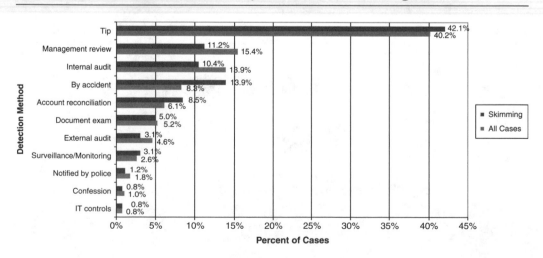

Exhibit 3.6   *2009 Global Fraud Survey*: Perpetrators of Skimming Schemes

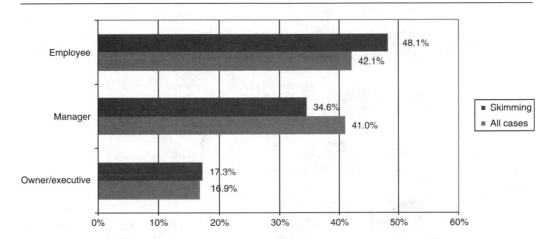

broke down the data based on position, we found that the median loss for schemes committed by owner/executives rose to $550,000, or more than nine times the overall median. (See Exhibit 3.7.)

Victims of Skimming Schemes

The data we gathered on the size of organizations that are victimized by skimming shows small companies (those with fewer than 100 employees) in our study were particularly vulnerable to this type of fraud. Although small companies made up 30.8 percent of all the victims in our study, they accounted for 46.6 percent of the victims in skimming cases. (See Exhibit 3.8.)

Our data also revealed that small organizations suffered disproportionately high median losses due to skimming schemes. The smallest organizations in our study (those with fewer than 100 employees) had a median loss of $67,000, which was the second highest median loss for all categories of organizations. (See Exhibit 3.9.)

Exhibit 3.7   *2009 Global Fraud Survey*: Median Loss by Perpetrator of Skimming Schemes

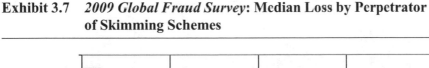
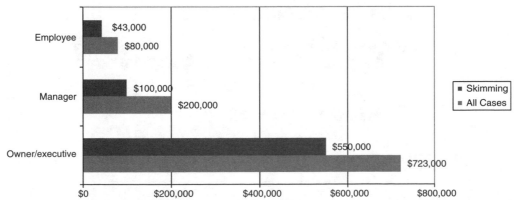

Exhibit 3.8 *2009 Global Fraud Survey*: Size of Victim in Skimming Schemes

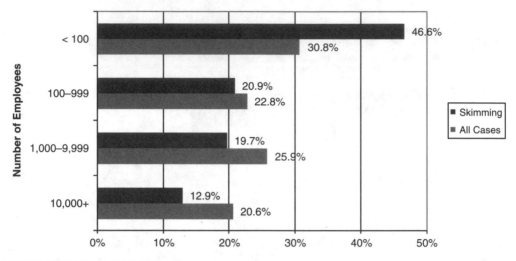

UNRECORDED SALES

The most basic skimming scheme occurs when an employee sells goods or services to a customer, collects the customer's payment, but makes no record of the sale. The employee pockets the money received from the customer instead of turning it over to the employer. (See Exhibit 3.10.) This was the method used by Dr. Brian Lee in the case study discussed previously. He was performing work and collecting money that his partners knew nothing about. As a result he was able to take approximately $200,000 without leaving any indications of his wrongdoings on the books. Had a patient not made an unexpected call for a copy of a billing statement, Lee's crime could have gone on indefinitely. The case of Dr. Lee illustrates why unrecorded sales schemes are perhaps the most dangerous of all skimming frauds.

Exhibit 3.9 *2009 Global Fraud Survey*: Median Loss by Size of Victim in Skimming Schemes

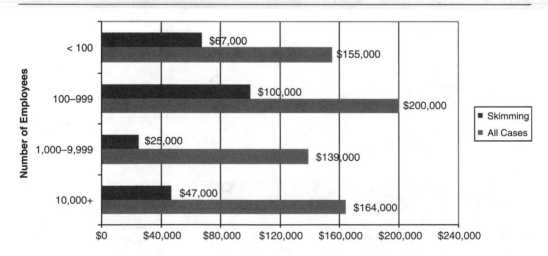

Exhibit 3.10   Unrecorded Sales

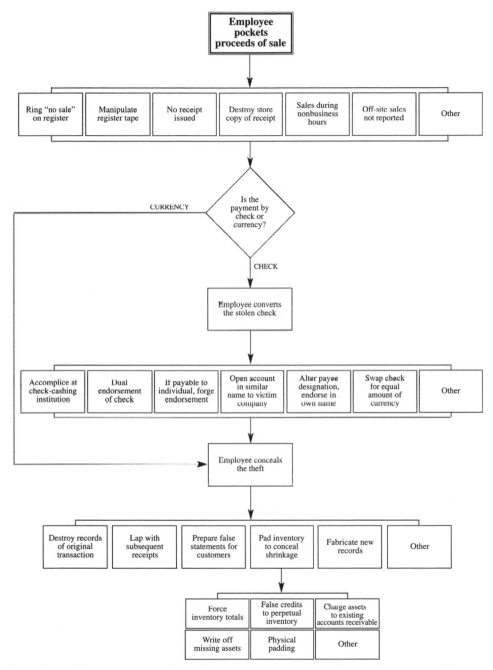

In order to discuss unrecorded sales schemes more completely, let us consider one of the simplest and most common sales transactions, a sale of goods at the cash register. In a normal transaction, a customer purchases an item and an employee enters the sale on the register. The register tape reflects that the sale has been made and shows that a certain amount of cash (the purchase price of the item) should have been placed in the register. By comparing the register tape to the amount of money on hand, it may be possible to detect thefts. For instance, if there were $500 worth of sales recorded on a particular register on a given day but only $400 cash in the register, it would be obvious that someone had stolen $100 (assuming no beginning cash balance).

When an employee skims money by making off-book sales of merchandise, however, it is impossible to detect theft by comparing the register tape to the cash drawer because the sale is not recorded on the register (that is why it is "off-book"). Instead, an employee pockets the customer's money. In order to create the appearance that the sale is being entered in the register, the fraudster might ring a "no sale" or some other noncash transaction. In one case, two employees in a midsize retail organization skimmed sales using this method.

Return to the example in which we compared the register tape to the cash on hand. Let us assume that a fraudster wants to make off with $100. Through the course of the day, there are $500 worth of sales at her register; one sale is for $100. When the $100 sale is made, the employee does not record the transaction on her register. The customer pays $100 and takes the merchandise home, but instead of placing the $100 in the cash drawer, the employee pockets it. Since the employee did not record the sale, at the end of the day the register tape will reflect only $400 in sales. There will be $400 on hand in the register ($500 in total sales minus the $100 that the employee stole) so the register will balance. Therefore, by not recording the sale, the employee is able to steal money without the missing funds appearing on the books.

The most difficult part in a skimming scheme at the register is that the employee must commit the overt act of taking money. If the employee takes the customer's money and shoves it into her pocket without entering the transaction on the register, the customer may suspect that something is wrong and report the conduct to another employee or manager. It is also possible that a manager, a fellow employee, or a surveillance camera will spot the illegal conduct.

Register Manipulation

As we said, some employees might ring a "no sale" or other noncash transaction to mask the theft of sales. The false transaction is entered on the register so that it appears a sale is being rung up when in fact the employee is stealing the customer's payment. To the casual observer it looks as if the sale is being properly recorded.

In other cases, employees have rigged their registers so that sales are not recorded on their register tapes. As stated, the amount of cash on hand in a register may be compared to the amount showing on the register tape in order to detect employee theft. It is thus not important to the fraudster what is keyed into the register but rather what shows up on the tape. If employees can rig the registers so that sales do not print, they can enter a sale that they intend to skim yet ensure that the sale never appears on the books. Anyone observing the employees will see the sale entered, see the cash drawer open, and so on, yet the register tape will not reflect the transaction. How is this accomplished? One service station employee hid stolen gasoline sales simply by lifting the ribbon from the printer. He then collected and pocketed the sales that were not recorded on the register tape. The fraudster then rolled back the tape to the point where the next transaction should appear and replaced the ribbon. The next transaction would be printed without leaving any blank space on the tape, apparently leaving no trace of the fraud. However, this fraudster overlooked the fact that the transactions on his register were prenumbered. Even though he was careful in replacing the register tape, he failed to realize that he was creating a break in the sequence of transactions. For instance, if the perpetrator skimmed sale #155, then the register tape would show only transactions #153, #154, #156, #157, and so on. The missing transaction numbers, omitted because the ribbon was lifted when they took place, indicated fraud.

Special circumstances can lead to more creative methods for skimming at the register. One movie theater manager figured out a way around the theater's automatic ticket dispenser. In order to reduce payroll hours, this manager sometimes worked as a cashier selling tickets. She made sure that at these times there was no one checking patrons' tickets outside the theaters. When a sale was made, the ticket dispenser would feed out the appropriate number of tickets, but the manager withheld tickets from some patrons and allowed them to enter the theater without them. When the next customer made a purchase, the manager sold the person one of the excess tickets instead of using the automatic dispenser. Thus, a portion of the ticket sales were not recorded. At the end of the night, there was a surplus of cash, which the manager removed and kept for herself. Although the actual loss was impossible to measure, it was estimated that this manager stole over $30,000 from her employer.

Skimming during Nonbusiness Hours

Another way to skim unrecorded sales is to conduct sales during nonbusiness hours. For instance, some employees have been caught running their employers' stores on weekends or after hours without the knowledge of the owners. They were able to pocket the proceeds of these sales because the owners had no idea that their stores were even open. One manager of a retail facility went to work two hours early every day, opening his store at 8:00 A.M. instead of 10:00 A.M., and pocketed all the sales made during these two hours. Talk about dedication! He rang up sales on the register as if it was business as usual, but then removed the register tape and all the cash he had accumulated. The manager then started from scratch at 10:00 as if the store was just opening and destroyed the tape so there was no record of the before-hours revenue.

Although we have discussed skimming in the context of cash register transactions, skimming does not have to occur at a register or even involve hard currency. Some of the most costly skimming schemes are perpetrated by employees who work at remote locations or without close supervision. This can include on-site salespeople who do not deal with registers, independent salespeople who operate off-site, and employees who work at branches or satellite offices. These employees have a high level of autonomy in their jobs, which often translates into poor supervision and in turn to fraud.

Skimming of Off-Site Sales

Several cases reported as part of the ACFE studies involved the skimming of sales by off-site employees. Some of the best examples of this type of fraud occurred in the apartment rental industry, where apartment managers handle the day-to-day operations without much oversight. A common scheme is for an on-site employee to identify the tenants who pay in currency and remove them from the books. This causes a particular apartment to appear as vacant on the records when, in fact, it is occupied. Once the currency-paying tenants are removed from the records, the manager can skim their rental payments without late notices being sent to the tenants. As long as no one physically checks the apartments, the fraudster can continue skimming indefinitely.

Another rental-skimming scheme occurs when apartments are rented out but no lease is signed. On the books, the apartment still appears to be vacant, even though there are rent-paying tenants on the premises. The fraudster can then steal the rent payments, which will not be missed. Sometimes the employees in these schemes work in conjunction with the renters and give them a ''special rate.'' In return, the renters' payments are made directly to the employee, and any complaints or maintenance requests are directed only to that employee so the renters' presence remains hidden.

Instead of skimming rent, the property manager in another case skimmed payments made by tenants for application fees and late fees. Revenue sources such as these are less predictable than rental payments, and therefore their absence may be harder to detect. The central office, for instance, knew when rent was due and how many apartments were occupied but had no control in place to track the number of people who filled out rental applications or how many tenants paid their rent a day or two late. Stealing only these nickel-and-dime payments, the property manager in this case was able to make off with approximately $10,000 of her employer's money.

A similar revenue source that is unpredictable and therefore difficult to account for is parking-lot-collection revenue. In one example, a parking lot attendant skimmed approximately $20,000 from his employer simply by not preparing tickets for customers who entered the lot. He would take the customers' money and wave them into the lot, but because no receipts were prepared, there was no way for the victim company to compare tickets sold to actual customers at this remote location. Revenue sources that are hard to monitor and predict, such as late fees and parking fees, are prime targets for skimming schemes.

Another off-site person in a good position to skim sales is the independent salesperson. A prime example is the insurance agent who sells policies but does not file them with the carrier. Most customers do not want to file claims on a policy, especially early in the term, for fear that their premiums will rise. Knowing this, the agent keeps all documentation on the policies instead of turning it in to the carrier. The agent then can collect and keep the payments made on the policy because the carrier does not know the policy exists. The customer continues to make payments, thinking that she is insured, when in fact the policy is a ruse. Should the customer eventually file a claim, some agents are able to backdate the false policies and submit them to the carrier, then file the claim so that the fraud will remain hidden.

Poor Collection Procedures

Poor collection and recording procedures can make it easy for an employee to skim sales or receivables. In one instance, a government authority that dealt with public housing was victimized because it failed to itemize daily receipts. This agency received payments from several public housing tenants, but at the end of the day, "money" received from tenants was listed as a whole. Receipt numbers were not used to itemize the payments made by tenants, so there was no way to pinpoint which tenant had paid how much. Consequently, the employee in charge of collecting money from tenants was able to skim a portion of their payments. She simply did not record the receipt of over $10,000. Her actions caused certain accounts receivable to be overstated where tenant payments were not properly recorded.

UNDERSTATED SALES AND RECEIVABLES

The cases just discussed deal with purely off-book sales. Understated sales work differently in that the transaction is posted to the books, but for a lower amount than the perpetrator collected from the customer. (See Exhibit 3.11.) In one case, an employee wrote receipts to customers for their purchases but removed the carbon paper backing on the receipts so that they did not produce a company copy. The employee then used a pencil to prepare company copies that showed lower purchase prices. For example, if the customer had paid $100, the company copy might reflect a payment of $80. The employee skimmed the difference between the actual amount of revenue and the amount reflected on the fraudulent receipt. This can also be accomplished at the register when the fraudster underrings a sale, entering a sales total lower than the amount actually paid by the customer. The employee skims the difference between the actual purchase price of the item and the sales figure recorded on the register. Rather than reduce the price of an item, an employee might record the sale of fewer items. If 100 units are sold, for instance, a fraudster might record the sale of only 50 units and skim the excess receipts.

A similar method is used when sales are made on account. The bill to the customer reflects the true amount of the sale, but the receivable is understated in the company books. For instance, a company might be owed $1,000, but the receivable is recorded as $800. (Sales also will be understated by $200.) When the customer makes payment on the account, the fraudster can skim $200 and post the $800 to the account. The books will reflect that the account has been paid in full.

False Discounts

Finally, sales or receivables might be understated by the use of false discounts. Employees with the authority to grant discounts may use this authority to skim revenues. In a false discount skimming scheme, an employee accepts full payment for an item but records the transaction as if the customer had been given a discount. It therefore appears that the customer paid less than full price for the item. The fraudster skims the amount of the discount. For example, on a $100 purchase, if an employee granted a false discount of 20 percent, he could skim $20 and leave the company's books in balance. The key to this scheme is to give the customer a receipt reflecting the full price paid and to provide a different (usually altered) receipt for bookkeeping purposes.

Exhibit 3.11   Understated Sales

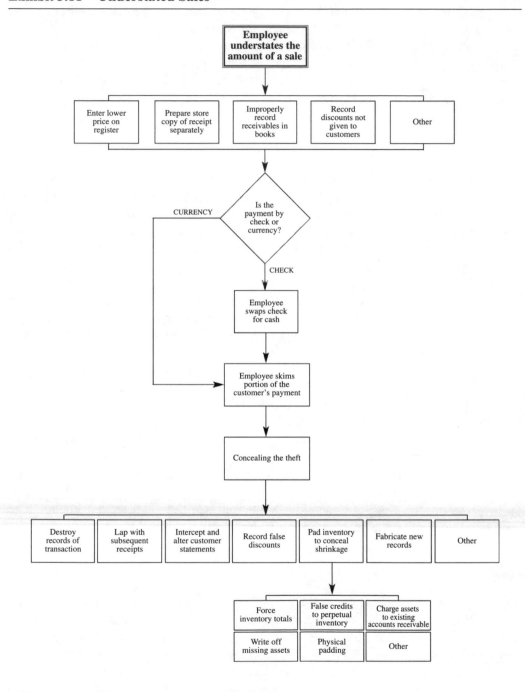

THEFT OF CHECKS THROUGH THE MAIL

Checks received through the mail are a frequent target of employees seeking illicit gains. Theft of incoming checks usually occurs when a single employee is in charge of opening the mail and recording the receipt of payments. This employee simply takes one or more of the incoming checks; since these checks are not logged as received, the payment is not posted to the customer account. (See Exhibit 3.12.) It appears as if the check had never arrived. When the task of receiving and recording incoming payments is left to a single person, it is all too easy for that employee to slip an occasional check into his pocket.

Exhibit 3.12   Theft of Incoming Checks

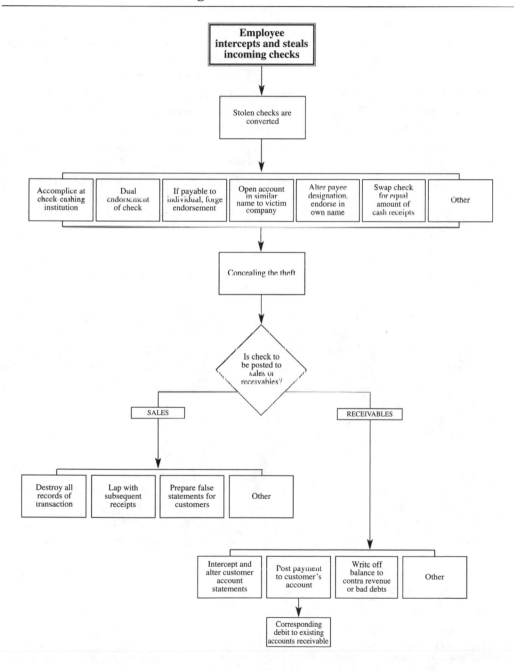

An example of a check theft scheme occurred in one case where a mailroom employee stole over $2 million in government checks arriving through the mail. This employee simply identified and removed envelopes delivered from a government agency known to send checks to the company. Using a group of accomplices acting under the names of fictitious persons and companies, this individual was able to launder the checks and divide the proceeds with his cronies.

Although the theft of checks usually is not complicated, it may be more difficult to conceal a check theft scheme than other forms of skimming. If the stolen checks were payments on the victim company's receivables, then these payments were expected. As receivables become past due, the victim company will send notices of nonpayment to its customers. Customers are likely to complain when they receive a second bill for a payment they have already made. In addition, the cashed check will serve as evidence that customers made payments. In other forms of skimming, such as unrecorded sales schemes, there is no such evidence that cash has been received. We discuss the methods used to conceal check thefts later in this chapter.

The next case study is an example of one person's check theft scheme. Stefan Winkler skimmed money by taking checks received in the mail, failing to record these checks, and substituting them for collections of currency. Winkler's control over his company's revenue streams allowed him to skim hundreds of thousands of dollars before he was caught. The case also describes how CFE Don Stine unraveled the specifics of Winkler's fraud.

Case Study: Beverage Man Takes the Plunge

For most people, Florida shines brightly from postcards and televisions, as brilliant as it must have seemed to the first Europeans who hoped to find the Fountain of Youth there. The contemporary image is a little gaudier than ancient myth, but still going strong. And when most people go to Florida, the vacation schedule and the tourist industry can make it seem as if the postcard image lives and breathes.

There really is something for the entire family: a tropical paradise for Mom and Dad, lots of noise and colors for the kiddies. But televisions switch off, and tourists go home. The land remains a place where people work, where they live and breathe and raise their families. This is the story of one of those people.

Stefan Winkler* worked for a beverage company in Pompano Beach, Florida. As director of accounting and controller, Stefan touched the flow of money into and out of the company at every point, though he was particularly focused on how money came in. The beverage company—call it Mogel's, Inc.—collected from customers in two ways: either the delivery drivers brought in cash or checks from their route customers, or credit customers sent checks in the mail.

The cash and checks from drivers were counted and put in the bank as route deposits; the checks arriving by mail from credit customers were filed as office deposits. Drivers gave their daily collections to a cashier who made out the route deposit slip

---

*Some names have been changed to preserve anonymity.

and sent it to Winkler. Any checks from office mail went directly to Winkler, who verified the money according to the payment schedule—30 days for some customers, 60 for others, and so on. Winkler's job was to combine office deposits and route deposits for the final accounting before bank deposit. Theoretically, then, Mogel's had two revenue streams, both of which converged at Winkler's desk and poured smoothly into the bank.

But Winkler had other plans. He siphoned off the cash from the route deposits through a lapping operation, covering the money he lifted from one account with funds from another. Winkler took large amounts of cash from the route deposits and replaced each cash amount with checks from the credit customers. He might filch $3,000 in cash from the transportation bags and put in $3,000 worth of checks from the mail. That way, the route deposit total matched the amount listed by the cashier on the deposit slip. There was no gap in office deposits, because Winkler never listed the check as received. Instead, he would extend the customer's payment schedule outward, sometimes indefinitely. He occasionally covered the amount later with other embezzlements. Like a kiting operation, lapping takes a continual replenishment of money, forcing the perpetrator to extend the circles of deception wider if the scheme is to continue to produce. And like kiting, lapping is destined to crumble, unless the person can find a way to replace the original funds and casually walk away. Winkler probably told himself he would replace the money sometime, preferably sooner than later. Maybe he figured he would make a killing in the stock market or win big at the track and set everything right again. Only he knows what he was thinking; he never admitted to taking anything. Acting as his own lawyer, he announced at trial, "There are other people besides me who could have taken that money." The prosecution, then, had to prove that Winkler, and not those other people, had actually stolen the money. How that happened is, as they say, the rest of the story. Mogel's operated in Pompano Beach as a subsidiary of a larger company from Delaware. Oversight was casual; auditors generally prepared their reports by dispatches from the local office. This gave Winkler as accounting director lots of room to maneuver. But perhaps there was too much room.

Over the course of a year and a half, Winkler's superiors became increasingly dissatisfied with his performance. Winkler was, fatefully enough, fired on the Friday morning before auditors were to arrive the following Monday. He did not have the money to replace what he had stolen, so he used the time to rearrange what he could of his misdealings and throw the rest into disarray. He took cash receipts journals, copies of customer checks, deposit slips, and other financial records from the office and removed his personnel file. He altered electronic files too, backdating accounts receivable lines to make them current and increasing customer discounts. Examiners would eventually discover "an extremely unusual general ledger adjustment of $303,970.25" made just before Winkler was fired. As the prosecuting attorney, Tony Carriuolo, puts it, "He attempted, through computers and other manipulations, to alter history."

When the auditors arrived on Monday, they started the long haul of reconstructing what had actually happened. This was, as Carriuolo and certified fraud examiner Don

Stine put it, ''the fun part, even though it was exhausting, of piecing together what happened and who did it, with documents missing and nothing that we could use to point directly at Winkler and say, 'There it is, he did it.''' Auditors for Mogel's set about evaluating the mess Winkler had left behind, working through bank statements, total deposit schedules, accounting records, and reports from delivery drivers.

They caught on to Winkler's method during the first efforts to reconstruct the previous two years' activity. An auditor found two checks totaling $60,000 on a route deposit slip but no entry in the accounts receivable brought forward for that month. (This was for July, a little over a month before Winkler was fired.) The deposit slip, someone pointed out, was not in the cashier's handwriting but in Winkler's.

Still, making the case would not be as simple as locating route deposits with checks in them. Some customers paid with checks, and the company's cashier routinely used route money to cash employees' paychecks. Thus, deposits regularly contained checks as well as cash. Examiners would have to cover each deposit and its constituent parts, and compare this against what actually hit the bank and the accounts receivable entries in the office deposits. Carriuolo says, ''I can't tell you how many times we had to compare the deposit slips from the cashier—some of which we had, and some we didn't—with the actual composition going to the bank.'' Because Winkler had removed so much from the office, sometimes the only way to verify what had come through the mail was to go to customers and reconstruct payments based on their records.

Once the auditors had gone through the material, they hired Don Stine to confirm their findings and help Carriuolo make the case against Winkler. Reviewing their work, Stine agreed that approximately $350,000 had been taken and that Winkler was the man. Mogel's left itself wide open for this hit because it had no controls covering what happened with the checks that came in the mail, in effect giving Winkler ''total authority'' to manipulate the accounts. Stine says that the situation at Mogel's is all too common, with managers and employees not recognizing a financial crime in progress until it is too late. ''There are plenty of things to alert people missing deposit slips, cash and credit reconciliations between a company and a customer that don't match. There are signs, but it doesn't hit them in the head, and then when something comes out, they say, 'How did this happen?' '' Auditors did ask by phone why customers were paying later and later, but they took Winkler's word for it when he put the delays down to computer systems and reorganizations inside the companies.

First contacts with Winkler did not pan out. He skipped meetings, stonewalled, and acted sullen and defiant. ''I didn't do it,'' he said. ''Trust me. Other people had access, they could have done it too.'' But Stine and Carriuolo were ready for this. Winkler admitted that several clerks and cashiers had worked at Mogel's during a two-year period but that losses had occurred continually. Unless the company was consistently hiring crooks in those positions, Carriuolo argued, the answer lay elsewhere. Besides, the manipulations required someone with accounting skills above the level of the average clerk. The one constant, it turns out, was Stefan Winkler. Two other workers actually had been there during the entire time period, but they had neither the access nor the skills necessary to redirect cash flow on the scale that had occurred.

And there was the physical evidence. When he came to Mogel's, Winkler was in a bind. He had lost his house, and his finances were a mess. But his tenure at the beverage company brought a wave of prosperity. He bought luxury watches, expensive clothing, and several cars, among them a $40,000 Corvette—paid for in cash. Winkler set up several businesses, including a limousine service, a jewelry distributorship, and facilities for a daycare center he planned to establish with his wife. He spent lots of money gambling, which he used as an explanation for his *Rich and Famous* mode of living. "I gamble a lot. I win a lot," he said. "The pit bosses in the Bahamas taught me how to play, so I win almost all the time—simple as that. Just lucky, I guess." Stine knew this was bunk. Nobody was that lucky, not over two years. Winkler's wave of wealth pushed the "Lifestyle Changes, You Lose" button in the game of fraud examination. "You see this in many of these employee defalcation, or employee fraud, cases," comments Stine. "Someone is making $50,000 a year, but he's buying a $500,000 home, driving a $75,000 car. And unless someone died and left him an inheritance, it doesn't add up."

In the civil trial for fraud and negligence, Winkler maintained his innocence—and his arrogance. Carriuolo and Stine presented evidence to show how the route deposits cash had been embezzled and covered for by the office deposits, explaining to the jury with charts and graphs and crash-course accounting presentations what crimes had occurred. The employee records, and the broad authority necessary to pull the scheme off, pointed the finger at Winkler. No one else, Carriuolo maintained, had the "unique access to, and knowledge of Mogel's Inc.'s computerized accounting systems" besides Winkler. Winkler's response? He dismissed (or lost) his attorney and declared he would represent himself. Little or no legal expertise was necessary for his defense: "It wasn't me, it must have been one of those other guys." When he cross-examined Don Stine, who has 12 years in litigation consulting, Winkler announced he had only one question: "Mr. Stine, do you know for certain who took the money?" Stine answered, "No," not with absolute, unconditional, ontological certainty. Happy to show there was no smoking gun, Winkler rested his case.

But the jury was unconvinced by Winkler's tactics. After a brief recess, they returned a guilty verdict for the $353,000 lost by Mogel's, plus treble damages, for a total judgment of over $1 million. And it seems that Winkler remains unreconstructed, since he was recently named in a complaint filed by the company he worked for after Mogel's. His high life keeps seeking new lows.

SHORT-TERM SKIMMING

Short-term skimming is not a distinct method for stealing sales and receivables but rather a distinct way of using skimmed money. Any of the methods discussed earlier—unrecorded sales, understated sales, or theft of incoming checks—could be used in a short-term skimming scheme. (See Exhibit 3.13.) The peculiar aspect to short-term skimming

Exhibit 3.13   Short-term Skim

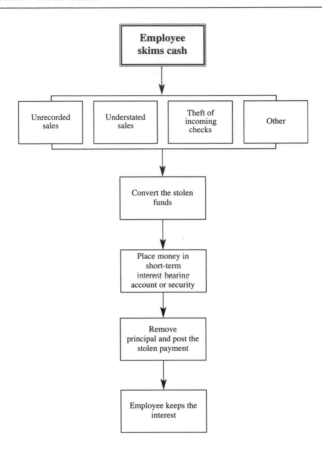

is that the fraudster keeps the stolen money only for a short while before eventually passing the payment on to the employer. The employee merely delays the posting.

In a short-term skimming scheme, employees steal an incoming payment and then place the skimmed funds in an interest-bearing account or in a short-term security. Employees earn interest on the skimmed payments while funds remain under their control. Eventually they withdraw the principal and apply it to the customer's account but retain the interest for themselves.

Payments from several sources can be routed through employees' personal interest-bearing accounts, where they will earn a return for the perpetrators. The proceeds from these schemes, over time, can be quite large. In one case in our study, an employee made approximately $10,000 in prohibited gains by using a short-term skimming scheme.

Employees who engage in short-term schemes often do not view their activity as fraudulent because the stolen payments eventually are returned to the victim company. Everyone gets his or her money in the end, they believe, and the employees simply make a little profit in between. In truth, of course, the employees are stealing the time value of the money, interest that could have been earned for their employer. The fraud is in depriving the company of the use of its money.

CONVERTING STOLEN CHECKS

As we have mentioned, intelligent fraudsters generally prefer to steal currency rather than checks, if given the opportunity, and the reasons why are obvious. Currency is harder to trace than a check. A cashed check eventually returns to the person who wrote it and may provide evidence of who cashed it or where it was spent. Endorsements, bank stamps, and the like may indicate the identity of the thief. Currency, however, disappears into the economy once it is stolen. One $20 bill is as good as another, and unless the victim has recorded the serial numbers, there is no way to determine where it has gone once someone steals it.

The second reason that currency is preferable to a check is the difficulty in converting the check. When currency is stolen, it can be spent immediately. A check must be endorsed and cashed or deposited before thieves can put their hands on the funds it represents. How do fraudsters go about converting checks they have skimmed?

Dual Endorsements

When checks are payable to a business, they can be endorsed simply by writing the company's name on the back of the check. Fraudsters do not have to forge the signature of another person the way they would if the stolen check were payable to an individual. The problem for the employees is that this endorsement, by itself, is not sufficient for them to convert the check. The company's endorsement only provides for the check to be deposited into a company account—something that does the perpetrators no good. A second endorsement will be required if the employees are to cash the check or deposit it into an account they control.

The problem of a second endorsement can be overcome if fraudsters have an accomplice at a check-cashing institution. In one case, a trusted secretary stole over $50,000 from her employer with the aid of an accomplice in a local bank. In this case, checks sometimes were made payable to the secretary's boss individually rather than to the partnership of which he was a part. When these checks arrived, the boss would endorse them and instruct his secretary to deliver them to the partnership's bookkeeper. Instead, the secretary took several of the checks to her boss's bank. There she was able to cash the checks with the assistance of her accomplice.

In the absence of an accomplice at a check-cashing institution, however, perpetrators will have to make a second endorsement on the back of the check, making the check payable to themselves, an accomplice, or another entity. Once this is done, employees can cash the check or deposit it into an account they control. In another case, a manager skimmed checks intended for a state agency and deposited them into his own account by signing his own name as the second endorser. Because the funds in this case were not very predictable, they were not likely to be missed if stolen. Consequently, the fraudster was able to continue his scheme for approximately three years and misappropriate over $1 million.

Generally, fraudsters prefer not to endorse a stolen check in their own name. If a victim company investigates the whereabouts of missing payments, a canceled check bearing a fraudster's endorsement will leave little doubt as to his guilt. Obviously, then, it is beneficial for fraudsters to endorse stolen checks in a false name. This simple tactic leaves a gap in the audit trail between the employees and the conversion of the stolen check. We have already alluded to a case in which a mailroom employee stole over $2 million in checks and used several accomplices, acting under fake names, to ''launder'' the check. This is an excellent example of how employees can convert a stolen check and simultaneously conceal their identities. In that case, the stolen checks were converted by several different people, all acting under false names and using false addresses.

The trick with this sort of scheme, of course, is in opening the accounts necessary to launder the funds. Personal identification, such as a driver's license and Social Security card in the name of the fictitious individual, usually are required. When a shell company is used to launder funds, fraudsters also may need to produce articles of incorporation or an assumed name certificate for the ''company.'' If these false documents can be obtained, fraudsters can distance themselves from their crimes.

If an employee works for a sole proprietor, incoming checks may be made out in the personal name of that proprietor. In these instances, the perpetrator likely will be able to convert stolen checks by forging that person's name (although fake ID in the payee's name probably still will be required).

False Company Accounts

Some cases involve the use of ''similar name'' accounts to launder skimmed funds. A similar name account is one that fraudsters open independently of the company. As an illustration, suppose ABC Company, Inc.'s account is maintained at Bank A. An employee goes to Bank B and opens an account in the name of ABC Corporation, Inc. The employee typically would provide false documents to Bank B to open the account. When the employee steals checks from ABC Company, Inc., she can deposit them in her ABC Corporation, Inc. account at Bank B because of the similarity of names. Bank B usually will not question the deposit. When the check is returned to the victim company, the fraudster relies on no one noticing the difference in the endorsement.

One example of the false account method occurred when an employee of a hospital laboratory opened a company account at a local bank in the name of her employer. She intercepted over $100,000 worth of incoming checks and deposited them into this account. The employee was able to write checks on this ''company'' account to withdraw the stolen money. Canceled checks eventually revealed the existence of the fake account that the employee had opened in her own name.

A twist to the practice of converting checks through the use of fake company accounts occurred in another case, where an employee discovered a seldom-used company account that management thought had been closed. No one in the company was monitoring this forgotten account. The perpetrator of the scheme, an accounts receivable employee, managed to obtain signatory authority on the forgotten account. She then stole incoming checks and deposited them into the hidden account, from which she wrote checks to extract the stolen funds.

Altered Payee Designation

A more direct way for an employee to convert a stolen check is to alter the check so that it is payable to that employee or an accomplice. In most cases, it is not possible to change the payee designation without defacing the stolen check. However, some employees in our study did manage to add their own names to stolen checks. When this is accomplished, converting the check is easy. No fake identification or hidden accounts are required; fraudsters can deposit the check directly into their own bank accounts. In one example, a credit manager picked up checks from customers and typed his own name on the face of the check above the company name. He was able to convert six checks through this method, amounting to nearly $90,000 in stolen proceeds. Eventually, however, a bank teller noticed the alteration of one of the checks and the scheme was uncovered.

Other than typing their own names on faces of stolen checks, fraudsters might tack on additional information to the payee designation or simply write a new name over the existing payee. Depending on the quality of the alteration, these checks may or may not pass muster when fraudsters attempt to convert them. Most alterations to the faces of checks are noticeable and will prevent a stolen check from being converted. As a result, employees do not usually prefer this method. A more detailed discussion of alterations can be found in Chapter 5.

Check-for-Currency Substitutions

As the preceding discussion should illustrate, it can be quite difficult for employees to convert a stolen check. Even when a stolen check is converted successfully, the canceled check may remain as evidence of the perpetrator's identity. As we said earlier, if possible, fraudsters usually attempt to steal currency rather than checks. Currency is instantly liquid and allows employees to forgo much of the messiness we have been discussing.

A common skimming scheme is to take unrecorded checks that a perpetrator has stolen and substitute them for receipted currency. Stefan Winkler used this method in the Mogel's case study. Another example of a check-for-cash substitution occurred when an employee responsible for receipting ticket and fine payments on behalf of a municipality abused her position and stole incoming revenues for nearly two years. When this individual received payments in currency, she issued receipts, but when checks were received, she did not. The check payments were therefore unrecorded revenues—ripe for skimming. She placed these unrecorded checks in the days' receipts and removed an equal amount of cash. The receipts matched the amount of money on hand except that payments in currency had been replaced with checks.

The check-for-currency substitution was very common among skimming schemes in the 1996 study. Although these substitutions make it easier for fraudsters to convert stolen payments, the problem of concealing the theft still remains. The stolen checks that were not posted mean that some customers' accounts are in danger of becoming past due. If this happens, the fraudster's scheme is in danger because these customers will almost surely complain about the misapplication of their payments. The methods used by employees to deal with this and other problems are discussed next.

CONCEALING THE FRAUD

Skimming schemes generally are easier to conceal than most other types of occupational fraud. Sales skimming schemes, particularly unrecorded sales, are easily hidden because the stolen money and the transaction that generated the payment were never on the books. Therefore, there is no direct audit trail. In many skimming schemes, fraudsters take no action at all to conceal their crimes.

Destroying or Altering Records of the Transaction

When perpetrators do take affirmative steps to cover their tracks, one method often used is to destroy the records of the original transaction. For instance, we already have discussed the need for a salesperson to destroy the store's copy of a receipt in order for the sale to go undetected. Similarly, cash register tapes may be destroyed to hide an off-book sale. In one case, two management-level employees skimmed approximately $250,000 from their company over a four-year period. These employees tampered with cash register tapes that reflected transactions in which sales revenues had been skimmed. The perpetrators either destroyed entire register tapes or cut off large portions where the fraudulent transactions were recorded. In some circumstances, the employees then fabricated new tapes to match the cash on hand and make their registers appear to balance.

Discarding register tapes may signal fraud by raising suspicions that they were destroyed to conceal fraudulent transactions. Nevertheless, without the tapes, it may be very difficult to reconstruct the missing transactions and prove that someone actually skimmed money. Furthermore, it may be difficult to prove who was involved in the scheme.

The fraudsters operated a more refined scheme than simply destroying records. By fabricating completely new tapes, the culprits were able to conceal not only their identities but also the fraud itself. Not knowing that it was being robbed, the victim company took no action to shore up controls and prevent future thefts. Therefore, the scheme was able to continue for an extended time. It is obviously favorable for fraudsters, if possible, to keep employers unaware that thefts are occurring. Most of the high-dollar-loss schemes in our study owed their profitability, at least in part, to the quality of the concealment efforts of their perpetrators.

Concealing Receivables Skimming Schemes

We have alluded to the fact that skimming receivables may be more difficult to conceal than skimming sales because receivables payments are expected. The victim company knows the customer owes money and is waiting for the payment. In a revenue skimming scheme where a sale goes unrecorded, it is as if the sale never existed. Receivables skimming, by contrast, may raise questions about missing payments. When a customer's monthly payment is skimmed, the absence of the payment appears on the books as a delinquent account. In order to conceal a skimmed receivable, then, a fraudster somehow must account for the payment that was due to the company but never received.

Lapping

Lapping customer payments is one of the most common methods of concealing skimming and may be particularly useful to employees who skim receivables. Lapping is the crediting of one account through the abstraction of money from another account. It is the fraudster's version of robbing Peter to pay Paul. Suppose a company has three customers: A, B, and C. When A's payment is received, the fraudster takes it instead of posting it to A's account. Customer A expects that her account will be credited with the payment she has made, but this payment actually has been stolen. When A's next statement arrives, she will see that her check was not applied to her account and will complain. To avoid this, some action must be taken to make it appear that the payment was posted.

When B's check arrives, the fraudster takes this money and posts it to A's account. Payments now appear to be up to date on A's account, but B's account is short. When C's payment is received, the perpetrator applies it to B's account. This process continues indefinitely until one of three things happens: (1) someone discovers the scheme, (2) restitution is made to the accounts, or (3) some concealing entry is made to adjust the accounts receivable balances.

In the Mogel's case study, one of the ways Stefan Winkler concealed his thefts was to lap payments on customer accounts. Anecdotal evidence indicates that lapping is perhaps the most common concealment technique for skimming schemes in our study. Although more commonly used to conceal skimmed receivables, lapping also can be used to disguise the skimming of sales. In another case, for instance, a store manager stole daily receipts and replaced them with the following day's incoming cash. She progressively delayed the banking as she took more and more money. Each time a day's receipts were stolen, it took an extra day of collections to cover the missing money. Eventually the banking irregularities became so great that an investigation was ordered. It was discovered that the manager had stolen nearly $30,000 and had concealed the theft by lapping her store's sales.

Because lapping schemes can become very intricate, fraudsters sometimes keep a second set of books on hand detailing the true nature of the payments received. In many skimming cases, a search of the fraudster's work area will reveal a set of records tracking the actual payments made and how they have been misapplied to conceal the theft. It may seem odd that people would keep records of their illegal activity on hand, but many lapping schemes become increasingly complicated as more and more payments are misapplied. The second set of records helps perpetrators keep track of what funds they have stolen and what accounts need to be credited to conceal the fraud. Uncovering these records, if they exist, will greatly aid the investigation of a lapping scheme.

The most extreme version of how to conceal a lapping scheme I ever investigated involved an employee of a data processing company. Nelson was his name. The company he worked for essentially acted as in-house data processors for a variety of banks and other financial institutions.

Nelson was one of the original employees of this now multibillion-dollar firm with three initials. He had been with the company for nearly ten years when he began stealing. The company, it seems, wanted to promote Nelson from its Dallas office to be the chief programmer for one of its largest clients, a bank in New Orleans.

The company provided Nelson a $15,000 advance to make the move. It was supposed to be repaid after he sold his house in Dallas. But the company didn't know that

Nelson was in debt up to his eyeballs, with creditors calling him constantly. So he took the money from the sale of his house in Dallas and paid as many debts as he could.

When the company did not get back its money on time, it began applying pressure on Nelson. He agreed to pay out the loan on an installment basis, then promptly gave the company a rubber check for his first payment. His manager called him in and said, "Nelson, Dallas has called again about this loan. Let me put it in terms you can understand: You have 30 days to pay off this loan, or the company is going to make me fire you." Nelson understood.

The first thing he did was open a checking account under the name of an uncle at his client bank in New Orleans. Once that was done, he started engaging in a series of programming tricks to move money into and out of the uncle's account, over which he had signature authority. The money ultimately came out of the accounts of real bank customers.

The programming trick was to remove money not directly from the checking account itself but from one of the fields on the customer's account statement. More specifically, Nelson programmed his computer to debit the ending balance field of the individual account statement the day after customers' monthly statements were mailed to them. That gave Nelson exactly 29 days to reverse the entry before the next statement would be mailed.

Nelson chose the ending balance field on the statement because it did not leave a trail on the customer's statement the following month—provided he moved the money back to the account on the twenty-ninth day. If he had simply debited the customer's checking account itself, the computer would automatically print the transaction on the depositor's statement, thereby causing suspicion.

The scheme itself was made possible by the fact that the bank's computers were programmed to close and mail a portion of customers' monthly statements each business day of the month. Customer Adams would get a statement on the first of the month, but customer Zane would receive one on the last day of the month.

Nelson wrote his own little program to track the movement of money in and out of customer accounts. His computer would tell him when it was time to move money from the Adams account to the Zane account. This is complicated enough when one is dealing with only one transaction. But how about hundreds? Nelson did not stop with "borrowing" enough money to pay back the company; he eventually "lent" himself money from customer accounts to bail himself out of debt.

Nelson's downfall came when it was inadvertently discovered that his how-to-move-money-around program had some sort of logic error embedded in it. As a result, a customer received a statement for May with an ending balance of $1,300. But her June statement reflected a beginning balance of $500. The bank, assuming the problem was a programming error by the data processing servicing company, gave the statement to Nelson's boss. The boss also assumed it was a programming error and gave the statements to Nelson. His face went white right in front of the boss.

In the following days, many more customers started receiving nonsensical checking account statements, and Nelson's boss finally figured out what was going on. I was called in as a private fraud examiner to document the case and work with the lawyers and authorities. Nelson fully confessed and helped me gather the documentary evidence to convict him. Because of the way the money was bouncing around from account to account, it would have taken me weeks to figure it out by myself. He had stolen about $150,000 in total.

Nelson's cooperation in documenting the losses did not cut much soap with the judge, who sent the family man to prison for a year or two. The last I heard—and this crime occurred in the mid-1980s—was that Nelson had been released from the joint and was working as an accountant for the Jimmy Swaggart Ministries. I kid you not.

Stolen Statements

Another method used by employees to conceal the misapplication of customer payments is the theft or alteration of account statements. If a customer's payments are stolen and not posted, the account will become delinquent. When this happens, the customer should receive late notices or statements that reflect that the account is past due. The purpose of altering customers' statements is to keep them from complaining about the misapplication of their payments.

To keep customers unaware of the true status of their accounts, some fraudsters intercept account statements or late notices; this might be accomplished, for example, by changing a customer's address in the billing system. The statements will be sent directly to the fraudster's home or to an address where he can retrieve them. In other cases, the address is changed so that the statement is undeliverable, which causes the statements to be returned to the fraudster's desk. In either situation, once the employee has access to the statements, he can do one of two things.

The first option is to throw the statements away, but this will not be particularly effective if the customers ever request information about their accounts after not receiving a statement. Therefore, the fraudster usually alters the statements or produces counterfeit statements to make it appear that customers' payments have been posted properly. The employee then sends these fake statements to the customers. The false statements lead customers to believe that their accounts are up to date, keeping them from complaining about stolen payments.

False Account Entries

Intercepting customers' statements will keep them in the dark as to the status of their accounts, but the problem still remains: As long as a customer's payments are being skimmed, the account is slipping farther and farther past due. The fraudster must find some way to bring the account back up to date in order to conceal the crime. As we have discussed, lapping is one way to keep accounts current as the employee skims from them. Another way is to make false entries in the victim company's accounting system.

Debit Accounts

An employee might conceal the skimming of funds by making unsupported entries in the victim company's books. If a payment is made on a receivable, for instance, the proper entry is a debit to cash and a credit to the receivable. Instead of debiting cash, the fraudster might choose to debit an expense account. This transaction still keeps the company's books in balance, but the incoming cash is never recorded. In addition, the customer's receivable account is credited, so it will not become delinquent.

Debiting Existing or Fictitious Accounts

Fraudsters use the same method just discussed when they debit existing or fictitious accounts receivable in order to conceal skimmed cash. In one case, for example, an office manager in a healthcare facility took payments from patients for herself. To conceal her activity, she added the amounts taken to the accounts of other patients that she knew would soon be written off as uncollectible. Employees who use this method generally add the skimmed balances to accounts that either are very large or that are aging and about to be written off. Increases in the balances of these accounts are not as noticeable as in other accounts. In the case just mentioned, once the old accounts were written off, the stolen funds would be written off along with them.

Rather than using existing accounts, some fraudsters set up completely fictitious accounts and debit them for the cost of skimmed receivables. The employees then simply wait for the fictitious receivables to age and be written off, knowing that they are uncollectible. In the meantime, they carry the cost of a skimming scheme where it will not be detected.

Writing Off Account Balances

In one instance, an employee skimmed cash collections and wrote off the related receivables as "bad debts." Similarly, in another case, a billing manager was authorized to write off certain patient balances as hardship allowances. This employee accepted payments from patients, then instructed billing personnel to write off the balance in question. The payments were never posted; they were intercepted by the billing manager. She covered approximately $30,000 in stolen funds by using her authority to write off patients' balances.

Instead of writing off accounts as bad debts, some employees cover their skimming by posting entries to contra revenue accounts such as "discounts and allowances." If, for instance, an employee intercepts a $1,000 payment, he would create a $1,000 "discount" on the account to compensate for the missing money.

Inventory Padding

A major concealment problem for fraudsters is a company's inventory, if it has one. Off-book sales of goods will always leave an inventory shortage and a corresponding rise in the cost of goods sold. When a sale of goods is made, the physical inventory is reduced by the amount of merchandise sold. If a retailer sells a pair of shoes, for instance, it has one less pair of shoes in the stockroom. However, if this sale is unrecorded, the shoes remain on the inventory records. Thus, there is one less pair of shoes on hand than the records indicate. Such a reduction in the physical inventory without a corresponding reduction in the perpetual inventory is known as shrinkage.

When an employee skims sales of services, there is no shrinkage (because there is no inventory for services), but when sales of goods are skimmed, shrinkage always occurs. Some amounts of shrinkage are expected due to customer theft, faulty products, and spoilage, but high levels of shrinkage serve as a warning that a company could be a victim of occupational fraud. The general methods used to conceal inventory shrinkage are discussed in detail in Chapter 9.

DETECTION

Some detection methods that may be effective in detecting skimming schemes follow.

Receipt- or Sales-Level Detection

- Key analytical procedures, such as vertical and horizontal analysis of sales accounts, can be used for skimming detection on a grand scale. These procedures analyze changes in the accounts and possibly can point to skimming problems including understated sales.
- Ratio analysis also can provide keys to the detection of skimming schemes. These procedures are discussed in detail in Chapter 13.
- Detailed inventory control procedures also can be utilized to detect inventory shrinkage due to unrecorded sales. Inventory detection methods include statistical sampling, trend analysis, reviews of receiving reports and inventory records, and verification of material requisition and shipping documentation as well as actual physical inventory counts. These procedures are reviewed in Chapter 9.

Check Conversion Detection

Red flags may arise when an employee attempts to convert a stolen check.

- A bank or check-cashing institution employee questions the validity of the check.
- A dual endorsement is not allowed or causes check verification at the cashing institution.
- Canceled checks with dual endorsements should be scrutinized.
- A forged endorsement is discovered.
- It is discovered that an employee has opened a bank account with a name similar to the victim company.
- An alteration of the check payee or endorsement is discovered.

Additional conversion detection techniques are found in Chapter 5.

Journal Entry Review

Skimming frauds sometimes can be detected by reviewing and analyzing all journal entries made to the cash and inventory accounts. Journal entries involving these topics should be examined:

- False credits to inventory to conceal unrecorded or understated sales
- Write-offs related to lost, stolen, or obsolete product
- Write-offs of accounts receivable
- Irregular entries to cash accounts

PREVENTION

Receipt- or Sales-Level Control

As with most fraud schemes, internal control procedures are a key to preventing skimming schemes. An essential part of developing control procedures is management's communication to employees. Controlling whether an employee will not record a sale, understate a sale, or steal incoming payments is extremely difficult.

Check Conversion Controls

Banks and other financial institutions have stepped up detection and prevention methods. But as with most things, the criminal element is usually one step ahead. Companies should work in a cooperative effort with banks to prevent check fraud. Additional check conversion and tampering controls are detailed in Chapter 5.

General Controls

Sales entries and general ledger access controls should include documented policies and procedures, which are communicated directly from management. The control procedures generally cover these subjects:

- Appropriate segregation of duties and access control procedures regarding who makes ledger transactions will be followed.
- Transactions must be recorded properly as to amount, date of occurrence, and ledger account.
- Proper safeguard measures will be adopted to ensure physical access to the account systems. Additional measures should ensure the security of company assets.
- Independent reconciliations as well as internal verification of accounts will be performed on ledger accounts.[2]

Skimming Controls

The discovery of thefts of checks and cash involves proper controls on the receipt process. Deficiencies in the answers to these typical audit-program questions may be red flags.

- Is mail opened by someone independent of cashier, accounts receivable bookkeeper, or other accounting employees who may initiate or post journal entries?

- Is the delivery of unopened business mail prohibited to employees having access to the accounting records?
- Does the employee who opens the mail:
  - Place restrictive endorsements (''For Deposit Only'') on all checks received?
  - Prepare a list of the money, checks, and other receipts?
  - Forward all remittances to the person responsible for preparing and making the daily bank deposit?
  - Forward the total of all remittances to the person responsible for comparing it to the authenticated deposit ticket and amount recorded?
- Is a lockbox used?
- Do cash sales occur? If yes:
  - Are cash receipts prenumbered?
  - Is an independent check of prenumbered receipts done daily and reconciled to cash collections?
  - Do cash refunds require approval?
- Are cash receipts deposited intact daily?
- Are employees who handle receipts bonded?
- Is the accounts receivable bookkeeper restricted from:
  - Preparing the bank deposit?
  - Obtaining access to the cash receipts book?
  - Having access to collections from customers?
- Are banks instructed not to cash checks drawn to the order of the company?
- Is the cashier restricted from gaining access to the accounts receivable records and bank and customer statements?
- Are areas where physical handling of cash takes place reasonably safeguarded?
- Is the person making postings to the general ledger independent of the cash receipts and accounts receivable functions?
- Does a person independent of the cashier or accounts receivable functions handle customer complaints?[3]

NOTES

1. Association of Certified Fraud Examiners, *Fraud Examiners' Manual* (Austin, TX: 2011).
2. George Georgiades, *Audit Procedures* (New York: Harcourt Brace Professional Publishing, 1995).
3. Ibid.

CHAPTER 4

Cash Larceny

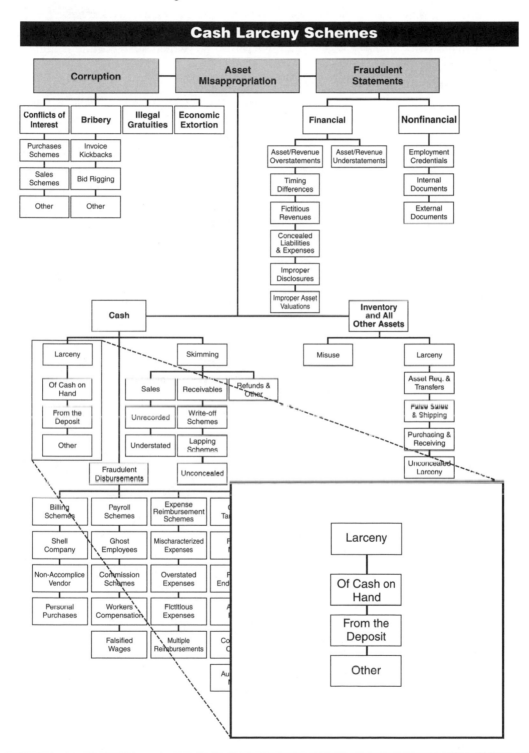

Case Study: Bank Teller Gets Nabbed for Theft

Laura Grove* had worked at Rocky Mountain Bank in Nashville, Tennessee, for five years. As a teller, she thought to herself, she wasn't getting any richer. She and her husband owed about $14,000 in credit card bills, which seemed to get higher and higher each month, especially after adopting a five-year-old girl the year before.

When she transferred to a branch bank in Cheetboro, Tennessee, the bank promoted her to head teller. In this new position, Laura had authority to open the night depository vault with another teller. For security reasons, the bank allowed each teller to possess only half the combination to the vault.

Every morning, Laura saw the bank night deposit vault door open and close after the removal of all customer night deposit bags. The bank placed only one camera on the night vault, which was turned on at 8:00 A.M. when the bank opened for business. Laura thought it would be easy to get into the night depository and take the bags. These thoughts were reinforced when a customer reported his bag missing and the bank quickly paid his money without a thorough investigation. So one Friday morning, Laura made up her mind that she could take about $15,000 with little risk of being identified. But before she actually took the money, she observed. When she opened the night vault with her coworker Frank Geffen, she saw him dial the first half of the combination and was careful to memorize the numbers. After entering the second half of the combination, they opened it as usual, removed and listed each night deposit bag, and shut the vault behind them. This time, however, Laura did not lock the vault.

It was here that Laura made her first mistake. She thought she could leave the vault door open and return Monday to take the money. But just before the bank closed and employees prepared to leave, teller Melissa Derkstein checked the vault one more time. Seeing that the vault was open, she spun the dial, shaking the handle to ensure the door was locked.

Laura and the other bank employees punched their security codes on the outside door and left for the day. During the weekend, Laura considered her plot. Should she enter the combination by herself this time and place the money into a personal tote bag? Should she stay at work all day with the goods beneath her feet?

Monday morning, she still was not sure how to pull it off but had resolved to go through with the plan anyway. Arriving at 7:15 A.M., Laura was the first person in the bank that morning. After punching in her security code, she placed her tote bag and personal belongings on her chair. Immediately, she went to the night vault and dialed the full combination. Nothing happened. Her mind raced. "Maybe this won't work; this is too risky." Her fingers tried the combination again, and once again, until she heard a click and the vault opened.

Inside, Laura removed the two customer deposit bags, ones that she knew contained large sums of cash. She placed both bags in her tote bag and walked back to her teller window. She stuffed her Weight Watchers book and purse inside the tote bag, on top of the deposit bags. She then hung her bag on the door of the storage room and returned to the teller window, straightening up her work area.

*Several names and details have been changed to preserve anonymity.

Fifteen minutes later, the branch manager, Harvey Lebrand, entered, looking surprised that Laura was already at her desk. He asked Laura why she had come into work so early this Monday.

"Oh, I just needed to get organized early, because I need to take my Bronco into the shop later today and knew I wouldn't have much time," Laura said.

"You need to get your truck repaired?" Mr. Lebrand asked. "Why don't you go now?"

"Okay, I can get my mother to give me a ride back," Laura said. "See you soon, Mr. Lebrand."

Laura rushed to the storage area, grabbed the tote bag, and left the bank. She drove directly to her home and emptied the contents of the bag, watching the many bills and checks spill onto her bed. She lit up with uneasy excitement. Sorting the checks into a separate pile, she gathered the money into a large heap and did a quick count. She estimated she had taken about $15,000. Placing the bills into manila envelopes, she hid them in the headboard storage compartment of the bed. She placed the checks in a small plastic bag. She then phoned her mother and asked her to meet her at the Sears Auto Center.

Laura knew there was an apartment complex next to Sears that had a large blue Dumpster. After she had deposited the checks in the Dumpster, Laura drove to Sears. Her mother arrived a little later to take her back to work.

A day later, Rocky Mountain Bank Audit Investigator Stacy Boone received a call from Laura's manager, informing her that two customers had not gotten credit for the deposits they'd made the night before. Each deposit was for $8,000.

Boone's investigation quickly led her to suspect Grove. The first one in the bank that morning, Grove also came in before the surveillance cameras turned on. As head teller, she had one-half of the combination to the night depository. Other employees said they "didn't trust her." But when the investigators questioned her, Grove strongly denied any knowledge of the theft.

"During our interview with her, she broke out in a red rash" (which suggested stress). "I have seen innocent people break out into a red rash, but she was the only one we interviewed that day who did," Boone said.

Boone also suspected Grove because the branch bank from which she'd transferred "had a lot of unexplained shortages, and she was a suspect there, but we could never pin down that she took the money. She had bought a lot of new jewelry, wore a lot of expensive clothes, but had filed bankruptcy at one point that year."

The investigation came to a swift conclusion, however, when Boone received a call on her answering machine from Grove's husband, a former neighbor. "I was afraid he wanted to know why we were investigating his wife and hesitated to call him right back," Boone said.

Boone decided she "might as well get this over with and tell him I could not talk about it [the investigation]. When I called him, he told me he found the bank's money in his attic and suspected his wife. His wife had told him of the bank's investigation but had not admitted any theft.

"Their daughter had overheard a conversation they had the day of the theft" in which Laura had expressed anxiety to her husband about the bank's investigation, Boone said. "His daughter had told him that she saw [Laura] put something in the attic. So, when she wasn't there, the husband went up in the attic and looked, and found two bags of money."

Boone said the husband was also suspicious because his wife had lied to him before. "He told me that his mother-in-law, her mother, always won all these prizes. She had even won a car through a contest. One night he came home and found a new big-screen LCD HDTV in the living room and asked his wife where it came from. She said 'Oh, Mom won that.' At the time, he really didn't think anything about it. But a couple days later, Kirby's Electronics, where the TV came from, called in regard to her credit application. They told him that she charged that TV."

Faced with this evidence, Laura and her husband delivered the $16,000 in cash as restitution. The bank dismissed Grove, and she was prosecuted for the crime but received probation in lieu of prison time.

A year later, Boone received a call from one of the bank's tellers who had seen Grove working at another bank in a small city outside of Nashville. Boone called one of the personnel employees there and talked with her. "They were a bank that did not do fingerprint checks, so they had no knowledge that she had been convicted. She did get into another bank to work, but not for very long."

OVERVIEW

In the occupational fraud setting, a the term "cash larceny" may be defined as the intentional taking away of an employer's cash (the term "cash" includes both currency and checks) without the consent and against the will of the employer. In our first case study, Laura Grove's theft of approximately $16,000 from her employer is an example of a cash larceny.

How do cash larceny schemes differ from other cash frauds? In order to understand the distinction in our classifications, it is helpful to break down the cash schemes into two broad groups, the first being the *fraudulent disbursement schemes* and the second being what we will loosely term the *cash receipts schemes*. Fraudulent disbursement schemes are those in which a distribution of funds is made from some company account in what appears to be a normal manner. The method for obtaining the funds may be the forging of a check, the submission of a false invoice, the doctoring of a timecard, and so forth. The key is that the money is removed from the company in what appears to be a legitimate disbursement of funds. Fraudulent disbursements are discussed later in Chapters 5 through 8.

Receipts schemes are what we typically think of as the outright stealing of cash. Perpetrators do not rely on the submission of phony documents or the forging of signatures; they simply grab the cash and take it. Receipts schemes fall into two categories: *skimming*, which we have already discussed, and *larceny schemes*. Remember that skimming was defined as the theft of off-book funds. Cash larceny schemes involve the theft of money that has already appeared on a victim company's books.

Exhibit 4.1   *2009 Global Fraud Survey*: **Frequency of Cash Misappropriations**

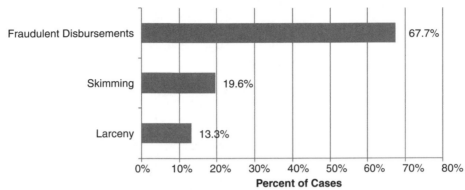

CASH LARCENY DATA FROM ACFE *2009 GLOBAL FRAUD SURVEY*

Frequency and Cost

In our study, cash larceny schemes were the least common and least costly forms of cash misappropriations. Thirteen percent of all cash schemes in our survey involved cash larceny. (The sum of these percentages exceeds 100 percent because some cases involved multiple fraud schemes that fell into more than one category. Various charts in this chapter may reflect percentages that total in excess of 100 percent for similar reasons.) The median loss for these cases was $100,000, which is more than the median loss for skimming schemes but only two-thirds as much as the median loss for fraudulent disbursements. (See Exhibit 4.1 and 4.2.)

Exhibit 4.3 shows the distribution of cash larceny losses compared with the distribution for all occupational frauds. Like skimming schemes, cash larceny schemes were more likely to fall into the lower-level ranges, with almost 45 percent of all cash larceny cases causing losses below $50,000.

Exhibit 4.2   *2009 Global Fraud Survey*: **Median Loss of Cash Misappropriations**

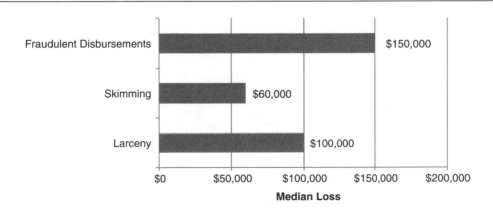

Exhibit 4.3 *2009 Global Fraud Survey*: **Dollar Loss Distribution for Cash Larceny Schemes**

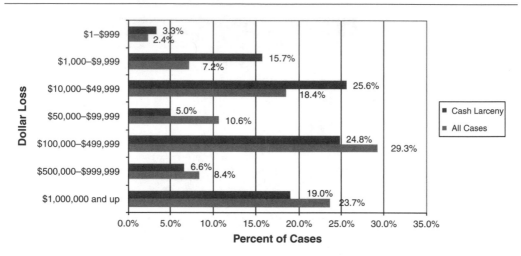

Detection of Cash Larceny Schemes

We received 180 responses in which the method of initial detection for cash larceny cases was identified. The most commonly cited detection methods were tips, management review, and internal audit. Additionally, both account reconciliation and external audit were responsible for detecting a greater percentage of cash larceny schemes than all schemes in general. (See Exhibit 4.4.)

Perpetrators of Cash Larceny Schemes

The distribution of perpetrator positions for cash larceny schemes was quite similar to that of all schemes for our 2009 study. Employees were responsible for 41.3 percent of

Exhibit 4.4 *2009 Global Fraud Survey*: **Detection of Cash Larceny Schemes**

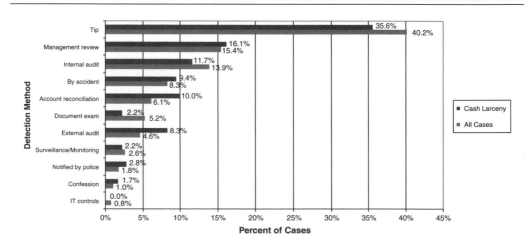

Exhibit 4.5   *2009 Global Fraud Survey*: Perpetrators of Cash Larceny Schemes

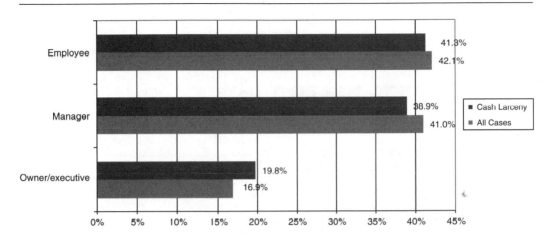

the 167 responses in which the position of the perpetrator in a cash larceny case was identified while managers and owner/executives were responsible for 38.9 percent and 19.8 percent, respectively. (See Exhibit 4.5.)

As with other types of occupational frauds, the median loss for cash larceny schemes rose with the position level of the principal perpetrator. Cash larceny cases involving managers caused a median loss of $116,000, which was more than three times the median loss of $34,000 associated with schemes committed by employees. Median losses in the 33 cases perpetrated by owner/executives were significantly larger than both other categories, at $225,000. (See Exhibit 4.6.)

Exhibit 4.6   *2009 Global Fraud Survey:* Median Loss by Perpetrator of Cash Larceny Schemes

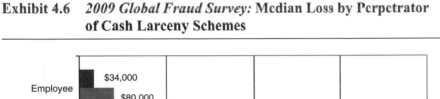
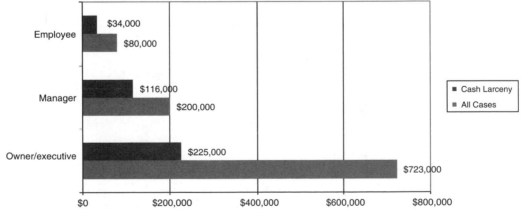

Exhibit 4.7 *2009 Global Fraud Survey*: Size of Victim in Cash Larceny Schemes

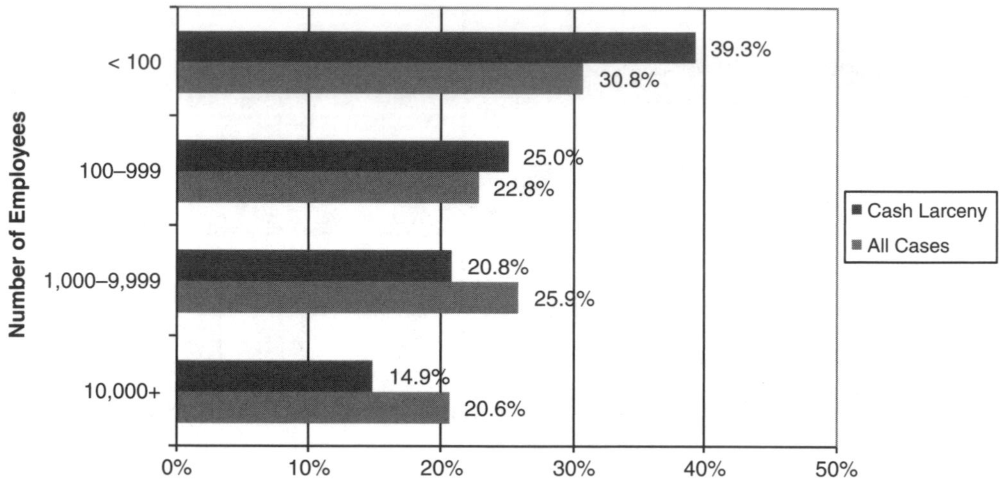

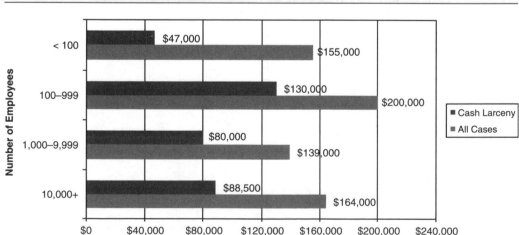

Victims of Cash Larceny Schemes

Exhibit 4.7 shows the breakdown of cash larceny cases in our study based on the number of employees in the victim organization. As was the case with skimming (see Chapter 2), cash larceny cases were much more common in small organizations than were occupational frauds in general.

Reflected in Exhibit 4.8 are the median losses associated with cash larceny cases based on the size of the victim organization. Interestingly, organizations with between 100 and 1,000 employees suffered the largest median loss, at $130,000, which was more than two and a half times as much as the loss suffered by companies with fewer

Exhibit 4.8 *2009 Global Fraud Survey*: Median Loss by Size of Victim in Cash Larceny Schemes

than 100 employees ($47,000). Losses at the largest companies—those with more than 1,000 employees—fell in between these two categories.

INCOMING CASH

Theft of Cash from the Register

A large percentage of the cash larceny schemes in our survey occurred at the cash register, and for good reason—the register is where the currency is. The register (or similar cash collection points like cash drawers or cash boxes) is usually the most common point of access to ready cash for employees, so it is understandable that the register is where larceny schemes frequently occur. Furthermore, there is often a great deal of activity at the register and multiple transactions requiring the handling of cash by employees. This activity can serve as a cover for the theft of cash. In a flurry of activity, with cash being passed back and forth between customer and employee, a fraudster is more likely to be able to slip currency out of the register and into a pocket without getting caught.

This is the most straightforward scheme: Open the register and remove currency. (See Exhibit 4.9.) It might be done as a sale is being conducted to make the theft appear to be part of the transaction or perhaps when no one is around to notice the perpetrator digging into the cash drawer. In one case, for instance, a teller simply signed on to a register, rang a "no sale," and took currency from the drawer. Over a period of time, the teller took approximately $6,000 through this simple method.

Exhibit 4.9 Cash Larceny from the Register

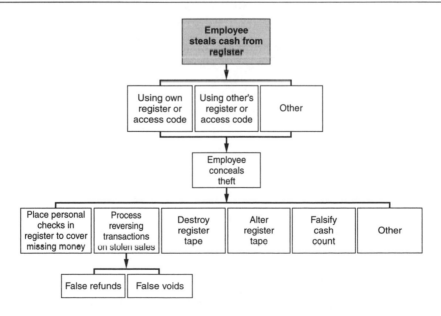

101

Recall that the benefit of a skimming scheme is that the transaction is unrecorded and the stolen funds are never entered on company books. The employee who is skimming either underrings the register transaction so that a portion of the sale is unrecorded or completely omits the sale by failing to enter it at all on the register. This makes the skimming scheme difficult to detect because the register tape does not reflect the presence of the funds that have been taken. In a larceny scheme, the funds that the perpetrator steals are already reflected on the register tape. As a result, an imbalance will result between the register tape and the cash drawer. This imbalance should be a signal that alerts a victim company to the theft.

The actual method for taking money at the register—opening the register and removing currency—rarely varies; it is the methods used by fraudsters to avoid getting caught that distinguish larceny schemes. Oddly, in many instances, perpetrators have no plan for avoiding detection. A large part of fraud is rationalizing; fraudsters convince themselves that they are somehow entitled to what they are taking or that what they are doing is not actually a crime. Register larceny schemes frequently begin when perpetrators convince themselves that they are only "borrowing" the funds to cover a temporary monetary need. These people might carry the missing currency in their registers for several days, deluding themselves that they will one day repay the funds and hoping their employers will not perform a surprise cash count on their register until the missing money is replaced.

Employees who do nothing to camouflage their crimes are easily caught; more dangerous are those who take active steps to hide their misdeeds. One basic way for employees to disguise the fact that they are stealing currency is to take money from someone else's register. In some retail organizations, employees are assigned to certain registers. Alternatively, one register is used and each employee has an access code. When cash is missing from a cashier's register, the most likely suspect for the theft is obviously that cashier. Therefore, by stealing from another's register or by using someone else's access code, the fraudster makes sure that another employee will be the prime suspect in the theft. In the case just discussed, for example, the employee who stole money did so by waiting until another teller was on break, then logging on to that teller's register, ringing a "no sale," and taking the cash. The resulting cash shortage appeared in the register of an honest employee, deflecting attention from the true thief. In another case we reviewed, a cash office manager stole over $8,000, in part by taking money from cash registers and making it appear that the cashiers were stealing.

A very unsophisticated way to avoid detection is to steal currency in very small amounts over an extended period of time. This is the death-by-a-thousand-cuts larceny scheme; $15 here, $20 there—and slowly, the culprit bleeds the company. Because the missing amounts are small, the shortages may be credited to errors rather than theft. Typically, employees become dependent on the extra money they are pilfering, and their thefts increase in scale or become more frequent, which causes the scheme to be uncovered. Most retail organizations track overages or shortages by employee, making this method largely ineffectual.

A register is balanced by comparing the transactions on the register tape to the amount of cash on hand. Starting at a known balance, sales, returns, and other register transactions are added to or subtracted from the balance to arrive at a total for the period in question. The actual cash is then counted, and the two totals are compared. If the register tape shows that there should be more cash in the register than what is present, it may be because of larceny.

Personal Checks

One way for employees to conceal larceny schemes is to leave personal checks in their registers to cover the amount of money they have stolen. The employee writes a personal check for the missing amount and places it in the cash drawer so that the register is always in balance. This method is used to avoid the danger of a larceny scheme being discovered during a surprise cash count. (Of course, the presence of the employee's personal check in the register might itself raise concerns of theft.) The employee obviously never allows the check to be deposited, so the "balance" on the register is really an illusion.

In one case, a bank teller used a similar concealment method, but instead of a personal check, she used a transfer ticket to cover the cash she had stolen. A transfer ticket is a document in a teller's cash drawer that shows that a certain amount of money was transferred to another location. It is a debit to the drawer of the teller who holds the ticket and a credit to the teller who receives the cash in exchange for the ticket. The teller stole over $57,000 and was not detected for a little more than a year as she carried a transfer ticket in her drawer for the amount that she had embezzled. Although her cash was counted quarterly by management, the fraudulent transfer ticket was not validated. In other words, no one traced the offsetting credit on the ticket to another teller. Had they done so, the fraud would have been easily discovered.

Reversing Transactions

Another way to conceal a cash larceny is to use reversing transactions, which cause the register tape to reconcile to the amount of cash on hand after the theft. By processing false voids or refunds, an employee can reduce the amount of cash reflected on the register tape. In one instance, a cashier received payments from a customer and recorded the transactions on her system. She stole the payments from the customers, then destroyed the company's receipts that reflected the transactions. To complete the cover-up, the cashier went back and voided the transactions that she had entered at the time the payments were received. The reversing entries brought the receipt totals into balance with the cash on hand. (These schemes are discussed in more detail in Chapter 6.)

Instead of using reversing entries, some employees manually alter the register tape or the cash count. Again, the purpose of this activity is to force a balance between the cash on hand and the actual cash received over the period. An employee might use correction fluid to cover up a sale whose proceeds were stolen or simply cross out or alter the numbers on the tape so that the register total and the cash drawer balance. A department manager altered and destroyed cash register tapes in one case to help conceal a fraud scheme that went on for four years.

Altering Cash Counts

Instead of falsifying the company's record of receipts, some fraudsters alter the cash counts on their registers. An employee in one example not only discarded register tapes to conceal her thefts but also erased and rewrote cash counts for the registers from which she pilfered. The new totals on the cash count envelopes were overstated by the amount of money she had stolen, reflecting the actual receipts for the period and balancing with the cash register tapes. Under the victim company's controls, this employee was not supposed to have access to cash. Ironically, coworkers praised her dedication for helping them count cash when it was not one of her official duties.

Destroying Register Tapes

If the fraudster cannot make the cash and the tape balance, the next best thing is to prevent others from computing the totals and discovering the imbalance. Employees who are stealing from the register sometimes destroy detail tapes that would implicate them in a crime. When detail tapes are missing or defaced, it may be because someone does not want the information on them to be known.

Other Larceny of Sales and Receivables

Not all receipts arrive via the cash register. Although most of the larceny schemes in our study involved the theft of cash from the register, there is no reason that employees cannot steal money received at other points. One of the more common methods for those stealing incoming money is to post the customer's payment to the accounting system but take the cash. (See Exhibit 4.10.) There was one example in which an employee posted all records of customer payments to date but stole the money received. In a four-month period, this employee took over $200,000 in incoming payments. Consequently, the cash account was significantly out of balance, which led to discovery of the fraud. This was one of the cases in our study, incidentally, in which the employee justified the theft by saying she planned to pay the money back. This case illustrates the central weakness of cash larceny schemes—the resulting imbalances in company accounts. This case is very similar to many of the skimming schemes discussed in Chapter 3, except that in those frauds the stolen receipts were not posted to the cash receipts journal.

Fraudsters who have total control of a company's accounting system can overcome the problem of out-of-balance accounts. In one case, an employee stole customer payments and posted them to the accounts receivable journal in the same manner as the fraudster discussed in the last example. As in the previous case, this employee's fraud resulted in an imbalance in the victim company's cash account. The difference between the two frauds is that this perpetrator had control over the company's deposits and all its ledgers. She therefore was able to conceal her crime by making unsupported entries in the company's books, which produced a fictitious balance between receipts and ledgers. This case illustrates how poor separation of duties can allow the perpetuation of a fraud that ordinarily would be easy to detect.

Exhibit 4.10   Other Cash Larceny

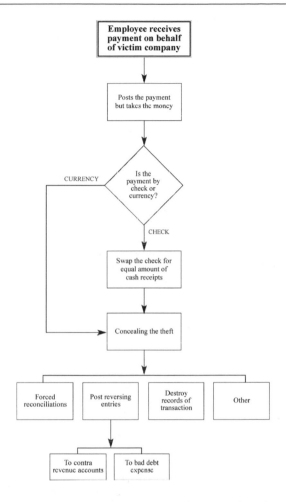

In circumstances in which payments are stolen but nonetheless posted to the cash receipts journal, reversing entries can be used to balance the victim company's accounts. For instance, an office manager stole approximately $75,000 in customer payments from her employer. In a number of these cases she posted the payment to the customer's account, then later reversed the entry on the books with unauthorized adjustments, such as "courtesy discounts."

A less elegant way to hide a crime is simply to destroy all records that might prove that the perpetrator has been stealing. Destroying records en masse does not prevent the victim company from realizing that it is being robbed, but it may help conceal the identity of the thief. This slash-and-burn concealment strategy was used by a controller in one case. The controller, who had complete control over the books of her employer, stole approximately $100,000. When it became evident that her superiors were suspicious of her activities, the perpetrator entered her office one night after work, stole all the cash on hand, destroyed all records, including her personnel file, and left town.

CASH LARCENY FROM THE DEPOSIT

At some point in most revenue-generating businesses, someone must physically take the company's currency and checks to the bank. This person or persons, literally left holding the bag, will have an opportunity to take a portion of the money prior to depositing it into the company's accounts.

Typically, when cash is received by a company, someone is assigned to tabulate the receipts, list the form of payment (currency or check), and prepare a deposit slip for the bank. Then another employee, preferably one not involved in the preparing of the deposit slip, takes the cash and deposits it in the bank. One copy of the slip generally is retained by the person who made out the deposit. This copy is matched to a receipted copy of the slip stamped by the bank when the deposit is made.

This procedure is designed to prevent theft of funds from the deposit, but thefts still occur, often because the process is not adhered to. (See Exhibit 4.11.) For

Exhibit 4.11   Cash Larceny from the Deposit

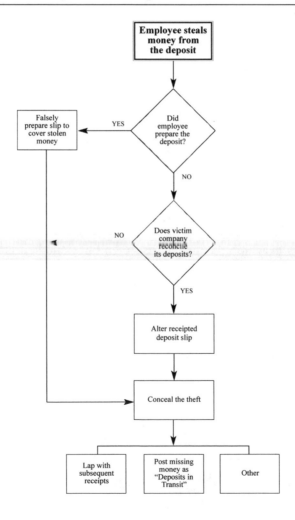

example, an employee in a small company was responsible for preparing and making the deposits, recording the deposits in the company's books, and reconciling the bank statements. This employee took several thousand dollars from the company deposits and concealed it by making false entries in the books that corresponded to falsely prepared deposit slips. Similarly, in another case, in a retail store where cash registers were not used, sales were recorded on prenumbered invoices. The controller of this organization was responsible for collecting cash receipts and making the bank deposits. This controller was also the only person who reconciled the totals on the prenumbered receipts to the bank deposit. Therefore, he was able to steal a portion of the deposit with the knowledge that the discrepancy between the deposit and the day's receipts would not be detected.

Another oversight in procedure is failure to reconcile the bank copy of the deposit slip with the office copy. When the person making the deposit knows that his company does not reconcile the two copies, he can steal cash from the deposit on the way to the bank and alter the deposit slip so that it reflects a lesser amount. In some cases, sales records also will be altered to match the diminished deposit.

When cash is stolen from the deposit, the receipted deposit slip will, of course, be out of balance with the company's copy of the deposit slip (unless the perpetrator also prepared the deposit). To correct this problem, some fraudsters alter the bank copy of the deposit slip after it has been validated. This brings the two copies back into balance. For example, in the course of a year, one employee altered 24 deposit slips and validated bank receipts to conceal the theft of over $15,000. These documents were altered with correction fluid or ballpoint pen to match the company's cash reports. Of course, as the cash was stolen, the company's book balance would not match its actual bank balance. If another employee regularly balances the checking account, this theft should be easily detected.

Another mistake that can be made in the deposit function, and one that is a departure from common sense, is entrusting the deposit to the wrong person. For instance, a bookkeeper who had been employed for only one month was put in charge of making the deposit. She promptly diverted the funds to her own use. This is not to say that all new employees are untrustworthy—but it is advisable to have some sense of a person's character before handing that person a bag full of money.

Still another commonsense issue is the handling of the deposit on the way to the bank. Once prepared, the deposit immediately should be put in a safe place until it is taken to the bank. In a few of the cases we studied, the deposit was left carelessly unattended. For example, a part-time employee learned that it was the bookkeeper's habit to leave the bank bag in her desk overnight before depositing it the following morning. For approximately six months, this employee pilfered checks from the deposit and got away with it. He was able to endorse the checks at a local establishment, without using his own signature, in the name of the victim company. The owner of the check-cashing institution did not question the fact that this individual was cashing company checks because, as a pastor of a sizable church in the community, the fraudster's integrity was thought to be above reproach.

As with all cash larceny schemes, stealing from the company deposit can be rather difficult to conceal. In most cases, these schemes are successful for a long duration only when the person who counts the cash also makes the deposit. In any other circumstance, the success of the scheme depends primarily on the inattentiveness of those charged with preparing and reconciling the deposit.

Deposit Lapping

One method sometimes successfully used to evade detection is the lapping method. Lapping occurs when an employee steals the deposit from day 1, then replaces it with day 2's deposit. Day 2's deposit is replaced with day 3's, and so on. Perpetrators are always one day behind, but as long as no one demands an up-to-the minute reconciliation of the deposits to the bank statement and if the size of the deposits does not drop precipitously, they may be able to avoid detection for a period of time. In one case, a company officer stole cash receipts from the company deposit and withheld the deposit for a time. Eventually the deposit was made, and the missing cash was replaced with a check received at a later date. Lapping is discussed in more detail in Chapter 3.

Deposits in Transit

A final concealment strategy with stolen deposits is to carry the missing money as deposits in transit (d.i.t.). In one instance, an employee was responsible for receiving collections, issuing receipts, posting transactions, reconciling accounts, and making deposits. Such a lack of separation of duties leaves a company extremely vulnerable to fraud. This employee took over $20,000 in collections from her employer over a five-month period. To hide her theft, the perpetrator carried the missing money as deposits in transit, meaning that the missing money would appear on the next month's bank statement. Of course, it never did. The balance was carried for several months as "d.i.t." until an auditor recognized the discrepancy and put a halt to the fraud.

The next case study provides an example of how an employee stole cash from his company's bank deposits. Bill Gurado, a branch manager for a consumer-loan finance company, took his branch's deposits to the bank himself, where he placed the money into his own account rather than his employer's. CFE Harry Smith audited Gurado's branch to determine the scope of his scheme. This case provides an excellent example of how an employee's perception of his company's controls can be valuable in preventing and detecting fraud.

Case Study: The Ol' Fake Surprise Audit Gets 'em Every Time

Some people would say that auditors have no sense of humor—that they are a straight-laced, straight-faced bunch. Bill Gurado* knows better.

Gurado worked as a branch manager for Newfund, a consumer-loan finance company in New Orleans. He was the highly respected leader of the company's oldest, largest, and most successful branch. With such a high profile, Gurado

---

*Several names and details have been changed to preserve anonymity.

commanded a lot of respect. Other managers wanted to be like him. Employees respected him. Everyone in the company considered him a good guy.

For reasons not entirely clear, Gurado began stealing from the company. He did not take a lot of money. His scheme was less than brilliant. And because he did not appreciate an auditor's sense of humor, his fraud was brought to light just weeks after it began.

Newfund employed good controls, both from an accounting and from a management standpoint. One control on which Barry Ecker, the company's internal auditor, relied was the surprise audit. He normally sprang surprise audits at least once, and sometimes twice, a year on each of Newfund's 30 branches. Due to the size of Gurado's branch, Ecker could not perform a surprise audit by himself. He would have to coordinate with the external audit staff. During these surprise audits, Ecker came in and took control from the start. He was extremely thorough. Harry J. Smith, one of the external auditors whose team would accompany him, describes Ecker as "your typical old-time sleuth-type auditor. A little bitty, short, pudgy guy who got a lot of psychic pleasure out of scaring the hell out of branch people. He'd come in and he'd be quiet and very secure about his papers and his area. He'd stare people down. He'd stare at ledger cards looking for irregularities. He'd just make people quake." Adds Smith, "He was really fun to watch. When he was in his character, he was one for the books." Having been through several surprise audits, Gurado knew the extent of Ecker's investigating. He probably had that in the back of his mind when he ran into Ecker at a store by chance over the weekend.

They had a brief conversation, and as might be expected from someone like Ecker, who enjoyed putting a little fear into people, he mentioned he was about to launch a surprise audit at Gurado's branch. "Well, I'll see you Monday," he said without cracking a smile. "Harry and I are going to pull an audit on your branch on Monday morning." Of course, he had no plans to audit the branch any time in the near future. As they parted, Gurado said, "Great. See you then." But Gurado was not looking forward to seeing Ecker at all. He knew that Ecker, with all his searching and checking, would find some irregularities. He would piece together Gurado's fraud without much trouble at all. It would not take much effort to learn that Gurado had diverted company money into his own bank account.

Newfund's clientele was such that it received a lot of cash. For about a week Gurado took the daily deposits to the bank himself and deposited the money in his personal account. He made certain all the daily reports were sent to headquarters as usual—except, of course, the receipted bank deposit slips. It was only a few thousand dollars. But he had not yet had a chance to replace any of the money (if he had ever intended to), and he would not have time to cover his tracks before the "surprise" audit.

"He was absolutely convinced that had we audited his branch, we would find it," says Smith. "And we probably would have. Barry Ecker did an old-style audit where you go in and seal the file cabinets and take immediate control of the cash drawers and the ledger tubs. It's a complete instantaneous control and tie-out.

I'm pretty sure we'd have found it. I know the branch manager was convinced his boat was sunk.''

Gurado did some deep soul-searching that weekend. On Sunday night, he called on the president of the company, a man with a reputation of being a hard-driving, authoritarian individual. ''I know it was a giant step for the branch manager to call him up that night,'' Smith says. At the president's house that Sunday evening, Gurado came clean. ''I know the auditors are coming tomorrow morning,'' he said. Then he confessed to taking money from the company. He was immediately fired.

On Monday morning, Ecker called Smith at the accounting firm. He told Smith what had transpired and then said, ''Look, we gotta go audit the branch.'' Smith and Ecker pulled out all the stops to get an audit team over to the branch to make sure there was nothing else going on.

They found exactly what Gurado had reported and nothing else. Looking back on this case, Smith feels certain the fraud would have been detected even without the misunderstood joke. Newfund practiced a control procedure that probably would have turned up the missing money within 15 days. Because of that fact, he surmises that Gurado might have been covering some kind of short-term debt with the intent of repaying it.

Since Gurado returned the funds immediately and because he had confessed, the company did not pursue any criminal or civil action against him, feeling it a better course of action to keep the matter out of the public eye.

Word did travel quickly around the company, however—upper management made sure of that. The fact that this esteemed branch manager tripped himself up and immediately got caught went a long way toward reinforcing the importance of following proper procedures.

''People commonly measure auditing's benefit by the substance of its findings and recommendations,'' Smith says. ''Auditing's role in preventing abuse is hard to observe and measure and is often unappreciated. But this case clearly shows that the specter of having an audit certainly affects peoples' behavior.''

MISCELLANEOUS LARCENY SCHEMES

Obviously, as the Gurado case illustrates, there are numerous ways to steal cash from one's employer. The method used to do so will depend, to a large extent, on the circumstances existing at the victim company. A few of the more interesting cases in our study will be discussed to illustrate the variety of methods we have encountered.

A large number of cash larceny schemes we analyzed came from the banking industry, which is no great surprise considering the vast amounts of currency present at most banks. A notable example is one in which a bank encoding clerk stole a check for nearly $400,000, which had been deposited into a customer's account. The check had been validated and sent to the proof area for posting when the clerk took it and mailed it to an accomplice in another state. The accomplice opened an account in the depositor's name and attempted to deposit the check in this new account. Fortunately, the error was detected before the culprits were able to make off with the money.

As with other types of occupational fraud, cash larceny schemes often flourish where controls are weak or nonexistent. A perfect example of this was found in a case in which an employee stole over $100,000 worth of checks from his employer. The checks, each of which was endorsed with the company's name and account number, were simply left unattended in a basket marked "cashier."

Cash schemes are usually, but not always, orchestrated by a single person. In some cases, a group of employees conspire to rob their company, and in other instances, an employee might enlist outside help. Such was the situation in one case, where a manager allowed her store to accumulate approximately $150,000 in cash and food stamps, then arranged for a group of accomplices to rob the store.

Although cash larceny schemes on the whole are perhaps the most varied of all the classifications in our study, within a particular business they should be among the easiest to prevent and detect. This is true primarily because, in these schemes, employees can attack the business only at a few discrete points: those places where money is physically received or distributed. Proper observation of separation of duties and account management, along with ordinary monitoring of the cash-handling process, should prevent the bulk of these offenses.

DETECTION

Receipt Recording

In-depth analysis of the cash receipts and recording process is the key to detecting a cash larceny scheme. Areas of analysis may include:

- Mail and register receipt points.
- Journalizing and recording of the receipts.
- The security of the cash from receipt to deposit.

In analyzing the cash receipt process, it is important to meet several control objectives:

- Cash receipts must be complete. Each day's receipts must be collected promptly and deposited in full.
- It must be assured that each receivable transaction recorded is legitimate and has supporting documentation.
- All information included in the transaction must be verified as to amount, date, account coding, and descriptions.
- The cash must be safeguarded while in the physical possession of the company.
- There must be appropriate personnel responsible for overseeing cash control processes.
- Cash register tape totals should be reconciled to the amount of cash in drawer.
- An independent listing of cash receipts should be prepared before the receipts are submitted to the cashier or accounts receivable bookkeeper.

- An independent person should verify the listing against the deposit slips.
- Authenticated deposit slips should be retained and reconciled to the corresponding amounts in the cash receipts records.
- The bank deposit should be made by someone other than the cashier or the accounts receivable bookkeeper.
- A person independent of the cash receipts and accounts receivable functions should compare entries to the cash receipts journal with:
  - ○ Authenticated bank deposit slips.
  - ○ Deposit per the bank statement.
- Areas where physical handling of cash takes place should be reasonably safeguarded.

Analytical Review

Analyzing the relationship among sales, cost of sales, and returns and allowances can detect inappropriate refunds and discounts.

- If a large cash fraud is suspected, a thorough review of these accounts may enlighten the examiner as to the magnitude of the suspected fraud.
- An analysis of refunds and returns and allowances with the actual flow of inventory may reveal some fraud schemes. The refund should cause an entry to inventory, even if it is damaged inventory. Likewise, a return will cause a corresponding entry to an inventory account.
- There should be a linear relationship between sales and returns and allowances over a relevant range. Any change in this relationship may point to a fraud scheme unless there is another valid explanation, such as a change in the manufacturing process, change in product line, or change in price.

Register Detection

- As cash is received, whether at a register or through the mail, it is important to ensure that the employees responsible for receiving and recording the incoming payments are informed of their responsibility and properly supervised.
- Access to the register must be closely monitored, and access codes must be kept secure.
- An employee other than the register worker should be responsible for preparing register count sheets and agreeing them to register totals.
- Popular concealment methods must be watched for. These methods, discussed earlier, include checks for cash, reversing transactions, register tape destruction or alteration, and sales cash counts.
- Complete register documentation and cash must be delivered to the appropriate personnel in a timely manner.

- Cash thefts sometimes are revealed by customers who have paid money on an account and have not received credit or, in some cases, when they notice that the credit they have been given does not agree with the payment they have made.

Cash Account Analysis

Cash larceny can be detected by reviewing and analyzing all journal entries made to the cash accounts. This review and analysis should be performed on a regular basis. If employees are unable to conceal the fraud by altering the source documents, such as the cash register tape, they may resort to making a journal entry directly to cash. In general (and except in financial institutions), there are very few instances in everyday business activity where an independent journal entry is necessary for cash. One of these exceptions is the recording of the bank service charge. However, this is an easy journal entry to trace to its source documentation, namely the bank statement. Therefore, all other entries directly to cash are suspect and should be traced to their source documentation or explanation. Suspect entries generally will credit the cash account and correspondingly debit various other accounts, such as a sales contra account or bad debt expenses.

PREVENTION

Segregation of Duties

The primary way to prevent cash larceny is to segregate duties. Whenever one individual has control over the entire accounting transaction (e.g., authorization, recording, and custody), the opportunity is present for cash fraud. Ideally, each of these duties and responsibilities should be segregated:

- Cash receipts
- Cash counts
- Bank deposits
- Deposit receipt reconciliation
- Bank reconciliations
- Posting of deposits
- Cash disbursements

If any one person has the authority to collect the cash, deposit the receipts, record that collection, and disburse company funds, the risk is high that fraud can occur.

Assignment Rotation and Mandatory Vacations

Many internal fraud schemes are continuous in nature and require ongoing efforts by the employee to conceal defalcations. Mandatory job rotation is an excellent method of detecting cash fraud. By establishing a mandatory job or assignment rotation, the concealment element is interrupted. If mandatory vacations are in the company's policies, it is important that, during the employee's absence, another individual performs the normal workload of that employee. The purpose of mandatory vacations is lost if the work is allowed to remain undone during the employee's time off.

Surprise Cash Counts and Procedure Supervision

Surprise cash counts and supervisory observations are a useful fraud prevention method if properly used. It is important that employees know that cash will be counted on a sporadic and unscheduled basis. These surprise counts must be made at all steps of the process from receiving the check to deposit.

Physical Security of Cash

- Ensure proper segregation of duties of key personnel.
- Review the check and cash composition of the daily bank deposit during un-announced cash counts and during substantive audit tests of cash receipts.
- Review the entity's records of the numerical series of printed prenumbered receipts, and verify that these receipts are used sequentially (including voided documents).
- Review the timeliness of deposits from locations to the central treasurer function.
- Observe cash-receipting operations of locations.
- Prepare and review a schedule of all cash-receipting functions from a review of revenue reports, from cash receipt forms at the central treasurer function, and from discussion with knowledgeable employees.
- Prepare and analyze an inventory of all imprest and change funds by purpose, amount, custodian, date, and location.
- Audit all revenue sources on a cycle.
- Periodically use comparative analytical reviews to determine which functions have unfavorable trends.
- Determine reason(s) why revenue has changed from previous reporting periods.
- Confirm responses obtained from managers by using alternative records or through substantive audit tests.
- Adhere to a communicated policy of unannounced cash counts.

CHAPTER 5

Check Tampering

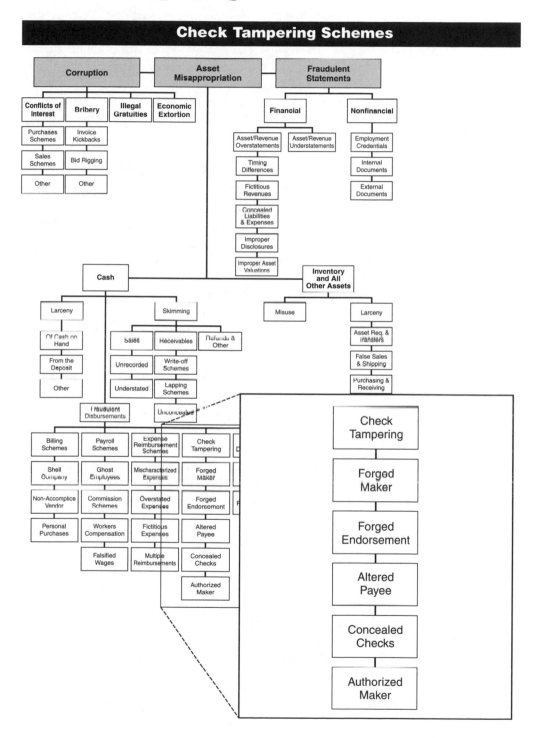

Case Study: A Wolf in Sheep's Clothing

Melissa Robinson* was a devoted wife and the mother of two adorable children. She was very active at her children's school and was known as a charitable person, giving both her time and money to various organizations throughout the community.

She spent a good portion of her time working for a worldwide charitable organization chapter in Nashville as the executive secretary. In fact, her fellow employees and club members perceived Robinson's donation of time and hard work as nothing less than a godsend. "Even if somebody had told [the board of directors] that this lady was stealing," recalls certified fraud examiner and CPA David Mensel, also a member of the organization, "they would have said 'Impossible, she'd never do it.'"

However, all these accolades could not obscure one cold fact: Melissa Robinson was a thief. As executive secretary, she was one of two people in the organization allowed to sign checks on its bank accounts. As a result, the club was bilked out of more than $60,000 over five years, until club members put an end to Robinson's scam.

The Nashville chapter of the organization was very much like other charitable entities—they engaged in fund-raising activities, such as selling peanuts or candy bars on street corners around the holiday seasons. Although a percentage came in check form, most of the fund-raising revenue was naturally cash.

"There was no oversight in those currency collections," says Mensel. "If I had gone out on a collecting route, I'd come back with a bag of money and drop it on the secretary's desk and be gone."

Mensel suspects that Robinson stole far more than the $60,800 that the audit team ultimately established, because the amount of currency that flowed through her office was undocumented. "It is just a supposition, given her behavior with the checking accounts," Mensel explains. "As well, we saw a basic decline in collections from some activities that the organization had been involved in for many years."

Robinson's fraudulent activities were made possible by the relaxed operations of the Nashville chapter's board of directors. The organization's charter mandated that an independent audit be performed annually. However, during Robinson's tenure as executive secretary, not one yearly audit was completed. Mensel describes the board of directors during that tenure as "lackadaisical."

Robinson arrived at the executive secretary's desk through hard work; she was one of the most dedicated employees the company had, giving as much time as she could to help out. Once she earned the executive secretary position, Robinson apparently began pilfering from the organization's three bank accounts a little at a time. Although the accounts required two signatures per check, Robinson was able to write checks to herself and others by signing her own name and forging the second signature. Mensel says she would usually write a check to herself or to cash and record the transaction in the organization's books as a check to a legitimate source. If anyone glanced at the books, they would see plenty of hotels and office supply stores, names that were expected to show up in the ledger.

---

*Several names and details have been changed to preserve anonymity.

"The club meetings were regularly held in a hotel in town or at one of these executive meeting clubs," Mensel recalls, "and those bills would run from $2,000 to $4,000 a month. The executive secretary would . . . post in the checkbook that she had paid the hotel, but the actual check would be made out to someone else."

Mensel also remembers that Robinson repeatedly refused to convert her manual checking system into the computerized system the organization wanted her to use. "Now we know why," says Mensel.

Mensel and another associate were very involved in a fund-raising operation when Robinson began her reign as executive secretary. Mensel observed that whenever he asked for any financial information from Robinson, she would stonewall him or make excuses. Mensel became suspicious and took the matter up with the board of directors. But when he told the board that he thought it was very peculiar that he couldn't get much financial data from Robinson, the board quite definitely sided with the executive secretary.

"The officers of the board essentially jumped down my throat, told me I was wrong and that I was being unreasonable," Mensel says. "And since I had no substantiation, just a bad feeling . . . I let it pass."

Mensel felt that the current treasurer was personally offended by his inquiry, as though he were suggesting that the treasurer was not doing his job properly. The treasurer acted defensively and did not check into Robinson's dealings.

As a result, the organization, which Mensel describes as previously "financially very sound," began to feel some financial strain. There simply wasn't as much money to run the organization as in the past, and it was at this point Robinson made what was perhaps her most ingenious maneuver. She convinced the board of directors that because the organization was experiencing some economic troubles, they ought to close the office space rented out for the executive secretary. This office was considered the financial center of the organization. Supposedly out of the goodness of her heart, Robinson told the board members that she would be happy to relinquish her precious space and run the financial matters of the club from her home. The board members agreed.

This allowed Robinson to carry out her embezzlement in small doses— Mensel recalls that Robinson wrote several checks for only $200 to $300. All this time, the board did nothing to impede Robinson's progress, even when she would not divulge financial information on request. When she came to club meetings, board members would sometimes ask her for information about the finances or ask to look at her books. Robinson would apologize and explain that she had forgotten them.

However, during the last year of the embezzlement, a new group of officers was elected, including a new treasurer. The first thing the treasurer did was ask Robinson for the books. Robinson repeatedly denied his requests, until the new chapter president went to Robinson's house and demanded them. "[The president] stood on her doorstep until she gave the books to him. He said he wouldn't leave until she gave them to him," Mensel recalls. "Once [the board] got their hands on the books . . . they could see that something was definitely very wrong."

In comparing the books with many of the returned checks, the organization could immediately see that not only had some checks been altered or forged but also many of the checks were simply missing. At that point, the board of directors assigned Mensel and two other club members, one a CPA, to investigate Robinson's alleged wrongdoings. As Mensel and the other audit committee members looked at the checks, they realized that Robinson hardly attempted to cover up her scams at all.

"She did physically erase some checks and sometimes even used correction fluid to rewrite the name of the payee that was in the checkbook after the check had cleared," Mensel says with a laugh. "But of course, on the back of the check was her name, as the depositor of the check."

The peculiar thing, in Mensel's mind, was the varying nature of Robinson's check writing. Although Mensel says several of the checks were written to casinos such as the Trump Taj Mahal and weekend getaway spots like the Mountain View Chalet, many more of the checks were written to other charities and to the school Robinson's children attended. She apparently didn't use the embezzled money to improve her lifestyle substantially, which Mensel describes as "a very standard middle-class life here in Nashville. She and her husband were not wealthy people by any means."

Robinson was immediately excused from her executive secretary position. She was indicted by a grand jury and was tried and found guilty. In addition, she was ordered to pay restitution to the club and its insurance company.

Robinson appeared to be one of the most dedicated volunteers in a charitable organization, giving of her time and efforts. The workers around her praised her generosity and work ethic, yet all the while she was stealing from them. If there is a lesson to be learned here, it is that audit functions are in place for a reason and should never be overlooked. Unfortunately, this charitable organization was reminded of this lesson the hard way.

OVERVIEW

Check tampering is unique among the disbursement frauds because it is the one group of schemes in which the perpetrator physically prepares the fraudulent check. In most fraudulent disbursement schemes, culprits generate a payment to themselves by submitting some false document to the victim company, such as an invoice or a time card. The false document represents a claim for payment and causes the victim company to issue a check that the perpetrators then convert. These frauds essentially amount to trickery; perpetrators fool the company into handing over its money.

Check tampering schemes are fundamentally different. As in the case of Melissa Robinson, fraudsters take physical control of checks and make them payable to themselves through one of several methods. Check tampering frauds depend on factors such as access to the company checkbook, access to bank statements, and the ability to forge signatures or alter other information on the face of the check. Five methods are used to commit check tampering frauds:

1. Forged maker schemes
2. Forged endorsements
3. Altered payees
4. Concealed check schemes
5. Authorized maker schemes

Because the vast majority of business payments currently still are made by check, the bulk of this chapter focuses on how traditional check-based payments can be manipulated by dishonest employees. However, businesses are increasingly using electronic forms of payment—such as wire transfers, Automated Clearing House (ACH) debits, and online bill-pay services—to pay vendors and other third parties. Consequently, the specific implications and considerations of these types of payments are discussed in a separate section at the end of this chapter.

CHECK TAMPERING DATA FROM ACFE *2009 GLOBAL FRAUD SURVEY*

Frequency and Cost

In Chapter 2, we saw that the vast majority of asset misappropriations target cash, as opposed to noncash assets. We also saw that cash misappropriations are subdivided into three categories in the fraud tree: *skimming, cash larceny*, and *fraudulent disbursements*. Skimming and cash larceny have already been covered, so we turn our attention in the next four chapters to fraudulent disbursement schemes. There are five major categories of fraudulent disbursement in the fraud tree:

1. Check tampering
2. Register disbursement schemes
3. Billing schemes
4. Payroll schemes
5. Expense reimbursement schemes

Among fraudulent disbursement cases in the 2009 study, 27 percent involved check tampering. (The sum of these percentages exceeds 100 percent because some cases involved multiple fraud schemes that fell into more than one category. Various charts in this chapter may reflect percentages that total in excess of 100 percent for similar reasons.) This ranked check tampering as the third most common form of fraudulent disbursement behind billing and expense reimbursement schemes. (See Exhibit 5.1.)

The median loss due to check tampering schemes in the 2009 survey was $131,000, making it the most expensive of the fraudulent disbursement schemes. (See Exhibit 5.2.)

In our 2009 study, 274 cases involved check tampering, and in 157 of those, the respondent provided data on the loss caused by the scheme. As Exhibit 5.3 shows, more check tampering schemes resulted in losses between $10,000 and $999,999, inclusive, than the general body of occupational fraud cases. Almost a quarter of the check tampering cases in our study caused at least $500,000 in losses.

Exhibit 5.1 *2009 Global Fraud Survey*: **Frequency of Fraudulent Disbursements**

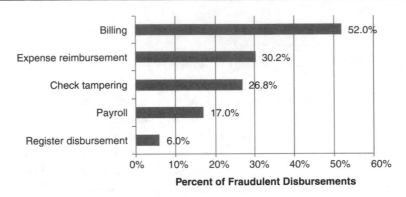

Percent of Fraudulent Disbursements

Exhibit 5.2 *2009 Global Fraud Survey*: **Median Loss of Fraudulent Disbursements**

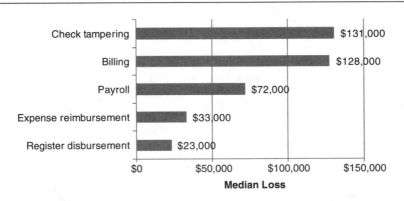

Median Loss

Exhibit 5.3 *2009 Global Fraud Survey*: **Dollar Loss Distribution for Check Tampering Schemes**

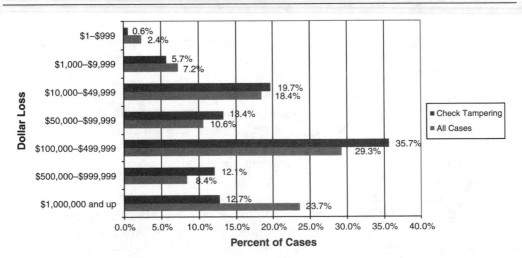

Percent of Cases

Exhibit 5.4 *2009 Global Fraud Survey*: Detection of Check Tampering Schemes

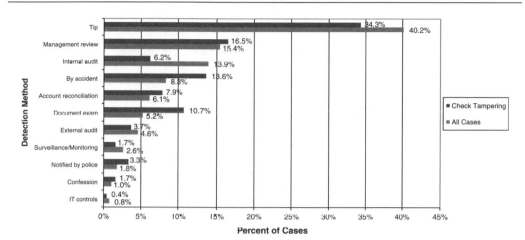

Detection of Check Tampering Schemes

We received 242 responses in which the method of initial detection for check tampering cases was identified. The most common means of detection was a tip, which occurred in 34 percent of the cases. However, this rate was notably lower for check tampering schemes than for the overall distribution of frauds studied, as was the rate of check tampering schemes uncovered by internal audit. By contrast, the numbers for detection by accident and through document examination were significantly higher for check tampering schemes than for the general body of occupational frauds. (See Exhibit 5.4.)

Perpetrators of Check Tampering Schemes

Nearly 42 percent of the check tampering schemes we reviewed were committed by employee-level fraudsters, while 36 percent were committed by managers and 22 percent involved owner/executives. Interestingly, the median loss for check tampering cases committed by managers was the highest of the three categories, at $201,000. This contrasts sharply with the general trend we observed of frauds committed by owner/executives causing the greatest damage. (See Exhibits 5.5 and 5.6.)

Victims of Check Tampering Schemes

Among all occupational frauds, 31 percent of the victim organizations had fewer than 100 employees, but a significantly larger percentage of the check tampering victims (59 percent) fell into this category. There is a good deal of anecdotal evidence suggesting that small businesses tend to have more lax internal controls than larger organizations; and perhaps because of a lack of personnel, it is noted frequently that small businesses fail to separate accounting functions adequately.

Exhibit 5.5 *2009 Global Fraud Survey*: **Perpetrators of Check Tampering Schemes**

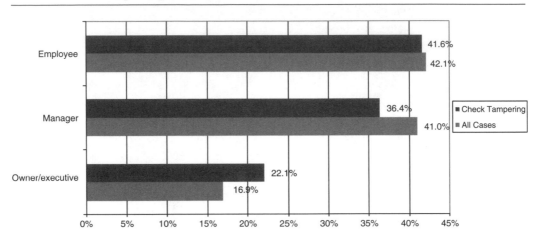

Thus, it is not uncommon to see a small business case in which a single person writes checks, posts disbursements, and reconciles bank accounts. As we explain in this chapter, the nature of check tampering makes it especially important (more so than in other fraudulent disbursement schemes) for the perpetrator to be able to post fraudulent checks and to have access to the bank statement in order to conceal defalcations. This may explain why so many check tampering schemes in our study attacked small businesses. (See Exhibit 5.7.)

The median losses from the check tampering schemes studied were directly related to the size of the victim organizations. While the greatest percentage of check tampering frauds was perpetrated at small companies, these schemes caused

Exhibit 5.6 *2009 Global Fraud Survey*: **Median Loss by Perpetrator of Check Tampering Schemes**

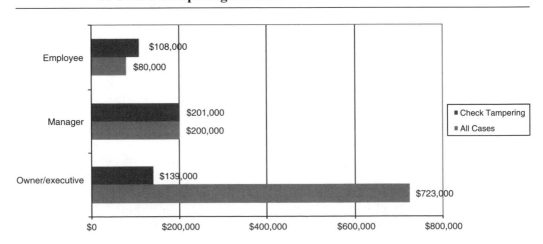

Exhibit 5.7 *2009 Global Fraud Survey*: Size of Victim in Check
Tampering Schemes

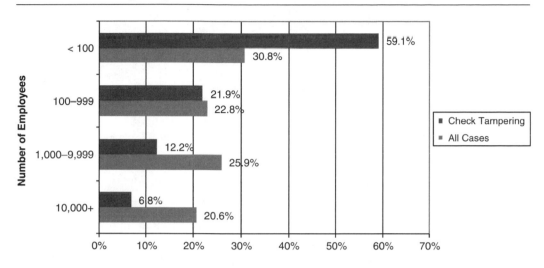

the lowest median loss, at $120,000. In contrast, check tampering schemes at the largest organizations caused a median loss of $200,000, as shown in Exhibit 5.8.

FORGED MAKER SCHEMES

The legal definition of forgery includes not only the signing of another person's name to a document (such as a check) with a fraudulent intent but also the fraudulent alteration of a genuine instrument.[1] This definition is so broad that it would encompass all check tampering schemes, so we have narrowed the term to fit our needs. Because we are interested in distinguishing the various methods used by individuals to tamper with

Exhibit 5.8 *2009 Global Fraud Survey*: Median Loss by Size of Victim
in Check Tampering Schemes

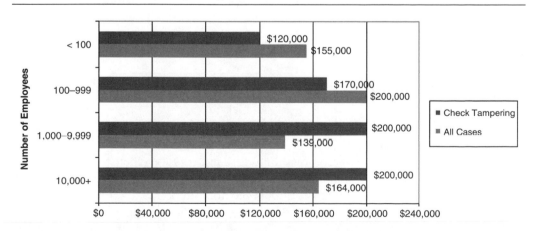

Exhibit 5.9   Check Graphic

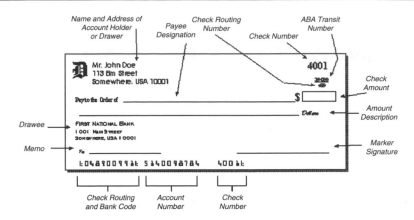

checks, we constrain the concept of "forgeries" to those cases in which an individual signs another person's name on a check. (See Exhibit 5.9.)

The person who signs a check is known as the "maker" of the check. A forged maker scheme, then, may be defined as a check tampering scheme in which an employee misappropriates a check and fraudulently affixes the signature of an authorized maker thereon. (See Exhibit 5.10.) Frauds that involve other types of check tampering, such as the alteration of the payee or the changing of the dollar amount, are classified separately.

As you might expect, forged check schemes usually are committed by employees who lack signatory authority on company accounts. Melissa Robinson's case is something of an exception because, although she did have signatory authority, her organization's checks required two signatures. Robinson therefore had to forge another person's signature.

In order to forge a check, employees must have access to a blank check, must be able to produce a convincing forgery of an authorized signature, and must be able to conceal the crime. If fraudsters cannot hide the crime from the employer, the scheme is sure to be short-lived. Concealment is a universal problem in check tampering schemes; the methods used are basically the same whether one is dealing with a forged maker scheme, an intercepted check scheme, a concealed check scheme, or an authorized maker scheme. Therefore, concealment issues are discussed as a group at the end of the chapter.

Obtaining the Check

Employees with Access to Company Checks

No one can forge a company check without first possessing a company check. The first hurdle that fraudsters must overcome in committing a forgery scheme is to figure out how to get their hands on a blank check. The results of our study indicate that most forgery schemes are committed by accounts payable clerks, office managers, bookkeepers, or other employees whose duties typically include the preparation of company

Exhibit 5.10   Forged Maker Schemes

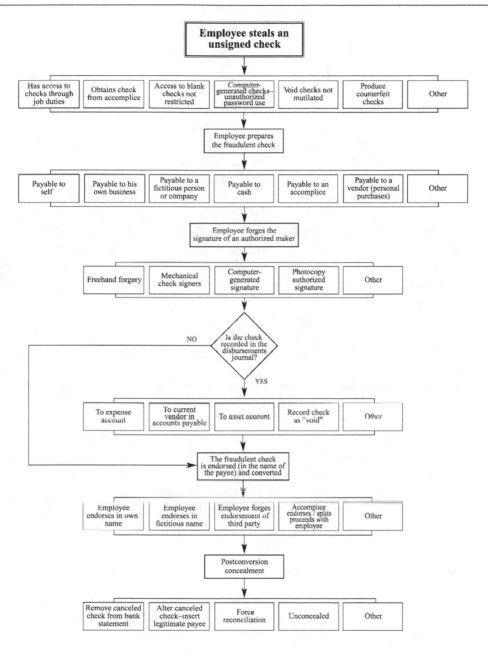

checks. Like Melissa Robinson, these are people who have access to the company checkbook on a regular basis and therefore are in the best position to steal blank checks. If an employee spends his workday preparing checks on behalf of his company, and if that employee has some personal financial difficulty, it takes only a small leap in logic (and a big leap in ethics) to see that his financial troubles can be solved by writing fraudulent checks for his own benefit. Time and again we see that employees tailor their fraud to the circumstances of their jobs. It stands to reason that those who work around the checkbook would be prone to committing forgery schemes.

Employees Lacking Access to Company Checks

If perpetrators do not have access to the company checkbook through their work duties, they will have to find other means of misappropriating a check. The method by which a person steals a check depends largely on how the checkbook is handled within a particular company. In some circumstances, the checkbook is poorly guarded, left in unattended areas where anyone can get to it. In other companies, the check stock may be kept in a restricted area, but the perpetrator may have obtained a key or combination to this area or may know where an employee with access to the checks keeps her own copy of the key or combination. An accomplice may provide blank checks for the fraudster in return for a portion of the stolen funds. Perhaps a secretary sees a blank check left on a manager's desk or a custodian comes across the check stock in an unlocked desk drawer.

In some companies, checks are computer-generated. In such cases, an employee who knows the password that allows checks to be prepared and issued usually can obtain as many unsigned checks as desired. There are an unlimited number of ways to steal a check, each dependent on the way in which a particular company guards its blank checks.

A fraudster also may be able to obtain a blank check when the company fails to properly dispose of unused checks. In one case, for example, a company used voided checks to line up the printer that ran payroll checks. These voided checks were not mutilated. A payroll clerk collected the voided checks after the printer was aligned and used them to issue herself extra disbursements through the payroll account.

An unusual method of obtaining blank checks was used by an employee in another case. This person had an accomplice who worked for a check-printing company and who printed blank checks with the account number of the perpetrator's company. The perpetrator then wrote over $100,000 worth of forgeries on these counterfeit checks. This case illustrates the creativity and intricacy of some schemes. Considering the amount of illegal gain that the fraudster realized, it should not be surprising that an employee would go to such trouble to obtain a blank check.

To Whom Is the Check Made Payable?

To the Perpetrator

Once a blank check has been obtained, fraudsters must decide to whom it should be made payable. They can write the check to anyone, although in most instances forged checks are payable to the perpetrators themselves so that they are easier to convert. A check made payable to a third person, or to a fictitious person or business, may be difficult to convert without false identification. The tendency to make forged checks payable to oneself seems to be a result of fraudsters' laziness rather than a decision integral to the successful operation of their schemes; checks payable to an employee are clearly more likely to be recognized as fraudulent than checks made out to other persons or entities.

If fraudsters own their own business or have established a shell company, they usually will write fraudulent checks to these entities rather than to themselves. When the payee on a forged check is a vendor rather than an employee of the victim company, the checks are not as obviously fraudulent on their faces. At the same time, these checks are easy to convert because the fraudsters own the entities to which the checks are payable.

To an Accomplice

Fraudsters working with an accomplice can make the forged check payable to that person; the accomplice then cashes the check and splits the money with the employee-fraudster. Because the check is payable to the accomplice in his true identity, it is easily converted. An additional benefit to using an accomplice is that a canceled check payable to a third-party accomplice is not as likely to raise suspicion as a canceled check to an employee. The obvious drawback to using an accomplice in a scheme is that the employee-fraudster usually has to share the proceeds of the scheme.

In some circumstances, however, the accomplice may be unaware that she is involved in a fraud. For example, in one case, a bookkeeper wrote several fraudulent checks on company accounts, then convinced a friend to allow her to deposit the checks in the friend's account. The fraudster claimed the money was revenue from a side business she owned and the subterfuge was necessary to prevent creditors from seizing the funds. After the checks were deposited, the friend withdrew the money and gave it to the fraudster.

To "Cash"

Fraudsters also may write checks payable to "cash" in order to avoid listing themselves as the payee. Checks made payable to cash, however, still must be endorsed. Fraudsters will have to sign their own name or forge the name of another in order to convert the check. In addition, checks payable to "cash" usually are viewed more skeptically than checks payable to persons or businesses. Some check-cashing institutions may refuse to cash checks made payable to "cash."

To Vendors

Employees who forge company checks may do so not to obtain currency but to purchase goods or services for their own benefit. When this is the case, forged checks are made payable to third-party vendors who are uninvolved in the fraud. For instance, several of Melissa Robinson's checks were written to casinos and hotels, apparently for personal vacations.

Forging the Signature

After employees have obtained and prepared a blank check, they must forge an authorized signature in order to convert the check. The most obvious method, and the one that comes to mind when we think of the word "forgery," is simply to take pen in hand and sign the name of an authorized maker.

Freehand Forgery

The difficulty fraudsters encounter when physically signing the authorized maker's name is in creating a reasonable approximation of the true signature. If the forgery appears authentic, the perpetrator probably will have no problem cashing the check. In truth, the forged signature may not have to be particularly accurate. Many fraudsters cash forged checks at liquor stores, grocery stores, or other institutions that are known to be less than diligent in verifying the accuracy of signatures and identification. A poorly forged signature can be a clear red flag. The maker's signature on canceled checks should be reviewed for forgeries during the reconciliation process.

Photocopied Forgeries

To guarantee an accurate forgery, some employees make photocopies of legitimate signatures and affix them to company checks. The fraudsters are thus assured that the signature appears authentic. This method was used by a bookkeeper in one case to steal over $100,000 from her employer. Using her boss's business correspondence and the company Xerox machine, she made transparencies of his signature. She placed these transparencies in the copy machine so that when she ran checks through the machine, the boss's signature was copied onto the maker line of the check. The bookkeeper now had a signed check in hand. She made the fraudulent checks payable to herself but falsified the check register so that the checks appeared to have been written to legitimate payees.

Automatic Check-Signing Mechanisms

Companies that issue a large number of checks sometimes utilize automatic check-signing mechanisms in lieu of signing each check by hand. Automated signatures are produced with manual instruments, such as signature stamps, or they are printed by computer. Obviously, a fraudster who gains access to an automatic check-signing mechanism will have no trouble forging the signatures of authorized makers. Even the most rudimentary control procedures should severely limit access to these mechanisms. Nevertheless, several of the forged maker schemes we reviewed were accomplished through use of a signature stamp. In one instance, a fiscal officer maintained a set of manual checks that were unknown to other persons in the company. The company used an automated check signer, and the custodian of the signer let the officer have uncontrolled access to it. Using the manual checks and the company's check signer, the fiscal officer was able to write over $90,000 worth of fraudulent checks to himself over a period of approximately four years.

The same principle applies to computerized signatures. Access to the password or program that prints signed checks should be restricted, specifically excluding those who prepare checks and those who reconcile the bank statement. The fraudster in one example was in charge of preparing checks. She managed to obtain the issuance password from her boss, then used this password to issue checks to a company she owned on the side. Using this method, she was able to bilk her employer out of approximately $100,000.

The beauty of automated check signers, from the fraudster's perspective, is that they produce perfect "forgeries." Nothing about the physical appearance of the check will indicate that it is fraudulent. Of course, forged checks are written for illegitimate purposes, so they may be detectable when the bank statement is reconciled or when accounts are reviewed. The ways in which fraudsters avoid detection through these measures are discussed later in this chapter.

Miscoding Fraudulent Checks

Miscoding a check is actually a form of concealment, a means of hiding the fraudulent nature of the check. We discuss the ways fraudsters code their forged checks in the concealment section of this chapter. It should be noted here, however, that miscoding typically is used as a concealment method only by those employees who have access to the cash disbursements journal. If a forged maker scheme is undertaken by employees without access to the cash disbursements journal, they usually make no entry whatsoever in the disbursements journal.

Converting the Check

In order to convert the forged check, perpetrators must endorse it. The endorsement typically is made in the name of the payee on the check. Since identification generally is required when one seeks to convert a check, fraudsters usually need fake identification if they forge checks to real or fictitious third persons. As discussed earlier, checks payable to "cash" require the endorsement of the person converting them. Without fake identification, fraudsters likely will have to endorse these checks in their own name. An employee's endorsement on a canceled check can be an obvious red flag.

INTERCEPTED CHECKS

Instead of forging a maker's signature on a check, some fraudsters wait until legitimate checks are prepared and signed, then steal these checks before they are delivered to their proper payees. These schemes are classified as intercepted check schemes. When fraudsters have intercepted a signed check, they can do one of two things in order to cash it: They can endorse the check by forging the true payee's signature, or they can alter the payee designation of the check. These schemes are typically more complicated than forgery schemes and create more concealment problems for fraudsters.

FORGED ENDORSEMENT SCHEMES

Forged endorsement frauds are those check tampering schemes in which an employee intercepts a company check intended for a third party and converts the check by signing the third party's name on the endorsement line of the check. (See Exhibit 5.11.) In

Exhibit 5.11   Forged Endorsement Schemes

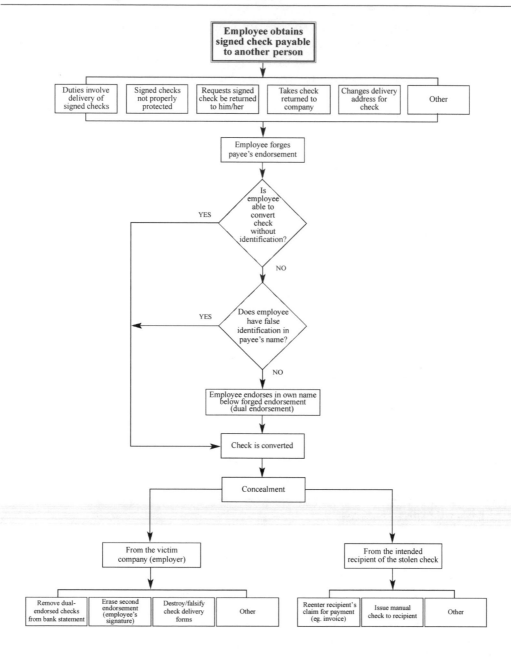

some instances, the fraudster also signs his own name as a second endorser. The term "forged endorsement schemes" would seem to imply that these frauds should be categorized along with the forged maker schemes discussed earlier. It is true that both kinds of fraud involve the false signing of another person's name on a check, but there are certain distinctions that cause forged endorsement schemes to be categorized separately rather than with the other forgeries.

In classifying fraud types, we look to the heart of the scheme. What is the crucial point in the commission of the crime? In a forged maker scheme, the perpetrator is normally working with a blank check. The trick to this kind of scheme is in gaining access to blank checks and producing a signature that appears authentic.

In a forged endorsement scheme, the perpetrator is tampering with a check that has already been written, so the issues involved in the fraud are different. The key to these schemes is obtaining the checks after they are signed but before they are delivered properly. If this is accomplished, the actual forging of the endorsement is somewhat secondary. For this reason, forged endorsements are classified as intercepted check schemes.

A fraudster's main dilemma in a forged endorsement case (and in all intercepted check cases, for that matter) is gaining access to a check after it has been written and signed. The fraudster must either steal the check between the point where it is signed and the point where it is delivered, or he must reroute the check, causing it to be mailed to a location where he can retrieve it. The manner used to steal a check depends largely on the way the company handles outgoing disbursements—anyone who is allowed to handle signed checks may be in a good position to intercept them.

Intercepting Checks before Delivery

Employees Involved in Delivery of Checks

Obviously, employees in the best position to intercept signed checks are those whose duties include the handling and delivery of signed checks. The most obvious example is a mailroom employee who opens outgoing mail containing signed checks and steals the checks. Other personnel who have access to outgoing checks might include accounts payable employees, payroll clerks, secretaries, and so on.

Poor Control of Signed Checks

Unfortunately, fraudsters often are able to intercept signed checks because of poor internal controls. In one instance, signed checks were left overnight on the desks of some employees because processing on the checks was not complete. A janitor on the overnight cleaning crew found these checks and took them, forged the endorsements of the payees, and cashed them at a liquor store. Another example of poor observance of internal controls occurred when a high-level manager with authority to disburse employee benefits instructed accounts payable personnel to return signed benefits checks to him instead of immediately delivering them to their intended recipients. These instructions were not questioned, despite the fact that they presented a clear violation of the separation-of-duties concept, due to the manager's level of authority within the company. The perpetrator simply took the checks that were returned to him and deposited them into his personal bank account, forging the endorsements of the intended payees.

This case represents what seems to be the most common breakdown of controls in forged endorsement frauds. We have seen repeated occurrences of signed checks being returned to the employee who prepared them. This situation typically occurs when a supervisor signs a check and hands it back to a clerk or secretary who presented it to the supervisor; it is done either through negligence or because the employee is highly trusted and thought to be above theft. Adequate internal controls should prevent the person who prepares company disbursements from having access to signed checks. This separation of duties is elemental; its purpose is to break the disbursement chain so that no one person controls the entire payment process.

Theft of Returned Checks

Another way to obtain signed checks is to steal checks that have been mailed but have been returned to the victim company for some reason, such as an incorrect address. Employees with access to incoming mail may be able to intercept these returned checks from the mail and convert them by forging the endorsement of the intended payee. In one example, a manager took and converted approximately $130,000 worth of checks that were returned due to noncurrent addresses. (He also stole outgoing checks, cashed them, and then declared them lost.) The fraudster was well known at his bank and was able to convert the checks by claiming that he was doing it as a favor to the real payees, who were "too busy to come to the bank." The fraudster was able to continue with his scheme because the nature of his company's business was such that the recipients of the misdelivered checks often were not aware that the victim company owed them money. Therefore, they did not complain when their checks failed to arrive. In addition, the perpetrator had complete control over the bank reconciliation, so he could issue new checks to those payees who did complain and then "force" the reconciliation, making it appear that the bank balance and book balance matched when in fact they did not. Stealing returned checks is obviously not as common as other methods for intercepting checks, and it is more difficult for a fraudster to plan and carry out on a long-term basis. But it is also very difficult to detect and can lead to large-scale fraud, as the previous case illustrates.

Rerouting the Delivery of Checks

The other way an employee can go about misappropriating a signed check is to alter the address to which the check is to be mailed. The check either is delivered to a place where the fraudster can retrieve it or is purposely misaddressed so that the fraudster can steal it when it is returned. As we have said before, proper separation of duties should preclude anyone who prepares disbursements from being involved in their delivery. Nevertheless, this control often is overlooked, allowing the person who prepares a check to address it and mail it as well.

In some instances in which proper controls are in place, fraudsters still are able to cause the misdelivery of checks. In one instance, the fraudster was a clerk in the customer service department of a mortgage company, where her duties included changing the mailing addresses of property owners. She was assigned a password that gave her access to make address changes. The clerk was transferred to a new department where one of her duties was the issuance of checks to property owners. Unfortunately, her supervisor forgot to cancel her old password. When the clerk realized this over-sight, she requested checks for certain property owners, then signed onto the system with her old password and changed the addresses of the property owners. The checks were then sent to her. The next day the employee used her old password to reenter the system and replace the proper address so that there would be no record of where the check had been sent. This fraudster's scheme resulted in a loss of over $250,000 to the victim company.

Converting the Stolen Check

Once the check has been intercepted, perpetrators can cash it by forging the payee's signature, hence the term "forged endorsement scheme." Depending on where they try to cash the check, perpetrators may or may not need fake identification at this stage. As we alluded to earlier, many fraudsters cash their stolen checks at places where they are not required to show identification.

If fraudsters are required to show identification in order to cash stolen checks, and if they do not have a fake ID in the payee's name, they may use a dual endorsement to cash or deposit the check. In other words, fraudsters forge the payee's signature as if the payee had transferred the check to them, then endorse the check in their own name and convert it. When the bank statement is reconciled, double endorsements on checks always should raise suspicions, particularly when the second signer is an employee of the company.

ALTERED PAYEE SCHEMES

The second type of intercepted check scheme is the altered payee scheme. This is a type of check tampering fraud in which an employee intercepts a company check in-tended for a third party and alters the payee designation so that the check can be con-verted by the employee or an accomplice. (See Exhibit 5.12.) The fraudster inserts her own name, the name of a fictitious entity, or some other name on the payee line of the check. Altering the payee designation eliminates many of the problems associated with converting the check that would be encountered in a forged endorsement fraud. The alteration essentially makes the check payable to the fraudster (or an accomplice), so there is no need to forge an endorsement and no need to obtain false identification. The fraudster or an accomplice can endorse the check in her own name and convert it.

Of course, if canceled checks are reviewed during reconciliation of the bank state-ment, a check made payable to an employee is likely to cause suspicion, especially if the alteration to the payee designation is obvious. This is the main obstacle that must be overcome by fraudsters in altered payee schemes.

Altering Checks Prepared by Others: Inserting a New Payee

The method used to alter the payee designation on a check depends largely on how that check is prepared and intercepted. (Incidentally, the amount of the check may be

133

Exhibit 5.12   Altered Payee Schemes

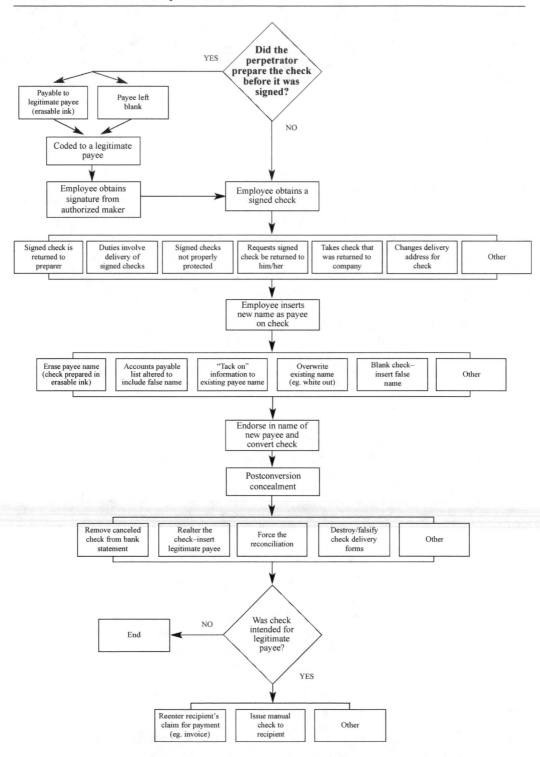

altered at the same time and by the same method as the payee designation.) Checks prepared by others can be intercepted by any of the methods discussed in the "Forged Endorsement Schemes" section. After intercepting a check that has been prepared by someone else, fraudsters can alter it in one of two methods. One way is to insert the false payee's name in place of the true payee's. This usually is done by rather unsophisticated means. The true name might be scratched out with a pen or gone over with correction fluid, and another name is entered on the payee designation. These kinds of alterations usually are simple to detect.

A more intricate method occurs when the perpetrator of the fraud enters the accounts payable system and changes the names of payees, as occurred in the next example. An accounts payable employee in this case was so trusted that her manager allowed her to use his computer password in his absence. The password permitted access to the accounts payable address file. This employee waited until the manager was absent, then selected a legitimate vendor with whom her company did a great deal of business. She held up the vendor's invoices for the day and after work used the manager's logon to change the vendor name and address to that of a fictitious company. The new name and address were run through the accounts payable cycle with an old invoice number, causing a fraudulent check to be issued. The victim company had an automated duplicate invoice test, but the fraudster circumvented it substituting "1" for "I" and "0" (zero) for capital "O." The next day the employee replaced the true vendor's name and address and mutilated the check register so that the check payable to the fictitious vendor was concealed. Approximately $300,000 in false checks were issued using this method.

Altering Checks Prepared by Others: "Tacking On"

The other method that fraudsters can use to alter checks prepared by others is "tacking on" additional letters or words to the end of the real payee designation. This rather unusual approach to check tampering occurred in one case in which an employee took checks payable to "ABC" company and altered them to read "A.B. Collins." She then deposited these checks in an account that had been established in the name of A.B. Collins. The simple inclusion of a filler line after the payee designation would have prevented the loss of over $60,000 in this case. In addition to altering the payee designation, the amount of the check can be altered by tacking on extra numbers if the person preparing the check is careless and leaves space for extra numbers in the "Amount" portion of the check.

Altering Checks Prepared by the Fraudster: Erasable Ink

When fraudsters prepare the checks that are to be altered, the schemes tend to be a bit more sophisticated. The reason for this is obvious: When perpetrators are able to prepare the checks themselves, they can prepare them with the thought of how the payee designation will be altered. But if perpetrators are preparing the checks themselves, why not make the checks payable to themselves or an accomplice to begin with? In order to get an authorized maker to sign the check, fraudsters must make it appear that the checks are made out to a legitimate payee. Only after a legitimate signature is obtained does the fraudster in an altered payee scheme set about tampering with the check.

One of the most common ways to prepare a check for alteration is to write or type the payee's name (and possibly the amount) in erasable ink. After the check is signed by an authorized maker, the perpetrator retrieves the check, erases the payee's name, and inserts his own. One example of this type of fraud occurred when a bookkeeper typed out small checks to a local supplier and had the owner of the company sign them. The bookkeeper then used her erasing typewriter to lift the payee designation and amount from the check. She entered her own name as the payee and raised the amount precipitously. For instance, the owner might sign a $10 check that later became a $10,000 check. These checks were entered in the disbursements journal as payments for aggregate inventory to the company's largest supplier, which received several large checks each month. The bookkeeper stole over $300,000 from her employer in this scheme. The same type of fraud can be undertaken using an erasable pen. In some cases, fraudsters even have obtained signatures on checks written in pencil!

We have already discussed how, with a proper separation of duties, a person who prepares a check should not be permitted to handle the check after it has been signed. Nevertheless, this is exactly what happens in most altered payee schemes. When fraudsters prepare checks with the intent of altering them later, they obviously have a plan for reobtaining the checks once they have been signed. Usually the fraudsters know that there is no effective separation of controls in place and know that the maker of the check will return it to them.

Altering Checks Prepared by the Fraudster: Blank Checks

The most egregious example of poor controls in the handling of signed checks is one in which perpetrators prepare a check, leave the payee designation blank, and submit it to an authorized maker who signs the check and returns it to the perpetrators. Obviously, it is quite easy for fraudsters to designate themselves or an accomplice as the payee when this line has been left blank. Common sense tells us not to give a signed, blank check to another person. Nevertheless, this happened in several cases in our studies, usually when the fraudster was a longtime, trusted employee. In one example, an employee gained the confidence of the owner of his company, whom he convinced to sign blank checks for office use while the owner was out of town. The employee then filled in his own name as the payee on a check, cashed it, and altered the check when it was returned along with the bank statement. The owner's blind trust in his employee cost him nearly $200,000.

Converting Altered Checks

As with all other types of fraudulent checks, conversion is accomplished by endorsing the checks in the name of the payee. Conversion of fraudulent checks has been discussed in previous sections and will not be reexamined here.

CONCEALED CHECK SCHEMES

Another scheme that requires a significant breakdown in controls and common sense is the concealed check scheme. These are check tampering frauds in which an employee prepares a fraudulent check and submits it, usually along with legitimate checks, to an authorized maker who signs it without a proper review. (See Exhibit 5.13.) Although not nearly as common as the other check tampering methods, it is worth mentioning for its simplicity, its uniqueness, and the ease with which it could be prevented.

The perpetrator of a concealed check scheme is almost always a person responsible for preparing checks. The steps involved in a concealed check scheme are similar to those in a forged maker scheme, except for the way in which the employee gets the fraudulent check signed. These schemes work in this way: The perpetrator prepares a check made out to herself, an accomplice, or a fictitious person. Instead of forging the signature of an authorized maker, the employee takes the check to the authorized maker, usually concealed in a stack of legitimate checks awaiting signatures. Typically the checks are delivered to the signer during a busy time of day when he is rushed and will be less likely to pay close attention to them. Generally, the checks are fanned out on the signer's desk so that the signature lines are exposed but the names of the payees are concealed. If a particular authorized maker is known to be inattentive, the checks are given to him.

The maker signs the checks quickly and without adequate review. Because he is busy or generally inattentive or both, he simply does not look at what he is signing. He does not demand to see supporting documentation for the checks and does nothing to verify their legitimacy. Once the checks have been signed, they are returned to the employee, who removes her check and converts it. This appears to be one of the methods used by Ernie Philips in the case study at the end of this chapter. Philips slipped several checks payable to himself into a stack of company checks, then took them to the operations manager, who was designated to sign checks when the business's owner was out of town. The operations manager apparently did not check the names of the payees and unknowingly signed several company checks to Philips.

A similar example of the concealed check method took place in a case where a bookkeeper took advantage of the owner of her company by inserting checks payable to herself into batches of checks given to the owner for signature. The owner simply never looked at whom he was paying when he signed the checks.

The perpetrator of a concealed check scheme banks on the inattentiveness of the check signer. If the signer were to review the checks he was signing, he certainly would discover the fraud. In these cases the fraudster could make the fraudulent check payable to an accomplice, a fictitious person, or a fictitious business instead of payable to himself. This is more common and certainly a lot less dangerous for the employee (but not nearly as exciting).

AUTHORIZED MAKER SCHEMES

The final check tampering scheme, the authorized maker scheme, may be the most difficult to defend against. An authorized maker scheme is a type of check

Exhibit 5.13   Concealed Check Schemes

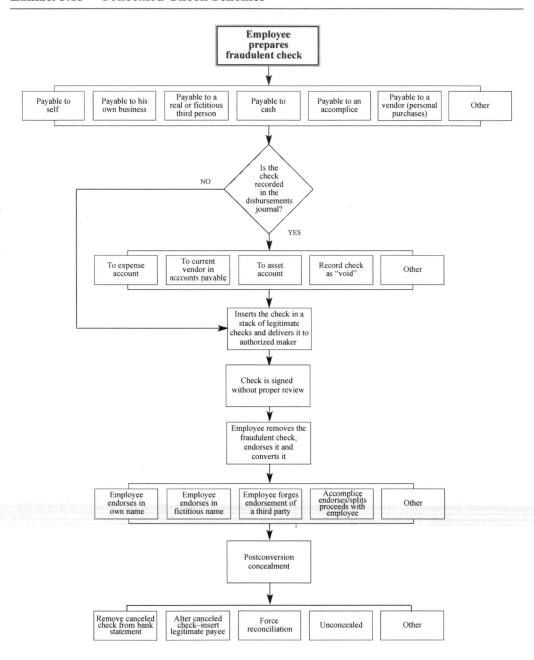

tampering fraud in which employees with signature authority on a company account write fraudulent checks for their own benefit and sign their own name as the maker. (See Exhibit 5.14.) Perpetrators in these schemes can write and sign fraudulent checks themselves. They do not have to alter a prepared instrument or forge the maker's signature.

Exhibit 5.14 Authorized Maker Schemes

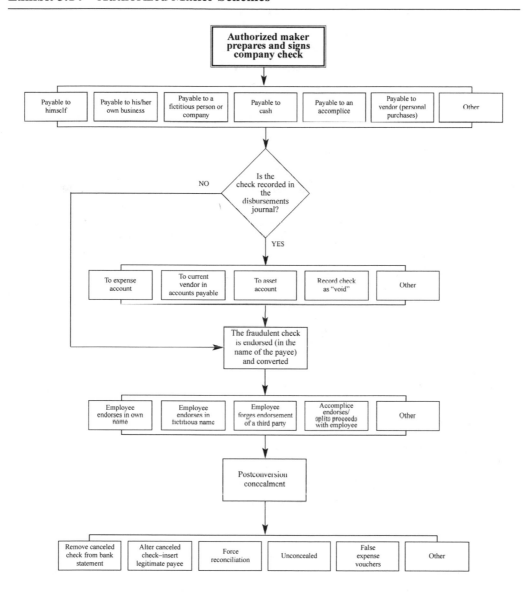

Overriding Controls through Intimidation

When a person is authorized to sign company checks, preparing the checks is easy. The employee simply writes and signs the instruments the same way he would with any legitimate check. In most situations, check signers are owners, officers, or otherwise high-ranking employees and thus have or can obtain access to all the blank checks they need. Even if company policy prohibits check signers from handling blank checks, normally the perpetrator can use her influence to overcome this impediment. What employee is going to tell the chief executive officer that she cannot have a blank check?

The most basic way an employee accomplishes an authorized maker scheme is to override controls designed to prevent fraud. We already have stated that most authorized signatories have high levels of influence within their companies. Perpetrators may use this influence to deflect questions about fraudulent transactions. The most common example is one in which a majority owner or sole shareholder uses a company as a sort of alter ego, paying personal expenses directly out of company accounts. If this arrangement is disclosed and agreed to by other owners, there may be nothing illegal about it—after all, one cannot steal from oneself. However, in the absence of an agreement between all owners, these disbursements amount to embezzlement. Instead of paying personal expenses, the fraudster might cut checks directly to himself, his friends, or his family. Using fear for job security as a weapon, the owner can maintain a work environment in which employees are afraid to question these transactions.

High-level managers or officers also may use their authority to override controls in those companies whose ownership is either absent or inattentive. Intimidation can play a large part in the commission and concealment of any type of occupational fraud where powerful individuals are involved. In one example, the manager of a sales office stole approximately $150,000 from his employers over a two-year period. This manager had primary check-signing authority and abused this power by writing company checks to pay his personal expenses. The manager's fraudulent activities were well known by certain members of his staff, but the perpetrator controlled these employees' careers. Fear of losing their jobs combined with lack of a proper whistleblowing structure prevented the manager's employees from reporting his fraud.

Poor Controls

Although overriding controls is the most blatant way to execute an authorized maker scheme, it is not the most common. Far more of these schemes occur because no one is paying attention to the accounts and few controls are present to prevent fraud. In one example, a manager of a small business wrote company checks to purchase assets for his own business. He took approximately $800,000 from his employer, hiding the missing money in accounts receivable because he knew that those accounts were reviewed only once a year. Before audits, the manager would borrow money from the bank to replace the missing funds, then begin the whole process again when the books were closed. This scheme ended in tragedy; the manager and his wife committed suicide when the fraud came to light. Setting aside the personal catastrophe that occurred in this case, it is obvious that if the books had been monitored more closely, or if there had been a threat of surprise audits in addition to the regularly scheduled reviews, this fraud may not have gotten so far out of hand.

The failure to monitor accounts closely is supplemented by lack of internal controls, specifically the absence of separation of duties in the cash disbursements process. In another instance, the perpetrator was in charge of signing all company checks as well as reconciling the bank accounts for a small business. This put the fraudster in perfect position to write fraudulent checks to herself and her husband. Similarly, in another case, the bookkeeper of a medium-size company was charged with paying all bills and preparing the company payroll. She had access to an automatic check signer and total control over company bank accounts. The bookkeeper wrote extra checks to herself, coded the expenditures to payroll, and destroyed the canceled checks when they were returned with the bank statement. Had the duties of preparing checks and reconciling accounts been separated, as they should be, the fraudster would not have been able to complete her scheme.

Special Project Accounts

Sometimes employees are given signature authority on limited project accounts rather than on company accounts in general. These project accounts are funded based on expected costs, and the employee in question has limited authority to disburse the funds as necessary for the completion of the project. In one case, an employee was in charge of project accounts and succeeded in taking almost $150,000 for his personal use. He accomplished this by charging the cost of supplies for his projects to regular departmental accounts rather than the specially funded project accounts. This left excess money in the project accounts, which the perpetrator removed by writing fraudulent checks under his own signature authority.

Tampering with the Signature Card

The preceding discussion has centered on cases where the perpetrator is authorized by the company to sign checks. In a few schemes we reviewed, employees were able secretly to add their names to the signature card of a company bank account. This allowed the perpetrators to write checks on the company account for their own benefit.

As might be expected, the presence of an unauthorized employee's signature on a check might set off alarms during reconciliation. In one specific case, an employee avoided this problem by adding a fictitious name to the signature card of a staff fund account. The addition of a fictitious maker to the signature card would assure that, even if the fraudulent checks were discovered, no one would know who actually had written them. Unfortunately for the victim company, this was not an issue because it did not perform an audit on the account until after the perpetrator retired, eight years later and $120,000 richer.

CONCEALMENT

Because most check tampering schemes do not consist of a single occurrence but instead continue over a period of time, concealing the fraud is arguably the most important aspect of the scheme. If a fraudster intended to steal a large sum of money and skip to South America, hiding the fraud might not be so important. But the vast majority of occupational fraudsters remain employees of their companies as they continue to steal from them. Therefore, hiding the fraud is extremely important. Concealment of the fraud means not only hiding the identity of the criminal but in most cases hiding the fact of the fraud. The most successful frauds are those in which the victim company is unaware that it is being robbed. Obviously, once a business learns that it is being victimized, it will take steps to stanch its bleeding and the end of the fraudster's scheme will be at hand.

Check tampering schemes can present especially tricky concealment problems for fraudsters. In other types of fraudulent disbursements, such as invoice or payroll schemes, the fraudulent payment is entered in the books as a legitimate transaction by someone other than the fraudster. Remember that the payments in those schemes are generated by the production of false documents that cause accounts payable personnel to think that money is owed to a particular person or vendor. When accounts payable issues a disbursement for a bogus invoice, it does so because it believes the invoice to be genuine. The payment then is entered in the books as a legitimate payment. In other words, perpetrators generally do not have to worry about concealing the payment in the books, because someone else unwittingly does it for them.

Check tampering schemes do not always afford this luxury to fraudsters. In forgery and authorized maker schemes, perpetrators are the ones writing the check, and they usually are the ones coding the check in the disbursements journal. They must "explain" the check on the books. Forged endorsement schemes and altered payee schemes are different because they involve the alteration of checks that were already prepared and coded by someone else. Nevertheless, they create a problem for fraudsters because the intercepted check was intended for a legitimate recipient. In short, someone is out there waiting for the check that the fraudsters have taken. Culprits in these schemes must worry not only about hiding the fraud from the employer but also about appeasing the intended payee. If the intended recipient of the check does not receive payment, he will complain to the fraudsters' employer about the nonpayment. This could trigger an investigation into the whereabouts of the missing check, something fraudsters definitely want to avoid.

Fraudster Reconciling the Bank Statement

A large portion of those who perpetrate check tampering frauds are involved in reconciling the company's bank statement. The bank statement that a company receives normally includes the canceled checks that have been cashed in the preceding period. People who reconcile the accounts are therefore in a position to hide the existence of any fraudulent checks that they have written to themselves. They can remove the fraudulent checks or doctor the bank statement, or both.

In forged maker and authorized maker schemes, perpetrators usually have to code the check in the disbursements journal. The most fundamental way to hide the check is to code it as "void" or to include no listing at all in the journal. Then, when the bank statement arrives, perpetrators remove the fraudulent check from the returned checks and destroy it or alter the bank statement. Now there is no record of the payment in the journal and no physical evidence of the check on hand. Of course, the bank will have a copy of the check, but unless someone questions the missing check, there is little chance that the company will discover the problem routinely. And since the perpetrators are the ones who reconcile the account, it is unlikely that anyone will even notice that the check is missing.

The problem with simply omitting the fraudulent check from the disbursements journal is that the bank balance will not reconcile to the book balance. For instance, if the fraudster wrote a $25,000 check to himself and did not record it, then the book balance will be $25,000 higher than the bank balance. (The fraudster took $25,000 out of the bank account, but it was not credited out of the company's cash account.) Fraudsters usually omit their illicit checks from the disbursement journal only in situations in which they personally reconcile the bank statement and no one reviews their work, thus allowing them to "force" the reconciliation. In other words, fraudsters report that the bank balance and book balance match when in fact they do not. These are circumstances in which the employer basically takes the perpetrators' word that the book balance and bank balance reconcile.

Some of the victim companies in our studies simply did not reconcile their accounts regularly. Because no one was reconciling the book balance and the bank balance, fraudsters were able to write checks without recording them. In a system in which controls are so lax, almost any concealment method will be effective to disguise fraud. In fact, in these circumstances, no effort to conceal the crime may be necessary.

Fraudsters might alter the bank statement physically to cause it to match the company's book balance. For instance, a person engaging in a forged maker scheme may decide to steal blank checks from the bottom of the check stock. These checks are out of sequence and therefore will be listed last on the bank statement. The employee then deletes this clump of checks and alters the final total to match the victim company's books. This method of concealment is used in the next case study.

In some cases, although an employee's duties do not include reconciling the bank accounts, he is nevertheless able to intercept bank statements and alter them to hide his crimes. In the next case study, Ernie Philips was able to persuade his company's bank to send the bank statements directly to him instead of to his boss. Philips then altered the bank statements to conceal his fraudulent activities. This case describes how Certified Fraud Examiner James Sell put an end to Philips's scheme.

Case Study: What Are Friends For?

Ernie Philips* had fallen on hard times. Several back operations left him barely able to move around. He became addicted to the pills that made the pain bearable. His CPA practice was going under. He and his wife had six adopted children to support. Not surprisingly, he suffered from depression and chronic anxiety. But Ernie's luck changed when he ran into his old friend, James Sell. The two men had worked together at a federal agency and known each other more than 20 years. Ernie talked about the trouble he was having, and James said he could help. At the time, Ernie was in a rehabilitation program for his substance abuse, so James told him, "Let me know when you're finished with that, and I'll have some work for you."

James rented Ernie an office and started sending a few small projects his way. "I wanted to try him out, see how he would do," Sell remarks. "He seemed like he was trying to get himself together." Ernie completed the work on time and performed well, so when James got a big account with the Arizona and Nevada

*Several names and details have been changed to preserve anonymity.

governments, he brought his friend into the main office. They agreed on a salary just over $68,000 a year, which James upped to $74,000 after six months.

Sell was appointed receiver for CSC Financial Services in Arizona and Nevada. CSC owners had been caught diverting $5.5 million of customer escrow funds from its operations in Arizona and Nevada. The computer equipment used in the operation dated from the 1960s, and a lack of supervision and proper controls obviously had allowed the embezzlement to take place. The company didn't use a double-entry system, so management could alter ending totals with wide latitude. Even after a regulatory audit discovered that things were in disarray at CSC, the Arizona administrators had allowed the offending owners to continue operating for a year and a half. So when Sell finally took over, he found a rather large mess. That's part of the game, he says: "When you get a company as receiver, you try to survive with what you inherit." The receivership involved more than 15,000 active accounts, with about $285 million in in-house payments each year and more than 30,000 transactions a month. Sorting out the trouble wouldn't be easy. Sell knew Ernie had experience, so he tapped him for the job. "One of the reasons I brought him in," Sell says, "was to establish controls where there were none before."

But Ernie had little respect for controls. When James asked the mailroom clerk about the bank statements for a particular month, he told him that Ernie had them. "Why is that?" James asked. "He knows those are supposed to come to me unopened. He shouldn't have them." The clerk said Ernie needed the statements for a reconciliation. James didn't want to overreact, but he was nervous. "There's limited control over any position and even less over a key financial position," he says, "and any time you lose a control point, you're in jeopardy. So you have to take a strong position in order to restore the process." He discussed the matter with Ernie and thought they had an understanding.

Ernie was having problems with other people in the company too. He and the operations manager had a heated exchange when the manager retrieved some account papers from Ernie's desk. Ernie had been out and the papers were needed right away. When Ernie aired his grievance, James sided with the operations manager. There shouldn't be any problem, James said. It wasn't like anyone was rifling Ernie's desk. Besides, Sell traveled frequently and spent a lot of time in the Nevada office, so having open access in the Arizona office allowed for informal oversight. Sell muses, "One of the best controls in the world is to create an atmosphere of uncertainty. Usually embezzlement doesn't occur unless the person thinks he can hide what he's doing. So I figured this would be a way to keep things on the up-and-up."

The uncertainty didn't prevent the fraud, but it did help detect what was going on. The operations manager discovered Ernie's scheme during a search for accounting records. He brought Sell a company check from Ernie's desk, made out in the name of Ernie Philips for $2,315. It wasn't Ernie's payroll check, so what was it? The check hadn't been cashed, but Sell's signature had been forged. Not sure yet about the situation, Sell arranged to meet Ernie away from the main office.

Sell had been out of town and needed some updates on the escrow operations, so he dropped by Ernie's private office one afternoon. After they finished their discussion, James said, "There's one more thing I wanted to ask you about." He pulled a copy of the check from his briefcase and told Ernie, "I was hoping you could explain this."

There was a long silence. Ernie stared at the check, pursing his lips and scratching his hands across the desktop. The pause stretched into what seemed like minutes. Finally he confessed, "I've been taking money."

"I could tell from the look on his face this was trouble," Sell reports. The worst was confirmed. He had been hoping there was an explanation, an innocuous one, despite all the signs. Still, he had come prepared. "I wanted to confront him away from the main office so if there was anything he could get to and destroy, I'd be protected." James had also brought a copy of the check so it wouldn't be apparent when he showed the check to Ernie that it wasn't cashed. "I wanted to make him believe I knew more than I did. Nailing down this operation would have meant reviewing pages and pages of bank statements, verifying checks and payments. Before I went to that trouble, I wanted to know there was a reason to look."

Sell barred Ernie from both his offices and began tracing his friend's activities over the past seven months. In some cases, Sell's name was forged onto the checks in handwriting that wasn't his and that bore a resemblance to Ernie's. Others were marked with the signature stamp that was supposed to remain locked in a clerk's office except when she was using it for a very limited set of transactions. Somehow Ernie had been able to slip the stamp away and mark his checks.

He covered his tracks by taking checks out of sequence so they would show up at the end of the bank statement. Then he'd intercept the statement and alter the report at the end, returning a copy of the statement to the clerk for filing. After the clerk told Sell about Ernie having the statement, Ernie arranged with the bank for the statements to come addressed to his attention. Without getting authorization, the bank agreed; Ernie could then doctor the statement, copy it, and send it down the line. If someone did ask about an unidentified disbursement, Ernie told them the money went to a supply vendor, and since he was the controller, he was taken at his word. He even managed on a couple of occasions to slip checks made out to himself into a regular batch, which the operations manager—who was authorized to sign checks in Sell's absence—signed.

Sell was, to put it mildly, chagrined. He had believed that his office was set up to avoid the kind of flagrant defalcation he was facing now. But, he admits, "No matter how good a system you design, one knowledgeable person can circumvent it. . . . The trick is to make sure the procedures you set up are followed. I don't know if there's a system in the world that's immune. The key is to limit and control the extent of any one person's action, so you can at least detect when things go awry."

Sell figured his losses at about $109,000. He got a complete run of the bank statements from Ernie's tenure, identified checks out of sequence or gaps in issued checks, and then verified to whom they were payable and the stated purpose. The scheme had required some footwork but wasn't terribly sophisticated. The checks were written in odd-number amounts—$4,994.16, for example—but Ernie had made the payments in his own name. He had left behind some of his personal bank statements, which showed deposits correlated with the money he'd taken from Sell. (The amounts didn't always match, because Ernie would take cash back from the deposit, but they were close enough to link the transactions.)

Ernie's brief era of good feelings had ended. He had used the proceeds from his finagling for a lavish family vacation, a new car, a new computer, and improvements on the house where he lived with his wife and their children, but in the fallout of his dismissal Ernie's house went into foreclosure. Around the same time he was charged with driving under the influence. The CPA board revoked his license and fined him for ethics violations. He made no defense at his civil trial, where a judgment was rendered against him for the $109,000 he took, plus treble damages. While he was out on bail for the criminal charges against him, Ernie took his family and fled; Sell was able to locate him through an Internet search service. But Ernie died shortly thereafter. "He threw everything away," Sell laments. "For $109,000 he fouled up his life and his family."

Sell takes the matter philosophically. There are plenty of cases that echo Ernie's. For example, Sell just investigated a paralegal who not only wrote company checks to herself but also sent one to the county attorney's office—to pay the fine she owed for writing bad checks. "Typically, these people don't take the time to set up a new identity or a dummy company," James says. "They just want the money fast and grab it the easiest way they can."

"And often enough," he adds, "they want to get caught. . . . Ernie knew he was out of control; we had been friends for so long. He knew he was doing more than just breaking the law. During one of our conversations after this he told me, 'You know, the first check was real hard to write. But I had clients I had borrowed from, I owed money all over the place, I had a family. As it went on, writing the checks just got easier.'"

Realteration of Checks

In altered payee schemes, it is common for perpetrators to take a check intended for a legitimate recipient, then doctor the instrument so that they are designated as the payee. A company check payable to an employee obviously will raise suspicions of fraud when the canceled check is reconciled with the bank statement. To prevent this, some employees realter their fraudulent checks when the bank statement arrives. We already have discussed how some fraudsters alter checks by writing the payee's name in erasable ink or type when the check is prepared. These employees obtain a signature for the check, then erase the true payee's name and insert their own. When these checks return with the statement, employees erase their own name and reenter the name of the proper payee; thus, there will be no appearance of mischief. The fraudster in one case used the realteration method to hide over $185,000 in fraudulent checks.

The realteration method is not limited to altered payee schemes; the concealment is equally effective in forged maker schemes, authorized maker schemes, and concealed check schemes. Realtered checks will match the names of legitimate payees listed in the disbursements journal.

Entering False Information in the Disbursements Journal

Rather than omit a fraudulent check from the disbursements journal or list it as void, perpetrators might write a check payable to themselves but list a different person as the payee on the books. Usually the fake payee is a regular vendor—a person or business that receives numerous checks from the victim company. Employees tend to pick known vendors for these schemes because one extra disbursement to a regular payee is less likely to stand out.

The false entry usually is made at the time the fraudulent check is written, but in some cases fraudsters make alterations to existing information on the books. In the opening case study in this chapter, for instance, Melissa Robinson used correction fluid and an eraser to change the payee names in her company's checkbook. Obviously, alterations found in a company's books should be scrutinized carefully to make sure they are legitimate.

Fraudsters also can conceal a fraudulent check by falsely entering the amounts of legitimate checks in the disbursements journal. They overstate the amounts of legitimate disbursements in order to absorb the cost of a fraudulent check. For instance, assume that a company owes $10,000 to a particular vendor. The fraudster would write a check to the vendor for $10,000 but enter the check in the disbursements journal as a $15,000 payment. The company's disbursements are now overstated by $5,000. The fraudster can write a $5,000 check to herself and list that check as void in the disbursements journal. The bank balance and the book balance will still match, because the cost of the fraudulent check was absorbed by overstating the amount of the legitimate check. Of course, the fact that the canceled checks do not match the entries in the journal should indicate potential fraud. This type of concealment really is effective only when the bank accounts are not closely monitored or when the employee is also in charge of reconciling the accounts.

Coding the Fraudulent Checks

If possible, fraudsters will try to code their fraudulent checks to existing accounts that are rarely reviewed or to accounts that are very active. For instance, in one case, the perpetrator charged his checks to an intercompany payables account because it was reviewed only at the end of the year, and not in great detail. The perpetrator in this case also might have coded his checks to an account with extensive activity in the hopes that his fraudulent check would be lost in the crowd of transactions on the account. In the cases we reviewed, most checks were coded to expense accounts or liability accounts.

This particular method can be very effective in concealing fraudulent checks, particularly when the victim company is not diligent in reconciling its bank accounts. For instance, one victim company reconciled its accounts by verifying the amount of the checks with the check numbers but did not verify that the payee on the actual check matched the payee listed in the disbursements journal. As a result, the company was unable to detect that the checks had been miscoded in the disbursements journal. As we discussed in the previous section, fraudsters also might intercept the bank statement before it is reconciled and alter the payee name on the fraudulent check to match the entry they made in the disbursements journal.

Reissuing Intercepted Checks

In intercepted check schemes, employees face detection not only through their employer's normal control procedures but also by the intended recipients of the checks they steal. After all, when these people do not receive their payments from the victim company, they are likely to complain; these complaints, in turn, could trigger a fraud investigation.

Some employees head this problem off by issuing new checks to the people whose checks they stole. In one case, for instance, an employee stole checks intended for vendors and deposited them into her own checking account. She then took the invoices from these vendors and reentered them in the company's accounts payable system, adding a number or letter to avoid the computerized system's duplicate check controls. This ensured that the vendors received their due payment and therefore would not blow the whistle on her scheme, which netted approximately $200,000.

Another example of reissuance was provided by an accounts payable troubleshooter. The employee in this case was in charge of auditing payments to all suppliers, reviewing supporting documents, and mailing checks. Every once in a while, she purposely would fail to mail a check to a vendor. The vendor, of course, called accounts payable about the late payment and was told that the invoice had been paid on a certain date. Since accounts payable did not have a copy of the canceled check (because the fraudster was still holding it), it would call the troubleshooter to research the problem. Unfortunately for the company, the troubleshooter was the one who had stolen the check; she told accounts payable to issue another check to the vendor while she stopped payment on the first check. Thus the vendor received his payment, and instead of stopping payment on the first check, the troubleshooter deposited it into her own account.

The difference between these two schemes is that in the latter, two checks were issued for a single invoice. The troubleshooter in the first example did not have to worry about this problem because she performed the bank reconciliations for her company and was able to "force" the totals. Once again, we see that access to the bank statement is a key to concealing a check tampering scheme.

Bogus Supporting Documents

Whereas some fraudsters attempt to wipe out all traces of their fraudulent disbursements by destroying the checks, forcing the bank reconciliation, and so on, others opt to justify their checks by manufacturing fake support for them. These fraudsters prepare false payment vouchers, including false invoices, purchase orders, or receiving reports, to create an appearance of authenticity. This concealment strategy is practical only when fraudsters write checks payable to someone other than themselves (e.g., an accomplice or a shell company). A check made payable to an employee may raise suspicions regardless of any supporting documents manufactured.

Conceptually, the idea of producing false payment vouchers may seem confusing in a chapter on check tampering. If the fraudster is using fake vouchers, shouldn't the crime be classified as a billing scheme? Not necessarily. In a check tampering scheme, fraudsters generate the disbursement by writing the check themselves. They may create fake support to justify the check, but the support—the voucher—had nothing to do with the disbursement being made. Had the fraudsters not created a fake invoice, they would still have had a fraudulent check.

In a billing scheme, fraudsters use the false voucher *to cause a payment to be generated*. Without a fake voucher in these schemes, there would be no fraudulent disbursement at all, because the employees depend on someone else actually to cut the check. In other words, the false voucher is a means of creating the unwarranted payment in these schemes rather than an attempt to hide it.

DETECTION

Account Analysis through Cut-off Statements

Bank cut-off statements should be requested for 10 to 15 days after the closing date of the balance sheet. These statements may be used to detect cash fraud during periods between monthly bank statements. Auditors often use cut-off statements to ensure that income and expenses are reported in the proper period. If employees know that at any time during the month a cut-off statement may be ordered and reviewed independently, cash fraud will be less likely.

A cut-off statement generally is ordered from the bank, delivered unopened to the auditor (or outsider), and reconciled. It can be ordered at any time during the accounting cycle. If cut-off bank statements are not ordered or received, the following period's bank statement should be obtained and account analysis and investigation should be performed.[2]

Bank Reconciliations

Copies of the bank reconciliations and account analysis should be obtained along with the complete set of bank statements on all checking and savings accounts as well as certificates of deposit and other interest-bearing and non-interest-bearing accounts. These nine tests should be performed:

1. Confirm the mathematical accuracy of the reconciliation.
2. Examine the bank statement for possible alterations.
3. Trace the balance on the statement back to the bank cut-off and bank confirmation statements.
4. Foot the balance to the company's ledger.

5. Trace the deposits in transit to the bank cut-off statement to ensure recording in proper period.

6. Examine canceled checks and compare to the list of outstanding checks.

7. Sample supporting documentation of checks written for a material amount.

8. Verify supporting documentation on outstanding checks written for a material amount.

9. Verify accuracy of nonoperational cash or cash-equivalent accounts (certificates of deposit and other investment accounts). Analysis should include the verification of the institution holding the funds, interest rate, maturity date, beginning and ending balances, and current period activity. Book and bank balances should be compared and any accruals of interest analyzed.[3]

Bank Confirmation

Another method related to the cut-off statement is the bank confirmation request. Unlike the cut-off statement, this detection method is merely a report of the balance in the account as of the date requested. This balance should be requested to confirm the statement balance as well as any other necessary balance date. If the fraud is occurring at the bank reconciliation stage, this independent confirmation may prove to be very helpful.

Check Tampering Red Flags

- *Voided checks* may indicate employees have embezzled cash and charged the embezzlement to expense accounts. When the expense is paid (from accounts payable), fraudulent checks are marked and entered as void and removed from distribution points. An account-balancing journal entry then is made. The list of voided checks should be verified against physical copies of the checks. Bank statements should be reviewed to ensure that voided checks have not been processed.

- *Missing checks* may indicate lax control over the physical safekeeping of checks. Stop payments should be issued for all missing checks.

- *Checks payable to employees*, with the exception of regular payroll checks, should be closely scrutinized. Such an examination may indicate other schemes such as conflicts of interest, fictitious vendors, or duplicate expense reimbursements.

- *Altered endorsements or dual endorsements* of returned checks may indicate possible tampering.

- *Returned checks* with obviously forged or questionable signature endorsements should be verified with the original payee.

- *Altered payees* on returned checks should be verified with the intended payee.

- *Duplicate or counterfeit checks* indicate fraud. These checks may be traceable to the depositor through bank check coding.

- *Questionable deposit dates* should be matched to the corresponding customer accounts.

- *Cash advances* should be examined to see that all are properly documented and that inappropriate payments have not been made to employees.
- *Customer complaints* regarding payments not being applied to their accounts should be investigated.
- *A questionable payee or payee address* on a check should trigger review of the corresponding check and support documentation.

PREVENTION

Check Disbursement Controls

To help tighten controls and possibly deter employees from giving in to the temptation to commit check fraud, make sure that:

- Checks are not prepared by a signatory on the account.
- Checks are mailed immediately after signing.
- Theft control procedures are adhered to.
- Accounts payable records and addresses are secure from possible tampering.
- Changes in vendor information are verified.
- Bank statements are reviewed diligently to ensure that amounts and signatures have not been altered.
- Bank reconciliations are completed immediately after monthly statements are received. The Uniform Commercial Code states that discrepancies must be presented within 30 days from the bank statement in order to hold the bank liable.
- Bank reconciliations are not made by signatories on the account.
- Bank statements are reconciled and reviewed by more than one person.
- Appropriate separation of duties is documented and adhered to.
- Detailed comparisons are made routinely between check payees and the payees listed in the cash disbursement journal.
- Personnel responsible for handling and coding checks are rotated periodically, keeping the total number of personnel involved to a minimum.

Bank-Assisted Controls

Companies should work in a cooperative effort with banks to prevent check fraud. Consider taking these control measures in regard to a firm's checking accounts.

- *Establish maximum dollar amounts* above which the company's bank will not accept checks drawn against the account.
- *Use positive pay banking controls.* Positive pay allows a company and its bank to work together to detect fraudulent items presented for payment. The company provides the bank with a list of checks and amounts that are written each day. The bank verifies items presented for payment against the company's list and

rejects items that are not on the list. Investigations are conducted as to the origin of "nonlist" items.

Physical Tampering Prevention

This list details check tampering prevention techniques that are being used today by some institutions to secure the check integrity of businesses. These methods can be used individually or in combination.

- *Signature line void safety band.* The word "VOID" appears on the check when photocopied.
- *Rainbow foil bar.* A horizontal, colored bar placed on the check fades and is shaded from one bar to the next. Photocopied foil bars appear solid.
- *Holographic safety border.* Holographic images are created in a way that reflects light to reveal a three-dimensional graphic.
- *Embossed pearlescent numbering.* Checks are numbered using a new technique that is revealed by a colored highlighter pen or by a bright light held behind the check.
- *Other chemical voids.* Checks reveal an image or the word "VOID" when treated with an eradicator chemical.
- *Microline printing.* Extremely small print is too small to read with the naked eye and becomes distorted when photocopied.
- *High-resolution microprinting.* Images are produced on the check in high resolution, 2,400 dots per inch or higher. This technique is very difficult to reproduce.
- *Security inks.* Checks contain inks that react with eradication chemicals, reducing a forger's ability to modify the check.
- *Chrome coloring.* The use of chromelike coloring deters photocopying even with color copiers. The chrome pattern or numbering develops solid black.
- *Watermark backers.* Hidden images can be seen only when the check is held at an angle. This image is very difficult to reproduce.
- *Ultraviolet ink.* This ink displays an image or message when held under ultraviolet lighting.

Check Theft Control Procedures

It is very important to provide internal controls that will minimize the possibility of check tampering and theft. Items on the next list should be incorporated into the company's policies and procedures to help deter check tampering.

- Purchase new checks from reputable, well-established check producers.
- Store unused checks in a secure area such as a safe, vault, or other locked area. Security to this area should be restricted to authorized personnel only. Routinely change keys and access codes to storage areas.
- Review all hiring procedures. One of the most important means of fighting fraud is not hiring people with questionable backgrounds. Develop a distinct separation of

duties in the accounts payable department, including written policies and procedures for all personnel who have the opportunity to handle checks, from mailroom clerks to the chief executive.

- Use electronic payment services to handle large vendor and financing payments, eliminating the use of paper checks.
- Report lost or stolen checks immediately.
- Properly and securely store canceled checks.
- Destroy unused checks for accounts that have been closed.
- Mail printed and signed checks immediately after signing.

ELECTRONIC PAYMENT TAMPERING

As businesses move to using electronic payments—such ACH payments, online bill payments, and wire transfers—in addition to or instead of traditional checks, fraudsters are adapting their methods to manipulate these payments as well. Some of these fraudsters abuse their legitimate access to their employer's electronic payment system; these schemes are similar to traditional check tampering frauds carried out by authorized makers. Others gain access through social engineering or password theft or by exploiting weaknesses in their employer's internal control or electronic payment system. Regardless of the means by which they log in to the system, dishonest employees use this access fraudulently to initiate or divert electronic payments to themselves or their accomplices.

As with other schemes, once the fraudulent payment has been made, the employee must cover his or her tracks. However, the lack of physical evidence and forged signatures can make concealment of fraudulent electronic payments less challenging than other check tampering schemes. Some fraudsters attempt to conceal their schemes by altering the bank statement, miscoding transactions in the accounting records, or sending fraudulent payments to a shell company with a name similar to that of an existing vendor. Others merely rely on the company's failure to monitor or reconcile its accounts.

PREVENTION AND DETECTION

Internal Controls

One of the most important internal controls for preventing and detecting electronic payment fraud is separation of duties. For example, in the case of online bill payments, such as those made through a bank's Web site or a third-party business-to-business payment service, separate individuals should be responsible for maintaining payments templates, entering payments, and approving payments. For wire transfers, duties for creating, approving, and releasing wires should be segregated. And to prevent attempts to conceal fraudulent electronic payment activity, no individual involved in the payment process should reconcile the bank statement or even have access to it. In addition to separating duties, companies should consider segregating their bank accounts in order to maintain better control over them—for example, separate accounts can be used for paper and electronic transactions.

Account monitoring and reconciliation should be performed daily so as to quickly spot and notify the bank of any unusual transactions. Depending on the accounting software in use at the company and the account reconciliation offerings of its bank, much of the reconciliation process can be automated. Additionally, many banks are able to provide daily itemized reports of outstanding payments in addition to a list of those payments that have already cleared.

In guarding against improper access to electronic payment systems, proper management and protection of user access and account information are essential. All log-in information, such as usernames and passwords, should be guarded heavily, with passwords changed frequently and user access immediately deactivated for any user who no longer has a need for it (e.g., a terminated employee or an employee who has changed roles). Although most electronic payment systems eventually will time out, users should log off immediately when they are finished using the system or if they need to leave their computer unattended, even if only for a short time. Unattended computers that are logged on to a payment system provide fraudsters with a free pass to the company's bank account. For example, in Case 5777, an employee who was working in the company's electronic payment system left his computer unattended for less than ten minutes so that he could grab a cup of coffee. During that time, another employee who shared an office with him was able to wire $3,273 to an existing vendor with whom he was in collusion. Because the victim company performed daily account reconciliations, the fraud was caught the next day. The fraudster was fired immediately, and the individual who left his computer unattended while logged into the system was reprimanded.

Bank Security Services

Most large banks offer a number of security services that can help business account holders mitigate fraud through early detection and prevention of fraudulent electronic payments. For example, ACH blocks allow account holders to notify their banks that ACH debits—whether authorized or not—should not be allowed on specific accounts. ACH filters enable account holders to provide their banks with a list of defined criteria (such as the sending company ID, account number, and transaction code) against which banks can filter ACH debits and reject any unauthorized transactions. Positive pay for ACH is another security feature offered by banks to their account holders, in which banks match the details of ACH payments with those on a list of legitimate and expected payments provided by the account holder. Only authorized electronic transactions are allowed to be withdrawn from the account; exceptions are reported to the customer for review.

Organizations can also set up their commercial banking software to restrict access to specific banking activities—such as viewing transactions, viewing bank statements, initiating electronic payments, or setting up ACH blocks or filters—to designated individuals. Companies should incorporate this feature into their internal control system to enhance separation of duties. For example, any individual authorized to make payments should not be permitted to set up ACH blocks or filters or to submit positive pay information. In addition, businesses can customize their banking software to incorporate features such as dual authorization for certain transactions and daily or individual transaction limits.

Companies can further enhance their protection against unauthorized access to an electronic payment system through the use of their banks' multifactor authentication tools, mechanisms that combine two or more methods to validate the identity of the person attempting to access the system. These tools—such as tokens (physical devices that authorized users provide in addition to their passwords to prove their identities electronically), digital certificates, smart cards, and voiceprint recognition software—can help businesses overcome the problem of compromised credentials, such as usernames and passwords.

NOTES

1. Henry Campbell Black, *Black's Law Dictionary*, 5th ed. (St. Paul, MN: West, 1979), p. 585.
2. George Georgiades, *Audit Procedures* (New York: Harcourt Brace Professional Publishing, 1995).
3. Ibid.

CHAPTER 6

Register Disbursement Schemes

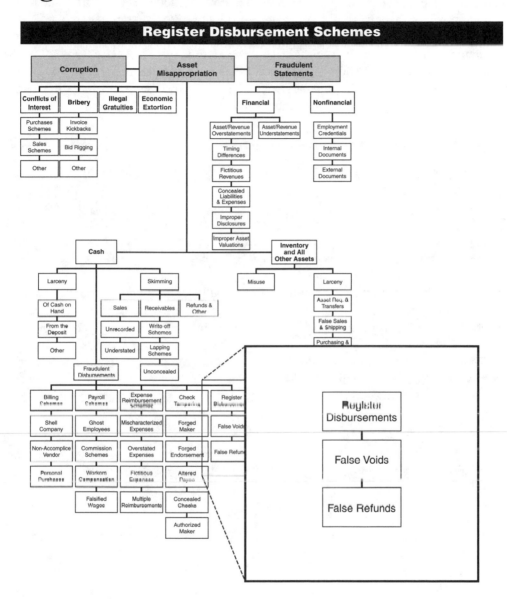

OVERVIEW

So far we have discussed two ways in which fraud is committed at the cash register—skimming and cash larceny. These schemes are what we commonly think of as theft. They involve the surreptitious removal of money from a cash register. When money is taken from a register in a skimming or larceny scheme, there is no record of the transaction—the money is simply missing.

In this chapter, we discuss fraudulent disbursements at the cash register. These schemes differ from the other register frauds in that when money is taken from the register, the removal of money is recorded on the register tape. A false transaction is recorded as if it were a legitimate disbursement to justify the removal of money. Bob Walker's fraudulent refunds in the next case study were an example of such a false transaction.

Two basic fraudulent disbursement schemes take place at the register: *false refunds* and *false voids*. Although the schemes are largely similar, there are a few differences between the two that merit discussing them separately.

Case Study: Demotion Sets Fraud in Motion

Following a demotion and consequent pay cut, Bob Walker* silently vowed to even the score with his employer. In six months Walker racked up $10,000 in ill-gotten cash from his employer, who was caught completely off guard, before someone blew the whistle.

The whistleblower was Emily Schlitz, who worked weekends as a backup bookkeeper at a unit of Thrifty PayLess, a chain of 1,000 discount drugstores crossing ten Western states.

One October, while reviewing her store's refund log, Schlitz noticed an unusually large number of protocol breaches by the head cashier—one Bob Walker—who naturally handled most refunds. In issuing cash refunds for big-ticket items, for instance, Walker frequently failed to record the customer's phone number. Often he neglected to attach sales receipts to the refund log, noting that the customers wanted to keep their receipts. Schlitz questioned the high proportion of these irregularities and notified the store manager, who in turn called the asset protection (security) department at headquarters to investigate what he termed "strange entries."

Thrifty PayLess pays serious attention to such phone calls, according to its director of asset protection, James Hansen, who celebrated his thirteenth anniversary with the retailer that year. In 57 percent of the fraud cases for that year, Hansen reported, investigators received their first alert directly from store managers, as in this case.

The strange entries that Schlitz found called for immediate action. Hansen dispatched a field investigator, Raymond Willis, to review the findings and conduct a brief background check of Walker—a 32-year-old single male who had been employed by Thrifty PayLess for five years.

Willis soon learned that six months earlier the store manager, citing poor performance, had demoted Walker from a management position to head cashier, which also brought a $300 a month pay cut for Walker. To Willis, that information alone raised some red flags that signal potential fraud by employees: personal or financial problems, lifestyle changes or pressures, and low morale or feelings of resentment.

Further inquiry revealed Walker blamed management for the demotion.

But those red flags paled next to the wealth of evidence Willis uncovered during his investigation. He began by calling customers listed in the refund log to inquire about the service they received at the drugstore, discreetly looking for verification

---

*Several names and details have been changed to preserve anonymity.

158

or vilification. Next, he compared the number of refunds for food processors—by far the most popular merchandise item Walker accepted for return—to the number originally received in shipment minus those sold. These numbers were in turn compared to the food processors actually in stock. The investigator discovered major discrepancies.

Willis brought the case to a conclusion in just three days. "He stayed awake nights working on this one because he quickly saw the enormity of the take," recalled boss Hansen. "It just fueled his fire."

"The perpetrator had really gotten carried away with his activity. As will often happen, over time he got greedy. And once Walker got greedy, he got careless and sloppy," said Hansen.

Although aggressive in his investigation, Willis kept it quiet. He limited his interviews to just two or three of Walker's fellow employees. "Several coworkers had previously told managers that Walker seemed disgruntled and somewhat upset. But outwardly, his frustration never peaked enough to warrant the need for management to keep an eye on this guy," explained Hansen.

At the end of Willis's third day in the field, it was time to interview Walker. Initially, Willis asked general questions about store policies and procedures. He went on to focus more on cashiering methods. Walker seemed at ease in the beginning, helpful and responsive. At one point, Walker even offered the suggestion that "more controls should be placed on refunds."

As the interview progressed, however, Walker got more and more nervous. The smooth talker began to stutter and stammer. Willis asked Walker if he knew the definition of shrinkage. He haltingly replied, "For one, loss of cash or inventory due to customer or employee theft."

Willis then asked, "What have you personally done to cause shrinkage?" Walker became very quiet. After a long pause, he asked in a hushed tone, "Well, what if I did do it?" Willis laid out the consequences and continued to query the formerly trusted employee.

Walker vented his anger toward the managers who had "unjustly" demoted him. He confessed to writing fake cash refunds in retaliation. While the fraud began in May as an occasional act, it soon increased in frequency and flagrancy. At first, to fulfill the blanks on the customer information part of the refund log, he pulled names at random from the phone book. Later he simply made up names and phone numbers, he said. As his greed escalated, he altered legitimate refunds that he had issued earlier in the day, adding merchandise to inflate their monetary value and pocketing the difference.

Although store policy dictated that management approval was required for refunds totaling more than $25 or in the absence of a sales receipt, Walker deliberately thumbed his nose at those rules and others. No one ever questioned the signature authority of this recently demoted member of the management team.

To further justify his actions, Walker detailed his previous financial problems, which he said were exacerbated by the $300 monthly pay cut.

Proceeds from the fraud initially went toward his two mortgage payments, which equaled $800 a month. His ongoing booty subsequently financed his insurance premiums and living expenses, which were now mounting. He easily paid off his credit cards. The single man also used the cash for fancy dinners out on the town.

During the two-hour confrontation, Walker claimed ignorance about the exact amount he'd filched, saying he had never tallied the score. He did admit, however, that he played this lucrative game with a growing ardor and intensity.

As it turned out, all three refunds Walker had issued the day of the interview proved fraudulent. Yet he still seemed shocked that his fraud totaled upward of $10,000—more than five-and-a-half times his total pay cut over the past six months.

In a store that generates $4 million in annual sales, $10,000 over six months represents a small percentage of loss. In the retail industry, such shrinkage may be explained away by shoplifting, bad checks, accounting or paperwork errors, breakage or spoilage, shipping shortages, or numerous other reasons. Employee theft, of course, is also a significant factor in shrinkage, said Hansen, who began his career as a store detective.

"In my mind, a comprehensive loss prevention program is well balanced between preventive and investigative efforts." He said Thrifty PayLess maintains an outstanding educational program for all employees. They attend mandated training classes in both the prevention and detection of fraud. Crucial to the success of the antifraud program, employees always are made to feel like integral parts of Thrifty PayLess's whole loss prevention effort. Hansen and his asset protection staff regularly visit the stores to introduce themselves, become familiar to employees, form and maintain rapport, and build a level of trust in confidentiality. To further encourage communication, the retailer established a hotline that employees can call with anonymous tips about suspected fraud or abuse.

As evidenced by the part-time bookkeeper's suspicions and subsequent actions in this case, Thrifty PayLess's efforts obviously work, said the head of security. "It's not that our controls were in any way inadequate; it's that a local manager was not properly enforcing those controls. Generally, he got lax with a 'trusted' employee." (Needless to say, the store manager suffered some repercussions as a result of this case.)

As a result of the Walker experience, manager approval is now required for all refunds over $5. A sales receipt must also accompany all refunds, said Hansen. Thrifty PayLess's internal audit and asset protection departments perform audits regularly, checking for compliance.

"Proper implementation is the key," Hansen said. "You cannot prevent fraud 100 percent. The best you can do is to limit it through your proactive educational, awareness, and audit programs. And, of course, aggressively investigating all red flags or tips as well." Hansen's asset protection department concludes over 1,400 employee theft and fraud cases and 30,000 customer shoplifting cases annually.

Owing to the grand scale of theft in this case, Walker was arrested immediately after his interview, booked on felony charges of embezzlement, and held pending bail. He faced criminal and civil prosecution. Walker made bail within hours, then disappeared without a trace. All investigative efforts to locate him thus far have failed.

To this day Bob Walker remains a fugitive of justice.

REGISTER DISBURSEMENT DATA FROM ACFE *2009 GLOBAL FRAUD SURVEY*

Frequency and Cost

Register disbursements were reported less frequently than any other fraudulent disbursement scheme in our 2009 survey; they accounted for 6 percent of the reported fraudulent disbursements. (The sum of these percentages exceeds 100 percent because some cases involved multiple fraud schemes that fell into more than one category. Various charts in this chapter may reflect percentages that total in excess of 100 percent for similar reasons.) It should be remembered, however, that our survey asked respondents to report only one case they had investigated; it was not designed to measure the overall frequency of various types of schemes within a particular organization. Thus, the low response rate for register disbursements does not necessarily reflect how often these schemes occur. Furthermore, the type of fraud that occurs within an organization is determined to some extent by the nature of business the organization conducts. For example, register disbursement schemes would tend to be much more common in a large retail store that employs several cash register clerks than in a law firm where a cash register would not even be present. Readers should keep in mind that the frequency statistics presented in this book represent only the frequency of cases that were reported by our respondents. (See Exhibit 6.1.)

In addition to being the least frequently reported type of fraudulent disbursement, register disbursements were the least costly, with a median loss of $23,000. The typical register disbursement scheme in our survey caused about one-sixth the losses of the typical check tampering scheme. (See Exhibit 6.2.)

Exhibit 6.3 shows the distribution of register disbursement schemes compared with the distribution of all occupational fraud schemes in our study. It should be noted that there were only 55 reported cases of register disbursements in this study, so the data in the charts may have questionable reliability in terms of providing generalized information about register disbursements. Nevertheless, we have presented the same comparisons here as in other chapters for the sake of completeness and to provide some insight into the nature of the register disbursement schemes we did review. We see that over 70 percent of the register disbursement schemes caused losses of less than $50,000.

Exhibit 6.1   *2009 Global Fraud Survey*: **Frequency of Fraudulent Disbursements**

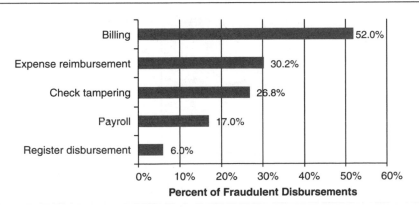

Exhibit 6.2 *2009 Global Fraud Survey*: **Median Loss of Fraudulent Disbursements**

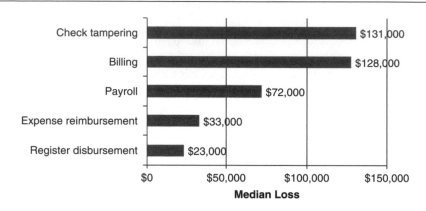

Detection of Register Disbursement Schemes

The method of initial detection was identified for all 55 register disbursement schemes in our study. Of these cases, 38.2 percent were uncovered by a tip and 21.8 percent were detected by internal audit. (See Exhibit 6.4.)

Perpetrators of Register Disbursement Schemes

The results of our survey included 53 register disbursement schemes in which the position of the principal perpetrator was identified. Of these cases, more than half were committed by employee-level fraudsters, 32.1 percent involved managers, and 17 percent involved owners/executives. It is not surprising that the majority of register

Exhibit 6.3 *2009 Global Fraud Survey*: **Dollar Loss Distribution for Register Disbursements Schemes**

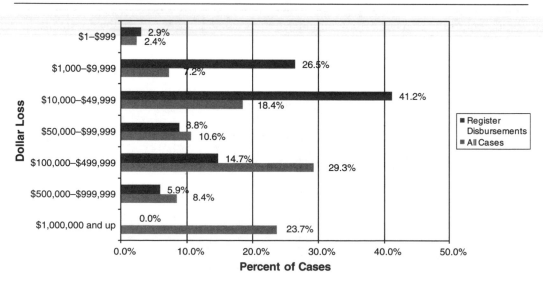

Exhibit 6.4 *2009 Global Fraud Survey*: Detection of Register Disbursement Schemes

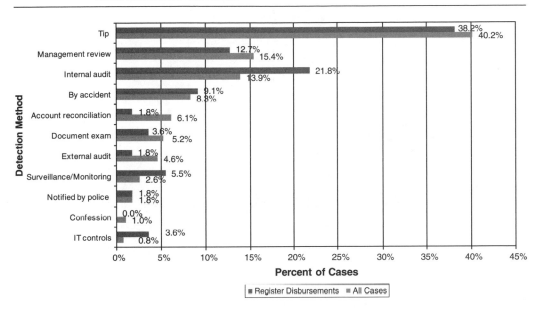

disbursement schemes in our study were perpetrated by employees, as dishonest managers and owners/executives generally utilize more sophisticated means of pilfering organizational cash. (See Exhibit 6.5.)

The trend of median losses for register disbursement cases based on perpetrator position was consistent with the trend for losses in all cases in our study, as shown in Exhibit 6.6. That is, as the position of the principal perpetrator rose within the organization, the monetary damage suffered by the organization increased.

Exhibit 6.5 *2009 Global Fraud Survey*: Perpetrators of Register Disbursement Schemes

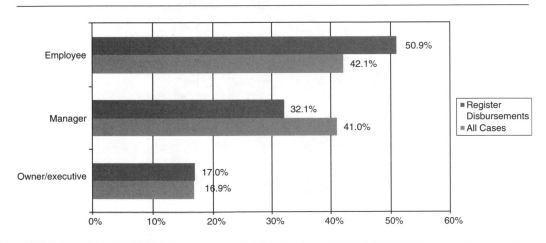

Exhibit 6.6 *2009 Global Fraud Survey*: **Median Loss by Perpetrator of Register Disbursement Schemes**

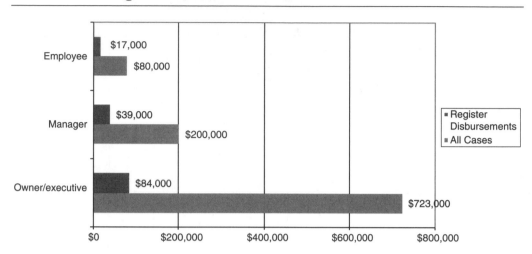

Victims of Register Disbursement Schemes

Of the 51 reported cases of fraudulent register disbursements for which size information about the victim organization was provided, one-quarter occurred at an organization with over 10,000 employees. Nearly a third of the cases occurred in small organizations with less than 100 employees. (See Exhibit 6.7.)

Exhibit 6.7 *2009 Global Fraud Survey*: **Size of Victim in Register Disbursement Schemes**

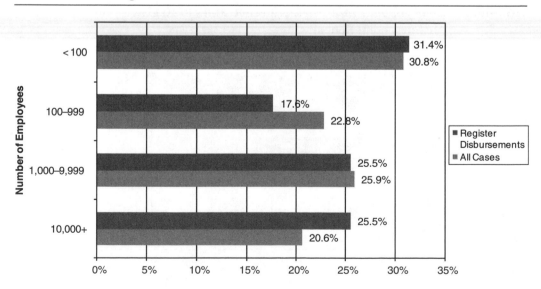

Exhibit 6.8   *2009 Global Fraud Survey*: **Median Loss by Size of Victim in Register Disbursement Schemes**

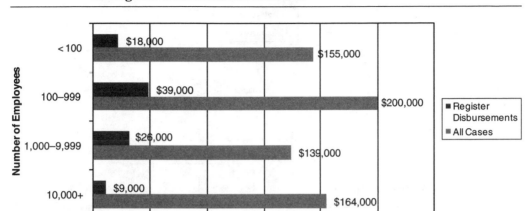

As Exhibit 6.8 shows, the median losses due to register disbursement schemes were much smaller for organizations of all sizes than the median losses from all the occupational fraud cases in our study. Additionally, the median loss from fraudulent register disbursements for the largest organizations was the smallest of all the categories, at $9,000.

FALSE REFUNDS

A refund is processed at the register when a customer returns an item of merchandise purchased from that store. The transaction that is entered on the register indicates that the merchandise is being replaced in the store's inventory and that the purchase price is being returned to the customer. In other words, a refund shows a disbursement of money from the register as the customer gets money back. (See Exhibit 6.9.)

Fictitious Refunds

In a fictitious refund scheme, a fraudster processes a transaction as if a customer were returning merchandise, even though no actual return takes place. Two things result from this fraudulent transaction. First, the fraudster takes cash from the register in the amount of the false return. Since the register tape shows that a merchandise return has been made, the disbursement appears legitimate. The register tape balances with the amount of money in the register, because the money that was taken by the fraudster is supposed to have been removed, given to a customer as a refund. These kinds of fraudulent transactions were used by Bob Walker in the case study.

As we also saw in that case study, the second thing that happens in a fictitious refund scheme is that a debit is made to the inventory system showing that the merchandise has been returned to the inventory. Because the transaction is fictitious, no merchandise

Exhibit 6.9 False Refunds

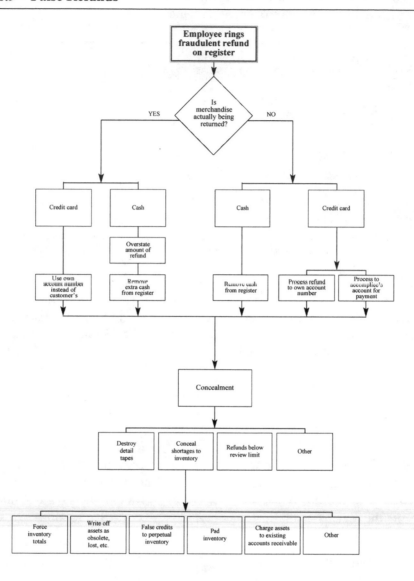

actually is returned. As a result, the company's inventory is overstated. In one case, a manager created $5,500 worth of false returns, resulting in a large shortage in the company's inventory. He was able to carry on his scheme for several months, however, because inventory was not counted regularly and because the perpetrator, a manager, was one of the people who performed inventory counts.

Overstated Refunds

Rather than create an entirely fictitious refund, some fraudsters merely overstate the amount of a legitimate refund and steal the excess money. This occurred in a case in which an employee sought to supplement his income by processing fraudulent refunds. In some cases, he rang up fictitious refunds, making up names and phone numbers for his customers. In other instances, he added to the value of legitimate refunds, overstating the value of a real customer's refund, paying the customer the actual amount owed for the returned merchandise and keeping the excess portion of the return for himself.

Credit Card Refunds

When purchases are made with a credit card rather than cash, refunds appear as credits to the customer's credit card rather than as cash disbursements. Some fraudsters process false refunds on credit card sales in lieu of processing a normal cash transaction. One benefit of the credit card method is that the perpetrator does not have to physically take cash from the register and carry it out of the store, the most dangerous part of a typical register scheme (since managers, coworkers, or security cameras may detect the culprit in the process of removing the cash). By processing the refunds to a credit card account, a fraudster reaps an unwarranted financial gain and avoids the potential embarrassment of being caught red-handed taking cash.

In a typical credit card refund scheme, the fraudster rings up a refund on a credit card sale, although the merchandise is not actually being returned. Rather than use the customer's credit card number on the refund, the employee inserts her own. As a result, the cost of the item is credited to the perpetrator's credit card account.

A more creative and wide-ranging application of the credit card refund scheme was used by Joe Anderson in the next case study. Anderson processed merchandise refunds to the accounts of other people and in return received a portion of the refund as a kickback. Certified fraud examiner (CFE) Russ Rooker discovered Anderson's scheme, which cost Greene's department store at least $150,000. This case is also a bribery scheme because Anderson took illicit payments in exchange for creating fraudulent transactions. It serves as an excellent example of how the cash register can be used as a tool for theft.

Case Study: A Silent Crime

"A silent crime"—that's the way Russ Rooker* refers to the theft he uncovered at a Detroit-area Greene's department store. "It takes only about 30 seconds, and you can have a thousand bucks," explains the regional investigation specialist.

Joe Anderson, a 15-hour-a-week employee in that store's shoe department, was an expert at that silent crime—ringing up fictitious returns and crediting credit cards for the cash.

During his five-year tenure with the store, Anderson did this time and time again. Rooker documented at least $150,000 in losses but believes it was closer to $500,000 and wouldn't be surprised if the fraud exceeded $1 million. "We're scared to even know," he says.

This was a scam that was right up Rooker's analytical alley. At the time of the investigation, he had worked in retail security for about a decade—first as a credit

---

*Several names and details have been changed to preserve anonymity.

167

fraud investigator checking the external, or customer, side of credit card fraud. Then he went into internal investigation, searching out employee theft and fraud.

At Greene's store, records showed that the store's shoe department was losing money because it had an exceedingly high rate of returns on its shoes. Rooker decided to investigate by using his FTM formula—follow the money.

He ordered up five months of sales data for the department from ten sales terminals. Rooker had returns divided into categories of cash, proprietary credit cards (i.e., Greene's cards), and third-party credit cards such as Visa and MasterCard.

And he saw a trend. Around the twenty-eighth of each month, certain credit card numbers would be credited for a return of approximately $300. "Two hundred ninety-seven dollars and sixty cents to be exact," says Rooker. There was never a corresponding sale recorded for the returns. And each month, each credit card number was credited only once—thus, if Rooker had chosen to study only one month's data, the crime would not have been discovered.

He eventually found that one part-time employee, Joe Anderson, was crediting more than 200 credit cards belonging to 110 persons. Each week, Anderson credited $2,000 to $3,000 in returns to his friends', neighbors', and relatives' accounts. In return, Anderson was paid up to 50 percent of the credit. For instance, if a friend was running $300 short at the end of the month and still needed to make his house payment, he'd phone Anderson. According to Rooker, the word around Detroit was if you needed money, "Call Joe. Give him $150 and he'll double your money."

The friend might contact Anderson at the home he shared with his girlfriend, or he might meet Anderson at the local bar or in the back of his souped-up van. Or he might simply text him a credit card number.

Either way, the friend gave Anderson his credit card number and promised to pay him $150 for the money. Then Anderson, in 30-second increments at the cash register, punched in the credit. Next, just as rapidly, he'd phone the friend and tell him the deal was done. Finally, the friend would go to the nearest ATM, swipe through his credit card, and—knowing that he had a $300 credit to his account—get $300 in cash.

"So it was basically turning the money right into cash," says Rooker. "You can see the drug connection here." Yet a drug connection was never actually proven. What was proven, to quote Rooker, was that a man who "worked fifteen hours a week at Greene's was living the high life. He dressed like a million bucks. He ate at fancy restaurants." And he wore lots of gold jewelry—and drove a "fully decked out" conversion van.

The majority of his "customers" looked as though they lived an upper-middle-class life too, but appearances can be deceiving. Most of them were in the lower-income bracket—Anderson had helped them move up. Sometimes he gave them a $300 pair of shoes to go along with their $300 credit; that way, they could go to another Greene's location, return the shoes, and get an additional $300. One customer was credited $30,000 in one year, says Rooker.

One regular customer was Anderson's girlfriend, who owned the house in which the two lived. And although she worked as a branch manager for a major bank in Detroit, she was not prosecuted; the Secret Service and the U.S. Attorney, whom Rooker called into the investigation upon his discovery of the perpetrator, decided who was prosecuted.

Anderson was well known by many; he had friends and acquaintances just about everywhere. The 15-hour-a-week employee with the big, illegal income was a mover and shaker of sorts. Rooker thinks that was part of Anderson's motive— Anderson hung out with the upper middle class and was well accepted in their stratum. He wanted to stay in that social group, but the only way he could find to do that was to commit fraud.

Rooker also believes that Anderson simply got "caught up in it" because people came to expect the fraud of him. In fact, they came directly into the store and asked for Anderson: Only he could wait on them. Those people were often the ones to whom he gave a pair of shoes as well.

The Secret Service told Rooker that if he would document a minimum of $10,000 in returns via video surveillance, they would go from there. So Rooker had video surveillance equipment installed throughout the shoe department and at the point-of-sale registers. The first day the equipment was up and running, Anderson was up and running as well; he credited $5,000 that day.

According to Rooker, Anderson simply reached into the inside pocket of his expensive suit jacket, pulled out a list, and started ringing up credits. One day he gave a single customer a $300 cash refund, a $300 credit refund, and a $300 pair of shoes.

This wreaked havoc on the Greene's inventory. Let's say the store's inventory reports showed that there were 10 pairs of style 8730 in stock. But then along came Anderson, ringing up a return for style 8730. Suddenly the inventory reports showed 11 pairs of style 8730 in stock, even though there were still only the original 10 pairs.

Five thousand dollars of returns in one day caused inventory to be overstated by approximately 17 pairs of shoes. Seventeen pairs of shoes, five workdays a week, 4.3 weeks per month—and Greene's had a lot of invisible shoes in stock.

Six weeks after the start of in-store surveillance, $30,000 in losses was recorded on videotape—put another way, that's 100 pairs of nonexistent shoes that were falsely reported as in stock.

Most of those losses were documented at the end of each month, because by then, Anderson's customers were in a typical end-of-the-month money crunch. "They came to really depend on this money," explains Rooker.

The CFE next started matching customers to credit card numbers. That was easy to do with the Greene's cards, but it was a slightly harder task for the third-party cards, which were responsible for the majority of the returns.

By working his professional connections, Rooker was able to contact fraud investigators at various banks to find out informally "what was going on" from the banks' perspectives. That's how he learned that some of Anderson's customers were the man's friends and relatives.

Ironically, the part-time employee never had his own credit card. He was a cash-only customer. His only known asset was his conversion van. As mentioned, the house he shared with his girlfriend was held in her name.

The Secret Service put Anderson under surveillance. Over two weeks, they discovered how he was making his contacts. All day long, friends, relatives, and neighbors streamed in and out of the home he shared with his banker girlfriend. In essence, his 15-hour-a-week job demanded more than 15 hours a week. And often the same people who were observed going into his home received credits that same day.

Anderson had apparently started his "side" job as a bit of a lark and charged only 10 percent of the fictitious refund as his fee. As the scam and his renown grew, he upped his percentage to 25, then 50 percent. Everyone in town and everyone in the shoe department knew he was doing something fishy, reports Rooker, but they were scared to report him. Anderson allegedly carried a gun. And although many liked Anderson, many also feared him.

But that did not deter Rooker and the Secret Service. "The Secret Service was very aggressive," he explains.

Its agents promised to pursue any co-conspirator who had earned at least $5,000 in returns over two years. That led the agents to Ohio, where they interviewed a middle-age couple. (Most of Anderson's customers were between the ages of 30 and 50.)

This couple had once lived in the Detroit area. After getting them to turn state's evidence (as the Secret Service did with numerous co-conspirators during this investigation), the law enforcement officers learned Anderson's entire scam.

Soon thereafter, four armed U.S. Secret Service agents entered the store, grabbed Anderson, pulled him through the stockroom, and arrested him. When confronted with the crime, Anderson told the agents and Rooker, "Pound sand." He had $5,000 in cash stuffed into his socks. In his coat pocket, he had a list of 15 third-party credit card numbers with dollar amounts to credit.

Having those 15 numbers on his person, says Rooker, was enough to charge the perpetrator. Eventually, though, Rooker learned that $60,000 in refunds had been credited to those 15 numbers over the previous two years.

Anderson was led through the mall, in handcuffs, by the Secret Service. As he exited, mall store manager after store manager stood at their doors and yelled, "Hey, Joe, what's going on?"

They were worried. They were losing one of their best cash customers.

Local and federal charges for embezzlement and financial transaction card fraud against Anderson and 27 conspirators are pending.

Not pending are new internal controls at Greene's. Rooker implemented them immediately. Over time, another 50 to 60 employees were determined to be pulling off the same scam, at losses of $10,000 to $30,000 to Greene's. The only difference was that these employees were crediting their own charge cards; Anderson credited other people's charge cards, silently, in 30-second increments.

FALSE VOIDS

Fictitious voids are similar to refund schemes in that they generate a disbursement from the register. When a sale is voided on a register, a copy of the customer's receipt usually is attached to a void slip, along with the signature or initials of a manager that indicate that the transaction has been approved. (See Exhibit 6.10.) In order to process a false void, then, the first thing fraudsters need is the customer's copy of the sales receipt. Typically, when employees set about processing a fictitious void, they simply withhold the customer's receipt at the time of the sale. If the customer requests the receipt, the clerks can produce it, but in many cases customers simply do not notice that they did not receive a receipt.

With the customer copy of the receipt in hand, the culprits ring a voided sale. Whatever money the customer paid for the item is removed from the register as if it were being returned to a customer. The copy of the customer's receipt is attached to the void slip to verify the authenticity of the transaction.

Before the voided sale will be perceived as valid, it generally must be approved by a manager. In many of the cases in our studies, the manager in question simply neglected to verify the authenticity of the voided sale. Such managers signed essentially anything presented to them, leaving themselves vulnerable to a voided sales scheme. An example of this kind of managerial nonchalance occurred in a case where a retail clerk kept customer receipts and ''voided'' their sales after the customers left the store; the store manager signed the void slips on these transactions without taking any action to verify their authenticity. A similar breakdown in review was detected in another case where an employee processed fraudulent voids, kept customer receipts, and presented them to her supervisors for review at the end of her shift, long after the alleged transactions had taken place. Her supervisors approved the voided sales, and the accounts receivable department failed to notice the excessive number of voided sales processed by this employee.

It was not a coincidence that the perpetrators of these crimes presented their void slips to a manager who was lackadaisical about authorizing them. Generally, such managers are essential to the employee's schemes.

Because not all managers are willing to provide rubber-stamp approval of voided sales, some employees take affirmative steps to get their voided sales ''approved.'' This usually amounts to forgery, as in the retail clerk case whereby the fraudster eventually began forging his supervisor's signature as his false voids became more and more frequent.

Finally, it is possible that a manager will conspire with a register employee and approve false voids in return for a share of the proceeds. Although we did not encounter any cases like this in our studies, we did come across several examples of managers helping employees to falsify time cards or expense reimbursement requests. There is no logical reason why the same kind of scheme would not work with false voids.

CONCEALING REGISTER DISBURSEMENTS

As discussed, when a false refund or void is entered into the register, two things happen. First, the employee who is committing the fraud removes cash from the register; second, the item allegedly being returned is debited back into the inventory. This

Exhibit 6.10   False Voids

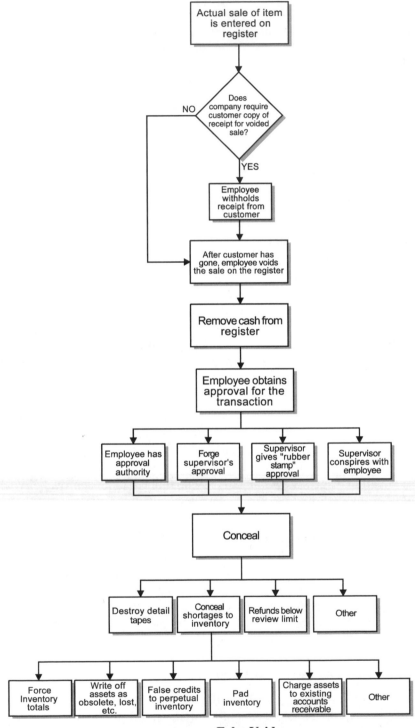

False Voids

leads to shrinkage: a situation in which there is less inventory actually on hand than the inventory records reflect. A certain amount of shrinkage is expected in any retail industry, but too much shrinkage raises concerns of fraud. It is therefore in the fraudster's best interests to conceal the appearance of shrinkage on the books.

Remember: Inventory is essentially accounted for by a two-step process. The first part of the process is the perpetual inventory, which is essentially a running tabulation of how much inventory *should be on hand*. When a sale of merchandise is made, the perpetual inventory is credited to remove this merchandise from the records; the amount of merchandise that should be on hand is reduced. Periodically, someone from the company takes a physical count of the inventory, going through the stockroom or warehouse and counting the amount of inventory that *is actually on hand*. The two figures then are compared to see if there is a discrepancy between the perpetual inventory (what should be on hand) and the physical inventory (what is on hand).

In register disbursement schemes, shrinkage often is concealed by overstating inventory during the physical count, especially if taking inventory is one of the fraudster's duties. The fraudster simply overstates the amount of inventory on hand so it matches the perpetual inventory. For a more detailed analysis of methods used to conceal inventory shrinkage, see Chapter 9.

Small Disbursements

Another way for employees to avoid detection in a refund scheme is to keep the sizes of the disbursements low. Many companies set limits below which management review of a refund is not required. When this is the case, fraudsters simply process copious numbers of refunds that are small enough that they need not be reviewed. In one example, an employee created over 1,000 false refunds, all under the review limit of $15. Eventually he was caught because he began processing refunds before store hours; another employee noticed that refunds were appearing on the system before the store opened. Nevertheless, before his scheme was detected, the employee made off with over $11,000 of his employer's money.

Destroying Records

As with many kinds of fraud, one final means of concealing a register scheme is to destroy all records of the transaction. Most concealment methods are concerned with keeping management from realizing that fraud has occurred. When employees resort to destroying records, however, they typically have conceded that management will discover the theft. The purpose of destroying records is usually to prevent management from determining who the thief is. In one case, a woman was creating false inventory vouchers that were reflected on the register tape. She then discarded all refund vouchers, both legitimate and fraudulent. Because documentation was missing on all transactions, it was extremely difficult to distinguish the good from the bad. Thus, it was hard to determine who was stealing.

DETECTION

Fictitious Refunds or Voided Sales

Fictitious refunds or voided sales often can be detected by closely examining the documentation submitted with the cash receipts.

- *Evaluate the refunds or discounts given by each cashier or salesperson.* This analysis may point out that a single employee or group of employees has a higher incidence of refunds or discounts than others. Further examination is then necessary to determine if the refunds are appropriate and properly documented.
- *Hang signs in the register area asking customers to ask for and examine their receipts use the customer as part of the internal control system.* This helps ensure that the cashier or salesperson is accounting for the sale properly and prevents employees from using customer receipts as support for false voids or refunds.
- *Make random service calls to customers who have returned merchandise or voided sales to verify the legitimacy of transactions.*

Register Scheme Red Flags

- There is inappropriate employee segregation of duties. For example, the cashier should not perform register counting and reconciling.
- Cashiers, rather than supervisors, have access to the control keys that are necessary for refunds and voids.
- Register employees have authority to void their own transactions.
- Register refunds are not methodically reviewed.
- Multiple cashiers operate from a single cash drawer without separate access codes.
- Personal checks from the cashier are found in register.
- Voided transactions are not documented properly or not approved by a supervisor.
- Voided cash receipt forms (manual systems) or supporting documents for voided transactions (cash register systems) are not retained on file.
- There are missing or obviously altered register tapes.
- There are gaps in the sequence of transactions on register tape.
- There is an inordinate number of refunds, voids, or no-sales on register tape.
- Inventory totals appear forced.
- There are multiple refunds or voids for amounts just under the review limit.

PREVENTION

- Review the segregation of duties of key employees who staff the register as well as the duties of their supervisors.
- Ensure that employees responsible for recording incoming cash are informed of their responsibilities and are properly supervised as cash is received.

- An employee other than the register worker should be responsible for preparing register count sheets and agreeing them to register totals.
- Complete register documentation and cash must be delivered to the appropriate personnel in a timely manner.
- Cash thefts sometimes are revealed by customers who have paid money on an account and have not received credit or, in some cases, who have been credited for an amount that does not agree with the payment they have made. Complaints and inquiries also are received frequently from banks.
- Access to the register must be closely monitored, and access codes must be kept secure.
- Analyze the quantity of refunds to detect multiple small refunds.
- Communicate and adhere to company policy of performing unannounced cash counts.
- Maintain supervision over the cash register area.
- Review supporting documents for voided and refunded transactions for propriety (i.e., legitimacy and approvals).
- Review the numerical sequence and completeness of cash register tapes.

CHAPTER 7

Billing Schemes

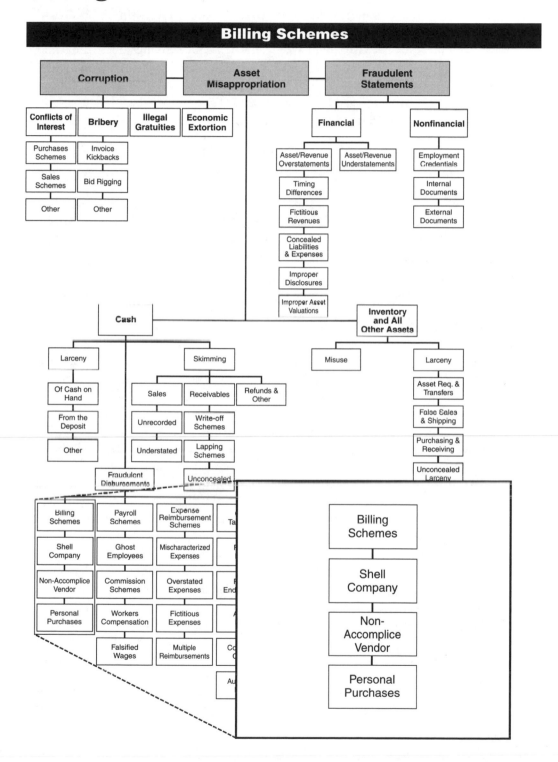

Case Study: Medical School Treats Fraud and Abuse

Fraud seemed to plague a certain southeastern medical college, with one bad case erupting after another. One supervisor's minor transgression opened a Pandora's box of fraud perpetrated by his assistant. It all began when Bruce Livingstone,* a married supervisor at the college's three-person business office, took his girlfriend on a business trip using school funds drawn from a suspense account (a temporary account in which entries of credits or charges are made until their proper disposition can be determined). Livingstone did not submit an expense report to offset the charges that month, a violation of a policy governing the college's extensive travel budget.

Once officials realized that employees had grown lax about submitting timely expense reports, they attempted to reconcile the suspense account by requiring employees to settle their own accounts before receiving their paychecks.

Not wanting his indiscretion revealed, Livingstone had to disguise the additional expense of taking his girlfriend on a business trip. He submitted a phony expense report in which he unwisely named a female senior auditor at the college as his traveling partner. He forged the auditor's signature on a letter that stated she had participated.

As luck would have it, the unsuspecting auditor herself reviewed the bogus report. She was quite surprised to find she'd taken a trip with Livingstone. She immediately informed Harold Dore, the director of internal audit for the institution, of the forgery. Dore alerted others.

Following a short interview with college officials, Livingstone admitted his wrongdoing and was promptly terminated. The executive vice president authorized Dore to conduct a full fraud examination. As they were soon to find out, they had not seen the worst of it yet. Livingstone's amorous business trip was just the tip of the iceberg.

"Whenever there's fraud found here," said Dore, "I automatically conduct what I call a 'magnitude investigation.'" He has learned that perpetrators rarely limit themselves to the fraud initially uncovered: "Chances are, they did something else."

As part of the information-gathering portion of his investigation, Dore decided to interview Cheryl Brown, the 30-year-old administrative assistant who had worked under Livingstone for three years. The interview was to be conducted with the dean of the dental school president, so Dore headed across campus toward the business office.

But Brown left before Dore arrived. She told coworkers that her uncle had been shot and that she had to depart for California immediately. In her haste to get away, she even left her paycheck behind.

Taking that as a sign, Dore immediately sealed the empty office Brown and Livingstone shared and began searching its contents. The search uncovered bags of expensive dental tools and prostheses, which it turned out Livingstone had been illegally selling to dental students for years.

Knowing vendor kickbacks are common—and since one of the main functions of the business office was to process invoices submitted by vendors—Dore started

---

*Several names and details have been changed to preserve anonymity.

178

by reviewing the master file. The list had never been purged and contained tens of thousands of names—all the vendors who had ever supplied goods and services as part of the college's annual budget of $55 million. He selected 50 vendors, deliberately choosing those without a phone number or street address.

Then Dore took his list to the next stop in the payment process, the accounts payable department. After methodically pulling all corresponding documentation, he quickly focused on one vendor: Armstrong Supply Company. It regularly billed two or three times a month for strange items named but unknown by Dore, and always for amounts under $4,500, thus eliminating the necessity of two authorized signatures. All of the request-for-funds forms attached to the invoices either bore the signature of Livingstone or the dean of the dental school. Furthermore, Dore could find no vendor application on file for Armstrong Supply. He also failed to find any competitive bidding process in place.

"Once I looked at the actual invoices, that really got me going," said the fraud examiner. Some carried invoice numbers; others did not, but they did carry a four-digit post office box number. (Subsequent research revealed that postal authorities had switched to five-digit and six-digit PO boxes years earlier.) Billed items included such things as "3 dozen TPM pins" (the identity of which baffled even the longtime stockroom manager).

"The invoices just smelled fake," said Dore, who packs more than 20 years of auditing experience. What's more, he later found blank invoices for Armstrong Supply in one of Brown's desk drawers. He even noticed one completed invoice that had been readied for submission. (Apparently, Brown left in too much of a hurry to dispose of the smoking gun.)

Based on those questionable invoices, the accounts payable department would issue a check for the stated amount. On the request-for-funds forms attached, Brown always indicated that she would personally present the check to Armstrong Supply. (Due to lax controls, vendors and employees were allowed to pick up checks.) Canceled checks revealed that a man named Claude Armstrong III cashed them at various check-cashing services, which sometimes called Cheryl Brown for additional verification, as noted on the backs of the checks.

Further research showed yet another scam, according to Dore. The office mail contained a department store gift card with a note from a vendor to Brown, thanking her for her recent business. The California vendor had billed the college for roughly $42,000 worth of copy machine cartridges—running $4,500 apiece—and Brown had processed the invoices. After a fruitless search for this valuable cache in the school's storerooms and copy centers, Dore called local dealers and discovered that their most expensive cartridge cost only $483. Under his direction, private investigators located the vendor's "corporate headquarters" in a rental unit at a retail postal center, but the college abandoned its long-distance pursuit of recovery when it proved too costly.

Although Dore tried to keep his three-month-long investigation quiet, the campus buzzed with news of his activities. Brown's many friends, including two in the accounts payable department, kept her abreast of his movements.

Next Dore pulled in Livingstone for a chat about the new evidence supporting vendor fraud and kickbacks as well as his backroom sale of orthodontic supplies. According to Dore, it became apparent during the interview that the philanderer knew nothing about the vendor schemes. Brown had perpetrated the $63,000 vendor fraud without Livingstone's help. He seemed quite taken aback that it had occurred under his nose by someone he trusted so much. In some cases, Brown had forged the signatures of her supervisor and the dean of the dental school. In others, the unwitting bosses actually signed the bogus forms.

At the same time the Livingstone interview was being conducted, the school's general counsel received a call from Brown's lawyer. "He asked if we had ever given leniency to an errant employee in the past, if he were to admit to everything," said Dore. Once the general counsel deemed it a possibility, they scheduled a meeting for September. It was to be attended by both attorneys, Dore, the executive vice president of the college, and Brown, who had never returned to work since her hasty departure. Her lawyer also relayed her request to bring along a friend as a character witness, a nurse for whom she had once worked and who could attest to the good nature of this unmarried mother supporting three small children.

Brown was quiet and cooperative at the meeting. Dore took her through his voluminous file folder on Armstrong Supply, the sham company she had created. She willingly identified each and every document that detailed her duplicity, which had begun five months after her hire. Dire cash emergencies prompted the first few deceptions, she said. As Brown realized how easy it was in light of the weak controls, her confidence grew and she stepped up her thefts with no signs of stopping. "It became addictive, in her words," recalled Dore.

To illustrate her need, she explained that her husband had developed a drug and alcohol problem and that she had been dragged into drug abuse as well. She claimed that after she had become addicted, her husband abandoned her and the small children. She then broke down and cried, the first of many times during the interview. Brown went on to point out that she was seeing a doctor for her addictive behavior. When Dore asked how long she had been seeing her doctor, "She said her first visit was going to be next week." (Months later, a casual conversation between Dore and a coworker who had once dated Brown raised doubts about her excuses. "He swore she never touched drugs or alcohol," said Dore.)

She said her accomplice, Claude Armstrong III, was a friend with a history of drug abuse. (Background checks showed an arrest and conviction on drug charges for Armstrong; Brown had no prior arrests or convictions, and her references proved favorable.) She also admitted that her cover story about the uncle in California was fabricated.

After Brown expressed remorse over the fake invoices, Dore asked her about her relationship with the phony cartridge supply firm. She totally disavowed any knowledge of that scam. She insisted that the invoices were legitimate and the cartridges were stacked in a storeroom. (Note: No one has found the cartridges to date.)

Even without owning up to the recent $42,000 cartridge scam, Brown seemed surprised to learn that her Armstrong Supply fraud had netted $63,000 over two years.

Given the small percentage of the annual budget that was pilfered, college officials were not surprised that the fraud went undetected by the Big Four firm that served as their external auditor. Their contract stated that "audit tests are not all-inclusive and not designed to find fraud," a disclaimer that auditors rely on to absolve them from possible culpability. "If they were that detailed, nobody could afford an external audit," said Dore, also a certified internal auditor.

Looking back, he saw that some good stemmed from the frauds. Since then, the college has instituted much stronger controls and makes sure to enforce them. Dore said tales of his dogged investigation enhanced respect for the audit function, "[a]nd probably instilled a bit of fear among the 4,500 employees, because the college officials did pursue a criminal prosecution against Brown."

During the course of her trial, the district attorney informed Dore that his testimony was not needed, even though it would have shown hell-bent intent on the part of the defendant. With her lawyer acting on her behalf, Brown struck a deal with the prosecutor. She was placed on probation and ordered to pay partial restitution. (Brown was found three-fourths culpable and Armstrong one-fourth. Because half of the stolen funds came from federal grants, $30,000 was charged off to the federal granting authority.)

As part of the deal, Brown was also sentenced to six months' house arrest—with exceptions granted for her to attend work and church.

OVERVIEW

The asset misappropriation schemes discussed up to this point—skimming, larceny, check tampering, and register schemes—all require the perpetrator of the scheme to physically take cash or checks from the employer. In the typical cash larceny, skimming, or register scheme, the perpetrator pockets cash—in the form of currency and checks—and carries it off company premises. In the check tampering schemes, an employee takes a check and prepares it in such a way that she is able to convert her employer's funds to her own use.

In this and the next chapter, we discuss a different kind of asset misappropriation scheme, one that allows perpetrators to misappropriate company funds without ever actually handling cash or checks while at work. These schemes attack the cash disbursements and payables cycle and are loosely called *bogus claims*, for they succeed by making a false claim for payment on the victim company. The bogus claims schemes induce victim companies to issue fraudulent payments for goods or services that they have not received. This group consists of *billing schemes* (which assail the purchasing function of a company), *payroll schemes*, and *employee-expense reimbursement schemes*. The most common such scheme is the billing scheme.

Exhibit 7.1   *2009 Global Fraud Survey*: **Frequency of Fraudulent Disbursements**

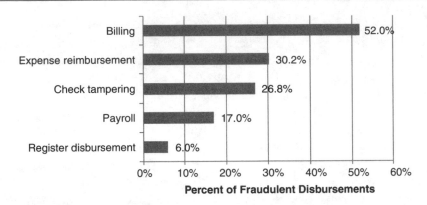

Percent of Fraudulent Disbursements

BILLING SCHEME DATA FROM ACFE *2009 GLOBAL FRAUD SURVEY*

Frequency and Cost

Among the fraudulent disbursement categories, billing schemes were most commonly reported in the *2009 Global Fraud Survey*. Of 921 reported fraudulent disbursement cases, 52 percent involved billing fraud. (The sum of these percentages exceeds 100 percent because some cases involved multiple fraud schemes that fell into more than one category. Various charts in this chapter may reflect percentages that total in excess of 100 percent for similar reasons.) Billing schemes were also the second most costly form of fraudulent disbursement, with a reported median loss of $128,000. (See Exhibits 7.1 and 7.2.)

Of the 316 billing scheme cases in which a dollar loss was reported, 54 percent of these caused losses of at least $100,000, and almost 20 percent caused losses of at least $1 million. The distribution of median losses from billing scheme cases closely

Exhibit 7.2   *2009 Global Fraud Survey*: **Median Loss of Fraudulent Disbursements**

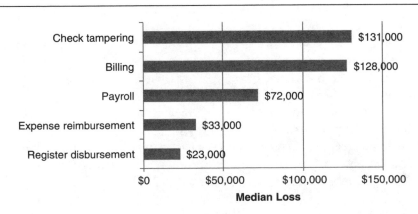

Median Loss

Exhibit 7.3   *2009 Global Fraud Survey*: **Dollar Loss Distribution for Billing Schemes**

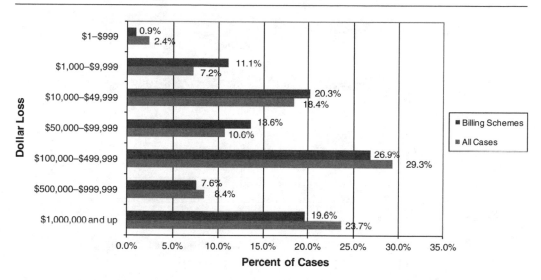

resembled the distribution of median losses for all of the occupational frauds in our study. (See Exhibit 7.3.)

Detection of Billing Schemes

The most common method of detection for billing schemes was through tips, which was cited in 38.9 percent of the billing fraud cases we reviewed. Detection through management review was also cited in almost 20 percent of billing schemes. (See Exhibit 7.4.)

Exhibit 7.4   *2009 Global Fraud Survey*: **Detection of Billing Schemes**

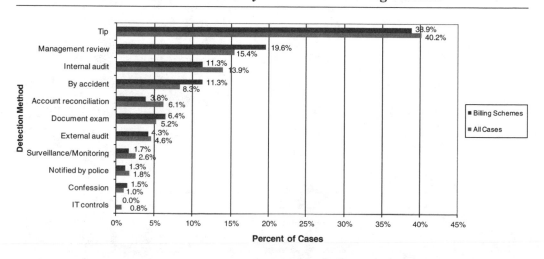

Exhibit 7.5 *2009 Global Fraud Survey*: **Perpetrators of Billing Schemes**

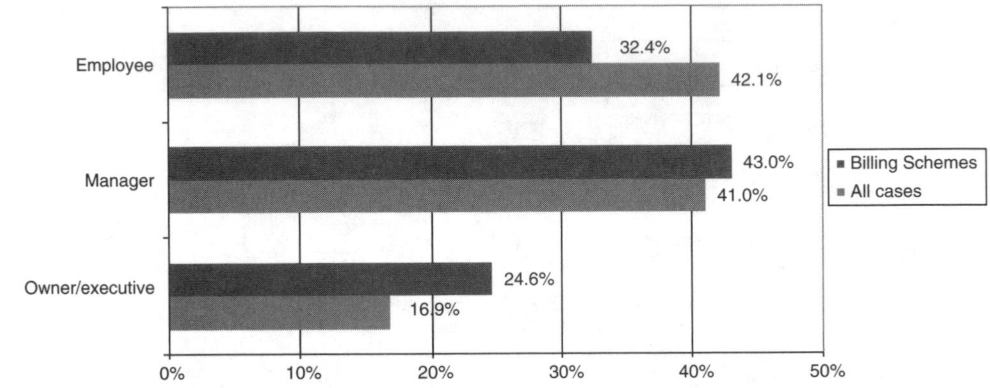

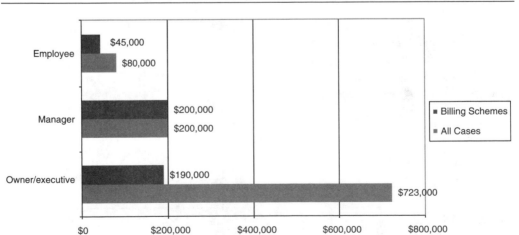

Perpetrators of Billing Schemes

Of 451 billing schemes in which the job position of the perpetrator was identified, 32.4 percent were committed by employees, 43 percent were committed by managers, and 24.6 percent were committed by owner/executives. (See Exhibit 7.5.)

The median loss in billing schemes committed by employees was $45,000, which was less than one-quarter the median loss caused by higher-level perpetrators. Managers and owner/executives who undertook billing schemes caused median losses of $200,000 and $190,000, respectively. (See Exhibit 7.6.)

Victims of Billing Schemes

Exhibit 7.7 shows the breakdown of billing cases in our study based on the number of employees in the victim organization. This distribution is fairly similar to the overall distribution.

Exhibit 7.6 *2009 Global Fraud Survey*: **Median Loss by Perpetrator of Billing Schemes**

Exhibit 7.7 *2009 Global Fraud Survey*: Size of Victim in Billing Schemes

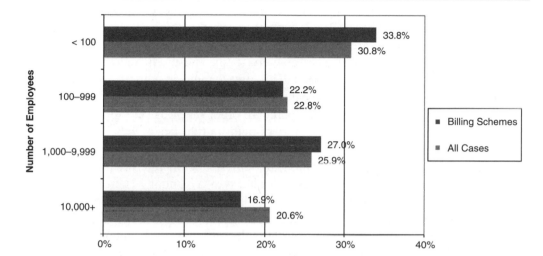

The median losses associated with billing fraud cases based on the size of the victim organization are illustrated in Exhibit 7.8. The median loss for billing schemes exceeded the median loss for all cases in organizations with more than 10,000 employees.

There are three main types of billing schemes:

1. Invoicing via shell companies
2. Invoicing via nonaccomplice vendors
3. Personal purchases with company funds

Exhibit 7.8 *2009 Global Fraud Survey*: Median Loss by Size
of Victim in Billing Schemes

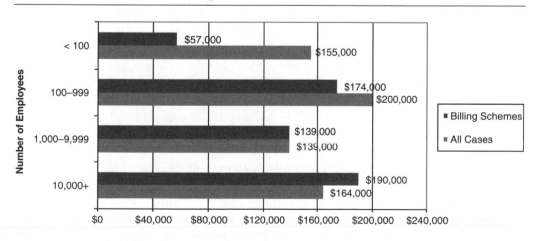

CASH-GENERATING SCHEMES

In a cash-generating scheme, an employee creates false vouchers or submits false invoices to the employer. These false documents cause the employer to issue payments for goods or services that are either fictitious or overstated in price. The perpetrator then collects the fraudulent checks and converts them. These schemes are distinct from the purchases schemes (to be discussed later in this chapter) in which an employee buys personal goods or services at her company's expense.

A *voucher* is a file that includes the purchase order that was sent to the vendor, the vendor invoice listing the cost and quantity of items purchased, and the internal receiving reports that verify that purchased items have been delivered. In the typical purchasing cycle, a completed voucher containing all of these documents is required before the accounts payable department will issue a check to a vendor. Therefore, a billing scheme might necessitate the falsification or alteration of any of these documents.

In general, cash-generating billing schemes are built around invoices from shell companies or employee-owned businesses. In other circumstances, a corrupt employee may utilize invoices from legitimate vendors to generate fraudulent disbursements.

INVOICING VIA SHELL COMPANIES

Forming a Shell Company

Shell companies, for the purposes of this book, are fictitious entities created for the sole purpose of committing fraud. As we saw in the case study at the beginning of this chapter, they may be nothing more than a fabricated name and a post office box that an employee uses to collect disbursements from false billings. However, since the payments received will be payable to the shell company, the perpetrator normally will also set up a bank account in the new company's name, listing himself as an authorized signer on the account. (See Exhibit 7.9.)

In order to open a bank account for a shell company, a fraudster will probably have to present the bank with a certificate of incorporation or an assumed-name certificate. A company obtains these documents through a state or local government. These documents can be forged, but it is more likely that the perpetrator will simply file the requisite paperwork and obtain legitimate documents from the state or county. This usually can be accomplished for a small fee, the cost of which can be more than offset by a successful fraud scheme.

If it is discovered that a company is being falsely billed by a vendor, examiners for the victim company may try to trace the ownership of the vendor. The documents used to start a bank account in a shell company's name sometimes can assist examiners in determining who is behind the fraudulent billings. If the corrupt employee formed the shell company under his own name, a search of public records at the local court house may reveal him as the fraudster.

For this reason, corrupt employees sometimes form shell companies in the name of someone other than themselves. In one instance an employee stole approximately $1 million from his company via false billings submitted from a shell company set up in his wife's name. Using a spouse's name adds a buffer of security to an employee's

Exhibit 7.9   False Billing from Shell Companies

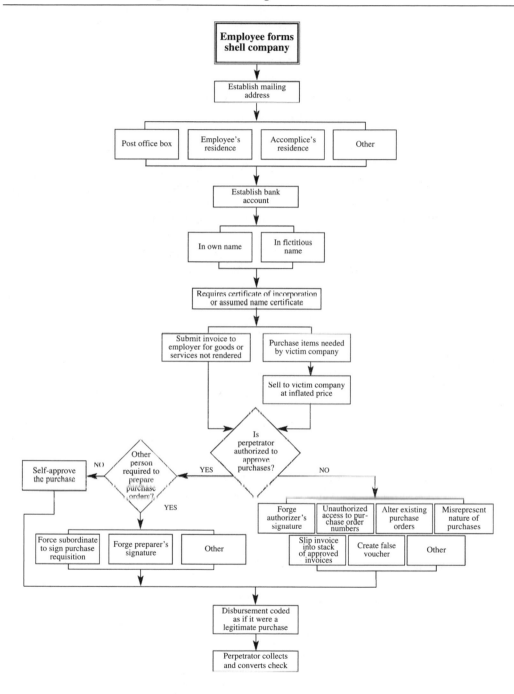

fraud scheme. When a male employee sets up a shell company, he sometimes does so in his wife's maiden name to further distance himself from the fictitious company.

A more effective way for fraudsters to hide connections to a false company is to form the company under a fictitious name. Take the case where an employee used a coworker's identification to form a shell vendor. The fraudster then proceeded to bill the employer for approximately $20,000 in false services. The resulting checks were deposited in the account of the shell company, and currency was withdrawn from the account through an automated teller machine.

The other issue involved in forming a shell company is the entity's address—the place where fraudulent checks will be collected. Often employees rent a post office box and list it as the mailing address of the shell company. Some employees list their home address instead. In one case, a department head set up a dummy company using his residence as the mailing address. Over a two-year period, this man submitted over $250,000 worth of false invoices. Eventually the scheme was detected by a newly hired clerk. The clerk was processing an invoice when she noticed that the address of the vendor was the same as her boss's address. (By a lucky coincidence, the clerk had typed a personal letter for her boss earlier that day and remembered his address.) Had the department head used a PO box instead of his home address on the invoices, his scheme might have continued indefinitely.

One reason employees might be hesitant to use PO boxes in shell company schemes is that some businesses are especially wary of sending checks to vendors that do not have street addresses. PO box addresses can signal fraud. For this reason, fraudsters may use the address of a relative, friend, or accomplice as a collection point for fraudulent checks.

Submitting False Invoices

Once a shell company is formed and a bank account has been opened, corrupt employees are in a position to begin billing the employer. Invoices can be manufactured by various means—a professional printer, a personal computer, or a typewriter. As we saw in the case study at the beginning of this chapter, false invoices do not always have to be of professional quality to generate fraudulent disbursements. The phony invoices Cheryl Brown used to bill from Armstrong Supply Company ''just smelled fake,'' according to Harold Dore, yet they were sufficient to generate checks.

Self-Approval of Fraudulent Invoices

The difficulty in a shell company scheme usually is not in producing the invoices but in getting the victim company to pay them. Authorization for the fictitious purchase (and therefore payment of the bill) is the key. In a large percentage of the shell company cases in our study, fraudsters were in a position to approve payment on the very invoices they were fraudulently submitting. In one example, a manager authorized payment of $6 million worth of phony invoices from a dummy company he had formed. Similarly, an employee in another case set up a bogus freight company and personally approved $50,000 worth of bogus invoices from it. It is only logical that those with authority to approve purchases would be among the most likely to engage in billing schemes, since they have fewer hurdles to overcome than other employees.

A slight twist to this method was used in a case where the victim organization properly required vouchers to be prepared and approved by different persons. The fraudster in this case had approval authority but was not allowed to prepare the vouchers that he approved. Therefore, he created false vouchers and forged a coworker's initials as the preparer. Then the perpetrator approved the voucher for payment under his own authority. It appeared that two employees had signed off on the voucher as mandated by the organization's controls.

Not all companies require the completion of payment vouchers before they will issue payments. In some enterprises, payments are issued based on less formal procedures. In one example, the chief executive officer of a nonprofit company simply submitted "check requests" to the accounting department. As the CEO, his "requests" obviously carried great weight in the organization. The company issued checks to whatever company was listed on the request in whatever amount was specified. The CEO used these forms to obtain over $35,000 in payments for fictitious services rendered by a shell company he had formed. In this case, invoices were not even required to authorize the payments. The check request forms simply listed the payee, the amount, and a brief narrative regarding the reason for the check. It was so easy for the CEO to generate fraudulent disbursements that he eventually had three separate companies billing the victim company at the same time. It is obvious that, as CEO, the fraudster in this case had a wide degree of latitude within the company and was unlikely to be obstructed by one of his subordinates. Nevertheless, this case should illustrate how the failure to require proper support for payments can lead to fraud.

"Rubber-Stamp" Supervisors

If employees cannot authorize payments themselves, the next best thing is if the person who has that authority is inattentive or overly trusting. "Rubber-stamp" supervisors like this are destined to be targeted by unethical employees. In one case, an employee set up a fake computer supply company with an accomplice and "sold" parts and services to his employer. The perpetrator's supervisor did not know much about computers and could not gauge accurately whether the invoices from the dummy company were excessive—or even necessary. The supervisor was forced to rely on the perpetrator of the scheme to verify the authenticity of the purchases. Consequently, the victim company suffered approximately $20,000 in losses.

Reliance on False Documents

When employees do not have approval authority for purchases and do not have the benefit of a rubber-stamp supervisor, they must run their vouchers through the normal accounts payable process. The success of this kind of scheme will depend on the apparent authenticity of the false voucher created. If the fraudsters can generate purchase orders and receiving reports that corroborate the information on the fraudulent invoice from the shell company, they can fool accounts payable into issuing a payment.

Collusion

Collusion among several employees sometimes is used to overcome well-designed internal controls of a victim company. For example, in a company with proper separation of duties, the functions of purchasing goods or services, authorizing the purchase, receiving the goods or services, and making the payment to the vendor should be separated. Obviously, if this process is adhered to strictly, it will be extremely difficult for any single employee to commit a false-billing scheme. As a result, we have seen schemes evolve in which several employees conspired to defeat the fraud prevention measures of their employer. In one case, a warehouse foreman and a parts ordering clerk conspired to purchase approximately $300,000 of nonexistent supplies. The parts ordering clerk initiated the false transactions by obtaining approval to place orders for parts he claimed were needed. The orders were then sent to a vendor who, acting in conjunction with the two employee fraudsters, prepared false invoices that were sent to the victim company. Meanwhile, the warehouse foreman verified receipt of the fictitious shipments of incoming supplies. The perpetrators were able to compile complete vouchers for the fraudulent purchases without overstepping their normal duties. Similarly, in a different case, three employees set up a shell company to bill their employer for services and supplies. The first employee, a clerk, was in charge of ordering parts and services. The second employee, a purchasing agent, helped authorize these orders by falsifying purchasing reports regarding comparison pricing. The clerk also was responsible for receiving the parts and services; a third conspirator, a manager in the victim company's accounts payable department, ensured that payments were issued on the fraudulent invoices.

These cases illustrate how collusion among several employees with separate duties in the purchasing process can be very difficult to detect. Even if all controls are followed, at some point a company must rely on its employees to be honest. One of the purposes of separating duties is to prevent any one person from having too much control over a particular business function; it provides a built-in monitoring mechanism whereby every person's actions are in some way verified by another person. But if *everyone* is corrupt, even proper controls can be overcome.

Purchases of Services Rather than Goods

Most of the shell company schemes in our survey involved the purchase of services rather than goods. Why is this so? The primary reason is that services are not tangible. If an employee sets up a shell company to make fictitious sales of goods to an employer, these goods will obviously never arrive. By comparing its purchases to its inventory levels, the victim company might detect the fraud. It is much more difficult for the victim company to verify that the services were never rendered. For this reason, many employees involved in shell company schemes bill their employers for things like ''consulting services.''

Pass-through Schemes

In the schemes discussed so far, the victim companies were billed for completely fictitious purchases of goods or services. This is the most common formula for a shell company fraud, but there is a subcategory of shell company schemes in which actual goods or services are sold to the victim company. These are known as pass-through schemes.

Pass-through schemes usually are undertaken by employees in charge of purchasing on behalf of the victim company. Instead of buying merchandise directly from a vendor, the employees set up a shell company and purchase the merchandise through that fictitious entity. They then resell the merchandise from the shell company to their employer at an inflated price, thereby making an unauthorized profit on the transaction.

One of the best examples of a pass-through scheme in our studies came from a case in which a department director was in charge of purchasing computer equipment. Because of his expertise on the subject and his high standing within the company, he was unsupervised in this task. The director set up a shell company in another state and bought used computers through the shell company, then turned around and sold them to his employer at a greatly exaggerated price. The money from the victim company's first installment on the computers was used to pay the shell company's debts to the real vendors. Subsequent payments were profits for the bogus company. The scheme cost the victim company over $1 million.

INVOICING VIA NONACCOMPLICE VENDORS

Pay-and-Return Schemes

Rather than use shell companies as vessels for overbilling schemes, some employees generate fraudulent disbursements by using the invoices of nonaccomplice vendors. In pay-and-return schemes, these employees do not prepare and submit the vendor's invoices; rather, they intentionally mishandle payments that are owed to the legitimate vendors. (See Exhibit 7.10.) One way to do this is to purposely double-pay an invoice. In one instance, a secretary was responsible for opening mail, processing claims, and authorizing payments. She intentionally paid some bills twice, then requested the recipients to return one of the checks. She would intercept these returned checks and deposit them into her own account.

Another way to accomplish a pay-and-return scheme is to pay the wrong vendor intentionally. This happened in a case where an accounts payable clerk deliberately put vendor checks in the wrong envelopes. After they had been mailed, she called the vendors to explain the "mistake" and requested that they return the checks to her. She deposited these checks in her own account and ran the vouchers through the accounts payable system a second time to pay the appropriate vendors.

Finally, an employee might pay the proper vendor but intentionally overpay him. In one example, an employee intentionally caused a check to be issued to a vendor for more than the invoice amount, then requested that the vendor return the excess. The fraudster deposited this money into her own account. Similarly, an employee might intentionally purchase excess merchandise, return the excess, and pocket the refund.

Overbilling with a Nonaccomplice Vendor's Invoices

In most instances where employees create fraudulent invoices to overbill their employer, they use a shell company. It is rare for employees to submit the invoice of an existing vendor. Nevertheless, in some instances, employees will undertake such a scheme by

Exhibit 7.10   Pay-and-Return Schemes

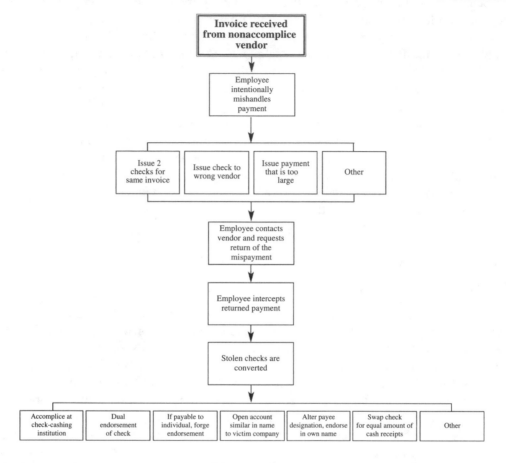

altering an existing-vendor invoice. In the next case study, Albert Miano took a copy of a contractor's invoice, replicated it, and used the resulting blank invoices to bill his employer for over $1 million worth of false work. Certified fraud examiner Terence McGrane put a stop to Miano's scheme.

Case Study: Cover Story: Internal Fraud

Sometimes fraud is discovered by chance instead of deliberate effort. In the $4 million embezzlement fraud by an employee of a magazine publisher, more than one coincidence brought down the perpetrator.

A popular magazine and large direct-mail publishing house decided to outsource much of its direct-mail operations to specialized mail vendors. The company began converting its plant in Pleasantville, New York, from a direct-mail-order factory to an office complex. Part of the office complex construction involved building an auditorium that was to be identical to another auditorium in historic Williamsburg, Virginia.

Terrence McGrane had just begun his third day on the job as chief internal auditor. In an effort to get to know his new company, he had scheduled a series of interviews with all the vice presidents. His first interview was with the vice president of administrative services, Harold J. Scott,* who was in charge of many construction projects and maintenance services. Because of the massive renovation project, it was not unusual for hundreds of invoices to be forwarded to Scott.

Coincidence 1: McGrane stopped by the accounts payable department and retrieved a series of recently submitted invoices for various trade expenses related to the auditorium construction project. "One of the things I wanted to accomplish was to understand how the accounting codes worked—what was capitalized; what was expensed; how it was recorded, etc." So he grabbed a stack of processed invoices with accounting codes and went up to the construction site to meet with the vice president for an hour-long interview.

As the two walked around the grounds, McGrane asked the vice president if he could explain the accounting codes to him. "He stared at the [top] invoice for approximately 30 seconds and said: 'That is not my signature on the invoice!' As he looked through the stack, he found what appeared to be about three or four other forgeries. He was completely baffled."

The initial investigation revealed that all of the forgeries were in the painting division, budgeted at approximately $500,000 a year. The company employed only one person to oversee the painting operations in its facilities department: Albert Miano.

Miano, a 35-year-old from New Fairfield, Connecticut, earned about $30,000 a year. It was his job to coordinate time-and-materials contracts with the scores of painters, carpenters, electricians, and plumbers who toiled daily on the renovation, repair, and construction of the building complex. As facilities supervisor, Miano regularly forwarded invoices to the vice president of administration services for approval.

Miano launched his scheme by crafting false invoices for the jobs done by the painters. He took a copy of a trade invoice from an existing painting contractor and, using his home computer, created a replica into which he would record slightly different hours for the trade contractors' work.

McGrane related a probable scenario of how Miano executed his scheme. "Let's say he knew that during the month of February, as an example," McGrane said, "there were 27 painters on the grounds during the course of one week." Miano also knew the total number of hours and the volume of materials used in that time. "He would create invoices that were similar in nature, but record only 11 painters on the grounds," McGrane said. Miano would not reinvoice exactly the same work done during a week, but he would make it look so similar that no one's suspicions were ever aroused. Effectively, there were no work orders on the "phantom work" he created on these invoices. Miano always listed fewer painters on the false invoice than the actual number who had worked that week, and he registered less time for their services than they had actually worked.

---

*Several names and details have been changed to preserve anonymity.

As part of his job, he regularly brought the trade invoices into the administrative vice president's office for signature approval. After delivering a stack of these invoices, he would return to collect them within the next day or two and deliver the approved invoices to the accounts payable department. "It was this opportunity," McGrane said, "that this individual was allowed to go and collect the approved invoices and insert his own replicated fraudulent invoices as approved. This was the first piece of an 'electronic circuit' that allowed him to commit the fraud." The second piece of the circuit for the fraud to ignite, McGrane said, was allowing this same employee to transport the invoices to the accounts payable department and ultimately to collect the check.

After seeing how easy it was to slip in his own false invoices in the stack of approved ones, Miano became bolder in his scheme. He began calling accounts payable, claiming that a carpenter or painter had arrived on the grounds and needed his check "immediately." To keep the project flowing, the employees in the accounts payable department accommodated him. Many employees knew and liked Miano, who had worked for the company for nearly 15 years.

Eventually, this routine became so familiar to employees in accounts payable that Miano did not even need to make up an excuse to pick up checks. Each time he would collect them, he stashed the check for the false invoice in his pocket. When he returned home to New Fairfield, Connecticut, he took the check to his bank, forged the contractor's name on the back, then endorsed it with his own name and deposited the check.

McGrane explains that Miano was able to pull off the scam due to failure of internal controls and employees not following standard accounting procedures. "For any business transaction, the invoices should be dispatched independently to the approving authority. Once signed, the approved invoices should be sent independently to accounts payable. When the check is prepared by accounts payable, they should mail it directly to the third party. Under a strong internal control system, the employees and/or contractors should not be allowed to come in and collect checks directly. Direct contacts with accounts payable personnel make it too tempting for someone to try to misappropriate funds."

Accounts payable also failed to combine the invoices into a single check—they wrote a check for each invoice. "Had they combined it," McGrane said, "his false invoice would have been added into the legitimate painter's monthly invoice summary, and the money would be mailed to the legitimate contractor," McGrane said. Accounts payable neglected to study the invoice signatures for forgeries, and the accounting department dropped the ball by not perusing processed checks for dual endorsements, another red flag for potentially misappropriated funds.

Miano's first transaction totaled $1,200. His second transaction jumped to $6,000—his third, $12,000. His largest single transaction came to over $66,000. Miano refined his strategy by pacing, on a parallel basis, a certain amount below the total due the painter. "If the painter submitted an invoice for $20,000 a month," McGrane said, "Miano would submit an invoice for, say, $14,000. If the painter submitted a $6,000 invoice, he'd submit one for $3,000." The individual invoice amounts, because of the continuing construction, would not have alarmed even an auditor.

Miano's behavior at the office was the same as ever. He dressed the same way, drove the same car to work, and shared little of his private life with other workers. He had not taken a vacation in over four years, and his boss thought he should be promoted (a move Miano resisted, for reasons now obvious). After hours, however, Miano was a different person.

Coincidence 2: McGrane's secretary was not only on Miano's bowling team, she was also his neighbor. They saw each other regularly at the local bowling alley. She took notice when Miano's behavior became somewhat extravagant. At first he took to buying the team drinks, a habit most appreciated by his teammates. However, the secretary began wondering where all the money was coming from when he showed up in his new Mercedes (one of five cars he bought) and talked about a new $18,000 boat. He also invested in real estate and purchased a second home costing $416,000.

McGrane's secretary approached Miano one night after he had spent some $800 on drinks for the team. "Did you win the lottery, or what?" she asked. He explained that his father-in-law had died recently and left a substantial inheritance to his wife and him. Miano's father-in-law was actually quite alive, but no one ever bothered to check out the claim. No one suspected Miano of doing anything sinister or criminal. All of his associates considered him "too dumb" to carry out such a scheme. One person described him as "dumb as a box of rocks."

Coincidence 3: After four years without a vacation, Miano took what he considered a well-deserved trip to Atlantic City. But he wasn't there long before he was called back to Pleasantville. One can imagine his chagrin at having to leave the casinos and boardwalks and head back to the office. Little did he know that things were about to get a lot worse.

Upon his return, Miano found himself confronted by the auditor, the vice president, and two attorneys from the district attorney's office. He readily admitted guilt. "He said he had expected to get caught," McGrane said. "He did it strictly based on greed. Miano claimed there was no one else involved, and the sum total of his fraud was about $400,000." But the internal audit found that Miano had forged endorsements on more than 50 checks in those four years, totaling $1,057,000. Ironically, the auditors could identify only about $380,000 spent on tangible items (boats, cars, down payment on a home, etc.). The investigators could not account for the other $700,000, although they knew Miano had withdrawn at least that much from the bank.

Miano served only two years of an eight-year sentence in a state penitentiary. At the time of his indictment, his wife filed for divorce, claiming she knew nothing of her husband's crimes. Miano told a reporter in jail that the loss of his family and the public humiliation had taught him his lesson.

"For a nickel or for $5 million, it doesn't pay," Miano said. "You enjoy the money for a while, but you lose your pride and your self-respect. It ends up hurting your family, and no money can ever change that."

PERSONAL PURCHASES WITH COMPANY FUNDS

Instead of undertaking billing schemes to generate cash, many fraudsters simply purchase personal items with their company's money, using company accounts to buy items for themselves, their businesses, their families, and so on. In one instance, a supervisor started a company for his son and directed work to the son's company. In addition to this unethical behavior, the supervisor saw to it that his employer purchased all the materials and supplies necessary for the son's business. The supervisor also purchased materials through his employer that were used to add a room to his own house. All in all, the perpetrator bought nearly $50,000 worth of supplies and materials for himself using company money.

Conceptually, one might wonder why a purchases fraud is not classified as a theft of inventory or other assets rather than a billing scheme. After all, in purchases schemes, the fraudster buys something with company money, then takes the purchased item for himself. In the case just discussed, the supervisor took building materials and supplies. How does this differ from those frauds discussed in Chapter 9, whereby employees steal supplies and other materials? On first glance, the schemes appear very similar. In fact, perpetrators of purchases fraud are stealing inventory just as they would in any other inventory theft scheme. Nevertheless, the heart of the scheme is not the *taking* of the inventory but the *purchasing* of the inventory. In other words, when employees steal merchandise from a warehouse, they are stealing an asset that the company needs, an asset that it has on hand for a particular reason. The harm to the victim company is not only the cost of the asset but the loss of the asset itself. In a purchasing scheme, the asset that is taken is superfluous. The perpetrator causes the victim company to order and pay for an asset that it does not really need, so the only damage to the victim company is the money lost in purchasing the particular item. This is why purchasing schemes are categorized as invoice frauds.

Personal Purchases through False Invoicing

In our studies, most of the employees who undertook purchases schemes did so by running unsanctioned invoices through the accounts payable system. Fraudsters in this type of fraud buy an item and submit the bill to the employer as if it represented a purchase on behalf of the company. (See Exhibit 7.11.) The goal is to have the company pay the invoice. Obviously, the invoice that the employees submit to the company is not legitimate. The main hurdle for fraudsters to overcome, therefore, is to avoid scrutiny of the invalid invoice and obtain authorization for the bill to be paid.

Fraudster as Authorizer of Invoices

As was the case in the shell company schemes we reviewed, the person who engages in a purchases scheme is often the very person in the company whose duties include *authorizing* purchases. Obviously, proper controls should preclude anyone from approving her own purchases. Such poorly separated functions leave little other than her conscience to dissuade an employee from fraud. Nevertheless, we saw several

Exhibit 7.11   Invoice Purchasing Schemes

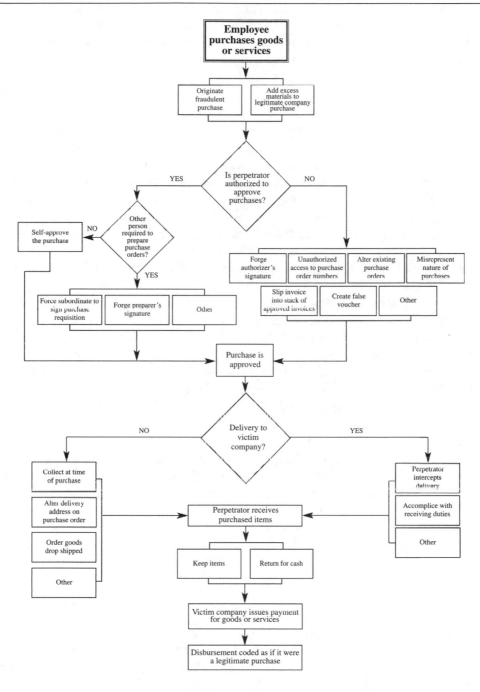

examples of companies in which this lapse in controls existed. As we continue to point out, fraud arises in part because of a perceived opportunity. An employee who sees that no one is reviewing his actions is more likely to turn to fraud than one who knows that his company diligently works to detect employee theft.

An example of how poor controls can lead to fraud was found in a case where a manager of a remote location of a large, publicly traded company was authorized to both order supplies and approve vendor invoices for payment. For over a year, the manager routinely added personal items and supplies for his own business to orders made on behalf of his employer. The orders often included a strange mix of items; technical supplies and home furnishings might, for instance, be purchased in the same order. Because the manager was in a position to approve his own purchases, he could get away with such blatantly obvious frauds. In addition to ordering personal items, the perpetrator changed the delivery address for certain supplies so that they would be delivered directly to his home or side business. This scheme cost the victim company approximately $300,000 in unnecessary purchases. In a similar case, an employee with complete control of purchasing and storing supplies for his department bought approximately $100,000 worth of unnecessary supplies using company funds. The employee authorized both the orders and the payments. The excess supplies were taken to the perpetrator's home, where he used them to manufacture a product for his own business. It should be obvious from these examples that not only do poor controls pave the way for fraud, a lack of oversight regarding the purchasing function can allow employees to take huge chunks out of a company's bottom line.

In some situations, perpetrators are authorized to approve purchases, but controls prevent them from also initiating purchase requests. This procedure is meant to prevent the kinds of schemes just discussed. Unfortunately, those with authority to approve purchases are often high-level employees with a good deal of control over their subordinates. These persons can use their influence to force subordinates to assist in purchases schemes. In one example at a certain utility company, purchases under $1,000 could be made with limited value purchase orders (LPOs), which required two signatures—the originator of a purchase request and the approver of the request. An LPO attached to an invoice for less than $1,000 would be paid by the accounts payable department. In this case, a manager bought goods and services on company accounts and prepared LPOs for the purchases. (In some cases, the LPO would falsely describe the item to conceal the nature of the purchase.) Once the LPO was prepared, the manager forced a clerk in his department to sign the document as the originator of the transaction. The clerk, intimidated by her boss, did not question the authenticity of the LPOs. With two signatures affixed, the LPO appeared to be legitimate and the bills were paid. The scheme cost the victim company at least $25,000.

Falsifying Documents to Obtain Authorization

Not all fraudsters are free to approve their own purchases; those who cannot must rely on other methods to get their personal bills paid by the company. The chief control document in many vouchers is the purchase order. When employees want to buy goods or services, they submit a purchase requisition to a superior. If the purchase requisition is approved, a purchase order is sent to a vendor. A copy of this purchase order, retained in the voucher, tells accounts payable that the transaction has been approved. Later, when an invoice and receiving report corresponding to this purchase order are assembled, accounts payable will issue a check.

In order to make their purchases appear authentic, some fraudsters generate false purchase orders. In one example, an employee forged the signature of a division controller on purchase orders; thus, the purchase orders appeared to be authentic, and the employee was able to buy approximately $3,000 worth of goods at his company's expense. In another instance, a part-time employee at an educational institution obtained unused purchase order numbers and used them to order computer equipment under a fictitious name. The employee then intercepted the equipment as it arrived at the school and loaded the items into his car. Eventually the employee began using fictitious purchase order numbers instead of real ones. The scheme came to light when the perpetrator inadvertently selected the name of a real vendor. After scrutinizing the documents, the school knew that it had been victimized. In the meantime, the employee had bought nearly $8,000 worth of unnecessary equipment.

Altering Existing Purchase Orders

Purchase orders also can be altered by employees who seek to obtain merchandise at their employer's expense. In one of the cases in our studies, several individuals conspired to purchase over $2 million worth of materials for their personal use. The ringleader of the scheme was a low-level supervisor who had access to the computer system that controlled the requisition and receipt of materials. This supervisor entered the system and either initiated orders of materials that exceeded the needs of a particular project or altered existing orders to increase the amount of materials being requisitioned. Because the victim organization had poor controls, it did not compare completed work orders on projects to the amount of materials ordered for those projects. The inflated orders were undetected. In addition, other employees involved in the scheme were in charge of receiving deliveries. These employees were able to divert the excess materials and falsify receiving reports to conceal the missing items. In addition, the victim institution did not enforce a central delivery point, meaning that employees were allowed to pick up materials from the vendors in their personal vehicles. This made it very easy to misappropriate the excess merchandise. The supervisor's ability to circumvent controls and initiate false orders or alter genuine ones, though, was the real key to the scheme.

False Purchase Requisitions

Another way for an employee to get a false purchase approved is to misrepresent the nature of the purchase. In many companies, those with the power to authorize purchases are not always attentive to their duties. If a trusted subordinate vouches for an acquisition, for instance, busy supervisors often give rubber-stamp approval to purchase requisitions. Additionally, employees sometimes misrepresent the nature of the items they are purchasing in order to pass a cursory review by their superiors. In one case, an engineer bought over $30,000 worth of personal items. The engineer dealt directly with vendors and also was in charge of overseeing the receipt of the materials he purchased. He therefore was able to misrepresent the nature of the merchandise he bought, calling it "maintenance items." Vendor invoices were altered to agree to this description.

Of course, the problem with lying about what one is buying is that when delivery occurs, it is the perpetrator's personal items that arrive, not the business items listed on the purchase requisition. In the case just discussed, detection at this stage of the crime was avoided because the engineer who made the fraudulent purchases was also in charge of receiving the merchandise. He could falsify receiving reports to perpetuate the fraud. We also have encountered cases in which fraudsters in the purchasing department enlisted the aid of employees in the receiving department to conceal their crimes.

Another way to avoid detection at the delivery stage is to change the delivery address for purchases. Instead of being shipped to the victim company, the items that the employee buys are sent directly to her home or business. In a related scenario, an accounts payable supervisor purchased supplies for her own business by entering vouchers in the accounts payable system of her employer. Checks were cut for the expenses during normal daily check runs. To avoid problems with receiving the unauthorized goods, the perpetrator ordered the supplies drop-shipped to a client of her side business.

Personal Purchases on Credit Cards or Other Company Accounts

Instead of running false invoices through accounts payable, some employees make personal purchases on company credit cards, purchasing cards, or running accounts with vendors. (See Exhibit 7.12.) As with invoicing schemes, the key to getting away with a false credit card purchase is avoiding detection. Unlike invoicing schemes, however, prior approval for purchases is not required. An employee with a company credit or purchasing card can buy an item merely by signing his name (or forging someone else's) at the time of purchase. Later review of the card statement, however, may detect the fraudulent purchase. In invoicing schemes, we saw how those who committed the frauds often were in a position to approve their own purchases. The same often is true in credit card and purchasing card schemes. A manager in one case reviewed and approved his own credit card statements. This allowed him to make fraudulent purchases on the company card for approximately two years.

Of course, only certain employees are authorized to use company credit cards or are issued purchase cards. The manager in the last case, for instance, had his own company card. Employees without this privilege can make fraudulent purchases with a company card only if they first manage to get hold of one. To this end, company cards sometimes are stolen or ''borrowed'' from authorized users. A more novel approach was used by an accountant in another case who falsely added her name to a list of employees to whom cards were to be issued. She used her card to make fraudulent purchases but forged the signatures of authorized cardholders to cover her tracks. Since no one knew she even had a company card, she would not be a prime suspect in the fraud even if someone questioned the purchases. For over five years this employee continued her scheme, racking up a six-figure bill on her employer's account. In addition, she had control of the credit card statement and was able to code her purchases to various expense accounts, thereby further delaying detection of her crime.

An executive secretary in one example used her access to the statement for a different purpose. After making hundreds of thousands of dollars' worth of fraudulent

Exhibit 7.12 Purchases on Credit Card or Company Account

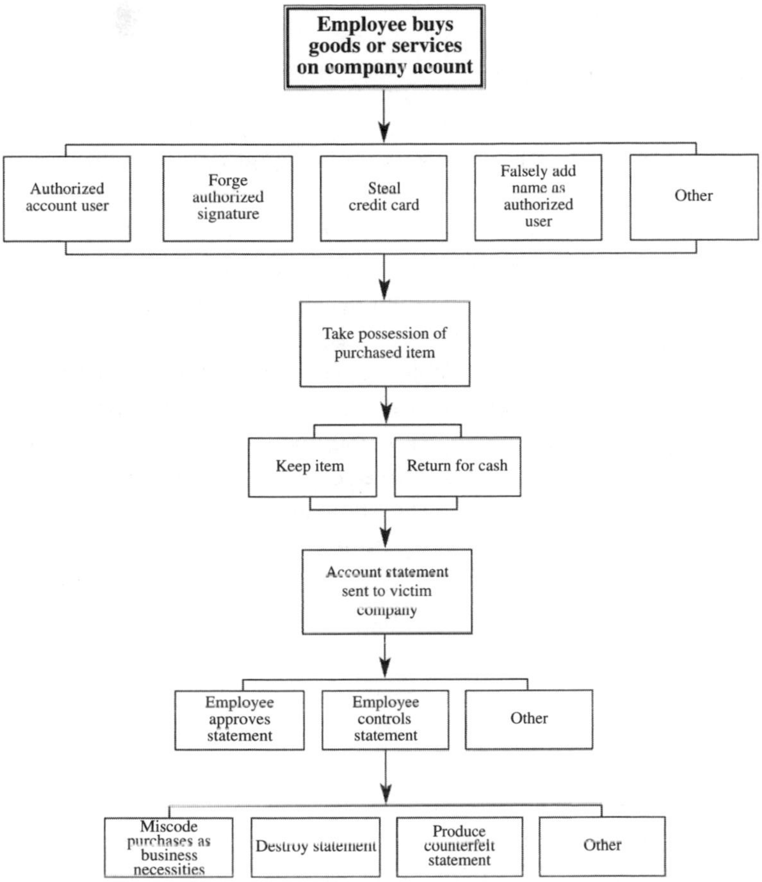

purchases on corporate cards, this employee destroyed both the receipts from her purchases and the monthly credit card statements. Eventually duplicate statements were requested from the credit card company, and the fraud was discovered. The fact that no statements were received by the company led to detection of the scheme. Some fraudsters, having destroyed the real copies of credit card statements, produce counterfeit copies that omit their fraudulent purchases. By taking this extra step, fraudsters are able to keep their employers in the dark about the true activity on the account.

Charge Accounts

Some companies keep charge accounts with vendors with whom they do regular business. Office supply companies are a good example of this kind of vendor. Purchases on charge accounts may require a signature or other form of authorization from a designated company representative. Obviously, that representative is in a position to buy personal items on the company account. Other employees might do the same by forging the signature of an authorized person at the time of a fraudulent purchase. In some informal settings, purchases can be verified by as little as a phone call, making it very easy to make fraudulent purchases.

Returning Merchandise for Cash

So far all the cases we have discussed in the fraudulent purchases section have involved the false purchase of merchandise for the sake of obtaining the merchandise. In some cases, however, fraudsters buy items and then return them for cash. The best example of this type of scheme in our survey was a case in which an employee made fraudulent gains from a business travel account. The employee purchased tickets for herself and her family through her company's travel budget. Poor separation of duties allowed her to order the tickets, receive them, prepare claims for payments, and distribute checks. The only review of her activities was made by a busy and rather uninterested supervisor who approved the employee's claims without requiring supporting documentation. Eventually the employee's scheme evolved. She began to purchase airline tickets and return them for their cash value. An employee of the travel agency assisted in the scheme by encoding the tickets as if the fraudster had paid for them herself. That caused the airlines to pay refunds directly to the fraudster rather than to her employer. In the course of two years, this employee embezzled over $100,000 through her purchases scheme.

DETECTION

These tests may be beneficial in detecting red flags to billing schemes.

- Does the company have a purchasing department? If yes, is it independent of (1) the accounting department, (2) the receiving department, or (3) the shipping department?
- Are purchases made only after the respective department heads sign purchase requisitions?
- Are purchases made by means of purchase orders sent to vendors for all purchases, or only for purchases over a predetermined dollar limit?
- Do purchase orders specify a description of items, quantity, price, terms, delivery requirements, and dates?
- Is a list of unfilled purchase orders maintained and reviewed periodically?
- Are purchase order forms prenumbered, and is the sequence accounted for periodically?
- Does the client maintain an approved vendors list?
- Are items purchased only after competitive bids are obtained? If so, are competitive bids obtained for all purchases, or only for purchases over a predetermined dollar limit?
- Is a log maintained of all receipts?

- Does the receiving department prepare receiving reports for all items received? If yes, are receiving reports (1) prepared for all items, (2) prepared only for items that have purchase orders, or (3) renumbered?

- At the time the items are received, does someone independent of the purchasing department check the merchandise before acceptance as to description, quantity, and condition?

- Are copies of receiving reports (1) furnished to the accounting department, (2) furnished to the purchasing department, or (3) filed in the receiving department?

- Are receipts under blanket purchase orders monitored, and are quantities exceeding authorized total returned to the vendor?

- Are procedures adequate for the proper accounting for partial deliveries of purchase orders?

- Are purchasing and receiving functions separate from invoice processing, accounts payable, and general ledger functions?

- Are vendors' invoices, receiving reports, and purchase orders matched before the related liability is recorded?

- Are invoices checked as to prices, extensions, footings, freight charges, allowances, and credit terms?

- Are controls adequate to ensure that all available discounts are taken?

- Are purchases recorded in a purchase register or voucher register before being processed through cash disbursements?

- Does a responsible employee assign the appropriate general ledger account distribution to which the invoices are to be posted?

- Are procedures adequate to ensure that invoices have been processed before payment and to prevent duplicate payment?

- Does a responsible official approve invoices for payment?

- Are procedures adequate to ensure that merchandise purchased for direct delivery to customers is billed to the customers promptly and recorded as both a receivable and a payable?

- Are records of goods returned to vendors matched to vendor credit memos?

- Are unmatched receiving reports, purchase orders, and vendors' invoices periodically reviewed and investigated for proper recording?

- Is the accounts payable ledger or voucher register reconciled monthly to the general ledger control accounts?

- Are statements from vendors regularly reviewed and reconciled against recorded liabilities?

- Do adjustments to accounts payable (e.g., writing off debit balances) require the approval of a designated official?

- Are budgets used? If yes, are budgets approved by responsible officials, and are actual expenditures compared with budgeted amounts and variances analyzed and explained?

- If excess inventory purchasing is suspected, is it verified that all inventory purchased was received (receiving report) at the proper location? Receiving reports or invoices examination might reveal alternative shipping sites.

PREVENTION

This list of billing-scheme-prevention methods may be helpful in the deterrence of billing fraud.

- Document and adhere to authorization procedures of purchase orders, invoicing, and payments.
- Periodically review the accounts payable list of vendors for strange vendors and addresses.
- Review payment codings for abnormal descriptions.
- Analyze vendor purchases for abnormal levels on both a monthly and a yearly basis.
- Compare and analyze purchases and inventory levels. (See Chapter 9.)
- Establish control methods to check for duplicate invoices and purchase order numbers.
- Establish a separation of duties among authorization, purchasing, receiving, shipping, and accounting.
- Periodically review payment of vouchers to ensure integrity of proper documentation.
- Review receiving and shipping reports for completeness and accuracy.
- Include purchasing trails and other information in asset information.
- Strictly scrutinize journal entries to inventory accounts.
- Periodically perform appropriate bank reconciliation and review procedures, checking for out-of-place vendors and endorsements.
- Review credit card and purchasing card statements often for irregularities.
- Verify the validity of invoices with post office box addresses.
- Install proper controls for the receipt and handling of return-to-sender checks.

CHAPTER 8

Payroll and Expense Reimbursement Schemes

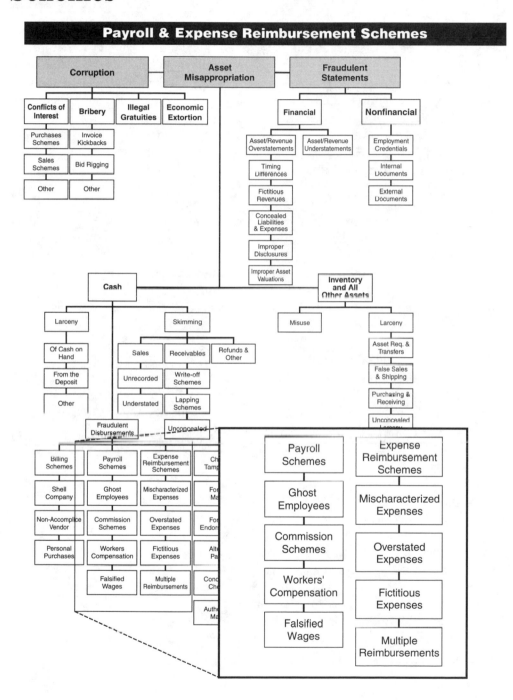

Case Study: Say Cheese!

Every once in a while, a person devises a fraud scheme so complex that it is virtually undetectable. Intricate planning allows the person to cheat a company out of millions of dollars with little chance of getting caught.

Jerry Harkanell* is no such person.

Harkanell's payroll scheme put only about $1,500 in his pocket before a supervisor detected his fraud, less than half a year after it began.

Harkanell worked as an administrative assistant for a unit of a large San Antonio hospital. His duties consisted mostly of clerical tasks, including the submission of payroll information for the unit.

An exception report for the month of March listed some unusual activity on Harkanell's time sheet. He had posted eight hours that resulted in overtime wages for a particular pay period. The pay period coincided with a time of low occupancy in Harkanell's unit. During times of low occupancy, there is no need for anyone—especially an administrative assistant—to work overtime.

When his supervisor confronted Harkanell about the eight hours, he confessed. He said he posted the time because of financial problems and threats from his wife to leave him. He immediately submitted his resignation, a hospital administrator accepted it, and Jerry Harkanell became a former hospital employee.

The hospital administrator shared the specifics of this incident with Oscar Straine, director of internal auditing for the hospital and a certified fraud examiner (CFE).

''Nobody leaves for just eight hours,'' Straine said. ''There must be a lot more there.''

When Straine delved into the records, he found exactly what he had suspected. Since October of the previous year, Harkanell had been overstating his hours. He had recorded hours that he had not actually worked; he had posted his hours to shifts for which pay was higher; and he had reported vacation time as time worked, drawing not only additional pay but extra vacation time too.

Unfortunately for Harkanell, his method of cheating his employer left a well-marked paper trail. In his administrative role, he collected and submitted the unit's manually prepared time sheets to his supervisor. She signed the time sheets, made copies to retain for her records, and returned them to Harkanell for delivery to the payroll department. Harkanell then altered his original time sheet before he delivered the approved documents to the payroll department. Amazingly, he completed his time sheets in pencil, allowing him simply to erase the old numbers and make changes.

The audit staff compared the supervisor's copies of time sheets with the time sheets on file in the payroll department. Discrepancies between the two stood out. The investigation lasted less than a month. The results revealed that during a 26-week period, Jerry Harkanell defrauded the hospital of $1,570.

Interviews conducted with coworkers and supervisors revealed one detail that might have tipped Harkanell's hand even earlier, had anyone recognized a suspicious act for what it was.

---

*Several names and details have been changed to preserve anonymity.

One Friday before payday when Harkanell had the day off, he showed up at the hospital anyway. This was more than a minor inconvenience since he didn't own a car. But Harkanell took the bus to work just so he could personally get the unit's time sheets approved and turned in to payroll. At the time, no one questioned why he didn't simply ask someone to cover for him.

At the completion of the investigation, the hospital filed a claim with the district attorney's office. Evidence consisted of copies of the approved time sheets, copies of the altered time sheets, and affidavits from Harkanell's supervisors.

An assistant district attorney in charge of the case called the hospital shortly after receiving the case. She had uncovered some interesting details about Harkanell's past during a routine background check. A computer search revealed that he had a criminal history and that he was currently on parole. In fact, the assistant district attorney reported, Harkanell previously had been sentenced to life in prison for armed robbery.

The news that the hospital had unknowingly hired a convicted felon distressed Oscar Straine. He discovered that the hospital's ability to conduct thorough background checks on prospective employees was restricted by money and access to records. The hospital routinely checked criminal records in Bexar County (where the hospital is located) and any counties in which an applicant reported having a history. But cost and time prohibited the hospital from checking records in all 254 Texas counties, especially when hiring a low-salaried employee like Harkanell.

The complaint against Harkanell went to the grand jury quickly. Straine testified, the grand jury issued an indictment, and a warrant was issued for Harkanell's arrest.

The sheriff's department attempted to locate Harkanell several times but with no success. He had moved and, not surprisingly, left no forwarding address. The DA's office notified the hospital that Harkanell had disappeared and that it had no immediate plans to continue the search.

Harkanell remained at large for several months, but luck was on the hospital's side—or, perhaps more accurately, stupidity was on Harkanell's. Just as he had done with his time sheet fraud, he left a clue behind, this time concerning his whereabouts. This was no subtle hint either. He might as well have mailed the hospital an invitation with a map.

The following January, Straine was talking to a woman in the Human Resources department who had worked on Jerry Harkanell's original case. Straine called this woman to talk about his continuing concerns over the hospital's inability to do a more thorough background check on prospective hires. During the conversation, the woman asked, "By the way, did you happen to see the paper a few weeks ago?"

"I don't know what you're talking about," he replied.

"Oh—well, Jerry Harkanell's picture was on the front page of the business section of the *Express.*"

"You have to be kidding." But she wasn't.

Straine immediately searched online for a copy of the article. Within minutes, he'd found a story about a nonprofit organization that helps low-income families buy houses with low-interest loans and no down payment.

Right in the middle of the article was a picture, and right in the middle of that picture was Jerry Harkanell. He and his family were sitting on the front porch of the new home the nonprofit group had helped him purchase. The article detailed Harkanell's story, commenting on how hard he had worked to get his house. And though it never mentioned the address, the article contained enough information to pinpoint the location. The Harkanells lived near a new shopping center and across the street from a park. Theirs was the only new house on the block.

From his office, it took Straine ten minutes to find the house. He knew the location of the shopping center, and he drove there, then located the park.

Straine said, "It was weird driving up the street with the photograph, and there's his house. We could even identify the design on the front door and match it with the photograph in the newspaper as we drove up the street."

As soon as he returned to his office, Straine called the assistant district attorney. Harkanell was arrested the next day.

Harkanell appealed for assistance from the nonprofit organization that had helped him buy his house. It agreed to help him—on the condition that he promise to come clean. The organization contacted the hospital's community outreach program to request that the charge be dropped, or at least decreased from a felony to a misdemeanor.

The hospital declined to drop the charge. The nonprofit group pleaded Harkanell's case, pointing out that he had a wife and a sick child who would have to go on welfare if he were convicted of a felony.

Straine made it clear that the hospital would pursue a conviction, whether a felony or a misdemeanor. The hospital's position was that Harkanell should at least have to face a judge. (Later, the assistant DA revealed that had Harkanell pleaded guilty to the felony charge, the judge would have sentenced him to 25 years.)

While Harkanell continued to try to get the charges dropped, another piece of his past caught up with him. A separate party filed a forgery claim with the district attorney's office. As soon as the nonprofit organization got word of this development, it refused to provide any additional assistance to Harkanell.

A judge sentenced Jerry Harkanell to 35 years in prison. Law enforcement officials escorted him from the courtroom directly to a jail cell.

OVERVIEW

Payroll and expense reimbursement schemes are similar to billing schemes. The perpetrators of these frauds produce false documents that cause the victim company to make a fraudulent disbursement unwittingly. In the previous chapter, the false document was usually an invoice (coupled, perhaps, with false receiving reports, purchase orders, and purchase authorizations). In this chapter, the false documents are items like time cards, sales orders, and expense reports. In the last case study, for example, Jerry Harkanell turned in false time sheets that caused his employer to overpay his wages. The major difference between these frauds and billing schemes is that payroll and expense frauds involve disbursements to employees rather than to external parties.

Exhibit 8.1   *2009 Global Fraud Survey*: **Frequency of Fraudulent Disbursements**

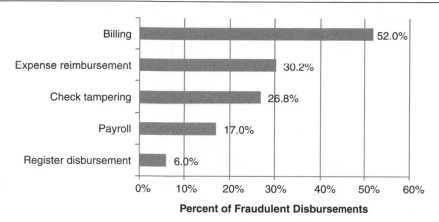

Percent of Fraudulent Disbursements

PAYROLL SCHEME DATA FROM ACFE *2009 GLOBAL FRAUD SURVEY*

Frequency and Cost

In our 2009 survey, payroll schemes ranked fourth among fraudulent disbursements in terms of frequency; 17 percent of the fraudulent disbursement cases we reviewed contained some form of payroll fraud. (The sum of these percentages exceeds 100 percent because some cases involved multiple fraud schemes that fell into more than one category. Various charts in this chapter may reflect percentages that total in excess of 100 percent for similar reasons.) (See Exhibit 8.1.)

The median loss among payroll frauds in our 2009 survey was $72,000. Payroll frauds ranked third among fraudulent disbursements in terms of median loss. (See Exhibit 8.2.)

Exhibit 8.3 shows the distribution of losses in the payroll cases in our 2009 study. Fewer than 5 percent of payroll schemes cases involved losses of greater than $1 million compared with 25 percent of all fraud cases. However, it is worth noting that over 45 percent of payroll cases still caused losses of at least $100,000.

Exhibit 8.2   *2009 Global Fraud Survey*: **Median Loss**
              of Fraudulent Disbursements

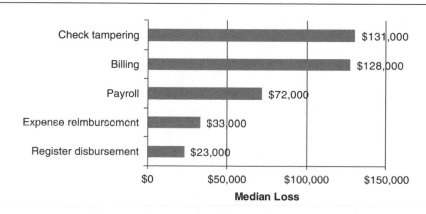

Median Loss

Exhibit 8.3 *2009 Global Fraud Survey:* **Dollar Loss Distribution for Payroll Schemes**

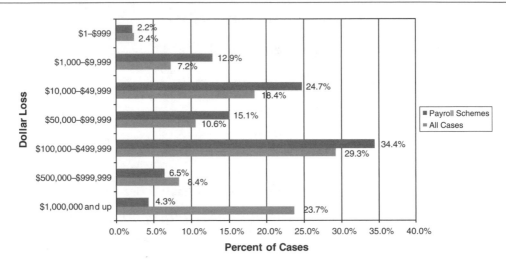

Detection of Payroll Schemes

In terms of how frauds were detected, payroll fraud schemes were significantly more likely to be detected by accident and through management review than were frauds in general but were less likely to be detected by tips, internal audits, and account reconciliation. (See Exhibit 8.4.)

Perpetrators of Payroll Schemes

The percent of payroll frauds committed by owner/executives was nearly double the rate of owner/executive fraud in all cases. Conversely, the percentage of frauds perpetrated by employees and managers in this category was slightly lower than in the general population of schemes we reviewed. (See Exhibit 8.5.)

Exhibit 8.4 *2009 Global Fraud Survey*: **Detection of Payroll Schemes**

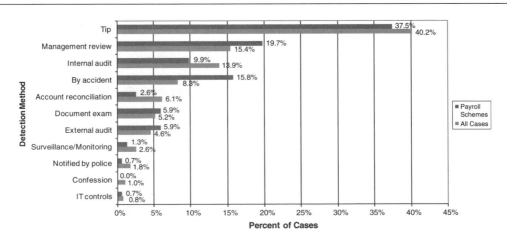

Exhibit 8.5   *2009 Global Fraud Survey*: **Perpetrators of Payroll Schemes**

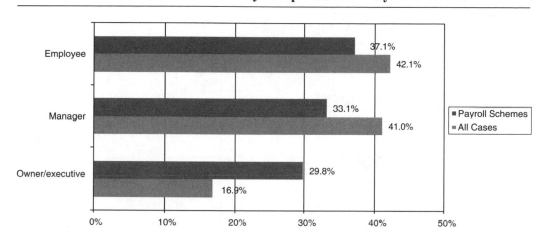

Typical of most forms of occupational fraud, median losses in payroll schemes rose with the position of the perpetrators. Schemes committed by managers were more than twice as costly as schemes committed by employees. Owner/executive schemes had a much lower median loss in payroll frauds than in all cases, but at $110,000 these schemes were still quite costly, on average. (See Exhibit 8.6.)

Victims of Payroll Schemes

Exhibits 8.7 and 8.8 illustrate how payroll schemes affected organizations based on the size of their workforce. In the first chart, we see that payroll frauds were more common in small organizations; 31 percent of the frauds in our study occurred in small organizations, but almost 50 percent of payroll frauds fell into this category.

Exhibit 8.6   *2009 Global Fraud Survey*: **Median Loss by Perpetrator of Payroll Schemes**

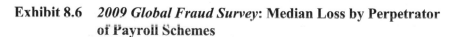

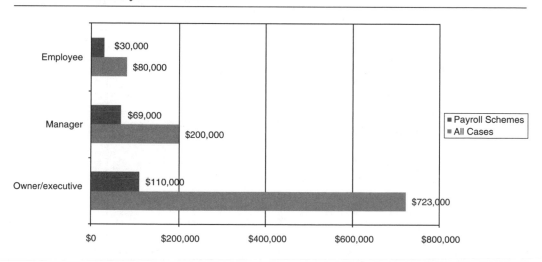

Exhibit 8.7 *2009 Global Fraud Survey*: Size of Victim in Payroll Schemes

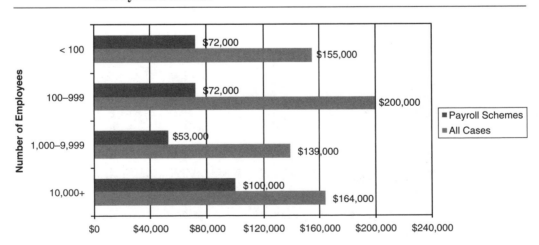

The median losses among payroll schemes were the highest in organizations with the largest workforces (those with 10,000 or more employees), at $100,000. In contrast, the median loss was $53,000 for organizations with 1,000 to 10,000 employees and was $72,000 for organizations in the two categories representing the smallest companies.

PAYROLL SCHEMES

There are three main categories of payroll fraud:

1. Ghost employee schemes
2. Falsified hours
3. Commission schemes

Exhibit 8.8 *2009 Global Fraud Survey*: Median Loss by Size of Victim in Payroll Schemes

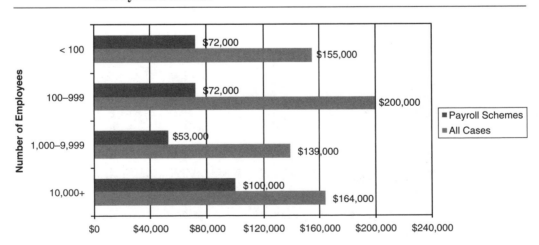

Ghost Employees

The term ''ghost employee'' refers to someone on the payroll who does not actually work for the victim company. Through the falsification of personnel or payroll records, a fraudster causes paychecks to be generated to a ghost. The fraudster or an accomplice then converts these paychecks. (See Exhibit 8.9.) Use of a ghost employee scheme by a fraudster can be like adding a second income to the household. The ghost employee

Exhibit 8.9   Ghost Employees

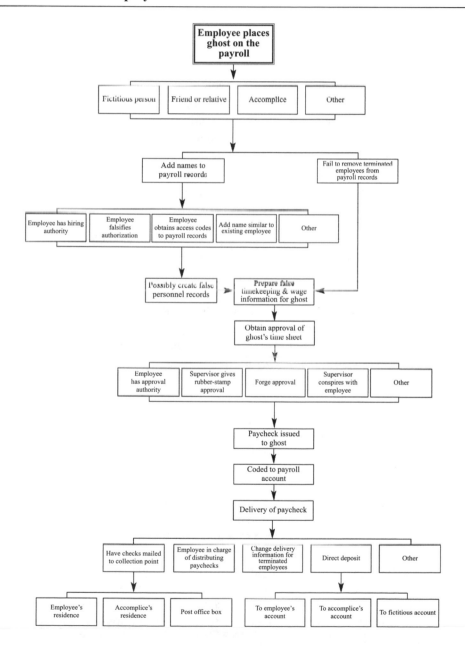

may be a fictitious person or a real individual who simply does not work for the victim employer. When the ghost is a real person, it is often a friend or relative of the perpetrator. In some cases, the ghost employee is an accomplice of the fraudster who cashes the fraudulent paychecks and then splits the money with the perpetrator.

For a ghost employee scheme to work, four things must happen:

1. The ghost must be added to the payroll.
2. Timekeeping and wage rate information must be collected.
3. A paycheck must be issued to the ghost.
4. The check must be delivered to the perpetrator or an accomplice.

Adding the Ghost to the Payroll

The first step in a ghost employee scheme is entering the ghost on the payroll. In some businesses, all hiring is done through a centralized personnel department; in others, the personnel function is spread over the managerial responsibilities of various departments. Regardless of how hiring of new employees is handled within a business, the person or persons who have authority to add new employees are in the best position to put ghosts on the payroll. In one example, a manager who was responsible for hiring and scheduling janitorial work added over 80 ghost employees to his payroll. The ghosts in this case were actual people who worked at other jobs for different companies. The manager filled out time sheets for the fictitious employees and authorized them, then took the resulting paychecks to the ghost employees, who cashed them and split the proceeds with him. This manager's authority in the hiring and supervision of employees enabled him to perpetrate this fraud.

Another area in which the opportunity to add ghosts exists is payroll accounting. In a perfect world, every name listed on the payroll would be verified against personnel records to make sure that those persons receiving paychecks actually work for the company, but in practice this does not always happen. Thus, persons in payroll accounting may be able to add fictitious employees to the roll. Access to payroll records usually is restricted, so it may be that only managers have access to make changes to records—making these managers the most likely suspects in a ghost employee scheme. However, lower-level employees often gain access to payroll records, either through poor observance of controls or by surreptitious means. In one case, an employee in the payroll department was given the authority to enter new employees into the payroll system, make corrections to payroll information, and distribute paychecks. This employee's manager gave rubber-stamp approval to the employee's actions because of a trusting relationship between the two. The lack of separation of duties and the absence of review made it simple for the culprit to add a fictitious employee into the payroll system.

One way to help conceal the presence of a ghost on the payroll is to create a fictitious employee with a name very similar to that of a real employee. The name on the fraudulent paycheck, then, will appear to be legitimate to anyone who glances at it. This method was used by the bookkeeper in a case in which she made off with $35,000 in fraudulent wages.

Instead of adding new names to the payroll, some employees undertake ghost employee schemes by failing to remove the names of terminated employees. Paychecks to the terminated employee continue to be generated even though he no longer works for the victim company. Perpetrators intercept these fraudulent paychecks and convert them to their own use. In one instance, an accountant delayed the submission of resignation notices of certain employees, then falsified time sheets for them to make it appear that they still worked for the victim company. This accountant was also in charge of distributing paychecks to all employees of the company, so when the fraudulent checks were generated, she simply took them out of the stack of legitimate checks and kept them for herself.

Collecting Timekeeping Information

The second thing that must occur in order for a paycheck to be issued to a ghost employee, at least in the case of hourly employees, is the collection and computation of timekeeping information. The perpetrator must provide payroll accounting with a time card or other instrument showing how many hours the fictitious employee worked over the most recent pay period. This information, along with the wage rate information contained in personnel or payroll files, will be used to compute the amount of the fraudulent paycheck.

Timekeeping records can be maintained in a variety of ways. In many organizations, computer systems are used to track employees' hours. Alternatively, employees might manually record their hours on time cards or might punch time clocks that record the time at which a person starts and finishes work.

When a ghost employee scheme is in place, someone must create documentation for the ghost's hours. This essentially amounts to preparing a fake time card showing when the ghost was allegedly present at work. Depending on the normal procedure for recording hours, a fraudster might log into the computerized system and record the ghost employee's hours, create a time card and sign it in the ghost's name, punch the time clock for the ghost, or so on. Preparation of the time card is not a great obstacle to the perpetrator. The real key to the timekeeping document is obtaining approval of the time card.

Time cards of hourly employees should be approved by a supervisor. This verifies to the payroll department that the employee actually worked the hours claimed on the card. A ghost employee, by definition, does not work for the victim company, so approval will have to be obtained fraudulently. Often the supervisor is the one who creates the ghost. When this is the case, the supervisor fills out a time card in the name of the ghost, then affixes his approval. The time card is thereby authenticated, and a paycheck will be issued. When a nonsupervisor is committing a ghost employee scheme, she typically forges the necessary approval and then forwards the bogus time card directly to payroll accounting, bypassing the supervisor.

In computerized systems, a supervisor's signature might not be required. In lieu of the signature, the supervisor inputs data into the payroll system. The use of the supervisor's password serves to authorize the entry. If an employee has access to the supervisor's password, he can input any data he wants, and it arrives in the payroll system with a seal of approval.

If the fraudster creates ghost employees who are salaried rather than hourly employees, it is not necessary to collect timekeeping information; salaried employees are paid a certain amount each pay period regardless of how many hours they work. Because the timekeeping function can be avoided, it may be easier for a fraudster to create a ghost employee who works on salary. However, because typically there are fewer salaried employees and they are more likely to be members of management, salaried ghosts may be more difficult to conceal.

Issuing the Ghost's Paycheck

Once a ghost is entered on the payroll and his time card has been approved, the third step in the scheme is the actual issuance of the paycheck. The heart of a ghost employee scheme is in the falsification of payroll records and timekeeping information. Once this falsification has occurred, the perpetrator generally does not take an active role in the issuance of the check. The payroll department issues the payment—based on the bogus information provided by the fraudster—as it would any other paycheck.

Delivery of the Paycheck

The final step in a ghost employee scheme is the distribution of the checks to the perpetrator. Paychecks might be hand-delivered to employees while at work, mailed to employees at their home addresses, or direct-deposited into employees' bank accounts. If employees are paid in currency rather than by check, the distribution is almost always conducted in person and on site.

Ideally, those in charge of payroll distribution should not have a hand in any of the other functions of the payroll cycle. For instance, the person who enters new employees in the payroll system should not be allowed to distribute paychecks because, as we saw in the case with the accountant who delayed resignation notices, this person can include a ghost on the payroll, then simply remove the fraudulent check from the stack of legitimate paychecks that she handles as she disburses pay. Obviously, when the perpetrator of a ghost employee scheme mails the checks to employees or passes them out at work, he is in the best position to ensure that the ghost's check is delivered to himself.

In most instances, the perpetrator does not have the authority to distribute paychecks and so must make sure that the victim employer sends the checks to a place from which he can recover them. When checks are not distributed in the workplace, they are either mailed to employees or deposited directly into employees' accounts.

If the fictitious employee was added into the payroll or personnel records by the fraudster, the problem of distribution is usually minor. When the ghost's employment information is input, the perpetrator simply lists an address or bank account to which the payments can be sent. In the case of purely fictitious ghost employees, the address is often the perpetrator's own. (The same goes for bank accounts.) The fact that two employees (the perpetrator and the ghost) are receiving payments at the same destination may indicate that fraud is afoot. Some fraudsters avoid this problem by having payments sent to a post office box or to a separate bank account. In one example, the perpetrator set up a fake bank account in the name of a fictitious employee and arranged for paychecks to be deposited directly into this account.

As we have said, the ghost is not always a fictitious person; it may instead be a real person who is conspiring with the perpetrator to defraud the company. In one instance,

216

an employee listed both his wife and his girlfriend on the company payroll. When real persons conspiring with the fraudster are falsely included on the payroll, the perpetrator typically sees to it that checks are sent to the homes or bank accounts of these persons in order to avoid the problem of duplicate addresses on the payroll.

Distribution is a more difficult problem when the ghost is a former employee who was simply not removed from the payroll. In one case, a supervisor continued to submit time cards for employees who had been terminated. Payroll records obviously will reflect the bank account number or address of the terminated employee in this situation. The perpetrator, then, has two courses of action.

In companies in which paychecks are distributed by hand or are left at a central spot for employees to collect, the perpetrator can ignore the payroll records and simply pick up the fraudulent paychecks. If the paychecks are to be distributed through the mail or by direct deposit, the perpetrator will have to enter the terminated employee's records and change the delivery information.

Falsified Hours and Salary

By far the most common method of misappropriating funds from the payroll is the overpayment of wages. For hourly employees, the size of a paycheck is based on two essential factors: the number of hours worked and the rate of pay. It is therefore obvious that for hourly employees to increase the size of their paycheck fraudulently, they must either falsify the number of hours worked or change the wage rate. (See Exhibit 8.10.) Because salaried employees do not receive compensation based on their time at work, in most cases these employees generate fraudulent wages by increasing their rates of pay.

When we discuss payroll frauds that involve overstated hours, we first must understand how an employee's time at work is recorded. As already discussed, time generally is kept by one of three methods. Time clocks may be used to mark the time when an employee begins and finishes work. The employee inserts a card into the clock at the beginning and end of work, and the clock imprints the current time on the card. In more sophisticated systems, computers may track automatically the time employees spend on the job based on login codes or some other similar tracking mechanism. Finally, paper or computerized time cards showing the number of hours an employee worked on a particular day often are prepared manually by the employee and approved by his manager.

Manually Prepared Time Cards

When hours are recorded manually, an employee typically fills out the time card to reflect the number of hours worked, then presents it to the supervisor for approval. The supervisor verifies the accuracy of the time card, signs or otherwise approves the card to indicate his authorization, then forwards it to the payroll department so that a paycheck can be issued. Most of the payroll frauds encountered in our study stemmed from abuses of this process.

Obviously, if an employee fills out his own time card, it may be easy to falsify his hours worked. He simply records the wrong time, showing that he arrived at work earlier or left later than he actually did. The difficulty is not in falsifying the time card

Exhibit 8.10   Falsified Hours and Salary

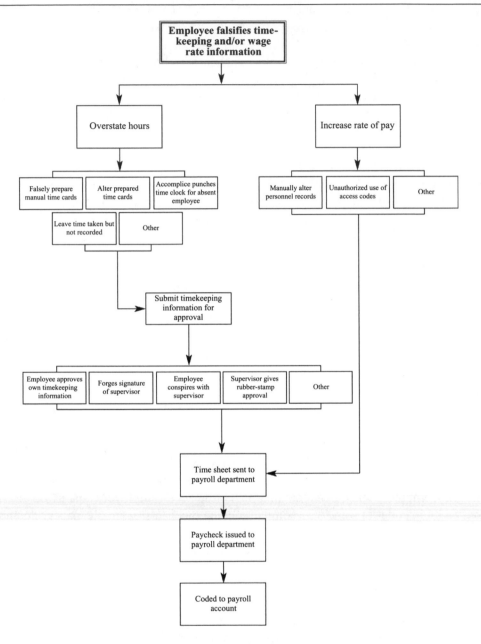

but in getting the fraudulent card approved by the employee's supervisor. There are basically three ways for the employee to obtain needed authorization.

Forging a Supervisor's Signature

When using the forging method, an employee typically withholds his paper time card from those being sent to the supervisor for approval, forges the supervisor's signature or initials, then adds the time card to the stack of authorized cards that are sent to payroll. In an electronic payroll environment, an employee who learns his or her supervisor's password can log into the system and authorize his or her own time card surreptitiously. The fraudulent time card then arrives at the payroll department with what appears to be a supervisor's approval, and a paycheck is subsequently issued.

Collusion with a Supervisor

The second way to obtain approval of a fraudulent time card is to collude with a supervisor who authorizes timekeeping information. In these schemes, the supervisor knowingly approves false time cards and usually takes a portion of the fraudulent wages. In some cases, the supervisor may take the entire amount of the overpayment. In one example, a supervisor assigned employees to better work areas or better jobs but in return demanded payment. The payment was arranged by the falsification of the employees' time cards, which the supervisor authorized. The employees were compensated for fictitious overtime, which was kicked back to the supervisor. It may be particularly difficult to detect payroll fraud when a supervisor colludes with an employee, because managers often are relied on as a control to ensure proper timekeeping.

But in payroll collusion schemes, the supervisor does not always take a cut of the overpayment. One case involved a temporary employee who added fictitious hours to her time sheet. Rather than get the approval of her direct supervisor, she obtained approval from an administrator at another site. The employee was related to this administrator, who authorized her overpayment without receiving any compensation for doing so. In another case, a supervisor needed to enhance the salary of an employee in order to keep him from leaving for another job. The supervisor authorized the payment of $10,000 in fictitious overtime to the employee. Perhaps the most unique case we came across in our study, though, was committed by two part-time employees, who did not even bother to show up for work. One of the fraudsters did not perform any verifiable work for nine months, and the other was apparently absent for two years. The time cards for these employees were completed by a timekeeper based on their work schedules, and a supervisor approved the time cards. This supervisor was also a part-time employee who held another job, in which he was supervised by one of the fraudsters. Thus, the supervisor was under pressure to authorize the fraudulent time cards in order to keep his second job.

"Rubber-Stamp" Supervisors

The third way to obtain approval of fraudulent time cards is to rely on a supervisor to approve them without reviewing their accuracy. The lazy-manager method seems risky—so much so that one would think that it would be uncommon—but it actually occurs quite frequently. A recurring theme in our studies is the reliance of fraudsters on the inattentiveness of others. When an employee sees an opportunity to make a little extra money without getting caught, that employee is more likely to be emboldened to attempt a fraud scheme. The fact that a supervisor is known to rubber-stamp time cards, or even ignore them, can be a factor in an employee's decision to begin stealing from her company.

For instance, in one case, a temporary employee noticed that his manager did not reconcile the expense journal monthly. Thus, the manager did not know how much was being paid to the temporary agency. The fraudster completed fictitious time reports, which were sent to the temporary agency and which caused the victim company to pay over $30,000 in fraudulent wages. Because the fraudster controlled the mail and the manager did not review the expense journal, this extremely simple scheme went undetected for some time. In another example of poor supervision, a bookkeeper whose duties included the preparation of payroll checks inflated her checks by adding fictitious overtime. This person added over $90,000 of unauthorized pay to her wages over a four-year period before an accountant noticed the overpayments.

Poor Custody Procedures

One form of control breakdown that occurred in several cases in our studies was the failure to maintain proper control over time cards. In a properly run system, once time cards are authorized by management, they should be sent directly to payroll. Those who prepare the time cards should not have access to them after they have been approved. Similarly, computerized time sheets should be blocked from modification by the employee once supervisor authorization has been given. When these procedures are not observed, the person who prepared a time card can alter it after the supervisor has approved it but before it is delivered to payroll. This is precisely what happened in several cases in our studies. In the case study at the beginning of this chapter, for instance, Jerry Harkanell was in charge of compiling weekly time sheets (including his own), obtaining his supervisor's approval on the sheets, and delivering the approved sheets to payroll. As we saw, Harkanell waited until his supervisor signed the unit's time sheets, then overstated his hours or posted hours he had worked to higher-paid shifts. Since the time sheet had been authorized by the supervisor, payroll assumed that the hours were legitimate.

Another way hours are falsified is in the misreporting of leave time. This is not as common as time card falsification but can nevertheless be problematic. Incidentally, it is the one instance in which salaried employees commit payroll fraud by falsifying their hours. The way a leave scheme works is very simple. An employee takes a certain amount of time off work as paid leave or vacation but does not report this leave time. Employees typically receive a certain amount of paid leave per year. If a person takes a leave of absence but does not report it, those days are not deducted from her allotted days off. In other words, she gets more leave time than she is entitled to. The result is that the employee shows up for work less yet still receives the same pay. This was another method used by Jerry Harkanell to increase his pay. Another example of this type of scheme was found in which a senior manager allowed certain persons to be absent from work without submitting leave forms to the personnel department. Consequently, these employees were able to take excess leave amounting to approximately $25,000 worth of unearned wages.

Time Clocks and Other Automated Timekeeping Systems

In companies that use time clocks to collect timekeeping information, payroll fraud usually is not complicated. In the typical scenario, the time clock is located in an unrestricted area, and a time card for each employee is kept nearby. Employees insert their time cards into the time clock at the beginning and end of their shifts, and the clock imprints the time. The length of time an employee spends at work is thus recorded. Supervisors should be present at the beginning and end of shifts to ensure that employees do not punch the time cards of absent coworkers, yet often this simple control is overlooked.

We encountered very few time clock fraud schemes, and those we did come across followed a single, uncomplicated pattern. When one employee is absent, a friend of that person punches his time card so that it appears the absent employee was at work that day. The absent employee therefore is overcompensated on his next paycheck. This method came up in a couple of our cases.

Rates of Pay

Although the preceding discussion focused on how employees overstate the number of hours they have worked, it should be remembered that employees also can receive larger paychecks by changing their pay rate. Employees' personnel or payroll records reflect their rate of pay. If employees can gain access to these records or have an accomplice with access to them, they can adjust them to receive a larger paycheck.

Commission Schemes

Commission is a form of compensation calculated as a percentage of the amount of transactions a salesperson or other employee generates. It is a unique form of compensation that is not based on hours worked or a set yearly salary but rather on an employee's revenue output. A commissioned employee's wages are based on two factors: the amount of sales generated and the percentage of those sales she is paid. In other words, there are two ways employees on commission can fraudulently increase their pay: (1) falsify the amount of sales made, or (2) increase the rate of commission. (See Exhibit 8.11.)

Fictitious Sales

Employees can falsify the amount of sales they have made in three ways, the first being the creation of fictitious sales. In one example, an unscrupulous insurance agent took advantage of his company's incentive commissions, which paid $1.25 for every $1.00 of premiums generated in the first year of a policy. The agent wrote policies to fictitious customers, paid the premiums, and received his commissions, which created an illicit profit on the transaction. For instance, if the fraudster paid $100,000 in premiums, he received $125,000 in commissions, a $25,000 profit. No payments were made on the fraudulent policies after the first year.

The way in which fictitious sales are created depends on the industry in which the fraudster operates. A fictitious sale might be constructed by the creation of fraudulent sales orders, purchase orders, credit authorizations, packing slips, invoices, and so on. Or a fraudster simply might ring up a false sale on a cash register. The key is that a fictitious sale is created, that it appears to be legitimate, and that the victim company reacts by issuing a commission check to the fraudster.

221

Exhibit 8.11   Commission Schemes

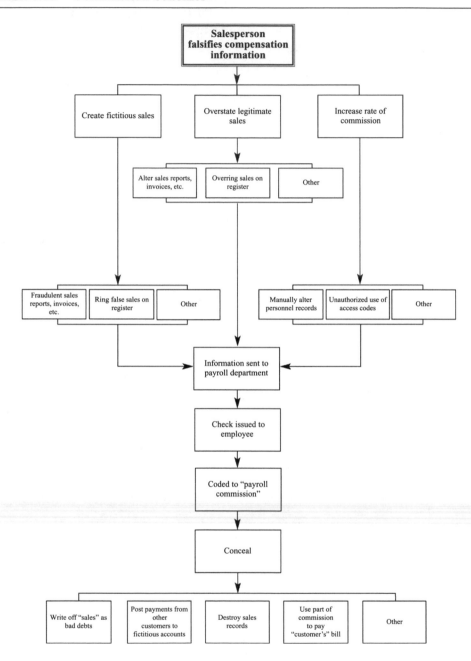

Altered Sales

The second way for fraudsters to falsify the value of sales they have made is to alter the prices listed on sales documents; in other words, fraudsters charge one price to a customer but record a higher price in the company books. This results in the payment of a commission that is larger than the fraudsters deserve. In one case, a salesman quoted a certain rate to his customers, billed them at this rate, and collected their payments—but overstated his sales reports. The fraudster intercepted and altered the invoices from these transactions to keep his customers from complaining. He also overstated the revenues received from his customers. Since the fraudster's commissions were based on the amount of revenues he billed out, he was overcompensated.

Converting Sales of Others

The third way employees can overstate sales is by claiming the sales of another employee as their own. Obviously, this method can be used only in a limited number of circumstances. In most cases, Salesman A cannot take credit for Salesman B's sale, because Salesman B also will claim it. However, the unique circumstances of one case allowed some employees to inflate their commissions fraudulently based on another person's sales. This incident involved a company that sometimes sold merchandise on layaway. Commissions on these sales were not paid until the fulfillment of the layaway contract, meaning that there could be a substantial period of time between the initial sales agreement and the resulting commission. Some layaway sales were initiated by employees who quit or were transferred before the completion of the layaway agreements, meaning that no one was slated to receive a commission on these sales. When customers made their final payments on these contracts, a manager at the location used his authority to cancel the layaway contracts and allowed current salespeople to reenter the transactions as their own. As a result, the salespeople received commission for the sales, even though they had not generated them. The manager received no benefit from this scheme other than the loyalty of his subordinates.

As mentioned, the other way to manipulate the commission process is to change the employee's rate of commission. This would likely necessitate the alteration of payroll or personnel records, records that should be off-limits to the sales staff.

Workers' Compensation

Workers' compensation is not a payroll account but rather an insurance expense. Nevertheless, it is essentially an employee benefit, entitling those persons who are injured on the job to compensation while they heal. Therefore, workers' compensation schemes are discussed in this chapter.

There was nothing tricky about any of the workers' compensation schemes we reviewed in our study. An employee simply fakes an injury and collects payments from the victim company's insurance carrier. Meanwhile, she does not work, even though she is physically able to do so. In some cases, the employee colludes with a doctor who processes bogus claims for unnecessary medical treatments, then splits the payments for these fictitious treatments with the "injured" employee.

The primary victim of a workers' compensation scheme is not the employer but the insurance carrier for the employer. It is the insurance carrier who pays for the perpetrator's fraudulent medical bills and unnecessary absences. Nevertheless, the employer is a tertiary victim of these crimes, as the bogus claims can result in higher premiums for the company in the future.

Case Study: Frequent Flier's Fraud Crashes

In his ten years at a regional office of Tyler & Hartford, Marcus Lane* had spent more time on the road than at home—which means he often whispered a long-distance goodnight to his kids over his cell phone. The 35-year-old Ph.D. traveled all over North and South America for his job as a geologist for the privately held firm specializing in environmental management and engineering services. Its extensive client list represented all types of industries and included municipalities, construction firms, petroleum companies, and manufacturers with multimillion-dollar projects. As part of a team assembled by a project manager from Tyler & Hartford, Lane was called on regularly to oversee drilling operations, conduct sampling tests, or assist with a formal site analysis.

Going from site to site, the road warrior adhered to the basic rules of business travel: Try to get a room on the top floor, away from the elevators and the ice machine. Request a seat in an emergency exit row on the airplane, where there is more legroom. Always get documentation for any travel expense—and so on. But Lane broke a basic rule of ethics: Never cheat on your expense report.

His transgression was discovered by Heidi McCullough, an accountant who worked out of Tyler & Hartford's East Coast headquarters. As she was processing Lane's most recent expense report, she noticed a discrepancy between the departure times listed on the flight receipt and boarding pass for Flight 4578 from Minneapolis to San Antonio. Whereas the receipt indicated that the flight had been scheduled to depart at 6:15 P.M., the boarding pass indicated a departure time of 6:15 A.M. McCullough figured that the discrepancy was most likely due to an error on the part of the airline. After all, Lane was a highly trusted and well-respected employee who traveled regularly on company business. But, being the prudent employee she was, she decided she'd better bring the discrepancy to the attention of Tina Marie Williams, manager of the internal audit department.

"I was immediately suspicious," recalled Williams, who was newly accredited as a CFE at the time. "Although it was possible that the airline had made an error, it seemed much more likely that the flight receipt, the boarding pass, or both had been doctored. This was a situation that needed to be looked into." The first thing Williams did was contact the airline to verify whether the flight number in question was even a legitimate flight, and, if so, what the correct scheduled departure time was. She learned that flight 4578 was, in fact, an actual flight and that it had been scheduled to depart—and did depart—at 6:15 P.M. But because Lane had booked the flight using his own credit card, she was unable to confirm with the airline whether he actually took the flight.

Next Williams proceeded to carefully review the rest of the Lane's travel receipts for his trip to San Antonio. Two of the receipts stood out. One was for a car rental, which indicated that the car was picked up by Lane at noon on the day of his flight to San Antonio. The second was a receipt for lunch at a restaurant located near the San Antonio International Airport, also on the day of the flight.

*Several names and details have been changed to preserve anonymity.

Williams suspected that Lane had not actually boarded flight 4578 but had created a phony boarding pass to make it appear as though he had. As an experienced auditor, Williams was familiar with a common expense reimbursement scheme in which an employee books two separate flights to the same location, but with a huge cost difference; he or she uses the cheaper ticket for the actual flight and returns the more expensive ticket for credit. And, of course, he or she submits the more expensive ticket for reimbursement.

"Company policy is that employees must book all travel through the company travel agent. But Lane has been booking his own travel since long before I started working here. When I mentioned my concerns over this to senior management, I was told to let it be—that Lane was a loyal and trustworthy employee and that I had nothing to worry about."

Playing by the book, Williams called the legal department at Tyler & Hartford to apprise it of the situation and ask for any advice on procedure. Williams said that the legal department put the case under protective privilege.

She then overnighted her collection of evidence along with her detailed analysis of the airfare scheme to Lane's immediate supervisor at the regional office, who in turn showed it to his boss at his earliest availability. The two managers scheduled a private meeting with Lane bright and early on the following Monday morning.

Without mincing words, one of the managers asked Lane, "How is it that you were able to pick up a rental car at noon and have lunch in San Antonio when your flight from Minneapolis didn't depart until 6 P.M.? Lane, knowing that he had been caught, immediately confessed to double-booking flights and creating fictitious boarding passes using his home computer, in order to make it appear as though he took a more expensive flight than he had actually taken. He explained that he was experiencing temporary financial problems as the result of his recent divorce, that he just needed some money to tide him over. He said that he intended to pay the money back as soon as possible. According to Williams, who heard the account secondhand, Lane vowed, "I only did it for four months." He swore that he padded his expense account for just a brief period; he urged the managers to check out all the other expense reports he had submitted in his ten years at Tyler & Hartford and voluntarily agreed to surrender his personal credit card and bank records. He also agreed to provide his own accounting of the crime.

All in all, Lane had swindled the company out of $4,100. He agreed to pay back the stolen money. "He paid us $2,000 in one lump sum initially, then $150 every two months after that," Williams recalled.

Lane was terminated promptly, but Tyler & Hartford decided not to prosecute the geologist. They kept their month long investigation quiet as well. "No one found out about it except through the grapevine." Even then, others only knew that somebody got in trouble for fudging an expense report, said Williams.

True to the company's culture of taking decisive action, Williams and her team resolved this case in just under one month from the time of its detection. "This is the smoothest case we've ever had," she admitted.

"We discovered that it was a very easy fraud to perpetrate, especially since it is so simple to create phony airline tickets and boarding passes. On behalf of Tyler & Hartford, Williams later launched a target audit to uncover other travel scams, and found some. Lane's scam, unfortunately, was not an isolated incident.

After Lane's fraud was exposed, Williams received full support from senior management for clarification and better enforcement of the policy that all travel for the entire company, including all 50 regional offices, must be booked through the company travel agent using a designated company credit card. "That makes our auditing lives so much easier. It gives us better control as well as better cost data," said Williams.

Williams also recommended that employees only use a company credit card to charge all other business expenditures. Top management accepted the recommendation and issued a mandate. Williams was pleased, as the billing statement for a company credit card provides a strong audit tool and an easy-access audit trail.

EXPENSE REIMBURSEMENT DATA FROM ACFE *2009 GLOBAL FRAUD SURVEY*

Frequency and Cost

In our 2009 study, expense reimbursement fraud was cited in 30 percent of fraudulent disbursement cases, ranking second in terms of frequency. (The sum of these percentages exceeds 100 percent because some cases involved multiple fraud schemes that fell into more than one category. Various charts in this chapter may reflect percentages that total in excess of 100 percent for similar reasons.) In contrast, expense reimbursement fraud schemes were the second least costly form of fraudulent disbursement in our study, resulting in a median loss of $33,000. (See Exhibits 8.12 and 8.13.)

Exhibit 8.12 *2009 Global Fraud Survey*: **Frequency of Fraudulent Disbursements**

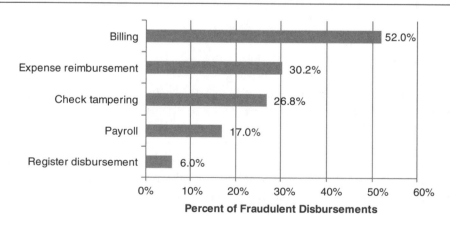

Exhibit 8.13 *2009 Global Fraud Survey*: **Median Loss of Fraudulent Disbursements**

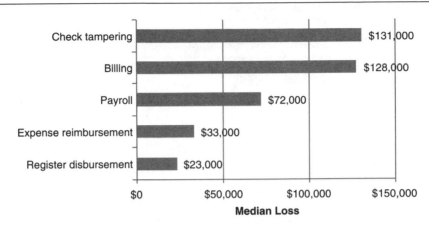

Exhibit 8.14 shows the distribution of dollar losses in expense reimbursement schemes compared with the distribution among all occupational frauds. Two-thirds of the expense reimbursement schemes studied caused losses of less than $100,000, compared to 38.6 percent of all cases.

Detection of Expense Reimbursement Schemes

We received 272 responses in which the method of initial detection for expense reimbursement cases was identified. Similar to the distribution of all cases, tips (38.6 percent) management review (21 percent), and internal audit (16.5 percent) were the three

Exhibit 8.14 *2009 Global Fraud Survey*: **Dollar Loss Distribution for Expense Reimbursement Schemes**

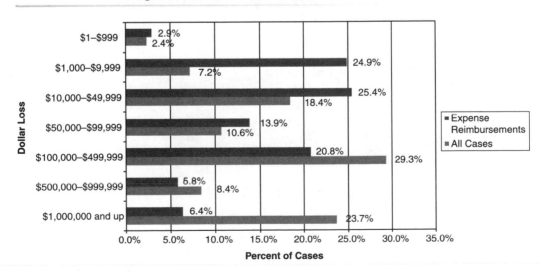

Exhibit 8.15 *2009 Global Fraud Survey*: Detection of Expense Reimbursement Schemes

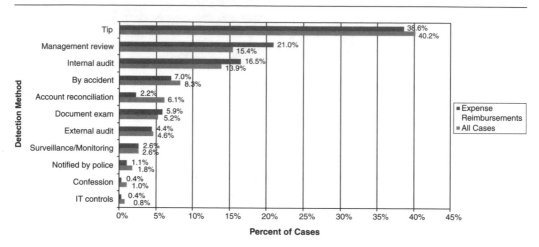

most commonly cited methods of detection for expense reimbursement schemes. (See Exhibit 8.15.)

Perpetrators of Expense Reimbursement Schemes

The general trend in our study was that the highest percentage of occupational frauds was committed by employees, but expense reimbursement schemes were more likely to be committed by higher-level perpetrators. Almost three-quarters of the cases involving expense reimbursement fraud were perpetrated by someone at the managerial or owner/ executive level. (See Exhibit 8.16.)

Exhibit 8.16 *2009 Global Fraud Survey*: Perpetrators of Expense Reimbursement Schemes

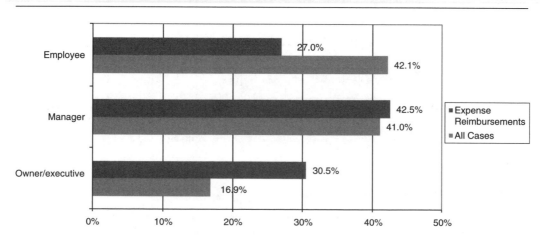

Exhibit 8.17 *2009 Global Fraud Survey*: Median Loss by Perpetrator Position in Expense Reimbursement Schemes

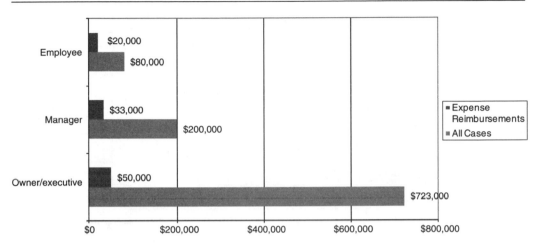

Although expense reimbursement cases were committed more commonly by managers and owners than was the case with occupational frauds as a whole, the losses committed by these two categories of perpetrators were much lower in expense reimbursement fraud than in all cases. (See Exhibit 8.17.)

Victims of Expense Reimbursement Schemes

Exhibits 8.18 and 8.19 compare the expense reimbursement frauds with all of the fraud cases in our study based on the number of employees in the victim organization.

Exhibit 8.18 *2009 Global Fraud Survey*: Size of Victim in Expense Reimbursement Schemes

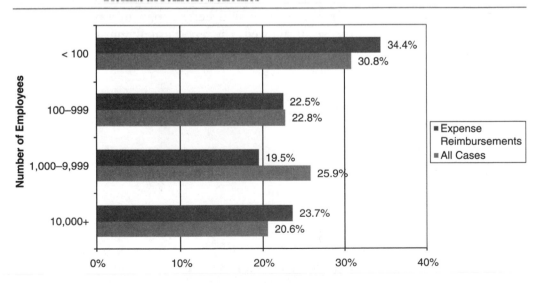

Exhibit 8.19 *2009 Global Fraud Survey*: **Median Loss by Number of Employees in Expense Reimbursement Schemes**

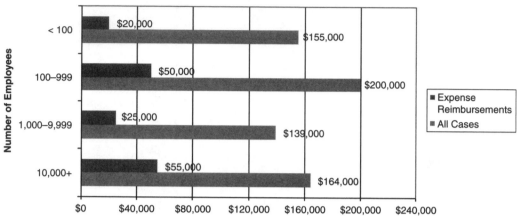

Expense reimbursement schemes occurred at a higher rate than fraud in general in organizations with fewer than 100 employees and those with more than 10,000 employees. Additionally, the median losses for expense account frauds were significantly less than for frauds in general for all organizational size categories.

EXPENSE REIMBURSEMENT SCHEMES

Companies usually pay expense reimbursements in this manner: An employee submits a report detailing an expense incurred for a business purpose, such as a business lunch with a client, airfare, hotel bills associated with business travel, and so on. In preparing an expense report, an employee usually must explain the business purpose for the expense as well as the time, date, and location in which it was incurred. Attached to the report should be support documentation for the expense—typically a receipt. In some cases, canceled checks written by the employee or copies of a personal credit card statement showing the expense are allowed. The report usually must be authorized by a supervisor in order for the expense to be reimbursed. The four main types of expense reimbursement schemes are:

1. Mischaracterized expenses
2. Overstated expenses
3. Fictitious expenses
4. Multiple reimbursements

Mischaracterized Expenses

Most companies reimburse only certain expenses of their employees. Which expenses a company will pay depends to an extent on policy, but in general, business-related travel, lodging, and meals are reimbursed. One of the most basic expense schemes is perpetrated simply by requesting reimbursement for a personal expense, claiming that it is business related. (See Exhibit 8.20.) Examples of mischaracterized expenses include claiming personal travel as a business trip, listing dinner with a friend as ''business development,'' and so on. Fraudsters may submit the receipts from their personal expenses along with their reports and provide business reasons for the incurred costs.

Exhibit 8.20   Mischaracterized Expenses

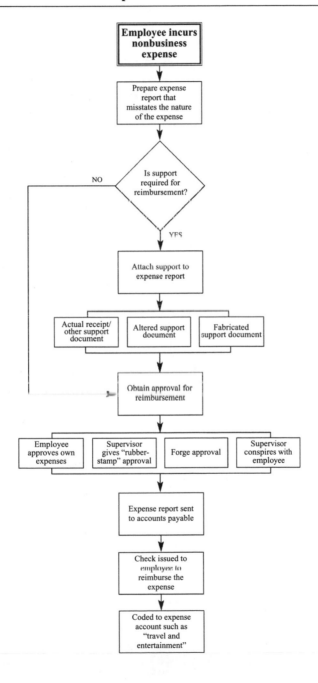

The false expense report induces the victim company to issue a check, reimbursing the perpetrator for personal expenses. A mischaracterization is a simple scheme, amounting to little more than fibbing. In cases involving airfare and overnight travel, a mischaracterization sometimes can be detected simply by comparing the employee's expense reports to her work schedule. Often the dates of the so-called business trip coincide with a vacation or day off. Detailed expense reports allow a company to make this kind of comparison and therefore are very helpful in preventing expenses schemes.

Requiring detailed information means more than just supporting documents; it should mean precise statements of what was purchased as well as when and where. In one case, a fraudster submitted credit card statements as support for expenses but submitted only the top portion of the statements, not the portion that describes what was purchased. Over 95 percent of his reimbursed expenses were of a personal rather than a business nature. Of course, in this particular example, the scheme was made easier because the perpetrator was the chief executive of the company, making it unlikely that anyone would challenge the validity of his expense reports.

Interestingly, many of the mischaracterized expense schemes in our studies were undertaken by high-level employees, owners, or officers. Many times, such a perpetrator actually has authority over the account from which expenses were reimbursed. In other cases, perpetrators simply fail to submit detailed expense reports, or even any expense reports at all. Obviously, when a company is willing to reimburse employee expenses without any verifying documentation, it is easy for an employee to take advantage of the system. Nevertheless, there does not seem to be anything inherent in the nature of a mischaracterization scheme that would preclude its use in a system in which detailed reports are required. As an example, suppose a traveling salesman goes on a trip and runs up a large bar bill one night in his hotel, saves his receipt, and lists this expense as ''business entertainment'' on an expense report. Nothing about the time, date, or nature of the expense would readily point to fraud, and the receipt would appear to substantiate the expense. Short of contacting the client who was allegedly entertained, there is little hope of identifying the expense as fraudulent.

One final note is that mischaracterization schemes can be extremely costly. They do not always deal with a free lunch here or there but instead may involve very large sums of money. In one example, two mid-level managers ran up $1 million in inappropriate expenses over a two-year period. Their travel was not properly overseen and their expense requests were not closely reviewed, allowing them to spend large amounts of company money on international travel, lavish entertainment of friends, and the purchase of expensive gifts. They simply claimed that they incurred these expenses entertaining corporate clients. Though this case was more costly than the average mischaracterization scheme, it should underscore the potential harm that can occur if the reimbursement process is not carefully attended to.

Overstated Expense Reports

Instead of seeking reimbursement for personal expenses, some employees overstate the cost of actual business expenses. (See Exhibit 8.21.) This can be accomplished in a number of ways.

Exhibit 8.21   Overstated Expenses

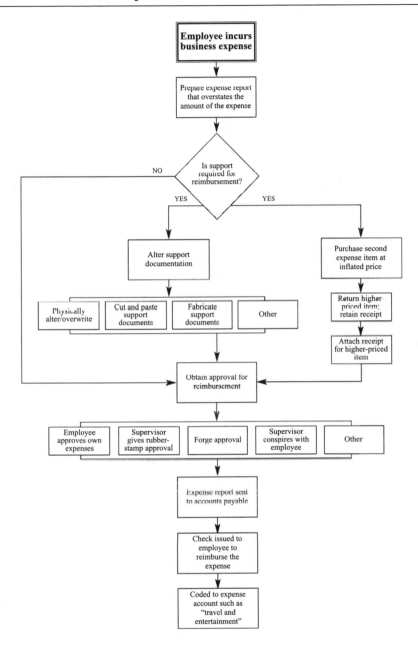

Altered Receipts

The most fundamental example of overstated expense reimbursement schemes occurs when an employee doctors a receipt or other supporting documentation to reflect a higher cost than what was actually paid. The employee may use correction fluid, a ballpoint pen, or some other method to change the price reflected on the receipt before submitting the expense report. If the company does not require original documents as support, the perpetrator generally attaches a copy of the receipt to the expense report. (Alterations are usually less noticeable on a photocopy than on an original document.) For precisely this reason, many businesses require original receipts and ink signatures on expense reports.

As with other expense frauds, overstated expense schemes often succeed because of poor controls. In companies in which supporting documents are not required, for example, fraudsters simply lie about how much they paid for a business expense. With no support available, it may be very difficult to disprove an employee's false expense claims.

Overpurchasing

The case of Marcus Lane illustrated another way to overstate a reimbursement form: the ''overpurchasing'' of business expenses. As we saw, Lane purchased two tickets for his business travel, one expensive and one cheap. He returned the expensive ticket but used the receipt for it, along with a phony boarding pass, to overstate his expense report. Meanwhile, he used the cheaper ticket for his trip. In this manner, he was able to be reimbursed for an expense that was larger than what he had actually paid.

Overstating Another Employee's Expenses

Overstated expense schemes are not only committed by the person who incurs the expense. They also may be committed by someone else who handles or processes expense reports. Such an example occurred in a case in which a petty cashier used correction fluid on other employees' requests for travel advances and inserted larger amounts. The cashier then passed on the legitimate travel advances and pocketed the excess. This method can be used for expense reimbursements as well as travel advances.

This kind of scheme is most likely to occur in a system in which expenses are reimbursed in currency rather than by a check, since perpetrators would be unable to extract their cut from a single check made out to another employee.

Orders to Overstate Expenses

Finally, we have seen a few cases in which employees knowingly falsified their own reports but did so at the direction of their supervisors. In one instance, a department head forced his subordinates to inflate their expenses and return the proceeds to him. The employees went along, presumably for fear of losing their jobs. The fraud lasted for ten years and cost the victim company approximately $6 million. Similarly, in another case, a sales executive instructed his salesmen to inflate their expenses in order to generate cash for a slush fund that was then used to pay bribes and to provide improper forms of entertainment for clients and customers.

Fictitious Expense Schemes

Employees sometimes seek expense reimbursements for wholly fictitious items. Instead of overstating a real business expense or seeking reimbursement for a personal

Exhibit 8.22   Fictitious Expenses

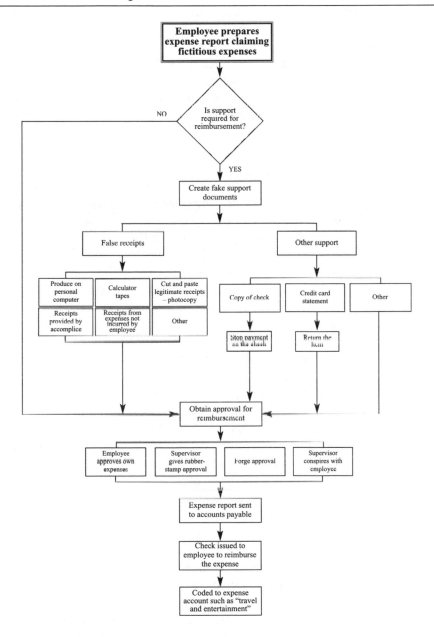

expense, an employee simply invents a purchase that needs to be reimbursed. (See Exhibit 8.22.)

Producing Fictitious Receipts

One way to generate a reimbursement for a fictitious expense is to create bogus support documents, such as false receipts. Personal computers enable employees to create realistic-looking counterfeit receipts at home. Such was the scheme in a case in which an employee manufactured fake receipts using his computer and laser printer. The counterfeits were very sophisticated, even including the logos of the stores in which he had allegedly made business-related purchases.

Computers are not the only means for creating support for a fictitious expense. The fraudster in the last case used several methods for justifying fictitious expenses as his scheme progressed. He began by using calculator printouts to simulate receipts, then advanced to cutting and pasting receipts from suppliers before finally progressing using computer software to generate fictitious receipts.

Obtaining Blank Receipts from Vendors

If receipts are not created by the fraudster, they can be obtained from legitimate suppliers in a number of ways. A manager in one example simply requested blank receipts from waiters, bartenders, and others. He then filled in these receipts to ''create'' business expenses, including the names of clients whom he allegedly entertained. The fraudster usually paid all his expenses in cash to prevent an audit trail. One thing that undid this culprit was the fact that the last digit on most of the prices on his receipt was usually a zero or a five. This fact, noted by an astute employee, raised questions about the validity of his expenses.

A similar scheme was found in a case in which an employee's girlfriend worked at a restaurant near the victim company. This girlfriend validated credit card receipts and gave them to the fraudster to submit with his expense reports.

Instead of asking for blank receipts, some employees simply steal them. In some cases, fraudsters steal an entire stack of blank receipts and submit them over time to verify fictitious business expenses. This type of fraud should be identifiable by the fact that the perpetrator is submitting consecutively numbered receipts from the same establishment even though her expense reports are spread out over time.

Claiming the Expenses of Others

Another way that fraudsters use actual receipts to generate unwarranted reimbursements is by submitting expense reports for expenses that were paid by others. Take, for instance, the case in which an employee claimed hotel expenses that had actually been paid by his client. Photocopies of legitimate hotel bills were attached to the expense report as if the employee had paid for his own room.

As we have stated, not all companies require receipts to be attached to expense reports. Checks written by the employee or copies of a personal credit card bill might be allowed as support in lieu of a receipt. In one case, a person wrote personal checks that appeared to be for business expenses, then photocopied these checks and attached them to reimbursement requests. In actuality, nothing was purchased with the checks; they were destroyed after the copies were made. This enabled the fraudster to receive a reimbursement from his employer without ever actually incurring a business expense. The same method can be used with credit cards, when a copy of a statement is used to support a purchase. Once the expense report is filed, the fraudster returns the item and receives a credit to her account.

In many expense schemes, the perpetrator is not required to submit any support at all. This makes it much easier to create the appearance of an expense that does not actually exist.

Multiple Reimbursements

Based on our study, the least common of the expense schemes is the multiple reimbursement. This type of fraud involves the submission of a single expense several times to receive multiple reimbursements. The most frequent example of a multiple reimbursement scheme is the submission of several types of support for the same expense. In one case, an employee used an airline ticket stub and a travel agency invoice on separate expense reports so that he could be reimbursed twice for the cost of a single flight. The fraudster had his division president authorize one report and the vice president authorize the other so that neither saw both reports. In addition, the perpetrator allowed a time lag of about a month between the filing of the two reports, so that the duplication would be less noticeable.

In cases in which a company does not require original documents as support, some employees use several copies of the same support document to generate multiple reimbursements.

Rather than file two expense reports, employees may charge an item to the company credit card, save the receipt, and attach it to an expense report as if they paid for the item themselves. The victim company therefore ends up paying twice for the same expense.

Perhaps the most interesting case of duplicated expenses in our study involved a government official who had responsibilities over two distinct budgets. The perpetrator took business trips and made expense claims to the travel funds of each of his budgets, thereby receiving a double reimbursement. In some cases, the culprit charged the expenses to another budget category and still submitted reports through both budgets, generating a triple reimbursement. Eventually this person began to fabricate trips when he was not even leaving town, which led to the detection of his scheme.

DETECTION OF PAYROLL SCHEMES

Independent Payroll Distribution

Ghost employee schemes can be uncovered by having personnel (other than the payroll department) distribute the payroll checks and by requiring positive identification of the payee.

Analysis of Payee Address or Accounts

If payroll checks are mailed or deposited automatically, a list of duplicate addresses or deposit accounts may reveal ghost employees or duplicate payments.

Duplicate Social Security Numbers

Because each employee is required to have a Social Security number, a listing of duplicate numbers may reveal ghost employees.

Overtime Authorization

Requiring employees to have overtime authorized by a supervisor, having the supervisor be responsible for the time cards, and having the supervisor refer the time cards directly to payroll will aid in reducing overtime abuses. In addition, the payroll department should scan the time reports and question obvious abuses, such as only one employee working overtime in a department or excessive overtime on a time card. By examining the source documentation, unauthorized overtime and falsified hours abuses may be detected.

Commissions

- Compare commission expenses to sales figures to verify linear correlation.
- Prepare a comparative analysis of commission earned by salesperson, verifying rates and calculation accuracy. Inordinately high earnings by an individual could signal fraud.
- Analyze sales by salesperson for uncollected sales amounts.
- Determine proper segregation of duties in calculation of commission amounts. Commissions should be independently provided by personnel outside the sales department.
- Contact a random sample of customers to confirm sales.

Analysis of Deductions from Payroll Checks

An analysis of payroll withholdings may reveal either ghost employees or trust account abuses. Ghost employees often will have no withholding taxes, insurance, or other normal deductions. Therefore, a listing of any employee without these items may reveal a ghost employee.

An analysis of withholding-tax deposits may reveal that trust account taxes have been "borrowed," even for a short period, before the taxes are deposited. Comparing the disbursement date with the deposit date should reveal if the trust account taxes have been borrowed. Additionally, any delinquent payroll tax notices from the Internal Revenue Service should serve as a red flag to potential trust account tax "borrowings."

DETECTION OF EXPENSE REIMBURSEMENT SCHEMES

Detecting personal expense reimbursement fraud involves two basic methods. The first of these is a review and analysis of expense accounts. The second detection method is a detailed review of expense reimbursements.

Review and Analysis of Expense Accounts

Generally, expense account review uses one of two methods: historical comparisons or comparisons with budgeted amounts. A historical comparison compares the balance expended this period to the balance spent in prior, similar periods. When performing this review, consider changes to the marketing, servicing, or other company operations.

Budgets are estimates of the money and/or time necessary to complete the task. They are based on past experience with consideration for current and future business conditions. Therefore, when comparing actual and budgeted expenses, it is important to determine inordinate expenses or inaccurate budget estimates.

Detailed Review of Expense Reimbursements

Overall, the best detection method is a detailed review of employee expense reimbursements. This method requires that the fraud examiner have, at the time of the examination, a calendar and a copy of the employee's schedule for the relevant period. The examiner should be familiar with the travel and entertainment policies of the company. Additionally, these two steps may help to detect and deter employee expense abuses:

1. Require employees to submit their expense reimbursements for a detailed review before payment is reimbursed. If employees know that expense reimbursements must be reviewed before payment is made, it is more likely that the expenses submitted will not be fraudulently prepared.
2. Periodically review employee expense reimbursements. This is particularly effective shortly before employee performance reviews.

PREVENTION OF PAYROLL SCHEMES

There are two basic preventive measures for payroll-related fraud: segregation of duties and periodic payroll review and analysis.

Segregation of Duties

These duties should be segregated:

- Payroll preparation
- Payroll disbursement (into payroll and withholding tax accounts)
- Payroll distribution
- Payroll bank reconciliations
- Human Resources departmental functions

If payroll is prepared by personnel not responsible for its distribution and reconciliation, it will be difficult for anyone to add ghost employees. Nor will people be able to "borrow" the trust account taxes because they will not have access to the disbursing function. In smaller companies, this function often is handled outside the firm at pennies per employee.

After the payroll checks are prepared, accounting should handle the transfer of funds from the general accounts to the payroll accounts. The personnel department should distribute checks and require identification in exchange for the payroll checks. This will curtail the opportunity to add ghost employees to the payroll. A suggested form of identification might be company-issued access passes, if available.

If the bank reconciliation function for the payroll account is assigned to someone other than those in the just-described functions, then all the payroll functions have been segregated. No one is able to add ghost employees or borrow the withholding taxes without the opportunity for discovery by someone else.

Periodic Review and Analysis of Payroll

Periodically, an independent review of the payroll might reveal that internal controls are not working as designed. Comparing deposit dates with dates of payroll disbursement or transfer may reveal ghost employees. An occasional independent payroll distribution may reveal ghost employees.

The presence of certain duplications or omissions may reveal the presence of ghost employees:

- More than one employee with the same address
- More than one employee with the same Social Security number
- More than one employee with the same bank account number (automatic deposit)
- Employees with no withholding

Red Flags of Payroll Fraud

In addition, the next questions will help spot red flags to payroll distribution fraud and help with installing control procedures:

- Are personnel records maintained independently of payroll and timekeeping functions?
- Is the payroll accounting function independent of the general ledger function?
- Are changes to payroll not made unless the personnel department sends approved notification directly to the payroll department?
- Are references and backgrounds checked for new hires?
- Are all wage rates authorized in writing by a designated official?
- Are signed authorizations on file for employees whose wages are subject to special deductions?
- Are bonuses, commissions, and overtime approved in advance and reviewed for compliance with company policies?
- Are sick leave, vacations, and holidays reviewed for compliance with company policy?
- Are appropriate forms completed and signed by employees to show authorization for payroll deductions and withholding exemptions?
- Is the payroll checked periodically against the personnel records for terminated employees, fictitious employees, and the like?
- Is a time clock used for office employees as well as factory workers?
- If a time clock is used, are time cards (1) punched by employees in the presence of a designated supervisor and (2) signed by a supervisor at the end of the payroll period?

- Are time cards and production reports reviewed and compared with payroll distribution reports and production schedules?
- Are payroll registers reviewed and approved before disbursements are made for (1) names of employees, (2) hours worked, (3) wage rates, (4) deductions, (5) agreement with payroll checks, and (6) unusual items?
- Are all employees paid by check out of a separate bank payroll account?
- Are payroll checks prenumbered and issued in numerical sequence?
- Is access restricted to unissued payroll checks and signature plates?
- Are checks drawn and signed by designated officials who do not (1) prepare payroll, (2) have access to the accounting records, or (3) have custody of cash funds?
- Are payroll checks distributed by someone other than the department head or the person who prepares the payroll?
- Is the distribution of the payroll rotated periodically to different employees without prior notice?
- Is the payroll bank account reconciled by a designated employee who (1) is not involved in the preparing of payroll, (2) does not sign the checks, or (3) does not handle the check distributions?
- Do payroll bank account reconciliations procedures include comparing the paid checks to the payroll and scrutinizing canceled check endorsements?
- Are the payroll registers reconciled to the general ledger control accounts?
- Is a liability account set up for all wages that have remained unclaimed for a certain period of time? If yes, (1) have these wages been redeposited in a special bank account, and (2) is identification required to be presented at the time of their subsequent distribution?
- Are distributions of hours (direct and indirect) to activity or departments reviewed and approved by supervisory personnel?
- Are actual payroll amounts reviewed and compared to budgeted amounts, and are variances analyzed regularly?
- Do adequate procedures exist for timely and accurate preparation and filing of payroll tax returns and related taxes?
- Are employee benefit plan contributions reconciled to appropriate employee census data?
- Are adequate, detailed records maintained of the entity's liability for vacation pay and sick pay? If yes, are they periodically reconciled to the general ledger control accounts?

PREVENTION OF EXPENSE REIMBURSEMENT SCHEMES

Detailed Expense Reports: Submission and Review

Detailed expense reports should require this information:

- Receipts or other support documentation
- Explanation of the expense including specific business purpose

- Time period expense occurred
- Place of expenditure
- Amount

It is not enough to have the detailed reports submitted if they are not reviewed. A policy requiring the periodic review of expense reports, coupled with examining the appropriate detail, will help deter employees from submitting personal expenses for reimbursement.

CHAPTER 9

Inventory and Other Assets

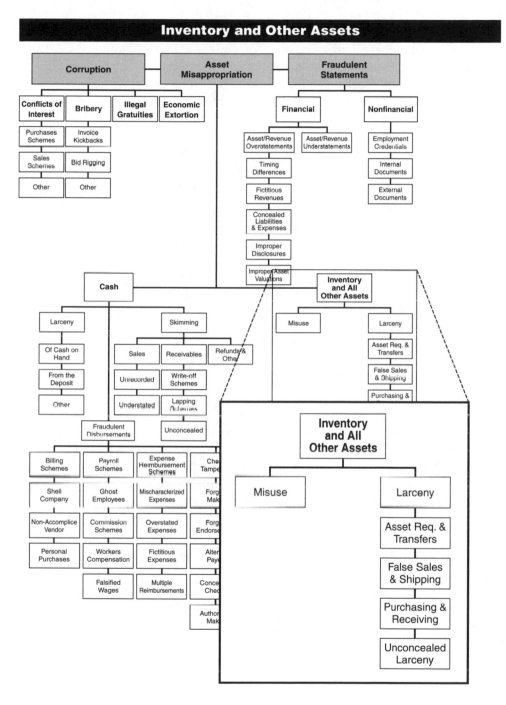

Case Study: Chipping Away at High-Tech Theft

Nineteen-year-old Larry Gunter* didn't know much about computers, but he worked as a shipping clerk in a computer manufacturer's warehouse. Like many other companies in Silicon Valley, this company produced thousands of miniature electronic circuits—microprocessor chips—the building block of personal computers.

Gunter didn't work in the plant's "clean room" building, where the chips were manufactured. The company moved the chips, along with other computer components, next door to the warehouse for processing and inventory. On the open market, one of these computer chips, which is comprised of hundreds of millions of transistors packed into a space no bigger than a fingernail, is worth about $40. Over 1,000 chips were packaged in plastic storage tubes inside a company-marked cardboard box.

Gunter knew they were worth something, but he didn't know how much. One day, he took a chip from a barrel in the warehouse and gave it to his girlfriend's father, Grant Thurman, whom he knew operated some type of computer salvage business. He told Thurman that the company had discarded the chip as "scrap."

"I asked him if he knew anyone who would buy scrap chips," Gunter said, and Thurman said he did. "So after about another week or two I stole three boxes of computer chips and brought them to Grant to sell them to his computer guy. Around a week later I got paid by Grant Thurman in the amount of $5,000 in a personal check."

Gunter knew the chips were not scrap, since the boxes, each about the size of a shoebox, bore the marking "SIMMS," signifying that the chips were sound. In fact, the manufacturer maintained a standard procedure for scrap chips, taking them to another warehouse on the company's grounds and sealing the components for shipment to another plant for destruction.

Gunter concealed the boxes from the security guards by placing them on the bottom of his work cart, with empty boxes on top. He pushed the cart out of the warehouse as if he were just taking empty boxes to the trash. Once in the parking lot, where there were no security guards, he loaded the three boxes of chips into his truck.

Shortly after the theft, an inventory manager filling an order noticed that many company chips were missing and immediately went to his supervisor, the warehouse manager. The manager verified that they were missing about ten cartons of chips, worth over $30,000. They contacted the company's director of operations, who accelerated the product inventory process at the plant. Instead of taking product inventory once a month, he began taking it once a week.

Gunter still found it easy to steal, he said, because the security guards didn't pay much attention and because it was easy to evade the stationary surveillance cameras in the warehouse. About two weeks after his first theft, he stole four boxes of new chips, for which Thurman paid him $10,000. Excited about his new conquest, Gunter told his young friend and coworker, Larry Spelber, about the easy profit to be made. The two could split $50,000 from a theft of six boxes of chips, he told Spelber—enough to quit work and finance their schooling.

---

*Several names and details have been changed to preserve anonymity.

By this time, however, the company had detected the second loss and contacted private investigator and fraud examiner Lee Roberts. Roberts, head of Roberts Protection & Investigations, had worked with the company's attorney before.

"They knew exactly how much of their product they were missing," Roberts said, "because no product was supposed to leave the building unless they had the paper for loading it on the truck to fill a specific order. However, there was a flaw in the system. The company's operation was separated in two buildings, about 300 feet apart. . . . They would receive an extremely valuable product, and it would go from one building to the other simply by being pushed by employees with carts through this 300-foot parking lot. Consequently, they would end up with an overstock of product that needed to leave the warehouse and be returned to Building One. Of course, that generated no internal paperwork; someone would simply say 'I'm taking this product to Building Two' or vice versa, and that was such a common occurrence that the security guards started to think nothing about it.

"My immediate concern was," Roberts said, "if we've got something leaving the building in the ordered process, then we must have supervisors involved, drivers involved, and the like. It would be a fairly massive operation, and maybe that was their concern."

Roberts suspected the thefts occurred between these interbuilding transfers. Since the employees who did these transfers were the 30 or so warehouse floor workers, he had many potential suspects.

To catch the thieves, however, a new video surveillance system would need to be set up at the warehouse. "We looked at their video surveillance system and found their cameras were improperly positioned, and they were not saving their tapes in the library long enough to go back and look at them." Roberts's firm, which partly specializes in alarms and security protection, set up an additional 16 hidden video cameras inside the warehouse as well as additional cameras in the parking lots.

"We agreed to pretend that nothing had happened," Roberts said of the thefts, "which would give the suspects a false sense of security, and the company agreed to restock the computer chips."

The warehouse manager and his assistant began to surreptitiously track interbuilding transfers on a daily basis. With access to the paperwork and new video, "we were able to freeze-frame images" in order to look at all sides of an employee's cart. This time, the warehouse manager knew exactly how many boxes an employee was supposed to be taking to the other building.

Unbeknownst to Gunter and Spelber, the video cameras recorded them talking in the aisleways and other areas of the warehouse. Coupled with the daily inventory check, the record showed that the two employees frequently had more than the number of boxes they were supposed to be moving.

About 3:30 one afternoon, Gunter and Spelber removed six boxes from the shelves, placed them on a cart with empty boxes on top, and moved the cart outside. In the parking lot, Spelber loaded the boxes into his truck and returned to work. After work, they drove their own vehicles down the street and transferred the boxes to Gunter's car.

At home, Gunter removed the company labels from the chips and drove to Thurman's house. Thurman promised to pay him $50,000 for this stock.

Gunter and Spelber never saw that money. The next day, company security confronted them with the evidence. They quickly admitted their guilt and identified Thurman as the receiver of the stolen equipment. When police interviewed Thurman at his home, he denied knowing that the computer chips were stolen, but he admitted to reselling the chips to an acquaintance named Marty for $180,000, paid for with cashier's checks.

Interviews with Marty, along with check receipts, revealed that the amount was actually much greater—Marty had paid approximately $697,000 to Thurman for the chips (a profit of about 50 cents on the dollar, as compared to the 10 cents on the dollar Gunter received). Although investigators could not uncover any stolen equipment, they believed that Marty had sold the goods to the aerospace industry and possibly to federal agencies.

The next day, police arrested Thurman after he attempted to make a large withdrawal from his credit union. Thurman and Gunter both served over a year in the state pen for grand theft and embezzlement; Spelber got nine months in a work furlough program. The police were never able to tag anything on Marty, who made the most money in the open market for the chips. Since none of the product could be found in his store, and since investigators could not prove he knew the property was stolen, they could not criminally prosecute him.

Roberts said the case was unique in that, at the time, it represented the largest internal theft in the history of this California county. The company, though unable to recover most of the stolen property, learned a valuable lesson from the fraud. Afterward, managers conducted tighter controls on transfers of property between buildings, produced more frequent inventory audits, and established enhanced physical security, which included a new chain-link fence between the two buildings.

"I think this fraud was difficult to detect because the audit controls that they set up, and the manner in which they had set them up, were improper," Roberts said. "That's a common thing that we see as fraud examiners or investigators. Often people spend a great deal of money to set up audit controls—they set up physical security; they install alarms—and we often say to them: Simply buying that piece of equipment or putting those procedures into place is not enough. You need a trained, experienced professional to tell you how to do it and how to use them. If you don't do it the right way, it's worthless."

OVERVIEW: NONCASH MISAPPROPRIATION
DATA FROM ACFE *2009 GLOBAL FRAUD SURVEY*

Frequency and Cost

Noncash schemes were not nearly as common as cash schemes in our survey, accounting for only 20 percent of asset misappropriations. (The sum of these percentages exceeds 100 percent because some cases involved multiple fraud schemes that fell into more than one category. Various charts in this chapter may reflect percentages that

Exhibit 9.1 *2009 Global Fraud Survey*: **Cash versus Noncash Schemes**

Scheme Type	Percent of Asset Misappropriation Cases	Median Cost
Cash Misappropriations (1,361 cases)	85.6%	$120,000
Non-Cash Misappropriations (322 cases)	20.3%	$90,000

total in excess of 100 percent for similar reasons.) Additionally, noncash schemes had a lower median cost than frauds that targeted cash. (See Exhibit 9.1.)

We received 251 noncash cases in which the dollar loss from the scheme was identified. As Exhibit 9.2 shows, the distribution of dollar losses for noncash schemes was fairly similar to that of all cases, but noncash schemes were more prevalent in the $1,000 to $50,000 loss range.

Types of Noncash Assets Stolen

By far, *physical assets*, including inventory and equipment, were the most commonly misappropriated noncash asset in our study. Fraudsters embezzled physical assets in 75 percent of the cases involving noncash misappropriations. (See Exhibit 9.3.)

Although securities were the least likely asset to be misappropriated (15 cases), the median loss in cases involving securities theft was significantly higher than in any other category, at $10,000,000. (See Exhibit 9.4.)

Detection of Noncash Theft Schemes

We received 316 cases that identified the means by which noncash schemes were initially detected. *Tips* were cited in 44 percent of these cases, which was a higher rate than we saw in the general body of occupational frauds. Noncash schemes were slightly

Exhibit 9.2 *2009 Global Fraud Survey*: **Dollar Loss Distribution for Noncash Schemes**

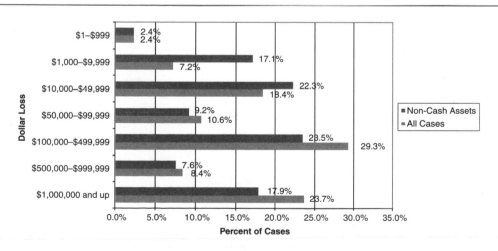

Exhibit 9.3 *2009 Global Fraud Survey*: Noncash Cases by Type of Asset Misappropriated

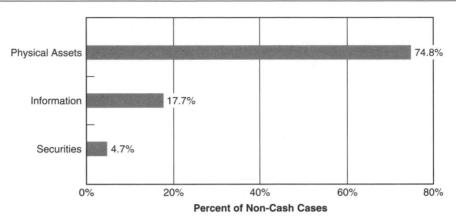

less likely to be detected by *management review or by document examination* than were other forms of occupational fraud. (See Exhibit 9.5.)

Perpetrators of Noncash Theft Schemes

There were 304 noncash schemes in which the position of the perpetrator was noted. In 43 percent of these, the perpetrator was an employee, while 42 percent of schemes were committed by managers and 15 percent involved owner/executives. This distribution was similar to the distribution of all occupational frauds. (See Exhibit 9.6.)

As one would expect, increasing levels of authority brought increasing losses in the noncash schemes we studied. Schemes committed by employees had a median loss of $72,000 while the median loss in schemes committed by managers was slightly higher, at $88,000. The noncash cases involving owner/executives had a median loss of $227,000, which was over three times greater than the median losses caused by employees. (See Exhibit 9.7.)

Exhibit 9.4 *2009 Global Fraud Survey*: Median Loss in Noncash Cases by Type of Asset Misappropriated

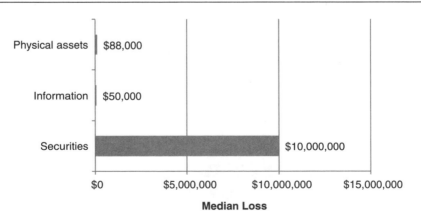

Exhibit 9.5 *2009 Global Fraud Survey*: Detection of Noncash Theft Schemes

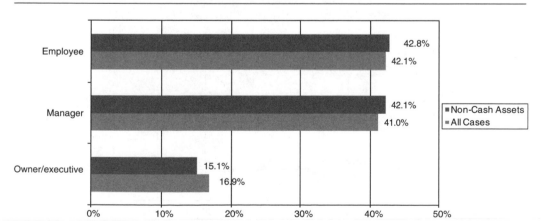

Victims of Noncash Theft Schemes

We received 299 cases that reported the size of the victim organization in noncash frauds. The distribution was similar to that for all occupational frauds, with slightly more victims falling in the two categories representing the largest organizations. (See Exhibit 9.8.)

Median losses in noncash frauds rose as with the size of the victim organization; however, the median losses for noncash schemes for all victim categories were lower than the median for all cases of categories of organizational size, as shown in Exhibit 9.9.

MISUSE OF INVENTORY AND OTHER ASSETS

There are basically two ways in which a person can misappropriate a company asset. The asset can be misused (or "borrowed"), or it can be stolen. Simple misuse is obviously the less egregious of the two. Assets that are misused but not stolen typically include company vehicles, company supplies, computers, and other office equipment. In one

Exhibit 9.6 *2009 Global Fraud Survey*: Perpetrators of Noncash Theft Schemes

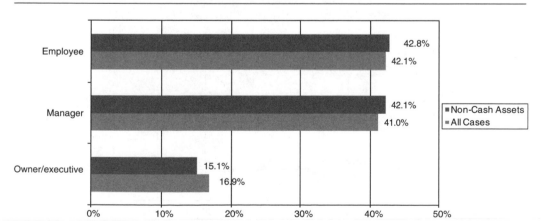

Exhibit 9.7 *2009 Global Fraud Survey*: **Median Loss by Perpetrator of Noncash Theft Schemes**

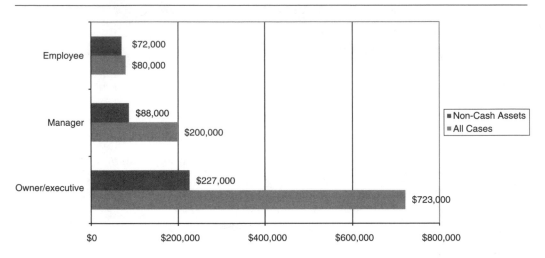

example, an employee made personal use of a company vehicle while on an out-of-town assignment. The employee provided false information, both written and verbal, regarding the nature of his use of the vehicle. The vehicle was returned unharmed, and the cost to the perpetrator's company was only a few hundred dollars, but such unauthorized use of a company asset does amount to fraud when a false statement accompanies the use.

Some employees also use computers, supplies, and other office equipment to do personal work on company time. For instance, an employee might use her computer at work to write letters, print invoices, or do other work connected with a business she runs on the side. In many instances, these side businesses are of the same nature as the employer's business, so the employee is essentially using his employer's

Exhibit 9.8 *2009 Global Fraud Survey*: **Size of Victim in Noncash Theft Schemes**

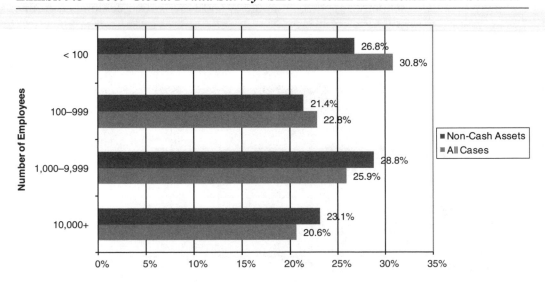

Exhibit 9.9   *2009 Global Fraud Survey*: Median Loss by Size of Victim in Noncash Theft Schemes

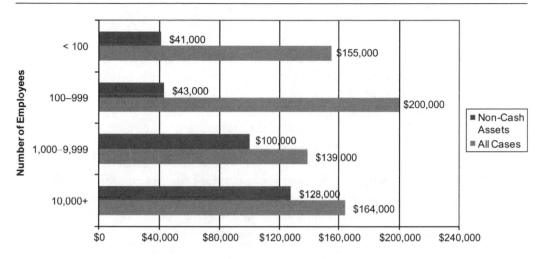

equipment to compete with the employer. An example of how employees misuse company assets to compete with their employers was provided in one case in which a group of employees not only stole company supplies but also used the stolen supplies, in conjunction with their employer's equipment, to manufacture their own product. The fraudsters then removed the completed product from their work location and sold it in competition with their employer. In a similar scheme, a perpetrator used his employer's machinery to run his own snow removal and excavation business for approximately nine months. He generally did his own work on weekends and after hours, falsifying the logs that recorded mileage and usage on the equipment. The employee formerly had owned all the equipment himself but had sold it in order to avoid bankruptcy. As a term of the sale, he had agreed to go to work for the new owner operating the equipment; in truth, however, he never stopped running his old business.

The preceding cases offer a good illustration of how a single scheme can encompass more than one type of fraud. Though the perpetrators in these schemes were misusing company materials and equipment—a case of asset misappropriation—they were also competing with their employers for business—a conflict of interest. The categories we have developed for classifying fraud are helpful in that they allow examiners to track certain types of schemes, noting common elements, victims, methods, and so on; but those involved in fraud prevention should remember that every crime will not fall neatly into one category. Frauds often expand as opportunity and need allow; a scheme that begins small may grow into a massive crime that can cripple a business.

Costs of Inventory Misuse

The costs of inventory misuse are difficult to quantify. Many individuals do not view this type of fraud as a crime but rather as "borrowing." In truth, the cost to a company from this kind of scheme often may be immaterial. When a perpetrator borrows a stapler for the night or takes home some tools to perform a household repair, the cost to the company is negligible, as long as the assets are returned unharmed.

But misuse schemes also can be very costly. Take, for example, situations such as those discussed previously in which an employee uses company equipment to operate a side business during work hours. Since the employee is not performing his work-related duties, the employer suffers loss in productivity. If the low productivity continues, the employer might have to hire additional employees to compensate, diverting more capital to wages. If the employee's business is similar to the employer's, then lost business could be an additional cost. If the employee had not contracted work for his own company, the business presumably would have gone to his employer. Unauthorized use of equipment also can mean additional wear and tear, causing the equipment to break down sooner than it would have under normal business conditions. Additionally, when an employee "borrows" company property, there is no guarantee that it will be brought back. This is precisely how some theft schemes begin. Despite some opinions to the contrary, asset misuse is not always a harmless crime.

THEFT OF INVENTORY AND OTHER ASSETS

Though the misuse of company property might be a problem, the *theft* of company property is obviously of greater concern. As we have seen, losses resulting from larceny of company assets can run into the millions of dollars. The means employed to steal company property range from simple larceny—just walking off with company property—to more complicated schemes involving the falsification of company documents and ledgers. Methods for stealing inventory and other assets include:

- Larceny schemes
- Asset requisitions and transfers
- Purchasing and receiving schemes
- False shipments

Larceny Schemes

The textbook definition of "larceny" is too broad for our purposes, as it would encompass every kind of asset theft. In order to gain a more specific understanding of the methods used to steal inventory and other assets, we have narrowed the definition. For our purposes, larceny is the most basic type of inventory theft, exhibited in schemes in which an employee simply takes inventory from the company premises without attempting to conceal it in the books and records. (See Exhibit 9.10.) In other fraud schemes, employees may create false documentation to justify the shipment of merchandise or tamper with inventory records to conceal missing assets, but larceny is more blunt. The culprit in these crimes simply takes company assets without trying to account for their absence. In the case study at the beginning of this chapter, for instance, Larry Gunter simply walked out of his warehouse with several hundred thousand dollars' worth of computer chips.

Exhibit 9.10 Noncash Larceny

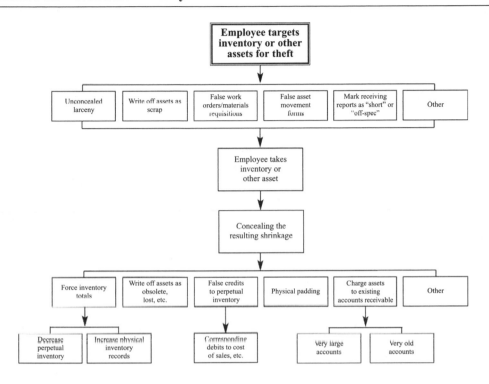

Most noncash larceny schemes are not very complicated. Typically they are committed by employees (such as warehouse personnel, inventory clerks, and shipping clerks) who have access to inventory and other assets. A technique representative of the unsophisticated nature of noncash larceny schemes is what may be termed a set-aside scheme. In this type of crime, an employee responsible for loading merchandise for shipment to customers withholds some of the merchandise and sets it aside with the intent of misappropriating it later. In one case, a perpetrator used the set-aside method, leaving the targeted inventory in plain sight on the warehouse floor as he went about his duties. Because the inventory was visible rather than hidden, the employee's coworkers did not suspect that it was marked for theft. If someone noticed that a shipment was short, the fact that the merchandise was sitting out in the open made it appear that the omission had been an oversight rather than an intentional removal. In most cases, however, no one noticed that shipments were short, leaving the excess inventory available for the perpetrator to take. If customers complained about receiving short shipments, the company sent the missing items without performing any follow-up to see where the missing inventory had gone. Eventually the culprit was caught when someone noticed that he was involved in the preparation of an inordinate number of short shipments.

When we speak of asset theft, we tend to conjure up images of late-night rendezvous at the warehouse or merchandise stuffed hastily under clothing as a nervous employee beats a path to her car. Although sometimes this is how employees go about stealing inventory and other assets, in many instances fraudsters do not have to go to these extremes. In several of the cases in our studies, employees took items openly during business hours, in plain view of their coworkers. How does this happen? The truth is that people tend to assume that their friends and acquaintances are acting honestly. When they see a trusted coworker taking something out of the office, people are likely to assume that the culprit has a legitimate reason for removing the asset. In most cases, people just do not assume that fraud is going on around them. Such was the situation in a case in which a university faculty member was leaving his offices to take a position at a new school. This person was permitted to take a small number of items to his new job but certainly exceeded the intentions of the school when he loaded two trucks full of university lab equipment and computers worth several hundred thousand dollars. The perpetrator simply packed up these stolen assets along with his personal items and drove away.

Though it is true that employees sometimes misappropriate assets in front of coworkers who do not suspect fraud, it is also true that employees may be fully aware that one of their coworkers is stealing yet may refrain from reporting the crime. There are several reasons why employees might ignore illegal conduct, among them a sense of duty to friends, a management-versus-labor mentality, intimidation by the thief, or poor channels of communication—or the coworkers are assisting in the theft. When high-ranking personnel are stealing from their companies, employees often overlook the crime for fear that they will lose their jobs if they report it. For example, a school superintendent in one case was not only pilfering school accounts but also stealing school assets. A search of his residence revealed a cellar filled with school property. A number of school employees knew or suspected that the superintendent was involved in illegal dealings, but he was very powerful and people were afraid to report him for fear of retaliation. As a result, he was able to steal from the school for several years. Similarly, in another example, a city manager ordered subordinates to install air conditioners—known to be city property—in his home and in the homes of several influential citizens. Although there was no question that this violated the city's code of ethics, no one reported the manager because of the lack of a proper whistleblowing procedure in the department.

Ironically, employees who steal inventory often are highly trusted within their organizations. This trust can provide employees with access to restricted areas, safes, supply rooms, or even keys to the business. Such access, in turn, makes it easy for employees to misappropriate company assets. An example of this kind of situation occurred when a long-term employee of a contractor was given keys to the company parts room. It was his job to deliver parts to job sites. He used his access to steal high-value items, which he then sold to another contractor. The scheme itself was uncomplicated, but because the employee had a long history of service to the company and because he was highly trusted, inventory counts were allowed to lapse and his performance went largely unsupervised. As a result, the scheme continued for over two years and cost the company over $200,000.

Employees who have keys to company buildings are able to misappropriate assets during nonbusiness hours, when they can avoid the prying eyes of their fellow employees as well as management and security personnel. We encountered several schemes in which employees entered their places of business to steal assets during weekends as well as before or after normal working hours. One case provided an example of this after-hours activity. In this scheme, two employees in management positions at a manufacturing plant would set finished items aside at the end of the day, then return the next day an hour before the morning shift and remove the merchandise before other employees arrived. These perpetrators had keys to the plant's security gate, which allowed them to enter the plant before normal hours. Over the course of several years, these two fraudsters removed and sold approximately $300,000 worth of inventory from their company.

It can be unwise for fraudsters physically to carry inventory and other assets off the premises of the company. This practice carries with it the inherent risk and potential embarrassment of being caught red-handed with stolen goods on their person. Some fraudsters avoid this problem by mailing company assets to a location where they can pick them up without having to worry about security, management, or other potential observers. In one example, a spare-parts custodian took several thousand dollars' worth of computer chips and mailed them to a company that had no business dealings with the custodian's employer. He then reclaimed the merchandise as his own. By taking the step of mailing the stolen inventory, the fraudster allowed the postal service to unwittingly do his dirty work for him.

Fake Sales

Asset misappropriations are not always undertaken solely by employees of the victim company. In many cases, corrupt employees use outside accomplices to help steal inventory. The fake sale is one method that depends on an accomplice for its success. Like most inventory thefts, the fake sale is not difficult. A fake sale occurs when the accomplice of the employee-fraudster "buys" merchandise, but the employee does not ring up the sale; the accomplice takes the merchandise without making any payment. To a casual observer, it appears that the transaction is a normal sale. The employee bags the merchandise and may act as if a transaction is being entered on the register, but, in fact, the "sale" is not recorded. The accomplice may even pass a nominal amount of money to the employee to complete the illusion. In one instance, the perpetrator went along with these fake sales in exchange for gifts from her accomplice, though in other cases the two might split the stolen merchandise.

Accomplices sometimes also are used to return inventory that an employee has stolen. This is an easy way for employees to convert inventory into cash when they have no need for the merchandise itself and have no means of reselling it on their own.

Asset Requisitions and Transfers

Asset requisitions and other forms that enable noncash assets to be moved from one location in a company to another can be used to facilitate the misappropriation of those assets. Fraudsters use internal documents to gain access to merchandise that they otherwise might not be able to handle without raising suspicion. Transfer documents do not account for missing merchandise the way false sales do, but they allow fraudsters to move assets from one location to another. In the process of this movement, the fraudsters take the merchandise for themselves. (See Exhibit 9.10.)

The most basic scheme occurs when an employee requisitions materials to complete a work-related project, then steals the materials instead. In some cases, fraudsters simply overstate the amount of supplies or equipment it will take to complete the work and pilfer the excess. In more extreme cases, fraudsters might completely fabricate a project that necessitates the use of certain assets they intend to steal. In one instance, an employee of a telecommunications company used false project documents to request approximately $100,000 worth of computer chips, allegedly to upgrade company computers. Knowing that this type of requisition required verbal authorization from another source, the employee set up an elaborate phone scheme to get the ''project'' approved. The fraudster used his knowledge of the company's phone system to forward calls from four different lines to his own desk. When the confirmation call was made, it was the perpetrator who answered the phone and authorized the project.

Dishonest employees sometimes falsify property transfer forms so that they can remove inventory or other assets from a warehouse or stockroom. Once the merchandise is in their possession, the fraudsters simply take it home with them. In one example, a manager requested that merchandise from the company warehouse be displayed on a showroom floor. But the pieces he requested never made it to the showroom, because he loaded them into a pickup truck and took them home. Sometimes he actually took the items in broad daylight and with the help of another employee. The obvious problem with this type of scheme is that the person who orders the merchandise usually is the primary suspect when it turns up missing. In many cases, fraudsters simply rely on poor communication between different departments in the company and hope no one will piece the crime together. The individual in this case, however, thought he was immune to detection because the merchandise was requested via computer, using a management-level security code. Because the code was not specific to any one manager, he thought there would be no way of knowing which manager had ordered the merchandise. Unfortunately for the thief, the company was able to record the computer terminal from which the request originated. The manager had used his own computer to make the request, which led to his undoing.

When inventory is stored in multiple locations, the transfer of assets from one building to another can create opportunities for employees to pilfer. Larry Gunter, in the case study at the beginning of this chapter, stole over $1 million worth of computer chips by adding extra merchandise to his cart as he transferred materials between two company buildings or as he took out the trash. He simply took a detour and loaded the stolen chips in his truck before continuing on his route. As is the case in many businesses, Gunter's company required no internal paperwork when product was moved between its two buildings, so it was very difficult to track the movement of assets. Consequently, it was easy for Gunter to steal from the company.

Purchasing and Receiving Schemes

The purchasing and receiving functions of a company also can be manipulated by dishonest employees to facilitate the theft of inventory and other assets. (See Exhibit 9.10.) It might at first seem that any purchasing scheme should fall under the heading of false billings, but there is a distinction between purchasing schemes that are classified as false billings and those classified as noncash misappropriations. If employees cause their company to purchase merchandise that the company does not need, this is a false billing scheme; the harm to the company comes in paying for assets for which it has no use. For instance, in one of our cases, a carpenter was allowed control over the ordering of materials for a small construction project. No one bothered to measure the amount of materials ordered against the size of the carpenter's project, so he was able to order excess, unneeded lumber, which was then delivered to his home to build a fence for himself. The essence of the fraud in this case was the *purchase* of unneeded materials.

If the assets were purchased intentionally by the company but simply misappropriated by the fraudster, this is classified as an inventory larceny scheme. In the preceding example, assume that the victim company wanted to keep a certain amount of lumber on hand for odd jobs. If the carpenter took this lumber home, the crime is a theft of lumber. The difference is that in the second example, the company is deprived not only of the cash it paid for the lumber but also of the lumber itself. It will now have to purchase more lumber to replace what it is missing. In the first example, the company's only loss was the cash it paid in the fraudulent purchase of the materials it did not need.

Falsifying Incoming Shipments

One of the most common ways for employees to abuse the purchasing and receiving functions is for a person charged with receiving goods on behalf of the victim company—such as a warehouse supervisor or receiving clerk—to falsify the records of incoming shipments. In one instance, two employees conspired to misappropriate incoming merchandise by marking shipments as short. If 1,000 units of a particular item were received, for example, the fraudsters would indicate that only 900 were received. They were then able to steal the 100 units that were unaccounted for.

The obvious problem with this kind of scheme is that if the receiving report does not match the vendor's invoice, there will be a problem with payment. In this example, if the vendor bills for 1,000 units but the accounts payable voucher shows receipt of only 900 units of merchandise, then someone will have to explain where the extra 100 units went. Obviously, the vendor will indicate that a full shipment was made, so the attention of the victim company will likely turn to whoever signed the receiving report.

In this case, the fraudsters attempted to avoid this problem by altering only one copy of the receiving report. The copy that was sent to accounts payable indicated receipt of a full shipment, so that the vendor would be paid without any questions. The copy used for inventory records indicated a short shipment so that the assets on hand would equal the assets in the perpetual inventory.

Instead of marking shipments short, fraudsters might reject portions of a shipment as not being up to quality specifications. The perpetrators then keep the "substandard" merchandise rather than sending it back to the supplier. The result is the same as if the shipment had been marked short.

False Shipments of Inventory and Other Assets

To conceal thefts of inventory and other assets, fraudsters sometimes create false shipping documents and false sales documents to make it appear that missing inventory was not actually stolen but was sold instead. (See Exhibit 9.11.) The document that tells the shipping department to release inventory for delivery is usually the packing slip. By creating a false packing slip, corrupt employees can cause inventory to be fraudulently delivered to themselves or to accomplices. The "sales" reflected in the

Exhibit 9.11   False Shipments of Inventory and Other Assets

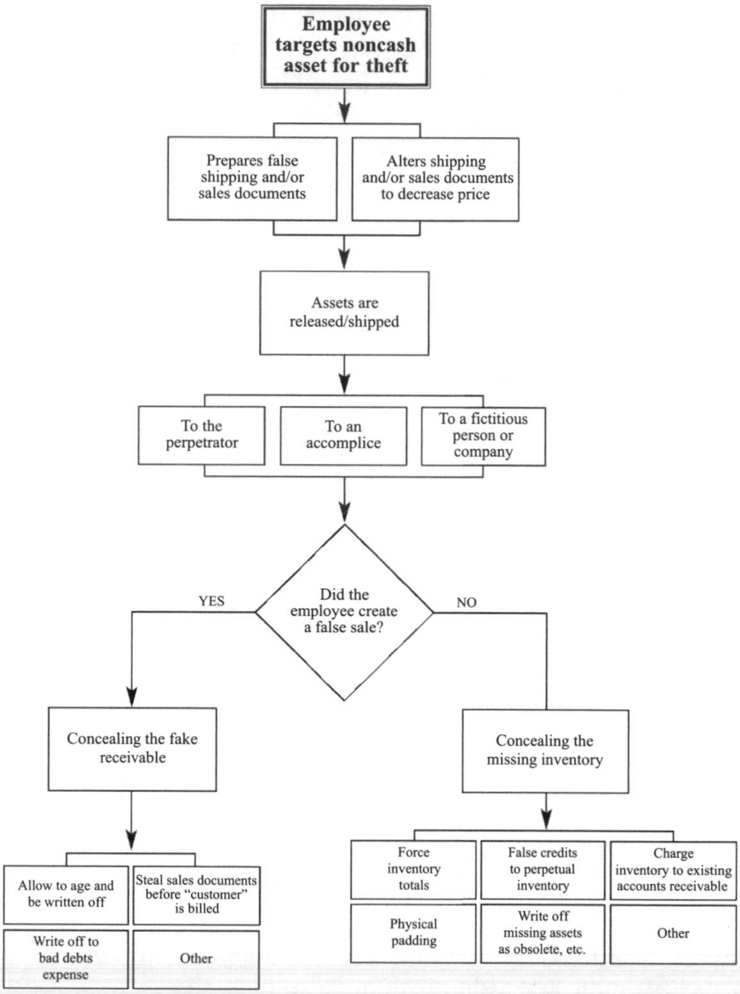

packing slips typically are made to a fictitious person, a fictitious company, or an accomplice of the perpetrator. In one example, an inventory control employee used his position to create fraudulent paperwork that authorized the shipment of over $30,000 worth of inventory to his accomplices. The fraudsters then were able to sell the inventory for their own profit.

One benefit to using false shipping documents to misappropriate inventory or other assets is that the product can be removed from the warehouse or storeroom by someone other than the fraudster. The perpetrator of the scheme does not have to risk being caught stealing company inventory. Instead, the victim company unknowingly delivers the targeted assets to the fraudster.

False packing slips allow inventory to be shipped from the victim company to the perpetrator, but they alone do not conceal the fact that inventory has been misappropriated. In order to hide the theft, fraudsters also may create a false sale so that it appears that the missing inventory was shipped to a customer. In this way, the inventory is accounted for. Depending on how the victim organization operates, the fraudster may have to create a false purchase order from the "buyer," a false sales order, and a false invoice along with the packing slip to create the illusion of a sale.

The result is that a fake receivable account goes into the books for the price of the misappropriated inventory. Obviously, the "buyer" of the merchandise will never pay for it. How do fraudsters deal with these fake receivables? In some cases, the fraudster simply lets the receivable age on the company's books until eventually it is written off as uncollectible. In other instances, the employee may take steps to remove the sale— and the delinquent receivable that results—from the books. In one of our cases, the perpetrator generated false invoices and delivered them to the company warehouse for shipping. The invoices were then marked "delivered" and sent to the sales office. The perpetrator removed all copies of the invoices from the files before they were billed to the fictitious customer. In other scenarios, the perpetrator might write off the receivables himself, as did a corrupt manager in another case; in a five-year scheme, the perpetrator took company assets and covered up the loss by setting up a fake sale. A few weeks after the fake sale went into the books, the perpetrator wrote off the receivable to an account for "lost and stolen assets." More commonly, however, the fake sale is written off to discounts and allowances or a bad debt expense account.

Instead of completely fabricated sales, some employees understate legitimate sales so that an accomplice is billed for less than is delivered. The result is that a portion of the merchandise is sold at no cost. In one instance, a salesman filled out shipping tickets, which he forwarded to the warehouse. After the merchandise was delivered, he instructed the warehouse employees to return the shipping tickets to him for "extra work" before they went to the invoicing department. But the extra work the salesman did was simply to alter the shipping tickets, reducing the quantity of merchandise on the ticket so that the buyer (an accomplice of the salesman) was billed for less than he received.

The next case study was selected as an example of a false shipping scheme. In this case, a marketing manager, with the help of a shipping clerk, delivered several computer hard drives to a computer company in return for a substantial cash payment. The victim company in this case had poor controls that allowed merchandise to be shipped without receipts, leaving the company extremely vulnerable to such a scheme. Certified fraud examiner Harry D'Arcy investigated this crime and eventually helped bring the culprits to justice.

Case Study: Hard Drives and Bad Luck

Someone had stolen 1,400 hard drives from a computer warehouse in Toronto, that much was certain. But the question remained: Who took them? The answer was more than academic; it could mean the difference between the distributor's continuing operation and a total crash. Swainler's Technology* averaged $8 to

*Several names and details have been changed to preserve anonymity.

$9 million a year in sales, but with an 8 percent profit margin, the company didn't have much financial room to maneuver. The company was a joint venture, overseen by a group of investors who were, to put it mildly, nervous. They had theft insurance, but a particularly sticky clause said that the policy wouldn't cover theft committed by a Swainler's employee. In order to collect on the $600,000 worth of disk drives missing from the warehouse, the investors had to show that the theft was an outside job.

The report showed just that. Employees and management agreed that the skids bearing the equipment had been safe and sound until the week that a competitor of Swainler's, Hargrove Incorporated, had sent delivery drivers over for an exchange. Evidently some of Hargrove's people had swiped the equipment during the several days they were working in the Swainler's warehouse. Hargrove and Swainler's worked together when they had to, but they were in hot competition, and at different times each company had lost business—and employees—to the other. Since all Swainler's employees checked out, management concluded that the theft must have been committed by someone from Hargrove.

Doug Andrews was an independent adjuster hired by Swainler's Technology's insurance company. Besides conducting routine loss estimates, he's also a CFE who is willing, as he puts it, "to see things other people either don't see or choose to ignore." Although the Swainler's board assured Andrews this was a simple case, he wasn't convinced: "I wasn't sure it wasn't an inside job. Too many questions were left hanging. How did the Hargrove people get the stuff out without being seen? The date management was setting for the loss seemed awfully convenient. It seemed like at the least someone at Swainler's had to be involved," Andrews remembers. He needed some help chasing down these hunches, so Andrews hired Harry D'Arcy to assist. D'Arcy worked for the Canadian Insurance Crime Prevention Bureau as a CFE and investigator. He and Andrews interviewed everyone at the warehouse and on the investors' board, returning two or three times if necessary to get their questions answered. They traced serial numbers and possible distribution routes to turn up some sign of the hard drives. D'Arcy says, "We met at least twice a week to come up with a way to solve this. It was like a think tank, bouncing ideas and options off each other: 'What tack should we take now? Should we call out to California? Do we need to go to that shop in Ottawa?' We knew we were being stymied. We just had to find a way around the blocks they put in front of us."

The main thing bothering D'Arcy was that the board was presenting the investigators with what appeared to be an open and shut case. Everyone's stories matched like precision parts. "It was too good to be true, too neat," D'Arcy says. The board members had seen the material on the Friday before Hargrove came; they noticed it was gone afterward; they had reason to suspect their competitor was behind it. Yes, they knew their insurance policy wouldn't pay if an employee did the hit, but that was beside the point. The board trusted its employees. Many of the people at Swainler's, from clerks to warehouse personnel, were either related to or friends of the management. D'Arcy and Andrews were encountering what Andrews later described as "an active campaign of misinformation."

Once he got a sense of the system of operation at Swainler's, D'Arcy had some material for a new round of questioning. He noticed that as skids of equipment were prepared for shipping, the entire apparatus was wrapped in a thick plastic sealant and moved from the warehouse floor into the shipping dock. "Now," he asked one of the investors, "if those disk drives were ready for shipping on the Friday you say, then they would have already been wrapped, right?"

"Sure."

"Then how did you know what you were seeing if the wrapping was already on? You can't see through the wrapping."

"I knew that batch was supposed to go out for the next week," the man replied.

"Then the skids should have been moved to the loading dock," D'Arcy interjected.

"I don't see your point."

"You said you saw them in the warehouse," D'Arcy reminded the man. "You couldn't have seen them in the warehouse if they had been moved to the dock for shipping."

The witness, feeling stymied himself, shifted and said, "Well, maybe they hadn't been taken over yet."

D'Arcy had a full house of questions for the initially talkative managers. Why would they notice a particular skid of drives on a particular day? Why were their memories so specific on this one shipment? How often did management tour the warehouse for an informal inventory? D'Arcy reports, "Once I had them shaken up, I would ask them point blank, 'Are you parroting something you heard somebody else say?'" The men would declare that, no, they'd seen the material themselves.

"Did you discuss this with other board members?" D'Arcy asked.

"We talked about it in board meetings, sure" came the answer.

"And did you all agree on what you would say when you gave a statement?"

"No."

"But your statements all match."

"We agreed that we remembered the drives being there on the same day."

Doug Andrews was feeling fed up: "We were getting this string of nonanswers. I felt like we were coming up dry."

Swainler's had hired a private investigator of its own to work the case. D'Arcy talked with the man, who was convinced he had the material to show an outside job. The PI had been to Hargrove and spoken with employees there, including a man who had once worked for Swainler's. "I don't know if somebody here took the stuff or not," the man said. "But those guys at Swainler's deserve everything they get." He claimed Swainler's required its employees to work long hours with little pay or benefits, that workers were little more than switches on a processing board. To Swainler's investigator, then, this was a classic case of employee resentment, a common excuse for fraud.

D'Arcy said he disagreed, but the investigator persisted. Swainler's Technology was now claiming its expenses for the investigation, finally totaling $125,000. During one week alone, the PI billed $45,000 when he conducted a stakeout in another city. An anonymous tip to the executive vice president at Swainler's placed the stolen disks at a storage facility in London, Ontario. The investigator took a team of people and equipment, and after a weekend surveillance, it observed a man opening the unit. When the team approached, it found nothing inside but the man's personal belongings.

Meanwhile, D'Arcy and Andrews pursued their own strategy. They notified the manufacturer's representatives throughout Canada and the United States to be on the lookout for a set of serial numbers. Sure enough, a call came in from a dealer in California; one of the disk drives had shown up for repair. Invoices showed the drive had been shipped from upstate New York and was purchased in Ottawa, Canada. The Ottawa shop had received the drive from a distributor in Montreal. Andrews went to the Montreal warehouse but found it empty. Canvassing the neighborhood, he was told the people renting the warehouse had moved to another area in northern Montreal.

When Andrews got to the new address, he questioned four or five of the workers there about his case. They had never heard of Swainler's and knew nothing about the stolen drives. But when Andrews pressured them to look through their records with him, he found documents matching his serial numbers. Then one of the missing drives turned up inside the warehouse.

Andrews wasn't ready to celebrate, though. "I was feeling beat. We'd been spending all this time, running back and forth, interviewing and reinterviewing. I said, 'I don't know, we may not get this one.' " The invoices he'd looked at were dated five weeks earlier than the time Swainler's had listed the theft. The discrepancy might help disprove the company's outside perpetrator theory but also could be used to throw Andrews's largely circumstantial case into further confusion. As he was driving back to Toronto, Andrews got a call from D'Arcy. "I've been doing some work based on what you found there," D'Arcy told him excitedly. "When you get back they'll be in chains."

Since D'Arcy now knew that at least some of the merchandise had gone through the warehouse in Montreal, he had looked for phone calls from that city in the phone logs at Swainler's. The marketing manager, Frederic Boucher, had not only received a large number of calls from Montreal, the calls were coming from the warehouse Andrews had just visited, the one where people claimed never to have heard of Swainler's. D'Arcy spoke again with people in the warehouse, one of whom admitted that the skids had disappeared much earlier than first reported. He guessed the actual date was about a month earlier than the one management had given. This, of course, coincided with the invoices Andrews had found in Montreal. At a special meeting, the board of directors reviewed D'Arcy's findings and confronted Frederic Boucher with the evidence pointing toward him. Boucher denied any involvement, and the board supported his story.

The next morning, Boucher told a different story. He had talked with his wife and a lawyer and was ready to come clean. He said he'd met the people from the Montreal warehouse at a conference. Together they worked out a deal in which Boucher would provide them with a supply of hard drives at a sweet price. With the help of a Swainler's shipping clerk, Boucher sent 60 low-end drives to Kingston, halfway between Montreal and Toronto, for $20,000 paid in cash. The atmosphere at Swainler's was ripe for this sort of offense. D'Arcy recalls, "The bookkeeping system wasn't controlled. It was nothing to find things going out with no receipts. The operation was mainly run on trust. The men who headed up the company were all old friends, and they hired people they knew or to whom they were connected in one way or another. It ran on blind trust and nepotism." Encouraged by their first success, Boucher and his accomplices then arranged to make the big sale: 1,400 top-quality hard drives for a $600,000 take. They didn't have to worry about covering their tracks, because management was eager to point the finger outside the company and collect on their insurance.

With Boucher's confession, Doug Andrews could make a happy report to his client that the insurance company was not liable for the claim. Boucher was sentenced to make restitution for the theft and to two years' imprisonment while the shipping clerk and the Montreal distributor were given one year each. All the sentences were suspended and the defendants placed on probation. The executives at Swainler's were, according to Harry D'Arcy, "cautioned regarding their complicity in the matter." Swainler's survived the loss but was later purchased by a prominent Canadian investment group and now operates under that umbrella.

Doug Andrews, who lectures and writes articles on insurance fraud in addition to conducting investigations, finds that people resist seeing cases like Swainler's as real crimes.

"There's a belief that perpetrating fraud against an insurer is a victimless crime." Reports from the KPMG accounting firm and the Canadian Coalition Against Insurance Fraud place the insurance losses in Canada between $1 billion and $2.6 billion a year. But Andrews believes that "[you can] take the middle figure of $2 billion and double it." Though a significant portion of those losses is related to occupational crimes, an accurate account is not yet available. That's because some of the major acts that occur in business felonies—such as supplier and kickback fraud—aren't included in the insurance industry figures. Nevertheless, these crimes are serious and proliferating. "They are frequent," Andrews says, "and often systematic and well organized. Especially since insurance companies don't advertise as aggressively in Canada as they do in the United States, people see insurance as a kind of faceless bureaucracy." With the tremendous amounts of money changing hands in this industry every day, "there's a mind-set that labels these companies fair game. . . . But people see the difference in the end, when they pay their premiums."

Other Schemes

Because employees tailor their thefts to the security systems, record-keeping systems, building layout, and other day-to-day operations of their companies, the methods used to steal inventory and other assets vary. The preceding categories comprised the majority of schemes in our studies, but a couple of other schemes, which did not fit any established category, merit discussion.

Write-offs often are used to conceal the theft of assets after they have been stolen. In some cases, however, assets are written off in order to make them available for theft. There was a case where a warehouse foreman abused his authority to declare inventory obsolete. He wrote off perfectly good inventory, then "gave" it to a dummy corporation that he secretly owned. This fraudster took over $200,000 worth of merchandise from his employer. Once assets are designated as scrap, it may be easier to conceal their misappropriation. Fraudsters may be allowed to take the "useless" assets for themselves, to buy them or sell them to an accomplice at a greatly reduced price, or simply to give the assets away.

Another unique example involved a scheme where a low-level manager convinced his supervisor to approve the purchase of new office equipment to replace existing equipment, which was to be retired. When the new equipment was purchased, the perpetrator took it home and left the existing equipment in place. His boss assumed that the equipment in the office was new, even though it actually was the same equipment that had always been there. If nothing else, this case illustrates that sometimes a little bit of attentiveness by management is all it takes to halt fraud.

CONCEALMENT

When inventory is stolen, the key concealment issue for fraudsters is shrinkage. Inventory shrinkage is the unaccounted-for reduction in the company's inventory that results from theft. For instance, assume that a computer retailer has 1,000 computers in stock. After work one day, an employee loads 10 computers into a truck and takes them home. Now the company only has 990 computers, but since there is no record that the employee took 10 computers, the inventory records still show 1,000 units on hand. The company has experienced inventory shrinkage in the amount of 10 computers.

Shrinkage is one of the red flags that signal fraud. When merchandise is missing and unaccounted for, the obvious question to ask is "Where did it go?" The search for an answer to this question can uncover fraud. The goal of fraudsters is to proceed with their schemes undetected, so it is in their best interests to prevent anyone from looking for missing assets. This means concealing the shrinkage that occurs from asset theft.

Inventory and other assets typically are tracked through a two-step process. The first step, the perpetual inventory, is a running count that records how much should be on hand. When new shipments of supplies are received, for instance, these supplies are entered into the perpetual inventory. Similarly, when goods are sold, they are removed from the perpetual inventory records. In this way, a company tracks its inventory on a day-to-day basis.

Periodically, companies should make a physical count of assets on hand. In this process, someone actually goes through the storeroom or warehouse and counts everything that the company has in stock. This total is then matched to the amount of assets reflected in the perpetual inventory. A variation between the physical inventory and the perpetual inventory totals is shrinkage. While a certain amount of shrinkage may be expected in any business, large shrinkage totals may indicate fraud.

Concealing Inventory Shrinkage

Altered Inventory Records

One of the simplest ways to conceal shrinkage is to change the perpetual inventory record so that it matches the physical inventory count. This is also known as a forced reconciliation of the account. Basically, the perpetrator just changes the numbers in the perpetual inventory to make them match the amount of inventory on hand. In one example, a supervisor involved in the theft of inventory credited the perpetual inventory and debited the cost of sales account to bring the perpetual inventory numbers into line with the actual inventory count. Once these adjusting entries were made, a review of inventory would not reveal any shrinkage. Rather than use correcting entries to adjust perpetual inventory, some employees simply alter the numbers by deleting or covering up the correct totals and entering new numbers.

There are two sides to the inventory equation, the perpetual inventory and the physical inventory. Instead of altering the perpetual inventory, a fraudster who has access to the records from a physical inventory count can change those records to match the total of the perpetual inventory. Going back to the computer store example, assume the company counts its inventory every month and matches it to the perpetual inventory. The physical count should come to 990 computers, since that is what is actually on hand. If the perpetrator is someone charged with counting inventory, she can simply write down that there are 1,000 units on hand.

Fictitious Sales and Accounts Receivable

We already have discussed how fraudsters create fake sales to mask the theft of assets. When the perpetrator made an adjusting entry to the perpetual inventory and cost of sales accounts in the previous example, the problem was that there was no sales transaction on the books that corresponded to these entries. Had the perpetrator wished to fix this problem, he would have entered a debit to accounts receivable and a corresponding credit to the sales account to make it appear that the missing goods had been sold.

Of course, the problem of payment then arises, because no one is going to pay for the goods that were ''sold'' in this transaction. There are two routes that a fraudster might take in this circumstance. The first is to charge the sale to an existing account. In some cases, fraudsters charge fake sales to existing receivables accounts that are so large that the addition of the assets that they have stolen will not be noticed. Other corrupt employees charge the ''sales'' to accounts that are already aging and will soon be written off. When these accounts are removed from the books, the fraudsters' stolen inventory effectively disappears.

The other adjustment that typically is made is a write-off to discounts and allowances or bad debt expense. In one case, an employee with blanket authority to write off up to $5,000 in uncollectible sales per occurrence used this authority to conceal false sales of inventory to nonexistent companies. The fraudster bilked his company out of nearly $180,000 using this method.

Writing Off Inventory and Other Assets

We have already discussed a case in which a corrupt employee wrote off inventory as obsolete, then "gave" the inventory to a shell company that he controlled. Writing off inventory and other assets is a relatively common way for fraudsters to remove assets from the books before or after they are stolen. Again, this is beneficial to fraudsters because it eliminates the problem of shrinkage that inherently exists in every case of noncash asset misappropriation. Examples of this method that we encountered included a case in which a manager wrote off supplies as lost or destroyed, then sold the supplies through his own company; in another case, a director of maintenance disposed of fixed assets by reporting them as broken, then took the assets for himself.

Physical Padding

Most methods of concealment deal with altering inventory records, either by changing the perpetual inventory or by miscounting during the physical inventory. As an alternative, some fraudsters try to make it appear that there are more assets present in the warehouse or stockroom than there actually are. Empty boxes, for example, may be stacked on shelves to create the illusion of extra inventory. In one case, employees stole liquor from their stockroom and restacked the containers for the missing merchandise. This made it appear that the missing inventory was present when in fact there were really empty boxes on the stockroom shelves. In approximately 18 months, this concealment method allowed employees to steal over $200,000 of liquor.

The most egregious case of inventory padding in our studies occurred when fraudsters constructed a facade of finished product in a remote location of a warehouse and cordoned off the area to restrict access. Although there should have been $1 million worth of product on hand, there was actually nothing behind the wall of finished product, which was constructed solely to create the appearance of additional inventory.

DETECTION

Statistical Sampling

Companies with inventory accounts typically have enormous numbers of source documents. Statistical sampling allows the fraud examiner to inspect key attributes on a smaller portion (or sample) of those documents. For example, the examiner may select a statistically valid, random sample of purchase requisitions to determine that all requisitions in the sample selected were approved properly. Statistical sampling enables the examiner to predict the occurrence rate for the population and, therefore, determine with some accuracy the error rate, or the potential for fraud.

Other items that may be sampled on a statistical basis include:

- Receiving reports
- Perpetual inventory records
- Raw materials requisitions

- Shipping documents
- Job cost sheets

The attributes tested for on these documents might include a specific date, item, or location.

Physical Inventory Counts

Physical inventory counts sometimes can give rise to inventory theft detection. However, because other explanations satisfy inventory shortages (i.e., shrinkage), historical analysis of inventory is usually necessary. Furthermore, if the only method used to detect inventory fraud is the year-end physical count, the perpetrators will have had all year to devise concealment methods to circumvent potential detection.

Analytical Review

By using analytical review, inventory fraud may be detected because certain trends become immediately clear. For example, if the cost of goods sold increases by a disproportionate amount relative to sales, and no changes occur in the purchase prices, quantities purchased, or quality of products purchased, the cause of the disproportionate increase in cost of goods sold might be one of two things: The ending inventory has been depleted by theft, or false entries have been made to the inventory account to conceal embezzlement.

An analytical review of all the component parts of the cost of goods sold should indicate to the examiner where to direct further inquiries. For example, assuming that the type of inventory purchased is the same and there is no change in the manufacturing process or purchase price, if sales and cost of sales change from $5,650,987 and $2,542,944 to $6,166,085 and $2,981,880, respectively, what is the data telling the examiner? To begin, sales have increased by 9.12 percent whereas cost of sales increased by 17.26 percent. The profit margin has decreased by 3 percent (from 55 to 52 percent). Based on this data, the fraud examiner might want to look further at the components of inventory, such as beginning inventory, purchases, and ending inventory. If beginning inventory was $1,207,898, purchases were $2,606,518 and $2,604,972, respectively, and ending inventory was $894,564, then an inventory matrix would look like Exhibit 9.12.

Inventory purchases, as a percentage of sales, have declined from 46.13 percent to 42.25 percent. From this example, we can hypothesize that (1) inventory purchases were purposely increased in year 1 only to be liquidated in year 2; (2) the increased

Exhibit 9.12   Sample Inventory Matrix

	Year 1	Year 2	% Change
Beginning Inventory	$ 1,207,898	$1,271,472	5.26%
Purchases	$ 2,606,518	$2,604,972	−0.06%
Goods Available for Sale	$ 3,814,416	$3,876,444	1.63%
Ending Inventory	$(1,271,472)	$ (894,564)	−29.64%
Cost of Sales	$ 2,542,944	$2,981,880	17.26%

Exhibit 9.13   Searches for Schemes

Searches	Schemes
Purchases by vendor	If same vendor is receiving favorable treatment
Inventory levels by types and dates	If inventory is being purchased at its reorder point or if excess inventory is being ordered
Inventory shipped by address	If vendor's address matches either an employee address or the address of another vendor
Cost per item	If discounts are properly credited to purchases
Direct labor by item	If excess labor hours are being added to a particular job or item
Direct materials by item	If materials are properly charged to the job (too much or the wrong materials)
Overhead per inventory item	If overhead is being properly applied, and applied only once
Disposals then reorders	If usable inventory is being designated prematurely as scrap
Shortages by inventory item	If there is inventory theft or reorder system is not functioning
Returns and allowances	If there is an unusually high incidence of returns and allowances
Sales allowances	If sales allowances are not properly credited to promotional allowances
Buyer	If buyer is not acting within scope of authority

sales in year 2 were unexpected and the purchase of inventory did not keep pace with the sales; or (3) there might be some fraud scheme in inventory. If, by interview, the examiner is unable to ascertain a reasonable explanation, such as (1) or (2) above, then further examination of the ending inventory may be warranted.

The fraud examiner next may look at the differences in the physical inventory procedures, to see if that created a more (or less) accurate inventory count at the end of either year 1 or year 2. If there is no other logical explanation, further investigation into these and other inventory accounts may be necessary to explain the anomalies occurring in inventory.

Computer-Generated Trend Analysis

Computers can be used to facilitate obtaining lists of items with specified attributes. For example, in a lumberyard operation, the computer can be programmed to list all purchases of 4 × 4 cedar fence posts, eight feet in length. The examiner can review all the source documents that are represented by the listing. By examining the source documents for each of these purchases, the examiner can plot trends to determine the occurrence of the following (or other) patterns. (See Exhibit 9.13.)

Detailed Audit Program

These questions also will be helpful in establishing inventory control:

- Do adequate, detailed, written inventory instructions and procedures exist? Do inventory procedures give appropriate consideration to the location and arrangement of inventories?
- Do inventory procedures give appropriate consideration to identification and description of inventories?
- Is the method of determining inventory quantities specified (e.g., weight, count)?

- Is the method used for recording items counted adequate (e.g., count sheets, prenumbered tags)?
- Are inventory tags used? If yes: (1) Are they prenumbered? (2) Is accounting for inventory tags adequate, and does it include control with respect to tags used, unused, and voided?
- Are adequate procedures in place to identify inventory counted, ensure that all items have been counted, and prevent double counting?
- Are obsolete, slow-moving, or damaged inventories properly identified and segregated?
- Is the inventory reasonably identifiable for proper classification in the accounting records (e.g., description, stage of completion)?
- Are inventory counts subject to (1) complete recounts by persons independent of the ones involved in the initial counts, (2) recounts only of merchandise having substantial value, or (3) spot checks by supervisory personnel?
- Are counts performed by employees whose functions are independent of the physical custody of inventories and record-keeping functions?
- Do proper accounting controls and procedures exist for the exclusion from inventory of merchandise on hand that is not property of the client (e.g., customers' merchandise, consignments in)?
- Do proper accounting controls and procedures exist for the inclusion in inventory of merchandise not on hand but the property of the client (e.g., merchandise in warehouses, out on repair, consignments out)?
- Will identical inventory items in various areas be accumulated to allow a tie-in to the total counts of a summary listing subsequent to the observation?
- Is the movement of inventory adequately controlled (e.g., shipping and receiving activities suspended) during the physical count to ensure a proper cut-off?
- Are significant differences between physical counts and detailed inventory records investigated before the accounting and inventory records are adjusted to match the physical counts?
- Will inventory at remote locations be counted?
- Will special counting procedures or volume conversions be necessary (e.g., items weighed on scale)?
- How will work-in-process inventory be identified?
- How will the stage of completion of work-in-process inventory be identified?
- Are there any other matters that should be noted for the inventory count?[1]

PREVENTION

Four basic measures, if properly installed and implemented, may help prevent inventory fraud. They are:

1. Proper documentation
2. Segregation of duties (including approvals)

3. Independent checks
4. Physical safeguards

Proper Documentation

Prenumber and control:

- Requisitions
- Receiving reports
- Perpetual records
- Raw materials requisitions
- Shipping documents
- Job cost sheets

However, not all inventories require the purchasing of raw materials. In these cases, the proper documentation might take the form of prenumbered and controlled tickets and receipts for sales.

Segregation of Duties

Different personnel should handle these duties:

- Requisition of inventory
- Receipt of inventory
- Disbursement of inventory
- Conversion of inventory to scrap
- Receipt of proceeds from disposal of scrap

Independent Checks

Someone independent of the purchasing or warehousing functions should conduct physical observation of inventory. The personnel conducting the physical observations also should be knowledgeable about the inventory.

Physical Safeguards

All merchandise should be physically guarded and locked; access should be limited to authorized personnel only. For example, strategic placement of security guards may aid in the detection and deterrence of potential theft schemes. Electronic methods also may be used, such as cameras and surveillance devices. The effectiveness of any device, however, will depend on the employee's knowledge that physical safeguard controls are adhered to and the type of inventory available for misappropriation.

MISAPPROPRIATION OF INTANGIBLE ASSETS

Misappropriation of Information

In addition to misappropriation of tangible noncash assets, organizations are vulnerable to theft of proprietary information, which can undermine their value, reputation, and competitive advantages and result in legal liabilities. According to the ACFE *2009 Global Fraud Survey*, fraudsters misappropriated information in 18 percent of the cases involving noncash misappropriations.

Companies frequently make sizable technological investments in protecting their information from external information thieves, but often the biggest threats are internal. Employees are the most likely to be in a position to exploit their employers' information security. After all, who has more insider information and access to proprietary records and data than an employee or former employee?

Information misappropriation schemes commonly include theft by employees of competitively sensitive information, such as customer lists, marketing strategies, trade secrets, new products, or details on development sites. For example, in Case 5565, an employee who felt a sense of entitlement for having contributed to a new product design stole the design in attempt to get ahead in a new job with a competitor. And in Case 5582, a disgruntled former employee sold a company trade secret to a competitor in order to retaliate for what he felt was unfair treatment.

It is critical that companies identify their most valuable information and take steps to protect it. This process must be a cross-departmental endeavor, involving specialists from corporate security/risk management, information technology, human resources, marketing, research and development, and so on. If in-house capabilities do not exist, companies can bring in information security experts to assist them in designing an effective information security system, including awareness training for employees. An information security system may include measures such as limiting access to networks, systems, or data to those who have a legitimate need for access; protecting company data through the use of firewalls and virus scanning software; implementing and enforcing confidentiality agreements and restrictive covenants where appropriate; performing adequate background checks on employees; establishing and enforcing a security policy; and much more.

Misappropriation of Securities

According to the ACFE *2009 Global Fraud Survey*, although securities were the least likely asset to be misappropriated (5 percent of cases), the median loss in cases involving securities theft was significantly higher than in any other category, at $10,000,000. (See Exhibits 9.3 and 9.4.) In order to avoid falling victim to a misappropriation of securities scheme, companies must maintain proper internal controls over their investment portfolio, including proper separation of duties, restricted access to investment accounts, and periodic account reconciliations.

In Case 5234, the director of accounting and finance, who was responsible for making trades, left his computer unattended for a short time while signed into one of the company's investment accounts. Another employee, a senior accountant, took the opportunity to access the director's computer to sell $15,000 worth of investments and have the proceeds mailed to the company. Due to lax internal controls, she was able to intercept the check and deposit it into her own bank account. Because this employee was in charge of reconciling the investment accounts and had the access needed to enter and post journal entries to the general ledger, she was able to hide her scheme by writing off a ''loss'' on investments to an expense account. It was not until almost a year later, when auditors were reviewing the company's books, that the scheme was uncovered. By that time, the thief was nowhere to be found.

NOTE

1. George Georgiades, *Audit Procedures* (New York: Harcourt Brace Professional Publishing, 1995).

PART II
CORRUPTION

CHAPTER 10

Bribery

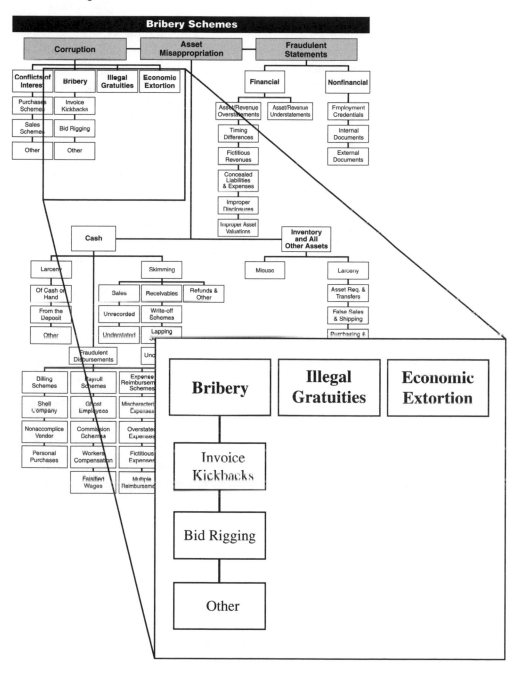

Case Study: Why Is This Furniture Falling Apart?

A number of years ago, the *Washington Post* ran a series of articles detailing charges of waste, fraud, and abuse in the General Services Administration (GSA), the federal government's housekeeping agency. In particular, for more than a decade, a furniture manufacturer in New Jersey had churned out $200 million worth of defective and useless furniture that the GSA purchased.

Despite years of complaints from the GSA's customers about the shoddiness of the furniture and equipment, the GSA had done little to investigate the contractor, Art Metal U.S.A.* Government agencies that had been issued the furniture, such as the Internal Revenue Service, the Central Intelligence Agency, and the State Department, told horror stories about furniture that fell apart, desks that collapsed, and chairs with one leg shorter than the others.

When federal employees complained to the GSA, they were ignored or rebuffed. "You didn't fill out the right form," the GSA would say, or "You have to pay to ship it back to the contractor and wait two years and you might get a replacement." After several years, this behavior naturally gave rise to the speculation that bribery and corruption were the cause of the problem.

A series of newspaper articles led to a congressional investigation. Peter Roman, then chief investigator for a subcommittee of the U.S. Senate Committee on Government Affairs, recalled when Senator Lawton Chiles of Florida, chairman of the subcommittee, called him to his office. "He wanted a full investigation into all the practices of GSA," Roman said. Unlike a private audit, a congressional investigation involves a thorough review of financial and operational records, interviews, and sworn testimony, when necessary. If there is enough evidence to show a crime has been committed, then the U.S. Justice Department prosecutes. Roman said this was "one of the few white-collar fraud investigations the Senate had done in years, with the exception of the Investigation Subcommittee's organized crime inquiries."

The first step in such an analysis involved general oversight hearings for the Subcommittee on Federal Spending Practices and Open Government. At one of the first hearings, Phillip J. Kurans, president of the Art Metal furniture company, appeared, uninvited, and demanded an opportunity to testify. He told Senator Chiles that his company produced good-quality furniture at bargain prices and challenged the subcommittee to prove otherwise. He invited the senator to the plant in Newark, New Jersey, to inspect their records.

"Chiles had me in his office the next morning," Roman recalls. "He said, 'Tell them we accept their offer. Get up to New Jersey and find out what happened.' "

Roman assembled an investigation team borrowed from other federal agencies. The principals were Dick Polhemus, certified fraud examiner, from the Treasury Department; and Marvin Doyal, CFE, CPA; and Paul Granetto from the U.S. General Accounting Office. "We agreed that the logical approach was to do a cash flow analysis," Roman recalls. "If the furniture was defective, then someone had

*Several names and details have been changed to preserve anonymity.

276

to generate cash to bribe somebody else to accept it. All of us had experience in following the money, so we went off to Newark to look for it.''

Together they paid a visit to Art Metal U.S.A. on behalf of the senator. Kurans grudgingly sent them into a large room filled with 30 years of financial records. In the past, the sheer volume of paper had caused two GSA investigations to end without incident and the company's own auditors to find nothing untoward. Half the team began controlling the checks, separating them out into operations and payroll, while the others reviewed the canceled checks to do a pattern analysis.

"Marvin Doyal and I still argue over which one of us first found the checks to a subcontractor which had been cashed rather than deposited," Roman says.

"As we began to review the operational checks," he remembers, "one of the items that stood out were checks made out to one company but under three different names: I. Spiegel, Spiegel Trucking Company, and Spiegel Trucking, Inc.'' Were the bookkeepers careless in writing the wrong name? The investigators discovered that the checks made out to I. Spiegel (which were folded into threes, like one would fold a personal check to be placed in a wallet) were cashed by one Isador Spiegel, unlike the other accounts. These checks were not run through any Spiegel Trucking Co. business account and had been used solely for cash. The checks to Spiegel Trucking Co. "looked like they had been used for actual delivery of furniture to various GSA depots or customers," Roman said.

The other item that caught the investigators' eyes involved checks made out simply to "Auction Expenses" for even sums of money. Kurans told them that the company bought used machinery for cash at auctions throughout the East Coast. That was the reason, he said, that the company spent large amounts of cash.

Yet when the team called operators of furniture auctions, they found that auctions required the buyer to show up with a certified check for 10 percent of the amount bought. The rest was also to be paid with certified checks. Over four years, Art Metal generated $482,000 in cash through so-called auction expenses. More than $800,000 flowing to Spiegel was converted into cash. This was enough evidence to garner Kurens a subpoena to appear before the subcommittee. The subpoena enabled investigators to obtain "literally a truck full of documents" from Art Metal, Roman said, "which filled a whole room in the basement of the Russell Senate Office Building."

With over $1 million in cash discovered, the next step for the investigating team was to look for evidence of bribery. They painstakingly interviewed every furniture inspector in the GSA's Region Two, eventually focusing on a former regional inspector of the GSA. Over the past four years, this man had bought 11 racehorses at an average price of $13,000 each—much more money than a GSA furniture inspector could afford. At this point, Senator Chiles authorized bringing in a special counsel. This was Charles Intriago, Esq., a former Miami Strike Force prosecutor. When confronted, the inspector availed himself of his Fifth Amendment rights, and the search for another witness continued. They found one: Louis Arnold, a retired bookkeeper at Art Metal. Arnold would testify that Art Metal management was paying off GSA inspectors. Arnold revealed a third source of cash, a petty cash fund totaling about $100,000 that was used to pay for the inspectors' lunches and hotel expenses.

Based on Arnold's testimony, investigators subpoenaed three banks that had photographed all of their cash transactions. "We found pictures of the treasurer, the plant manager, and occasionally one of the partners cashing these 'auction expense' checks and taking the money in twenties."

During the Senate hearings, several senior agency officials testified to the shoddiness of the furniture. Roman, who spent some time on the floor of the plant, saw many examples of shabby workmanship. For example, although plant managers claimed they had bought a quality paint machine to paint filing cabinets, Roman said all he ever saw was a man wearing a gas mask, with a hand-held paint sprayer, wildly spraying at cabinets that darted past him on a conveyor belt. "It was like seeing a little kid playing laser tag, and the target appears for half a second, and he takes a wild shot at it and hopes he hits the target," he said.

Marvin Doyal testified to the generation of $1.3 million in cash, a company official testified that the money had been used to bribe (unnamed) GSA inspectors, and company officials and GSA inspectors availed themselves of their Fifth Amendment rights. Interagency problems between the subcommittee and the Justice Department played a major role in a failed plea bargain with a former GSA official. At this point, Senator Chiles and the staff decided that the subcommittee had gone as far as it could go.

Why did Art Metal not make an attempt to hide its fraud? "In the first place," Roman said, "they thought nobody would ever come. Secondly, they had been the subject of two GSA-appointed investigations" that uncovered nothing.

The result of the investigations proved disappointing to Senator Chiles and the subcommittee staff.

"In the end," however, Senator Chiles later said, "we achieved our legislative mission. We were disappointed that the plea bargain and other subcommittee efforts didn't pay off as fully as it might have, but we sure got GSA's attention."

Embarrassed by the subcommittee disclosures, the GSA stopped awarding government furniture contracts to the Art Metal company. Having lost what amounted to its sole customer, Art Metal soon went bankrupt. Its plant manager and general counsel were convicted of related offenses within two years. The investigations into the GSA prompted a housecleaning of that agency. At the time of the hearings, the GSA had 27,000 employees; today it employs about 13,000. The GSA's role as the federal government's chief purchasing agent has been greatly diminished. The Art Metal case showed that centralized purchasing is not always a good idea.

OVERVIEW

Black's Law Dictionary defines "corrupt" as "spoiled; tainted; vitiated; depraved; debased; morally degenerate. As used as a verb, to change one's morals and principles from good to bad."[1] It further defines corruption as

> *an act done with an intent to give some advantage inconsistent with official duty and the rights of others. The act of an official or fiduciary person who unlawfully and wrongfully uses his station or character to procure some benefit for himself or for another person, contrary to duty and the rights of others.*[2]

My first official experience with bribery came when the FBI transferred me from El Paso, Texas, to New York, New York (''the town so nice they named it twice''). Sending me to New York was the FBI's cruel joke on someone who grew up in Duncan, Oklahoma. But I eventually learned to love the city. At the time I was transferred, about 1 out of every 7 FBI agents was assigned to the Manhattan office. As a result, the agents were divided into specialized squads, consisting of about 20 investigators and a supervisor.

Because there was an empty desk on the Bribery and Corruption Squad, that is where I found myself assigned. There was no other reason; I knew absolutely nothing about the topic. But I was about to learn. Over the next several years, I investigated part or all of several hundred cases. The most famous was the government's investigation of former U.S. Attorney John N. Mitchell for his role in Watergate. We sent him to prison. It seemed like a great accomplishment then—he did the crime, and he did the time. But later, after he was released and all the media fury died down, Mitchell died a broken man. My pride in that conviction has since turned to pity. As Lord Acton observed: ''Power corrupts. And absolute power corrupts absolutely.'' Perhaps many of us placed in the same circumstances as Mitchell would fall victim to temptation.

Although Watergate was my most famous case, it was not my first. And for those of us in the investigative field, the initial time we encounter a situation is frequently our most memorable. My first bribery case involved allegations against a highly placed government civil servant, Herman Klegman. He was with the Immigration and Naturalization Service (INS) and held the title of district director. Klegman's area covered all of New Jersey.

As district director for INS, Klegman had the ultimate authority to issue all green cards in his district. For the uninitiated, a green card gives a non–U.S. citizen the right to live and work in the country without becoming a permanent citizen. Green cards are strictly allotted by foreign country and can be very hard to come by legitimately, depending on the country of residence. At that time citizens from mainland China were especially likely to have their green card applications rejected, so many of them immigrated illegally. Once in the United States, these illegal immigrants would find their way into the Chinese community. In New York City, many of them would become employed by the numerous restaurants in Chinatown.

Unconfirmed rumors about Klegman's ethics apparently had circulated for years in INS circles. Finally someone—presumably an employee—wrote the FBI an anonymous letter claiming Klegman was ''on the take'' from a New York City Chinese restaurateur, Stanley Yee. No details were forthcoming, and I had no idea whatsoever where to start. So I spoke with the Corruption Squad's most experienced agent, Boyd Henry. He was a veteran of at least 1,000 bribery cases and really knew how to cut through the fog. I asked Boyd how to prove such a case.

''Joe,'' Boyd said, ''if someone is taking payoffs, then they're doing something they should not officially be doing. Look for what that something is, and you'll find the answer.'' Boyd was able to sum up the essence of investigating corruption in two sentences, and I have not forgotten it.

In Klegman's case, I reasoned that he must somehow be issuing green cards to Yee's workers in exchange for kickbacks. But this theory had an obvious flaw: Klegman's authority was limited to New Jersey only, and Yee's Chinese restaurants—20 of them—were all located in New York.

I discussed the theory with Boyd, who said, "That must be it—Klegman is probably somehow issuing green cards to Chinese restaurant workers in New York City through his office in New Jersey. You need to focus on exactly how he could pull that off." Boyd's approach made perfect sense to me. Sol Saletra, my contact at INS, explained that an application for a green card is filed in the district of the immigrant's residence. So if Klegman issued green cards to workers in New York City, they would show a New Jersey residence. Otherwise, it would look too suspicious to the compliance auditors at INS, who periodically check the procedure for issuing green cards. The first step in proving the address theory was to find the personnel records of all the employees of Yee's 20 eating establishments—about 400 people in total. We issued subpoenas to all the restaurants for their records. Once we had the names of Yee's Chinese workers, we searched them against INS records in New York and New Jersey.

Lo and behold, we hit pay dirt.

The search revealed a mysterious pattern with a dozen or so immigrants. It seemed their original immigration files were initiated in New York. Then each of these immigrants, at different times, sent a letter to the INS stating they had "moved" from New York to New Jersey. Their applications for green cards were thereafter processed in the New Jersey INS office by—you guessed it—Klegman himself. After their green cards were issued, each of these Chinese immigrants sent a letter to the New Jersey INS office, stating that they had "moved" back to New York. Interestingly, to the naked eye, all the letters looked like they had been prepared on the same typewriter.

I went back to Boyd Henry for more of his sage advice. "Yes, Joe, you're on to something," he said. "But you've still got a long way to go. You haven't quite proved that Klegman has done something he shouldn't have officially done." First, to put a circumstantial case together, Boyd reasoned that a highly placed INS official like Klegman would never personally approve green card applications, even though he had the authority to do so. Sol Saletra of the INS confirmed that it would be very unusual for the district director's signature to be on an application, as it was on these dozen or so Chinese immigrants' applications.

But Sol's observations would have to be confirmed for court purposes. I only knew one way to do that, and so did Sol: Someone would have to examine every immigration file in the District of New Jersey and inspect the approving official's signature. We reluctantly committed the staff power to do just that. Hundreds of hours of tedious labor later, we found exactly what we needed—out of thousands of immigration applications in his district, Klegman's signature appeared only on the dozen Chinese restaurant workers'.

Through Chinese FBI interpreters, we next interviewed the restaurant workers. The workers denied paying for their green cards. But during the interview process, we obtained bank account information from them and then subpoenaed those records. In each and every case, the restaurant workers had made a $10,000 cash withdrawal from their respective savings accounts. And each withdrawal closely coincided with the approval date of that immigrant's INS application.

Boyd Henry, my FBI mentor, smiled at my progress in the case. "In order to prove a bribery case, you're going to have to prove that Klegman got a 'thing of value' as required by the statute," he observed. "In most—but not all—cases, the 'thing of value' is going to be money. If you find where Klegman has stashed his bribe money, I think you have enough for a conviction.'' Finding the location of the stash proved more difficult than Henry thought. ''For some inexplicable reason,'' Boyd said, ''most people taking cash deposit some or all of it in their own bank account. Then they spend it. Look at his bank statements first,'' he suggested. I did. Nothing there. We then piecemealed a financial picture of Klegman indicating he was not living ostentatiously—no new homes, cars, or toys as far as we could tell. Then the Assistant United States Attorney, Robert ''Bolt'' Beller, who was interested in prosecuting the case, pulled Klegman before the grand jury. Klegman didn't take the Fifth—he cooperated fully but denied everything.

Then, as is standard in corruption cases, Bolt offered a deal to Stanley Yee that he could not refuse: Cooperate with the government and we will go easier on you. Eventually Yee came into the FBI office with his lawyer. In exchange for a reduced sentence, Yee furnished the key information. Yes, he had paid Klegman, he admitted. They had an arrangement—for every green card issued to one of Yee's restaurant workers, the illegal immigrant would pay Yee $10,000. In turn, Yee would pay that money to Klegman. The arrangement had been going on for years, and Yee estimated he had paid Klegman at least $250,000 in bribes.

But where did Klegman stash the ill-gotten gains? In Israel, Yee said, in a secret bank account Klegman had set up in Tel Aviv. We were able to confirm that through our international contacts. Klegman was indicted for bribery. A few days before his trial, Herman Simon Klegman entered a guilty plea and drew a modest prison term. Yee walked.

The lesson to be learned from such a difficult corruption case is that such cases are very hard to prove. And in almost all cases, it is necessary to make a deal with the proverbial ''bag man'' like Stanley Yee. Making such deals originally grated against me. But one learns in the criminal justice system to take what you can get. Otherwise, people like Klegman will go scot-free.

Corruption Classifications

In our study, *corruption schemes* were broken down into four classifications: *bribery, economic extortion, illegal gratuities,* and *conflicts of interest.* The first three classifications are very similar in nature and are discussed in this chapter. Conflict-of-interest schemes are covered in Chapter 11.

Before discussing how corruption schemes work, we must understand the similarities and differences that exist among bribery, extortion, and illegal gratuity cases. Bribery may be defined as the offering, giving, receiving, or soliciting anything of value to influence an official act.[3] The term ''official act'' means that traditional bribery statutes proscribe only payments made to influence the decisions of government agents or employees. In the case of Art Metal U.S.A., this is exactly what happened. The furniture supplier paid off government inspectors to accept substandard merchandise.

Many occupational fraud schemes, however, involve commercial bribery, which is similar to the traditional definition of bribery except that something of value is offered to influence a business decision rather than an official act of government. Of course, payments are made every day to influence business decisions, and these payments are perfectly legal. When two parties sign a contract agreeing that one will deliver merchandise in return for a certain sum of money, this is a business decision that has been influenced by the offer of something of value. Obviously, this transaction is not illegal. In a commercial bribery scheme, the payment is received by an employee without the employer's consent. In other words, commercial bribery cases deal with the acceptance of under-the-table payments in return for the exercise of influence over a business transaction. Notice also that *offering* a payment can constitute a bribe, even if the illicit payment is never actually made.

Illegal gratuities are similar to bribery schemes, except that something of value is given to an employee to *reward* a decision rather than influence it. In an illegal gratuities scheme, a decision is made that happens to benefit a certain person or company. This decision is not influenced by any sort of payment. The party who benefited from the decision then rewards the person who made the decision. For example, in one case, an employee of a utility company awarded a multimillion-dollar construction contract to a certain vendor and later received an automobile from that vendor as a reward.

At first glance, it may seem that illegal gratuities schemes are harmless if the business decisions in question are not influenced by the promise of payment. But most company ethics policies forbid employees from accepting unreported gifts from vendors. One reason is that illegal gratuities schemes can (and do) evolve into bribery schemes. Once an employee has been rewarded for an act such as directing business to a particular supplier, an understanding might be reached that future decisions beneficial to the supplier also will be rewarded. Additionally, even though an outright promise of payment has not been made, employees may direct business to certain companies in the hope that they will be rewarded with money or gifts.

Economic extortion cases are the pay-up-or-else corruption schemes. Whereas bribery schemes involve an offer of payment intended to influence a business decision, economic extortion schemes are committed when one person demands payment from another. Refusal to pay the extorter results in some harm, such as a loss of business. For instance, in one case, an employee demanded payment from suppliers and in return awarded those suppliers subcontracts on various projects. If the suppliers refused to pay the employee, the subcontracts were awarded to rival suppliers or held back until the fraudster got his money.

CORRUPTION DATA FROM ACFE *2009 GLOBAL FRAUD SURVEY*

Frequency and Cost

Of 1,843 cases in our 2009 survey, 33 percent involved a corruption scheme. (The sum of these percentages exceeds 100 percent because some cases involved multiple fraud schemes that fell into more than one category. Various charts in this chapter may reflect percentages that total in excess of 100 percent for similar reasons.) Although corruption schemes were far less common than asset misappropriations, which have been discussed already, they were much more costly. The median loss of corruption cases in our survey ($250,000) was nearly twice as large as the median loss of asset misappropriation schemes ($135,000). (See Exhibits 10.1 and 10.2.)

Exhibit 10.3 shows that corruption cases were much more heavily skewed to the highest dollar loss categories than occupational frauds in general. Of 418 corruption

Exhibit 10.1   *2009 Global Fraud Survey*: **Frequency of Three Major Fraud Categories**

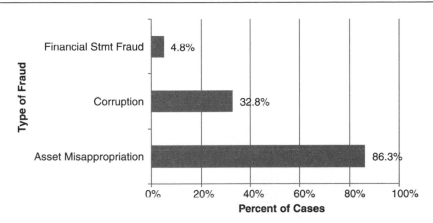

cases in which losses were reported, 33 percent caused losses in excess of $1 million, while only 24 percent of all occupational frauds fell in this category. Seventy percent of all corruption cases caused at least $100,000 in losses.

Types of Corruption Schemes

In the fraud tree, corruption schemes can be broken down into four distinct categories: bribery, conflicts of interest, economic extortion, and illegal gratuities. As Exhibit 10.4 shows, approximately 56 percent of the corruption cases we reviewed involved bribery while 53 percent involved conflicts of interest.

Detection of Corruption Schemes

The most common method of detection in corruption cases was a tip, which occurred in approximately half of the cases in our study. This was a higher rate than was found in

Exhibit 10.2   *2009 Global Fraud Survey*: **Median Loss of Three Major Fraud Categories**

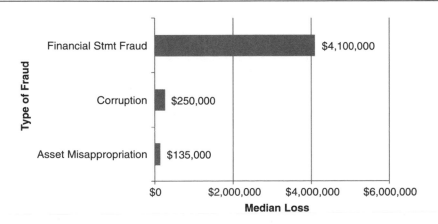

Exhibit 10.3   *2009 Global Fraud Survey*: **Dollar Loss Distribution for Corruption Schemes**

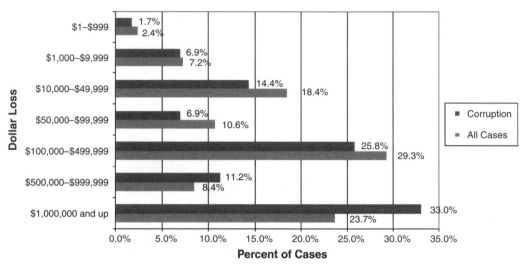

all fraud cases. In contrast, fewer corruption cases were detected by management review, accident, account reconciliation, and document examination than in the general body of occupational frauds. (See Exhibit 10.5.)

Perpetrators of Corruption Schemes

The corruption cases in our study were more likely to be committed by managers or owner/executives than were occupational frauds in general. While just under 41 percent of all cases were committed by managers, half of corruption cases fit this category. And while 17 percent of all cases involved owner/executives, 25 percent of corruption cases were in this category. (See Exhibit 10.6.)

Exhibit 10.4   *2009 Global Fraud Survey*: **Frequency of Corruption Schemes by Type**

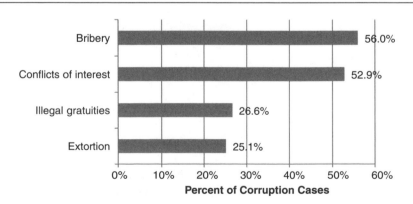

Exhibit 10.5 *2009 Global Fraud Survey*: **Detection of Corruption Schemes**

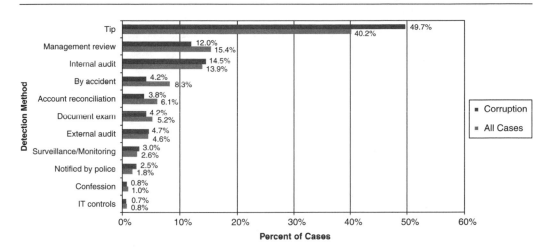

Among the corruption cases in our study, schemes committed by owner/executives had a median loss of $798,000, which was nearly eight times as high as the median loss in employee schemes. It was also more than twice as much as the median loss caused by managers who undertook corruption schemes, as shown in Exhibit 10.7.

Victims of Corruption Schemes

Exhibit 10.8 shows how the corruption cases in our survey were distributed based on the size of the victim organization. Corruption cases were slightly less likely to occur in small organizations than occupational frauds in general. Twenty-four percent of corruption cases occurred in the organizations with fewer than 100 employees, compared to 31 percent of all cases.

Exhibit 10.6 *2009 Global Fraud Survey*: **Perpetrators of Corruption Schemes**

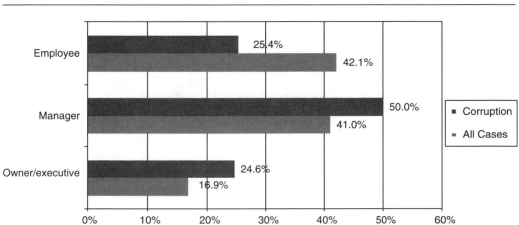

Exhibit 10.7 *2009 Global Fraud Survey*: **Median Loss by Perpetrator of Corruption Schemes**

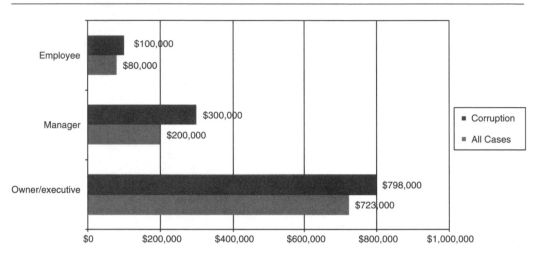

As mentioned previously, the corruption cases in our study caused greater losses, on average, than occupational frauds in general. Therefore, it is no surprise that the median losses caused by corruption schemes equaled or exceeded the median losses for all cases in every category of victim organization. (See Exhibit 10.9.)

BRIBERY SCHEMES

At its heart, a bribe is a business transaction, albeit an illegal or unethical one. As in the GSA case discussed earlier, a person "buys" something with the bribes she pays. What

Exhibit 10.8 *2009 Global Fraud Survey*: **Size of Victim in Corruption Schemes**

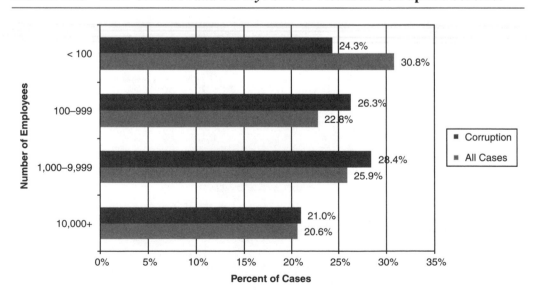

Exhibit 10.9 *2009 Global Fraud Survey*: Median Loss Size of Victim in Corruption Schemes

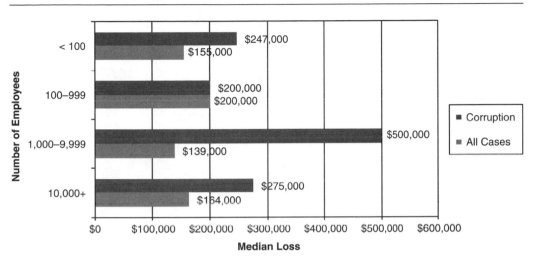

she buys is the influence of the recipient. Bribery schemes generally fall into two broad categories: *kickbacks* and *bid-rigging schemes*.

Kickbacks are undisclosed payments made by vendors to employees of purchasing companies. The purpose of a kickback usually is to enlist the corrupt employee in an overbilling scheme. Sometimes vendors pay kickbacks simply to get extra business from the purchasing company. Bid-rigging schemes occur when an employee fraudulently assists a vendor in winning a contract through the competitive bidding process.

Kickback Schemes

Kickback schemes are usually very similar to the billing schemes described in Part I of this book. They involve the submission of invoices for goods and services that are either overpriced or fictitious. (See Exhibit 10.10.)

Kickbacks are classified as corruption schemes rather than asset misappropriations because they involve collusion between employees and vendors. In a common type of kickback scheme, a vendor submits a fraudulent or inflated invoice to the victim company, and an employee of that company helps make sure that a payment is made on the false invoice. For that assistance, the employee-fraudster receives some form of payment from the vendor. This payment is the kickback.

Kickback schemes almost always attack the purchasing function of the victim company, so it stands to reason that these frauds often are undertaken by employees who have purchasing responsibilities. Purchasing employees often have direct contact with vendors and therefore have an opportunity to establish a collusive relationship. In one case, a purchasing agent redirected orders to a company owned by a supplier with whom he was conspiring. In return for the additional business, the supplier paid the purchasing agent over half the profits from the additional orders.

Exhibit 10.10   Kickback Schemes

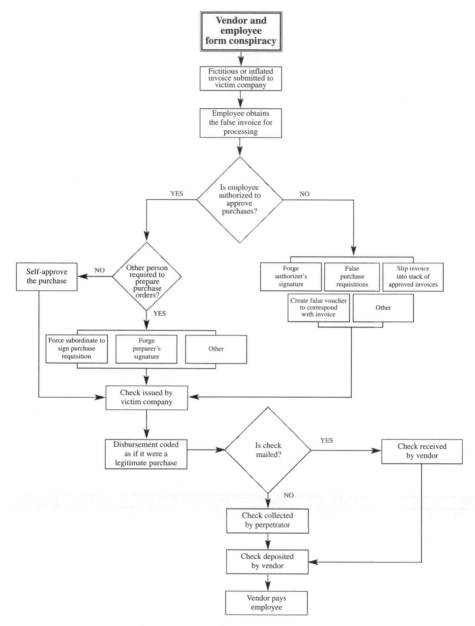

Diverting Business to Vendors

In some instances, an employee-fraudster receives a kickback simply for directing excess business to a vendor. There might be no overbilling involved in these cases; the vendor simply pays the kickbacks to ensure a steady stream of business from the purchasing company. In one instance, the president of a software supplier offered a percentage of ownership in his company to an employee of a purchaser in exchange for a major contract. Similarly, a travel agency in another case provided free travel and entertainment to the purchasing agent of a retail company. In return, the purchasing agent agreed to book all corporate trips through the travel agent.

If no overbilling is involved in a kickback scheme, one might wonder where the harm lies. Assuming the vendor simply wants to get the buyer's business and does not increase prices or bill for undelivered goods and services, how is the buyer harmed? The problem is that, having bought off an employee of the purchasing company, a vendor is no longer subject to the normal economic pressures of the marketplace. This vendor does not have to compete with other suppliers for the purchasing company's business and so has no incentive to provide a low price or quality merchandise. In these circumstances, the purchasing company almost always ends up overpaying for goods or services or getting less than it paid for. In the travel agency case just described, the victim company estimated that it paid $10,000 more for airfare over a two-year period by booking through the corrupt travel agency than if it had used a different company.

Once vendors know that they have an exclusive purchasing arrangement, their incentive is to raise prices to cover the cost of the kickback. Most bribery schemes end up as overbilling schemes even if they do not start that way. This is one reason why most business codes of ethics prohibit employees from accepting undisclosed gifts from vendors. In the long run, the employees' company is sure to pay for their unethical conduct.

Overbilling Schemes

Employees with Approval Authority

In most instances, kickback schemes begin as overbilling schemes in which a vendor submits inflated invoices to the victim company. The false invoices either overstate the cost of actual goods and services or reflect fictitious sales. In one example, an employee with complete authority to approve vouchers from a certain vendor authorized payment on over 100 fraudulent invoices in which the vendor's rates were overstated. Because no one was reviewing her decisions, the employee could approve payments on invoices at above-normal rates without fear of detection.

The ability to authorize purchases (and thus to authorize fraudulent purchases) is usually a key to kickback schemes. The fraudster in the case just mentioned was a nonmanagement employee who had approval authority for purchases made from the vendor with whom she colluded. She authorized approximately $300,000 worth of inflated billings in less than two years. Similarly, in a separate case, a manager was authorized to purchase fixed assets for his company as part of a leasehold improvement. The assets he ordered were of a cheaper quality and lower price than what was specified, but the contract he negotiated did not reflect this. Therefore, the victim company paid for high-quality materials but received low-quality materials. The difference in price between what the company paid and what the materials actually cost was diverted back to the manager as a kickback.

The existence of purchasing authority can be critical to the success of kickback schemes. If fraudsters can authorize payments themselves, they do not have to submit purchase requisitions to an honest superior who might question the validity of the transaction.

Fraudsters Lacking Approval Authority

Although the majority of the kickback schemes we reviewed involved people with authority to approve purchases, this authority is not an absolute necessity. When employees cannot approve fraudulent purchases themselves, they still can orchestrate a kickback scheme if they can circumvent accounts payable controls. In some cases, all that is required is the filing of a false purchase requisition. If a trusted employee tells a superior that the company needs certain materials or services, this is sometimes sufficient to get a false invoice approved for payment. Such schemes are generally successful when the person with approval authority is inattentive or when she is forced to rely on subordinates' guidance in purchasing matters.

Corrupt employees also might prepare false vouchers to make it appear that fraudulent invoices are legitimate. When proper controls are in place, a completed voucher is required before accounts payable will pay an invoice. One key is for the fraudster to create a purchase order that corresponds to the vendor's fraudulent invoice. The fraudster might forge the signature of an authorized party on the purchase order to show that the acquisition has been approved. In computerized payables systems, an employee who has access to a restricted password can enter the system and authorize payments on fraudulent invoices.

In less sophisticated schemes, a corrupt employee simply might take a fraudulent invoice from a vendor and slip it into a stack of prepared invoices before they are input into the accounts payable system. A more detailed description of how false invoices are processed may be found in Chapter 7.

Kickback schemes can be very difficult to detect. In a sense, the victim company is being attacked from two directions. Externally a corrupt vendor submits false invoices that induce the victim company to pay unwittingly for goods or services that it does not receive. Internally, one or more of the victim company's employees waits to corroborate the false information provided by the vendor.

Other Kickback Schemes

Bribes are not always paid to employees to process phony invoices. In some circumstances, outsiders seek other fraudulent assistance from employees of the victim company. In the case study at the beginning of this chapter, for instance, Art Metal U.S.A. paid huge sums to quality insurance inspectors so that its substandard equipment would be accepted by the General Services Administration. In this case, the vendor was not overbilling the agency; he was trying to dump substandard products in lieu of providing equipment that met government specifications.

In other cases, bribes come not from vendors who are trying to sell something to the victim company but rather from potential purchasers who seek a lower price from the victim company. In one of our cases, an advertising salesman not only sold ads but was authorized to bill for and collect on advertising accounts. He was also authorized to issue discounts to clients. In return for benefits such as free travel, lodging, and various gifts, this individual either sold ads at greatly reduced rates or gave free ads to those who bought him off. His complete control over advertising and a lack of oversight allowed this employee to "trade away" over $20,000 in advertising revenues. Similarly, in another case, the manager of a convention center accepted various gifts from show promoters. In return, he allowed these promoters to rent the convention center at prices below the rates approved by the city that owned the center.

Kickback Payments

Every bribe is a two-sided transaction. In every case in which a vendor bribes a purchaser, there is someone on the vendor's side of the transaction who is making an illicit payment. It is therefore equally likely that employees are paying bribes as accepting them.

In order to obtain the funds to make these payments, employees usually divert company money into a slush fund, a noncompany account from which bribes can be made. Assuming that bribes are not authorized by the briber's company, he must find a way to generate the funds necessary to illegally influence someone in another organization. Therefore, the key to the crime from the briber's perspective is the diversion of money into the slush fund. This fraudulent disbursement of company funds usually is accomplished by the writing of company checks to a fictitious entity or submitting false invoices in the name of the false entity. In one case, for example, an officer in a very large healthcare organization created a fund to pay public officials and influence pending legislation. This officer used check requests for several different expense codes to generate payments that went to one of the company's lobbyists, who placed the money in an account from which bribe money could be withdrawn. Most of the checks in this case were coded as "fees" for consulting or other services.

It is common to charge fraudulent disbursements to nebulous accounts such as "consulting fees." The purchase of goods can be verified by a check of inventory, but there is no inventory for these kinds of services. It is therefore more difficult to prove that the payments are fraudulent.

Bid-Rigging Schemes

As we have said, when one person pays a bribe to another, she does so to gain the benefit of the recipient's influence. The competitive bidding process, in which several suppliers or contractors are vying for contracts in what can be a cutthroat environment, can be tailor-made for bribery. Any advantage one vendor can gain over competitors in this arena is extremely valuable. The benefit of "inside influence" can ensure that a vendor will win a sought-after contract. Many vendors are willing to pay for this influence.

In the competitive bidding process, all bidders are legally supposed to be placed on the same plane of equality, bidding on the same terms and conditions. Each bidder competes for a contract based on the specifications set forth by the purchasing company. Vendors submit confidential bids stating the price at which they will complete a project in accordance with the purchaser's specifications.

The way competitive bidding is rigged depends largely on the level of influence of the corrupt employee. The more power a person has over the bidding process, the more likely the person can influence the selection of a supplier. Therefore, employees involved in bid-rigging schemes, like those in kickback schemes, tend to have a good measure of influence or access to the competitive bidding process. Potential targets for bribes include buyers, contracting officials, engineers and technical representatives, quality or product assurance representatives, subcontractor liaison employees, and anyone else with authority over the awarding of contracts.

Bid-rigging schemes can be categorized based on the stage of bidding at which the fraudster exerts influence. Such schemes usually occur in the presolicitation phase, the solicitation phase, or the submission phase of the bidding process. (See Exhibit 10.11.)

Exhibit 10.11 Bid-Rigging Schemes

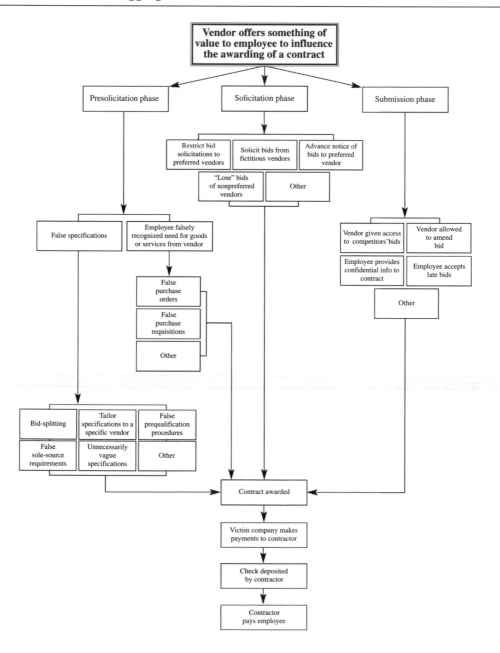

Presolicitation Phase

In the presolicitation phase of the competitive bidding process—before bids officially are sought for a project—bribery schemes can be broken down into two distinct types. The first is the need recognition scheme, whereby employees of a purchasing company are paid to convince their company that a particular project is necessary. The second reason to bribe someone in the presolicitation phase is to have the specifications of the contract tailored to the strengths of a particular supplier.

Need Recognition Schemes

The typical fraud in the need recognition phase of the contract negotiation is a conspiracy between the buyer and contractor whereby an employee of the buyer receives something of value and in return recognizes a "need" for a particular product or service. The result of such a scheme is that the victim company purchases unnecessary goods or services from a supplier at the direction of the corrupt employee.

Several trends may indicate a need recognition fraud. Unusually high requirements for stock and inventory levels may reveal a situation in which a corrupt employee is seeking to justify unnecessary purchase activity from a certain supplier. An employee also might justify unnecessary purchases of inventory by writing off large numbers of surplus items to scrap. As these items leave the inventory, they open up spaces to justify additional purchases. Another indicator of a need recognition scheme is the defining of a "need" that can be met only by a certain supplier or contractor. In addition, the failure to develop a satisfactory list of backup suppliers may reveal an unusually strong attachment to a primary supplier—an attachment that is explainable by the acceptance of bribes from that supplier.

Specifications Schemes

The other type of presolicitation fraud is a specifications scheme. The specifications of a contract are a list of the elements, materials, dimensions, and other relevant requirements for completion of the project. Specifications are prepared to assist vendors in the bidding process, telling them what they are required to do and providing a firm basis for making and accepting bids.

One corruption scheme that occurs in this process is the fraudulent tailoring of specifications to a particular vendor. In these cases, the vendor pays off an employee of the buyer who is involved in the preparation of specifications for the contract. In return, the employee sets the specifications of the contract to accommodate that vendor's capabilities. In one instance, a supplier paid an employee of a public utility to write contract specifications that were so proprietary that they effectively eliminated all competition for the project. For four years this supplier won the contract, which was the largest awarded by the utility company. The fraud cost the utility company in excess of $2 million.

The methods used to restrict competition in the bidding process may include the use of "prequalification" procedures that are known to eliminate certain competitors. For instance, the bid may require potential contractors to have a certain percentage of female or minority ownership. There is nothing illegal with such a requirement, but if it is placed in the specifications as a result of a bribe rather than as the result of other factors, then the employee has sold his or her influence to benefit a dishonest vendor—a clear case of corruption.

Sole-source or noncompetitive procurement justifications also may be used to eliminate competition and steer contracts to a particular vendor. Take the case of a requisitioner who distorted the requirements of a contract up for bid, claiming that the specifications called for a sole-source provider. Based on the requisitioner's information, competitive bidding was disregarded and the contract was awarded to a particular supplier. A review of other bids received at a later date showed that certain materials were available for up to $70,000 less than what the company paid in the sole-source arrangement. The employee had helped divert the job to the contractor in return for a promise of future employment. Competitive bidding also was disregarded in another case where management staff of a state entity took bribes from vendors to authorize purchases of approximately $200,000 in fixed assets.

Another type of specifications scheme is the deliberate writing of vague specifications. In this type of scheme, a supplier pays an employee of the purchasing company to write specifications that will require amendments at a later date. This will allow the supplier to raise the price of the contract when the amendments are made. As the buyer's needs become more specific or more detailed, the vendor can claim that, had he known what the buyer actually wanted, his bid on the project would have been higher. In order to complete the project as defined by the amended specifications, the supplier will have to charge a higher price.

Another form of specifications fraud is bid splitting. In one example, a manager of a federal employer split a large repair job into several component contracts in order to divert the jobs to his brother-in-law. Federal law required competitive bidding on projects over a certain dollar value. The manager broke the project up so that each sectional project was below the mandatory bidding level. Once the contract was split, the manager hired his brother-in-law to handle each of the component projects. Thus, the brother-in-law got the entire contract while avoiding competitive bidding.

A less egregious but still unfair form of bid-rigging occurs when a vendor pays an employee of the buyer for the right to see the specifications earlier than the competitors are able to. The employee does not alter the specifications to suit the vendor but rather simply gives the vendor a head start on planning his bid and preparing for the job. The extra planning time gives the vendor an advantage over competitors in preparing a bid for the job.

Solicitation Phase

In the solicitation phase of the competitive bidding process, fraudsters attempt to influence the selection of a contractor by restricting the pool of competitors from whom bids are sought. In other words, a corrupt vendor pays an employee of the purchasing company to ensure that one or more of the vendor's competitors do not get to bid on the contract. In this manner, the corrupt vendor is able to improve his chances of winning the job.

One type of scheme involves the sales representative who deals on behalf of a number of potential bidders. The sales representative (rep) bribes a contracting official to rig the solicitation, ensuring that only those companies represented by the rep get to submit bids. It is not uncommon in some sectors for buyers to "require" bidders to be represented by certain sales or manufacturing representatives. These reps pay a kickback to the buyer to protect their clients' interests. The result of this transaction is that the purchasing company is deprived of the ability to get the best price on its contract. Typically, the group of "protected" vendors does not actually compete against each other for the purchaser's contracts, but instead engages in "bid pooling."

Bid Pooling

Bid pooling is a process by which several bidders conspire to split contracts up and ensure that each gets a certain amount of work. Instead of submitting confidential bids, the vendors discuss what their bids will be so they can guarantee that each vendor will win a share of the purchasing company's business. For example, if vendors A, B, and C are up for three separate jobs, they may agree that A's bid will be the lowest on the first contract, B's bid will be the lowest on the second contract, and C's bid will be the lowest on the third contract. None of the vendors gets all three jobs, but they are all guaranteed to get at least one. Furthermore, since they plan their bids ahead of time, the vendors can conspire to raise their prices. Thus the purchasing company suffers as a result of the scheme.

Fictitious Suppliers

Another way to eliminate competition in the solicitation phase of the selection process is to solicit bids from fictitious suppliers. In the bid-splitting case discussed earlier, the brother-in-law submitted quotes in the names of several different companies and performed work under these various names. Although confidential bidding was avoided in this case, the perpetrator used quotes from several of the brother-in-law's fictitious companies to demonstrate price reasonableness on the final contracts. In other words, the brother-in-law's fictitious price quotes were used to validate his actual prices.

Other Methods

In some cases, competition for a contract can be limited by severely restricting the time for submitting bids. Certain suppliers are given advance notice of contracts before bids are solicited. These suppliers therefore are able to begin preparing their bids ahead of time. With the short time frame for developing bid proposals, the supplier with advance knowledge of the contract will have a decided advantage over the competition.

Bribed purchasing officials also can restrict competition for their co-conspirators by soliciting bids in obscure publications where they are unlikely to be seen by other vendors. Again, this is done to eliminate potential rivals and create an advantage for the corrupt suppliers. Some schemes also have involved the publication of bid solicitations during holiday periods when those suppliers not "in the know" are unlikely to be looking for potential contracts. In more blatant cases, the bids of outsiders are accepted but are "lost" or improperly disqualified by the corrupt employee of the purchaser.

Typically, when a vendor bribes an employee of the purchasing company to assist in any kind of solicitation scheme, the cost of the bribe is included in the corrupt vendor's bid. Therefore, the purchasing company ends up bearing the cost of the illicit payment in the form of a higher contract price.

Submission Phase

In the actual submission phase of the process, where bids are proffered to the buyer, several schemes may be used to win a contract for a particular supplier. The principal offense tends to be abuse of the sealed-bid process. Competitive bids are confidential; they are, of course, supposed to remain sealed until a specified date when all bids are opened and reviewed by the purchasing company. The person or persons who have access to sealed bids are often the targets of unethical vendors who are seeking an advantage in the process. In one example, gifts and cash payments were given to a majority owner of a company in exchange for preferential treatment during the bidding process. The supplier who paid the bribes was allowed to submit his bids last, knowing what prices his competitors had quoted or, alternatively, he was allowed actually to see his competitors' bids and adjust his own accordingly.

Vendors also bribe employees of the purchaser for information on how to prepare their bid. Take the case of the general manager for a purchasing company who provided confidential pricing information to a supplier that enabled the supplier to outbid his competitors and win a long-term contract. In return, both the general manager and his daughter received payments from the supplier. Other reasons to bribe employees of the purchaser include to:

- Ensure receipt of a late bid.
- Falsify the bid log.
- Extend the bid opening date.
- Control bid openings.

The next case study was selected to illustrate in greater detail a case of bid tampering at the submission phase. The story deals with Thad Ferguson, a corrupt salesman who consistently won bids for his clients because he had the buyer's plant manager in his back pocket. In return for cash payments and other gifts, the plant manager provided Ferguson with information that allowed him to narrowly outbid his competition. The study also describes in detail how CFE Gene Earle uncovered the scheme and shut it down.

Case Study: Keep Your Eye on the Salesman

CFE Gene Earle thought he was just going to a party. But the small talk was more than he bargained for. The party was thrown by Earle's employer, HydroCo, an air-separation company with over $600 million in annual sales.* HydroCo

*Several names and details have been changed to preserve anonymity.

isolates gases such as argon, oxygen, and hydrogen from the atmosphere and then distributes them for industrial use. While Earle sampled the hors d'oeuvres and drinks, he talked with the controller of a construction firm that had done several jobs for HydroCo.

"I'm gonna be frank with you," the man told Earle. "Your bid process on this asbestos work isn't fair." "What's the problem?" Earle asked. "Well, if you'll look into it you'll see that your work follows this one salesman. His name's Thad Ferguson. He's worked for different companies. But no matter who he works for, they end up getting your contracts. Where he goes, HydroCo business follows. Now, that's too wet to plow if you ask me." Besides that, the man said, Ferguson was known by insiders as a "sleazebag." What's a sleazebag in these circumstances? "You can apply any definition you want, and it'll describe this guy. He does it all," said the controller.

When Earle got to his office the next day, he started looking at the asbestos abatement projects. A government mandate branded asbestos a health hazard and demanded its immediate removal from all public buildings. Abatement was sensitive, headache-inducing work to say the least. From the outset, Earle learned that whatever he counted on could not be counted on. The purchasing department, a logical place to begin asking questions, had not handled the purchasing for these jobs. That had been deferred to the plant operations office.

Bid files at Operations were in a mess. Earle found precious little documentation of anything. Competitive bids had no verification, and safety compliance forms were either missing or incomplete. The papers that were present described work that did not measure up to the $300,000 and $400,000 contracts. Engineers had designed an overall abatement project amounting to a couple million dollars. The actual removal of the asbestos would be performed in phases at several hundred thousand dollars a phase. The disorganized files did not tell much of a story; though to Earle, "It looked like the work was being done, but not to the value we were paying for." HydroCo's chief engineer would later estimate that the company was bilked for between $250,000 and $400,000 on the first three phases of the abatement, which was settled with individual contractors. As for the bid-rigging fraud, Earle could not tell if his source's accusations were true or not, but he did find Thad Ferguson's name on several key papers.

Actually finding the abatement companies was the next hurdle. Because the work is so sensitive, webbed with regulations, and always a target for lawsuits, Earle had a hard time getting a clear picture of the various companies and their operations. "It's a nightmare trying to sort through the different layers of ownership and subsidiaries to find out where the company actually is, who is authorized to handle bids, approve bids, and oversee the process." Narrowing down the list of targets, Earle called one of Ferguson's old jobs and got nothing. The manager there said he had no idea what Earle was talking about. Ferguson had been there, he was gone, end of story. But the manager's company was still bidding for HydroCo jobs. If he wanted to remain competitive in the bidding, Earle hinted, it would be in everyone's interest for the man to stop talking nonsense. The manager thought for a second and made an offer. If he could be sure there would not be any legal or business repercussions, he would talk to Earle and show him the paperwork. But the man said they'd have to meet at a hotel. Earle thought this was a bit cloak-and-dagger but agreed to the meeting.

"When Ferguson came to work for us," the manager said bluntly, "he told us he had HydroCo in his back pocket. . . . He was going to be able to get your business regardless of who he worked for."

"Did he tell you how he was going to do this?" Earle asked.

"I didn't really want to know."

"I'm having a hard time believing that," Earle replied. The manager observed that it often pays to keep yourself in the dark.

Earle took another approach. "Ferguson was working for somebody else at the time. What did you have to do to get him on with you?"

"We made concessions on commissions."

"Were those pretty lucrative?"

"They were substantial," the manager said, emphasizing the word "substantial."

The conversation continued. "How did Ferguson say he was going to get our business for you?"

"We were going to have to buy a service, something called a 'travel evaluation report,' from your plant manager. Name of Ben Butler. . . . Butler's sister had some kind of travel agency. We were to purchase this evaluation from her."

"And how much was that?" asked Earle.

"Ten thousand dollars."

"How'd you pay for that?"

"With a check."

"One check?"

"One check, ten thousand dollars."

The manager said he had no idea what a travel evaluation report was. They never got anything from the travel agency. "We got the job," he deadpanned. He didn't like doing business that way. His company had gotten shafted twice on the project, he said. Besides the up-front money, Thad Ferguson's 19-year-old son was put on the construction payroll though he rarely, if ever, showed up for work. Just another perk in exchange for access to Ferguson's lucrative back pocket. At the end of the meeting, the manager gave Earle what he needed—a copy of the canceled check for $10,000 with Ben Butler's signature on the money line. A simple conversation with bank officials about authorized account signatures showed that Sun & Fun Travel did not belong to Butler's sister; Butler himself was the primary owner.

Back at the plant, Earle talked with people in the operations office where construction bids were processed. Oh yes, they all knew Ferguson. He dropped by at least once a month, more than that if a construction job was going on. He schmoozed everybody, brought flowers and candy to female workers, sprang for long lunches and drinks. A purchasing clerk told Earle that Ben Butler, as plant manager, handled the nuts and bolts of construction bids himself. "I did some of the paperwork," the woman said, "but that was just him giving me the numbers and I'd prepare the bid sheets . . . . For anything with Thad, Mr. Butler took care of that personally."

And Ferguson took care of Butler. The two of them disappeared for entire afternoons, touring the finest restaurants and topless bars in Houston. And quid pro quo, Ferguson's employers—whoever they happened to be—ended up filing a bid within 1% of the next lowest competitor. The purchasing clerk remembered one project during which she was first astounded, then confounded, then too worried to ask any questions. After a set of bids had been filed, a contractor called to say that he had misread a key requirement; he wanted to submit another version of his bid, and the clerk revised the numbers accordingly. Later, when the bids were unsealed, Ferguson's company had also revised its bid! It was just a little lower than the other contractor's new figure, and Ferguson got the job. As Earle's source declared at the party, this ground was too wet to plow.

Earle set up a meeting with Thad Ferguson. The salesman arrived in a nice suit and good spirits but was suffering from severe amnesia. He couldn't remember anything about Ben Butler or asbestos abatement. "He was slick," Earle says, "smiling, a fast talker, but you felt like you needed to take a bath after you left the room." Earle asked him about arranging for his old employer to buy a travel evaluation from Sun & Fun. Ferguson smirked and shook his head. "I never heard of such a thing. What do *you* think that is?" he asked in return. Earle got itchy as the interview went on, with nothing but smirks and denials from the charming Mr. Ferguson. "He knew I knew he was lying," Earle recalls bitterly, "but there wasn't anything I could do about it."

Ben Butler tried the amnesia track, but without Ferguson's luck. "I know Thad Ferguson, yes," Butler said. "Not very well, though. Just, I see him in the office, talk about jobs."

Earle listened patiently. "I needed for him to show his hand. We knew he had financial problems. Two of his adult children had moved back home, and he was supporting them. He had debts from a ranch he had bought a couple of years before." Plus, Earle had his ace—the contractor's canceled check with Butler's signature. About halfway through the six-hour interview, Earle put the check on the table. "We need to talk about this," he told Butler.

From there, the dam broke. Butler spilled out the whole story. "At first, it was just a business thing. We would go out, have lunch, go to a couple strip joints. Nothing out of line. After a while, we'd be talking and I'd give him a tip on jobs coming around, things like that." Eventually, Butler said, he felt trapped. He knew he was giving Ferguson more information than he should. So he had already crossed ethical lines. He might as well get something for his trouble. Butler and Ferguson set it up. Butler would provide inside information on jobs as they were let out for bids or adjust Ferguson's price in accordance with the other numbers the company received. Ferguson would see to it that his current employer took advantage of the value of Sun & Fun's multi-thousand-dollar evaluations.

No one was ever prosecuted. Butler was fired and forfeited the company contributions to his benefits plan, a substantial penalty since the former plant manager had been accruing funds for nearly 30 years. Thad Ferguson still makes his living in sales, although he has no welcome at HydroCo. Never mind. He keeps smiling and patting his pocket.

SOMETHING OF VALUE

Bribery was defined at the beginning of this chapter as "offering, giving, receiving, or soliciting *anything of value* to influence an official act or business decision." A corrupt employee like Ben Butler helps the briber obtain something of value, and in return the employee is given something of value. There are several ways for a vendor to "pay" an employee to aid the vendor's cause surreptitiously. The most common, of course, is money. In the most basic bribery scheme, the vendor simply gives the employee currency. This is what we think of in the classic bribery scenario—an envelope stuffed with currency being slipped under a table, a roll of bills hastily stuffed into a pocket. These payments preferably are made with currency rather than checks, because the payment is harder to trace. But currency may not be practical when large sums are involved. When this is the case, slush funds usually are set up to finance the illegal payments. In other cases, checks may be drawn directly from company accounts. These disbursements usually are coded as "consulting fees," "referral commissions," or the like. The $10,000 check to Ben Butler's sister in the last case study is an excellent example.

Instead of cash payments, some employees accept promises of future employment as bribes. In one case, a government employee gave a contractor inside information in order to win a bid on a multimillion-dollar contract in return for the promise of a high-paying job. As with money, the promise of employment might be intended to benefit a third party rather than the corrupt employee. In a different case, a consultant who worked for a particular university hired the daughter of one of the university's employees.

In one of the cases discussed earlier in this chapter, a corrupt individual diverted a major purchase commitment to a supplier in return for a percent of ownership in the supplier's business. This is similar to a bribe effected by the promise of employment but also contains elements of a conflict-of-interest scheme. The promise of part ownership in the supplier amounts to an undisclosed financial interest in the transaction for the corrupt employee.

Gifts of all kinds also may be used to corrupt an employee. The types of gifts used to sway an employee's influence can include free liquor and meals, free travel and accommodations, cars, other merchandise, and even sexual favors.

Other inducements include the paying off of a corrupt employee's loans or credit card bills, the offering of loans on very favorable terms, and transfers of property at substantially below-market value. The list of things that can be given to an employee in return for the exercise of influence is almost endless. Anything that the employee values is fair game and may be used to sway his or her loyalty.

ECONOMIC EXTORTION

As stated earlier, economic extortion is basically the flip side of a bribery scheme. Instead of a vendor offering a payment to an employee to influence a decision, the employee demands a payment from a vendor in order to make a decision in that vendor's favor. In any situation in which an employee might accept bribes to favor a particular company or person, the situation could be reversed so that the employee extorts money from a potential purchaser or supplier. In one example, a plant manager for a utility company started his own business on the side. Vendors who wanted to do work for the utility company were forced by the manager to divert some of their business to his own company. Those who did not play ball lost their business with the utility.

ILLEGAL GRATUITIES

As stated, illegal gratuities are similar to bribery schemes except there is not necessarily an intent to influence a particular business decision. One example of an illegal gratuity occurred in which a city commissioner negotiated a land development deal with a group of private investors. After the deal was approved, the commissioner and his wife were rewarded with a free international vacation, all expenses paid. Although the promise of this trip may have influenced the commissioner's negotiations, this would be difficult to prove. However, merely accepting such a gift amounts to an illegal gratuity, an act that is prohibited by most government and private company codes of ethics.

DETECTION

The next red flags may indicate that employees are involved in a bribery scheme.

General Purchasing

Questions such as the next ones may reveal that single-source vendors are being favored or that competitive bidding policies are not being followed.

- Are materials being ordered at the optimal reorder point?
- Are purchases often made from the same vendor?
- Are the established bidding policies being followed?
- Are the costs of materials out of line?

Prebid Solicitation

Prebid solicitation involves placing any restrictions in the solicitation documents that tend to restrict competition, such as:

- Tailoring specifications and statements of work to fit the products or capabilities of a single contractor.

301

- Using "prequalification" procedures to restrict competition.
- Unnecessary sole-source or noncompetitive procurement justifications:
  - Containing false statements.
  - Signed by unauthorized officials.
  - Bypassing necessary review procedures.
- The buyer providing information or advice to the contractor on a preferential basis.
- Using statements of work, specifications, or sole-source justifications developed by, or in consultation with, a contractor who will be permitted to bid.
- Permitting consultants who assisted in the preparation of the statements of work, specifications, or design to perform on the contract as subcontractors or consultants.
- Splitting costs into separate contracts to avoid review.
- Releasing information by firms participating in the design and engineering to contractors competing for the prime contract.
- Splitting up requirements so contractors can each get a fair share and can rotate bids.
- Using specifications that are not consistent with past similar procurement.

Bid Solicitation

- Limiting time for submission of bids so only those with advance information have adequate time to prepare bids or proposals.
- Revealing information to one contractor that is not revealed to all.
- Conducting a bidders' conference that permits improper communications among contractors, who then are in a position to rig bids.
- Failing to ensure a sufficient number of potential competitors are aware of the solicitation, such as:
  - Using obscure publications to publish bid solicitations.
  - Publishing bid solicitations during holiday periods.
- Vaguely wording bid solicitations as to the time, place, or other requirements for submitting acceptable bids.
- Providing inadequate internal controls over the number and destination of bid packages sent to interested bidders.
- Permitting improper communication by purchasers with contractors at trade or professional meetings, or improper social contact with contractor representatives.
- Allowing the purchasing agent to have a financial interest in the contractor's business.
- Permitting the purchaser to discuss possible employment with the contractor.
- Allowing the purchaser to assist the contractor in preparing his or her bid.
- Referring a contractor to a specific subcontractor, expert, or source of supply.
- Failing to amend solicitation to include necessary changes or clarifications in the bid, such as telling one contractor of changes that can be made after the bid.
- Falsifying documents or receipts to get a late bid accepted.

- Permitting a low bidder who withdraws to become a subcontractor on the same contract.
- Any indications of collusion between bidders.
- Falsifying the contractor's qualifications, work history, facilities, equipment, or personnel.

Bid or Contract Acceptance

- Restricting procurement to exclude or hamper any qualified contractor.
- Improperly accepting a late bid.
- Falsifying documents or receipts to get a late bid accepted.
- Changing a bid after other bidders' prices are known. (This is sometimes done by mistakes deliberately planted in a bid.)
- Withdrawing the low bidder, who may become a subcontractor to the higher bidder who gets the contract.
- Collusion or bid-rigging between bidders.
- Revealing one bidder's price to another.
- False certifications by contractor.
- Falsifying information concerning contractor qualifications, financial capability, facilities, ownership of equipment and supplies, qualifications of personnel, successful performance of previous jobs, and so on.

Behavior Profile of Bribery Recipient

The behavior profile of employees who are involved in bribery schemes may include these characteristics:

- Drug and/or alcohol addiction
- Personal financial problems
- Gambling habit
- Extravagant lifestyle
- Loan shark or other private debts
- Girlfriend supported by the subject
- Extraordinary medical expenses
- Significant, regular cash expenses for entertainment and/or travel

PREVENTION

Bribery Prevention Policy

The prevention of the use of bribery schemes can be difficult. The primary resource for heading off this complex act is a company policy that specifically addresses the problems and illegalities associated with bribery and related offenses. The purpose of the policy is to make the company's position absolutely clear. The absence of a clear policy leaves an opportunity for a perpetrator to rationalize a bribe or related offense or to claim ignorance of the wrongdoing. Examples of bribery prevention policies are presented next.

Gifts

No employee or member of his or her immediate family shall solicit or accept from an actual or prospective customer or supplier any compensation, advance loans (except from established financial institutions on the same basis as other customers), gifts, entertainment, or other favors that are of more than token value or that the employee would not normally be in a position to reciprocate under normal expense account procedures.

Under no circumstances should a gift or entertainment be accepted that would influence the employee's judgment. In particular, employees must avoid any interest in or benefit from any supplier that could reasonably cause them to favor that supplier over others. It is a violation of the code for any employee to solicit or encourage a supplier to give any item or service to the employee regardless of its value, no matter how small. Suppliers will retain their confidence in the objectivity and integrity of the company only if each employee strictly observes this guideline.

Reporting Gifts

An employee who receives, or whose family member receives, an unsolicited gift prohibited by these guidelines should report it to his or her supervisor and either return it to the person making the gift or, in the case of a perishable gift, give it to a nonprofit charitable organization.

Discounts

An employee may accept discounts on a personal purchase of the supplier's or customer's products only if such discounts do not affect the company's purchase price and are generally offered to others having a similar business relationship with the supplier or customer.

Business Meetings

Entertainment and services offered by a supplier or customer may be accepted by an employee when they are associated with a business meeting and the supplier or customer provides them to others as a normal part of its business. Examples of such entertainment and services are transportation to and from the supplier's or customer's place of business, hospitality suites, golf outings, lodging at the supplier's or customer's place of business, and business lunches and dinners for business visitors to the supplier's or customer's location. The services generally should be of the type normally used by the company's employees and allowable under the applicable company's expense account.

NOTES

1. Henry Campbell Black, *Black's Law Dictionary*, 5th ed. (St. Paul, MN: West, 1979), p. 311.
2. Ibid.
3. Association of Certified Fraud Examiners, *Fraud Examiners' Manual* (Austin, TX: Author, 2011).

Conflicts of Interest

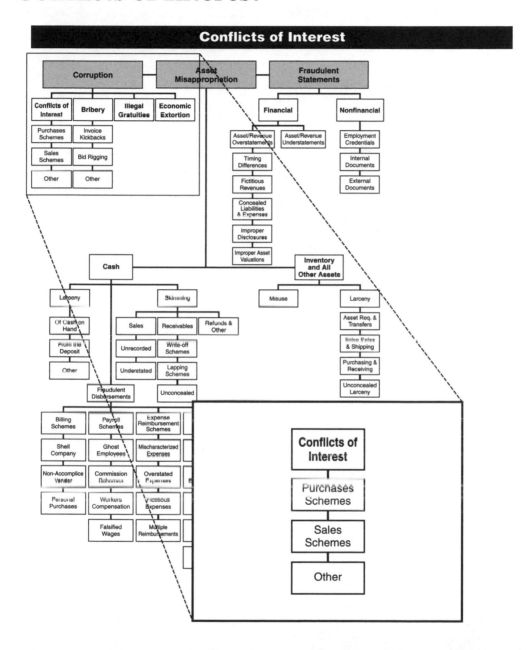

After grabbing a quick bite to eat at the mall, Troy Biederman* spent the rest of his lunch hour shopping for clothes. He liked to present a professional appearance as a

*Several names and details have been changed to preserve anonymity.

sales manager at ElectroCity, an electronics and appliance chain. While waiting on a charge approval at a small menswear store, Biederman spotted its promotion for a free La-Z-Boy recliner and tossed his business card into the drawing fishbowl on the counter. Suddenly his eye caught a familiar name on top of the pile—Rita Mae King, the full-time purchasing agent at ElectroCity. The card, however, read: Rita Mae King, account executive at Spicewood Travel.

"He put two and two together and it smelled fishy," explained Bill Reed, the vice president of loss prevention at ElectroCity. Biederman knew Spicewood Travel was the agency his company used to book incentive trips for its sales force, of which he was a member. He also knew King enjoyed close ties with Spicewood—now he wondered *how* close. Biederman snatched King's card from the pile and discreetly turned it in to his boss that afternoon.

Within two weeks, the business card had made its way up to the executive vice president of ElectroCity, a company that rings up annual sales of $450 million. Not wanting to jump to any conclusions, yet also suspecting that his purchasing agent might be in cahoots with a travel vendor, the executive vice president handed the card over to Bill Reed "to investigate the extent of the relationship."

Reed immediately requisitioned the accounts payable department for all corporate travel billings for the past three years. Early entries showed that the company had been using Executive Travel for most of its travel needs. In her first year as purchasing agent, however, King had introduced Spicewood and had placed it at the top of the travel vendor list. Reed said that although ElectroCity had never designated any one agency as its sole vendor, under the direction of the corporation's purchaser, Spicewood had squeezed out Executive Travel for the store's business, which now exceeded $200,000.

Corporate fraud examiners then phoned numerous other travel agencies, asking for quotes on similar services for the same period in an effort to compare prices. They found that many of the bills were inflated between 10 and 30 percent over the other agencies' package trips to destinations such as Trump Castle in Atlantic City and Bally's in Las Vegas. Calls to other branches of Spicewood Travel further confirmed significant overcharging by the local office, which King used exclusively.

Six days into his investigation, Reed took a statement from the corporate merchandising buyer at ElectroCity, who had experienced difficulties with King on several occasions about competitively priced trips. He said King was insistent on using Spicewood. In his written account of a recent episode, the merchandising buyer told of personally shopping for a better price on an incentive vacation to the Cayman Islands. "With this trip, I went to an outside agent first and then gave Rita Mae the information to price this trip. Spicewood came in almost $100 higher per person. Rita Mae did not book the trip through the lower-priced agent but went back and had Spicewood requote for what was supposed to be the same trip. When I asked to have Spicewood's now-lower requote spelled out exactly, I found that the airfare included an additional stopover, which lowered the cost."

In order to establish King's relationship with the travel agency, Reed had one of his investigators call its local office and ask to speak with account executive Rita

Mae King. Without missing a beat, the receptionist transferred him to Janet Levy, manager of corporate services. The investigator identified himself as an interested traveler who had King's business card and wanted her to book a good deal to the Bahamas. Levy assured him it would not be a problem since she worked closely with King. Levy then asked him to call King at another phone number. It turned out to be her number at ElectroCity.

"She was essentially running her own travel shop out of her office here," said Reed. Although she had no access to an online computer, she jerry-rigged a system for her travel customers. "Apparently, if King fed business to Spicewood, they would add that to her credit arrangement."

King operated out of a beehive of activity littered with paperwork, said Reed. The 51-year-old married woman often kept two or three conversations going in her workplace at the same time. "She was a very take-charge, bossy kind of person—very outgoing, but also caustic in a lot of her interactions with other employees. Also quick to denigrate and complain." On the flip side, "She can be very ingratiating and very nice when she wants." Through her work, King became well networked in the travel industry, with many friends and lots of contacts.

After having established an outside business link between King and Spicewood, Reed then reviewed personnel records for her travel activity. Working on a hunch, he homed in on a vacation King took the previous December when she and a companion flew to the Caribbean island of Antigua via American Airlines.

Reed, a former police officer, scrutinized King's personal credit card statements from that time. An examination of the statements revealed a MasterCard charge from the Royal Antiguan Hotel. Again, Reed had one of his investigators place a call. Posing as "Mr. Lowell King," the investigator phoned the hotel claiming to need help with his travel records in preparation for an Internal Revenue Service audit. The hotel bookkeeper graciously faxed the "guest" a copy of the King hotel bill.

On the bill, King had listed her occupation as a travel agent, giving her business address as the local office of Spicewood Travel. To receive a 50 percent discount on her room rate—a savings worth $412—she furnished the manager with her business card and an Airline Reporting Corporation number, a code issued by an international clearinghouse to identify every travel booking agency. Although Reed suspected King may have gone on other company-subsidized trips, "Antigua was the only one we flushed out. We only needed one."

Further analysis of King's credit statements showed that she charged three other airline tickets over a seven-month period and received three corresponding credits that canceled out the price of the trips, saving her $834.

The fraud examiners clearly proved that King had breached her duty to act in the company's best interests in connection with her role as the company's purchasing agent. And she also had derived some benefit from a vendor—another violation of corporate policy. ElectroCity's personnel handbook addresses both issues:

Employees must disclose any outside financial interest that might influence their corporate decisions or actions. If the company believes that such activities are in conflict with the company's welfare, the employee will be expected to terminate

*such interests. Such interests include but are not limited to personal or family own-
ership or interest in a business deemed a customer, supplier, or competitor.*

King broke other rules listed in the personnel handbook, as well: ''Employees
may not use corporate assets for their personal use or gain. Employees and their
families must never accept any form of under-the-table payments, kickbacks, or
rebates, whether in cash or goods, from suppliers.'' Contrary to company policy,
King had set up an offsite mini-agency using the company's phone, accepted travel
discounts from a vendor for continued and increased business, and received an estimated 10 percent of the agency's billings in kickbacks.

Based on their findings, the examiners also determined that King violated the
state's commercial bribery statute and could be liable for civil damages if the company decided to press charges. While Reed said that King's transgressions warranted immediate termination, the ex-cop recommended against pursuing criminal
action, given King's age and the ill health of her unemployed husband. ''When you
take someone to court, the only options you have are fines or prison.''

Reed takes full responsibility for the decision not to prosecute King. Like police
officers, security professionals must make appropriate assessments based on the
circumstances, Reed said. ''The bad ones always follow the book, regardless of
what's best for the community.

''We made the case, corrected the system within the company, and damaged her
professionally,'' Reed explained. ElectroCity now requires all vendors to sign
agreements acknowledging prohibited behavior and gifts to all its employees, who
now number 3,200. The errant employee was not required to make restitution.

Reed next brought the results of the fraud examination to the president of Spicewood Travel, who reacted with total silence and stunned disbelief. ''The documentation was there. They knew they were going to lose business.'' The company also
made verbal legal threats against the agency in the beginning. It held prolonged
negotiations to recover $20,000, an estimate of two years of overcharges, ''but an-
other VP dropped that ball,'' said Reed.

The corporation's director of investigations conducted a corporate interview
with King to make a final determination of the nature and extent of her relationship
with Spicewood and to elicit evidence of any other kickback arrangements that
might have adversely affected the company. Reed suggested that King be asked to
furnish investigators with a full written disclosure of her interests and activities in
connection with Spicewood and any other suppliers.

During the interview, King composed her thoughts in a handwritten letter to the
president of ElectroCity:

Dear Mr. Smith:

*I must say that I am sorry. It never dawned on me that what I did was in conflict of
my trusted position here at ElectroCity. I truly screwed up; there is no explanation
other than that. There was no consideration on my part that a reduced price was
anything other than that. I never even thought about it. I am truly sorry, especially
because I feel I have broken a trust that we have built over the years. Please*

understand that I meant nothing against ElectroCity or anyone. Additionally, I didn't even see that special rate as a benefit from a supplier, only as a manner by which I could save some dollars personally.

Respectfully,
Rita Mae King

King had misused her authority as a purchasing agent and had violated her duty to ElectroCity. "She was remorseful in the sense that she was now going to have to bite the bullet," said Reed. "I think she probably kicked herself because she didn't get more out of the scam. She felt that she was a woman who worked very hard at a very difficult job, was unappreciated, and was not compensated properly by a male-dominated class system in corporate America."

OVERVIEW

A *conflict of interest* occurs when an employee, manager, or executive has an undisclosed economic or personal interest in a transaction that adversely affects the organization.[1] As with other corruption cases, conflict schemes involve the exertion of an employee's influence to the detriment of his company. In the ElectroCity case, for instance, Rita Mae King used her influence to direct the bulk of her employer's travel business to Spicewood Travel. In the schemes discussed in Chapter 10, fraudsters were paid to exercise their influence on behalf of a third party. Conflict cases instead involve self-dealing by an employee. King overbilled ElectroCity to benefit herself and her other employer, Spicewood Travel.

The vast majority of conflict cases occur because the fraudster has an undisclosed economic interest in a transaction. But the fraudster's hidden interest is not necessarily economic. In some scenarios, an employee acts in a manner detrimental to the company in order to provide a benefit to a friend or relative, even though the fraudster receives no financial benefit from the transaction himself. In one instance, a manager split a large repair project into several smaller projects to avoid bidding requirements. This allowed the manager to award the contracts to his brother-in-law. Although there was no indication that the manager received any financial gain from this scheme, his actions nevertheless amounted to conflict of interest.

In order to be classified as a conflict-of-interest scheme, the employee's interest in the transaction must be undisclosed. The crux of a conflict case is that the fraudster takes advantage of the employer; the victim company is unaware that its employee has divided loyalties. If an employer knows of the employee's interest in a business deal or negotiation, there can be no conflict of interest, no matter how favorable the arrangement is for the employee.

Any bribery scheme discussed in Chapter 10 could be used in the conflict-of-interest context. The only difference is the fraudster's motive. For instance, if an employee approves payment on a fraudulent invoice submitted by a vendor in return for a kickback, this is bribery. If, however, an employee approves payment on invoices submitted by her own company (and if her ownership is undisclosed), this is a conflict of interest. This was the situation in one of our cases, where an office service employee recommended his own company to do repairs and maintenance on office equipment for his employer. The fraudster approved invoices for approximately $30,000 in excessive charges.

The distinction between the two schemes is obvious. In the bribery case, fraudsters approve the invoice in return for a kickback, while in a conflict case, they approve the invoice because of their own hidden interest in the vendor. Aside from the employee's motive for committing the crime, the mechanics of the two transactions are practically identical. The same duality can be found in bid-rigging cases, where employees influence the selection of a company in which they have a hidden interest instead of influencing the selection of a vendor who has bribed them.

Conflict schemes do not always simply mirror bribery schemes, though. There are vast numbers of ways in which employees can use their influence to benefit a company in which they have a hidden interest. This chapter discusses some of the more common methods that appeared in our study.

The majority of the conflict schemes in our survey fit into three categories: purchases schemes, sales schemes, and other schemes.

In other words, most conflicts of interest arise when a victim company unwittingly *buys* something at a high price from a company in which one of its employees has a hidden interest or unwittingly *sells* something at a low price to a company in which one of its employees has a hidden interest. Most of the other conflicts we have come across involved employees who stole clients or diverted funds from their employer.

PURCHASING SCHEMES

The majority of conflict schemes in our studies were purchasing schemes, and the most common of these was the overbilling scheme. We already have discussed conflict schemes involving billings. Because these schemes are very similar to the billing schemes discussed in Part I, it is helpful to discuss the distinction we have drawn between traditional billing schemes and purchasing schemes that are conflicts of interest.

Although it is true that any time employees assist in the overbilling of their company, there is probably some conflict of interest (the employees cause harm to their employer because of a hidden financial interest in the transaction), this does not necessarily mean that every instance of false billing is categorized as a conflict scheme. In order for the scheme to be classified as a conflict of interest, the employee (or a friend or relative of the employee) must have some kind of ownership or employment interest in the vendor submitting the invoice. This distinction is easy to understand if we look at the nature of the fraud. Why do fraudsters overbill their employers? If they engage in the scheme only for the cash, the scheme is a fraudulent disbursement billing scheme. However, if they seek to better the financial condition of their own business at the expense of their employers, this is a conflict of interest. In other words, the fraudsters' *interests* lie with a company other than the employer. When employees falsify the invoices of a third-party vendor to whom they have no relation, this is not a conflict-of-interest scheme because the employees have no interest in that vendor. The sole purpose of the scheme is to generate a fraudulent disbursement.

One might wonder, then, why shell company schemes are classified as fraudulent disbursements rather than conflicts of interest. After all, fraudsters in a shell company scheme own the fictitious company and therefore must have an interest in it. Remember, though, that shell companies are created for the sole purpose of defrauding the employer. The company is not so much an entity in the mind of the fraudsters as it is a tool. In fact, a shell company is usually little more than a post office box and a bank account. The fraudsters have no interest in the shell company that causes a division of loyalty; they simply use the shell company to bilk their employers. Shell company schemes therefore are classified as false billing schemes.

A rule of thumb can be used to distinguish between overbilling schemes that are classified as asset misappropriations and those that are conflicts of interest: If the bill originates from a *real company* in which a fraudster has an economic or personal interest, and if the fraudster's interest in the company is undisclosed to the victim company, then the scheme is a conflict of interest.

Now that we know what kinds of billing schemes are classified as conflicts of interest, the question is: How do these schemes work? The answer is somewhat anticlimactic. The schemes work the same either way. The distinction between the two kinds of fraud is useful only to distinguish the status and purpose of the fraudster. The mechanics of the billing scheme, whether conflict or fraudulent disbursement, do not change. (See Exhibit 11.1.) In one conflict-of-interest case, a purchasing superintendent defrauded his employer by purchasing items on behalf of the employer at inflated prices from a certain vendor. The vendor in this case was owned by the purchasing superintendent but established in his wife's name and run by his brother. The

Exhibit 11.1   Conflicts of Interest

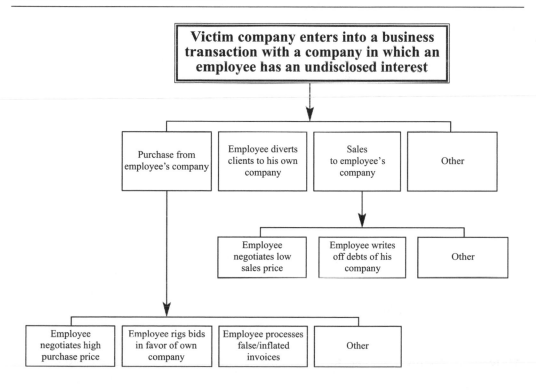

perpetrator's interest in the company was undisclosed. The vendor would buy items on the open market, then inflate the prices and resell the items to the victim company. The purchasing superintendent used his influence to ensure that his employer continued doing business with the vendor and paying the exorbitant prices. A more detailed analysis of overbilling frauds can be found in Chapter 7 of this book.

Fraudsters also engage in bid-rigging on behalf of their own companies. The methods used to rig bids are discussed in detail in Chapter 10 and will not be dealt with in depth here. Briefly stated, employees of the purchasing company are in a perfect position to rig bids because they have access to the bids of competitors. Since they can find out the amounts of the bids of other vendors, fraudsters can easily tailor their own company's bid to win the contract. Fraudsters also sometimes use bid waivers to avoid competitive bidding outright. In one instance, a manager processed several unsubstantiated bid waivers in order to direct purchases to a vendor in which one of his employees had an interest. The conflict was undisclosed, and the scheme cost the victim company over $150,000.

In other cases, fraudsters might ignore their employer's purchasing rotation and direct an inordinate number of purchases or contracts to their own company. Any way by which fraudsters exert their influence to divert business to a company in which they have a hidden interest is a conflict of interest.

Unique Assets

Not all conflict schemes occur in the traditional vendor-buyer relationship. Several of the cases in our survey involved employees negotiating for the purchase of some unique, typically large asset, such as land or a building, in which they had an undisclosed interest. It is in the process of these negotiations that the fraudsters violate their duty of loyalty to their employer. Because they stand to profit from the sale of the asset, the employees do not negotiate in good faith with their employer; they do not attempt to get the best price possible. After all, the fraudsters will reap a greater financial benefit if the purchase price is high.

One example of this type of scheme was reported. In it, a senior vice president of a utility company was in charge of negotiating and approving mineral leases on behalf of his company. Unknown to his employer, the vice president also owned the property on which the leases were made. The potential harm in this type of relationship is obvious—there was no financial motive for the vice president to negotiate a favorable lease for his employer.

Turnaround Sales

A special kind of purchasing scheme that we have encountered is called the *turnaround sale* or *flip*. In this type of scheme, employees know that their employer is seeking to purchase a certain asset and take advantage of the situation by purchasing the asset themselves (usually in the name of an accomplice or shell company). The fraudsters then turn around and resell the item to the employer at an inflated price. We already have seen one example of this kind of scheme in the purchasing superintendent case discussed earlier, in which a purchasing supervisor set up a company in his wife's name to resell merchandise to his employer. Another interesting example of the turnaround method occurred when the chief executive of a company, conspiring with a former employee, sold an office building to the CEO's company. What made the transaction suspicious was that the building had been purchased by the former employee on the same day that it was resold to the victim company, and for $1.2 million less than the price charged to the CEO's company.

SALES SCHEMES

Our studies identified two principal types of conflict schemes associated with the victim company's sales. The first and most harmful is the underselling of goods or services. Just as corrupt employees can cause employers to overpay for goods or services sold by a company in which the employees have a hidden interest, so too can they cause employers to undersell to a company in which the employees maintain a hidden interest. (See Exhibit 11.1.)

Underbillings

Perpetrators underbill the vendor in which they have a hidden interest. The victim company ends up selling its goods or services below fair market value, which results in a diminished profit margin or even a loss on the sale, depending on the size of the discount. This method was used in a case in which two employees sold their employer's inventory to their own company at reduced prices, causing a loss of approximately $100,000. Another example was found in which an employee disposed of his employer's real estate by selling it below fair market value to a company in which he had a hidden interest, causing a loss of approximately $500,000.

Writing Off Sales

The other type of sales scheme involves tampering with the books of the victim company to decrease or write off the amount owed by an employee's business. For instance, after an employee's company purchases goods or services from the victim company, credit memos may be issued against the sale, causing it to be written off to contra accounts, such as discounts and allowances. A plant manager in one of our cases used this method; this fraudster assisted favored clients by delaying billing on their purchases for up to 60 days. When the receivable on these clients' accounts became delinquent, the perpetrator issued credit memos against the sales to delete them.

A large number of reversing entries to sales may be a sign that fraud is occurring in an organization. The fraudster just discussed avoided the problem of too many write-offs by issuing new invoices on the sales after the "old" receivables were taken off the books. In this way, the receivables could be carried indefinitely on the books without ever becoming past due.

In other cases, perpetrators might not write off the scheme but simply delay billing. Sometimes this is done as a favor to a friendly client, not as an outright avoidance of the bill but rather as a dilatory tactic. The victim company eventually gets paid but loses time value on the payment, which arrives later than it should.

OTHER SCHEMES

Business Diversions

In one case, an employee started his own business that competed directly with his employer. While still employed by the victim company, this employee began siphoning off clients for his own business. This activity clearly violated the employee's duty of loyalty to his employer. There is nothing unscrupulous about free competition, but when a person acts as a representative of his employer, it certainly is improper to try to undercut the employer and take his clients. Similarly, a fraudster in another case steered potential clients away from his employer and toward his own business. There is nothing unethical about pursuing an independent venture (in the absence of restrictive employment covenants, such as noncompete agreements), but if employees fail to act in the best interests of their employers while carrying out their duties, then these employees are violating the standards of business ethics.

Resource Diversions

Finally, some employees divert the funds and other resources of their employers to the development of their own businesses. In one example, a vice president of a company authorized large expenditures to develop a unique type of new equipment used by a certain contractor. Another firm subsequently took over the contractor as well as the new equipment. Shortly after that, the VP retired and went to work for the firm that had bought out the contractor. The fraudster had managed to use his employer's money to fund a company in which he eventually developed an interest. This scheme involves elements of bribery, conflicts of interest, and fraudulent disbursements. In this particular case, if the VP financed the equipment in return for the promise of a job, his actions may have been properly classified as a bribery scheme. The case nevertheless illustrates a potential conflict problem. The fraudster could just as easily have authorized the fraudulent expenditures for a company in which he secretly held an ownership interest.

Although these schemes are clearly corruption schemes, the funds are diverted through the use of a fraudulent disbursement. The money could be drained from the victim company through a check-tampering scheme, a billing scheme, a payroll scheme, or an expense reimbursement scheme. For a discussion of the methods used to generate fraudulent disbursements, please refer to Part I of this book.

Financial Disclosures

Management has an obligation to disclose to the shareholders significant fraud committed by officers, executives, and others in positions of trust. Management does not have the responsibility of disclosing uncharged criminal conduct of its officers and executives. However, if and when officers, executives, or other persons in trusted positions become subjects of a criminal indictment, disclosure is required.

The inadequate disclosure of conflicts of interest is among the most serious of frauds. Inadequate disclosure of related-party transactions is not limited to any specific industry; it transcends all business types and relationships.

The next case study has been selected to illustrate the actual experience of one certified fraud examiner in dealing with a conflict-of-interest fraud. As we will see, James Larken used his influence to pour over $1 million of his employer's money into a struggling business in which he had a hidden interest. This study not only describes Larken's scheme but also shows how CFE Puyler Simonds went about uncovering his fraud.

Case Study: A Parasite Farm

James Larken had it going on.[*] As chief financial officer, he arranged for his employer to acquire another company. Then he supported the other company's operations from his employer's till. And because Larken never told his employers that they owned a subsidiary, he reaped all the benefits personally.

Larken worked for a large meat-packing house in the Midwest, for our purposes called Theriot's, Incorporated. Theriot's did in fact consider expanding its business into the supply end of the meat industry, approaching a feedlot operation that was in trouble but had potential. Upon closer inspection, the feedlot, Napa Farms, had nothing to offer but a little land and a lot of trouble, so Theriot's backed out of the deal.

Larken saw a different story. Since he did not have to use his own money, Napa Farms was nothing but potential. His authority at Theriot's was beyond question. Theriot's had an audit department but the staff reported to him. And they were scared of him. He had the power to do anything he wanted, or so he thought. "If this guy hadn't gotten greedy," says Puyler Simonds, the CFE who eventually brought down Larken's scheme, "he might have gotten away with it."

Larken exercised a stock option on Napa Farms that he had obtained secretly. Using his position inside Theriot's, he bought up Napa's receivables (money it was owed for livestock sold and services performed) and its inventory. With the help of a Theriot's certified public accountant, the money was tucked away as various credits on the accounting books.

Napa was ailing so badly, however, that the cash from the receivables sale was not enough. Larken decided to buy building equipment and vehicles for the feedlot. He ordered a truck, for example, on Theriot's account and had it delivered to Napa Farms. Larken had created a financial parasite. A couple months before Napa was sliding into bankruptcy; now it was drawing new life from Theriot's coffers.

But Larken's appetite exceeded his ability to cover his tracks. After a clerk discreetly voiced her suspicions about Larken and his relations with Napa Farms, the chief executive officer started going over the books. He was astounded by the receivables acquired from this company, the same one he had toured and considered buying. The same one that should have been defunct by now. All flags were flying when the CEO saw an invoice showing that Theriot's had bought a truck and sent it to Napa.

Simonds came in on behalf of the accounting firm working for Theriot's to check out the situation. Seizing Larken's files, Simonds's team found titles to

---

[*]Several names have been changed to preserve anonymity

317

equipment, bank records, signature cards, and other business documents, all signed by Larken on behalf of Napa. The people who worked with and under Larken were not slow about pointing the finger, even if their comments amounted to innuendo and suspicion.

They did not like him. Simonds remembers Larken as loud, aggressive, and harassing, especially to women. ''I don't think there was any love lost between this guy and the people he had working for him.''

Simonds next went to see the head of Napa Farms. Initially, Blain Fletcher dodged questions and avoided saying anything other than he knew Larken from past business. Fletcher eventually was persuaded to open his files, where Simonds found, ''almost by accident,'' the stock option in Larken's name. From there, it was a matter of following the footprints back to Larken. In eight months, he had funneled over $1 million into Napa using Theriot's cash. Charges were filed and the case was turned over to the police.

Unrepentant and arrogant as always, Larken nevertheless pled guilty and awaits sentencing. Bad news for him, though: You can buy the farm, but you can't take it with you.

DETECTION

Some of the more common methods that can be used to detect conflicts of interest are tips and complaints, comparisons of vendor addresses with employee addresses, review of vendor ownership files, review of exit interviews, comparisons of vendor addresses to addresses of subsequent employers, and interviews with purchasing personnel for favorable treatment of one or more vendors.

Tips and Complaints

If a particular vendor is being favored, competing vendors may file complaints. Additionally, employee complaints about the service of a favored vendor may lead to the discovery of a conflict of interest.

Comparison of Vendor Addresses with Employee Addresses

If nominee or related parties are used as owners of vendors, then the business address of the vendor may match that of the employee. Also, look for post office box addresses for vendors. This detection method is similar to that used for locating phony vendors.

Review of Vendor Ownership Files

When a vendor is selected, a complete file of the ownership of that vendor should be kept. This is particularly important for closely held businesses. If the vendor is required to update the file annually, then changes in ownership also will be disclosed. A computer comparison of the vendor ownership and the employee file may reveal conflicts of interest.

Review of Exit Interviews and Comparisons of Vendor Addresses to Addresses of Subsequent Employers

If a review of an employee's exit interview yields the name and address of the subsequent employer, a simple comparison of that name and address with the vendor file may reveal conflicts of interest wherein the employee has obtained employment from a contractor.

Interviews of Purchasing Personnel for Favorable Treatment of One or More Vendors

Employees are generally the first to observe that a vendor is receiving favorable treatment. Therefore, by asking employees if any vendor is receiving favorable treatment, the examiner may discover conflicts of interest that otherwise would have gone unnoticed. Another question that may be asked of employees is whether any vendor's service (or product) recently has become substandard.

PREVENTION

Conflict-of-interest schemes are variations of the rule that a fiduciary, agent, or employee must act in good faith, with full disclosure, in the best interest of the principal or employer. Most schemes are a violation of the legal maxim that a person cannot serve two masters. Some of the more common schemes involve an employee's, manager's, or executive's interest in a customer or supplier and receipt of gifts. Often the employee, manager, or executive is compensated for his or her interest in the form of "consulting fees."

Following the old saying that an ounce of prevention is worth a pound of cure, conflict-of-interest cases are prevented more easily than they are detected. Internal controls make it much more difficult for employees to run this kind of scheme. A policy requiring employees to complete an annual disclosure statement is an excellent proactive approach. Comparing the disclosed names and addresses with the vendor list may reveal real conflicts of interest and the appearance of such. Communication with employees regarding their other business interests is advisable.

NOTE

1. Association of Certified Fraud Examiners, *Fraud Examiners' Manual* (Austin, TX: Author, 2011).

PART III

FRAUDULENT STATEMENTS

CHAPTER 12

Fraudulent Statements

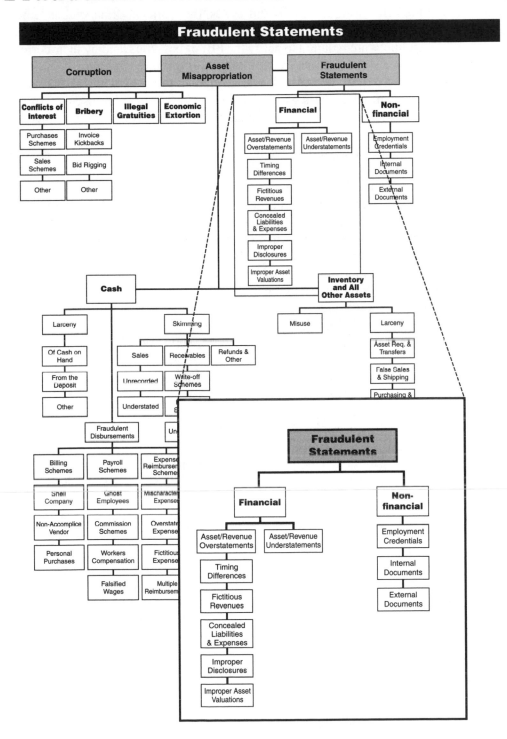

INTRODUCTION

When I was in the FBI during the 1970s and 1980s, the workaday financial statement fraud came from bank borrowers, either individual or corporate. Under the Bank Secrecy Act, financial institutions are required to notify the FBI of possible fraud by their borrowers in connection with a host of activities, most of it dealing with loan fraud.

The typical financial statement fraud case did not impress the typical FBI agent because many of us learned the hard way that some banks attempted to use the government as a collection agency. A common complaint by agents was that the banks would do little due diligence on borrowers before lending money. Many of the financial statements in bank loan files I examined would make an accountant laugh. Most were unaudited, a clue; and a number contained simple math errors on the balance sheet or income statement; in short, they did not even add up, another clue.

But in order for the financial statement fraud to be a violation of federal statutes, the lender was required to have relied on the false financials to some extent in making the loan. In most instances, the reality was that the numbers were in the bank's loan files only to conform with government regulations. Banks, in general, prefer hard collateral. And if the collateral loses its value or disappears when the loan goes into default, it is very tempting for even good bankers to run to the FBI crying financial statement fraud.

There is an obvious advantage, from the bank's point of view, in having an FBI agent show up at the door of a delinquent borrower. Even though the agents do not attempt to collect funds, it is amazing how many borrowers suddenly come up with the money to pay off their loans after being visited by the Federal Bureau of Investigation.

One memorable case, though, was not like that. Toward the latter part of my FBI career, I was assigned the investigation of Orange Associates, Inc. It was a start-up company supposedly specializing in a new concept: biofeedback equipment. Such equipment has come a long way since the 1970s and has been integrated into the mainstream of medical and psychological treatment.

The equipment has sensors that are placed on parts of the head, neck, and other areas. These sensors are connected by wire to a computer and screen. When the sensors are placed on strategic parts of a patient's body, it is possible actually to see and hear, in real time, increases and decreases in the level of stress in that person. By seeing and hearing the stress level, the patient is taught exercises that control the stress; hence, biofeedback.

The concept of Orange Associates actually was developed by an educator, whom I remember as David Aldridge, or something close to that. At any rate, Aldridge had a vague past as a ''consultant'' to the medical and psychological community. He eventually met a psychologist, Dr. Wayne Gaffney, who agreed to supply start-up capital for Orange. Their grand plan was to manufacture and distribute various models of biofeedback equipment.

Gaffney was a good choice for Aldridge. The former came from a long line of rice farmers in south Texas, where landholdings are so vast that they are quoted in the nearest 1,000 acres. Through inheritance of various real estate holdings from his family, Gaffney was worth millions. He was a gadget freak. Their initial plan was for Gaffney to be the money partner and for Aldridge to run the operation. Off they went to Travis Bank, where Gaffney pledged some of his rice land on a note for $1 million. That money was the initial seed capital. The loan proceeds went to the company checking account at what was then Austin State Bank.

Like so many other start-up operations, the initial seed money quickly proved inadequate; within months Orange needed additional working capital. Gaffney balked at borrowing more on his inheritance, so Aldridge prepared a loan package on Orange for submission to Austin State Bank.

Since Orange had no net worth, Aldridge, behind Gaffney's back, concocted a series of "contracts" the company supposedly had signed to sell its equipment in bulk to wholesalers. These "contracts" were pledged as accounts receivable on a second $1 million loan, this time at Austin State Bank. The "contracts" had one major flag that glowed like a neon light: The so-called customers were all Cayman Island corporations.

Aldridge's explanation for the Cayman customers was that they were resellers to the Japanese and Europeans. But Aldridge also said that the Japanese were manufacturing the biofeedback equipment for Orange. In essence, Aldridge claimed that the equipment was manufactured by one Japanese company and sold on paper to a company in the Caymans, and the Cayman company purchased the equipment from Orange. If the bank really had listened to what Aldridge was telling them, it would have noticed that his story made no sense whatsoever.

But the bank bought Aldridge's story, and so did his partner Gaffney, who still had to sign the Orange note individually as a guarantor before the bank would give them more working capital. Indeed, Orange Associates did get the money and Gaffney was now $2 million in debt.

Still Orange continued to bleed red. Aldridge's headquarters operations consisted of about a dozen administrators. Neither the bank nor Gaffney noticed that there was not one sales or marketing person in the lot. The rent was high. Research and development added to the costs. Soon Aldridge knew he had to go back to the well for more money or close the operation—an unthinkable option to him by this point.

Aldridge saw the problem coming six months before Orange actually applied for a third working capital loan. That was time enough for him to figure out that he needed to churn the operations checking account at Austin State Bank. After all, Aldridge reasoned, if the bank saw lots of activity, big deposits especially, it would be more likely to believe business at Orange was booming.

So Aldridge began kiting checks in the Austin State Bank demand deposit account. To create legitimate-looking sales, he deposited checks from a Cayman Island bank account into the Orange Associates operating account. Then he wire- transferred funds to a bank in Dallas, ostensibly for payment of equipment manufactured by the Japanese. In truth, the funds were going right back to the Cayman bank account to cover the check he had deposited at Austin State Bank.

When it came time to apply for a loan, the deposits in the Orange checking account looked pretty good to the bank; several hundred thousand dollars went into the account. But, of course, the money went right back out. Aldridge told the bank and Gaffney that business was so good they had to borrow more money to satisfy new orders. They would need about $2 million this time, Aldridge figured.

After reviewing the corporate accounts and yet another set of fraudulent statements, the bank bit one final time, but on this loan, it made a fatal error. It allowed Orange, which had been paying well on the other loans (albeit with the bank's money), to borrow on the equipment inventory alone. Gaffney did not even have to guarantee the note individually.

Orange managed to stay afloat, in total, about five years. This turned out to be a remarkable feat, considering the fact that the company never generated a cent of revenue. Instead, Aldridge had relied totally on bank financing to sustain the operations. He had lied to Gaffney and everyone else in the process. Orange Associates was largely a figment of David Aldridge's imagination.

The scheme came to light the fourth and final time Aldridge tried to go to the bank for more money. By this time, senior management at Austin State Bank had changed. It wanted Orange to reduce its loan balance, which was over $3 million. With nowhere else to turn for financing, Orange quickly ran out of money and began missing loan payments not only to Austin State Bank, but also to Travis Bank, where it still owed $1 million, more or less.

Both banks filed suit against Orange, Aldridge, and Gaffney to foreclose on their collateral. There was none. The combined losses completely wiped out the equity position of both banks. Rather than come up with more money, shareholders of both banks decided to sell. Because of the possibility of fraud, the FBI was contacted. That is where I came in.

I went to the United States Attorney's office and obtained a subpoena for Orange's financial and bank records. Then the real work began. One "Loan Ranger" FBI agent (me), without a staff or computer, spent the better part of six months simply scheduling debits and credits in and out of Orange's operating accounts.

The numbers told the real story: $4 million in loans and $5 million in expenses over five years. The expenses included a reasonable salary for Aldridge, but nothing outrageous. He had a rather large staff, spent millions on outside contractors for research and development, went on international trips to develop business, and paid lobbyists and other consultants. The expenses turned out to be legitimate.

After doing the financial homework, it was time to interview everyone in the loop. Aldridge's lawyer would not let him talk, but the other people talked. Gaffney, it turned out, was simply naive. For years he listened to Aldridge but never verified anything for himself. The employees of Orange Associates liked and respected Aldridge; however, they admitted to confusion over the business. The employees said Aldridge was both chief executive and de facto chief financial officer. The company bookkeeper, when I interviewed her, was clueless about the big picture.

In this case, the only culprit was Aldridge. I took my evidence to the United States Attorney's office to discuss a possible indictment. The prosecutor quickly honed in on the key question: If Aldridge did not particularly enrich himself, what was his motivation to concoct these patently fraudulent financial statements?

My investigation of Aldridge had turned up a curious contradiction. Aldridge was a good guy—well liked and respected by his employees, neighbors, and professional associates. He was as straight as an arrow—married, stable, college educated, a volunteer in the community, and a regular churchgoer.

By putting together the financial picture along with his personal profile, I told the prosecutor what I thought happened. When Aldridge first got involved with Gaffney and they borrowed the first million, Aldridge essentially misspent the money. He should have realized then that he was no businessman.

But instead, in order to cover his mistakes, he got Gaffney to borrow another million. Aldridge wasted a great deal of that money too. By that time, he had told too many lies to backtrack. He had to go forward and hope that by keeping the company alive long enough, Orange would start turning a profit. If that happened, his fraud would never be discovered.

The main reason Orange failed was because Aldridge was an egghead; he simply did not know what he was doing. The prosecutor agreed with that theory, and it bothered him. "Joe," he said, "other than his salary, Aldridge has received no personal benefit." I argued that the salary alone was derived principally from fraudulent activity.

"I know you are technically right, Joe," the prosecutor said. "But this doesn't have the jury appeal elements of a good criminal fraud case—someone the jury can hate because he is evil and greedy. This isn't such a man. I think we should decline criminal prosecution in favor of the bank taking civil action."

The prosecutor was right, I knew, but I still tried to sell him on the case. I guess my heart wasn't in it either, really. As I learned quickly working in the criminal justice system, you have to let many people go to concentrate on others. It is simply a question of resources.

Aldridge got off scot-free, without any criminal penalties. Both defrauded banks sued Aldridge and Gaffney, along with the defunct Orange Associates, Inc. I understand they got some money from Gaffney, but not enough to cover the losses. Gaffney was forced into bankruptcy; it seems the millions in real estate he had inherited were tied up mostly in a family trust. His family almost disowned him, I heard, because of the legal trouble he created.

In some financial statement fraud cases like Orange, the principals do not necessarily directly pocket ill-gotten gain. But like Aldridge, even top executives of major corporations do indeed have the motivation sometimes to cook the books; they look at this activity as vital to keeping their jobs. Unlike Aldridge, some corporate executives are paid millions, the ultimate motivator to lie. For others, the opportunity to benefit illegally through statement manipulation is irresistible.

FRAUD IN FINANCIAL STATEMENTS

Financial statement frauds like the one just described are caused by a number of factors occurring at the same time, the most significant of which is the pressure on upper management to show earnings. Preparing false financial statements is made somewhat easier by the subjective nature of the way books and records are kept. The accounting profession has long recognized that, to a large extent, accounting is a somewhat arbitrary process, subject to wide interpretation. The profession also indirectly recognizes that numbers are subject to manipulation. After all, a debit on a company's books can be recorded as either an expense or an asset. A credit can be a liability or equity. Therefore, there is tremendous temptation—when a strong earnings showing is needed—to classify those expenses as assets and those liabilities as equity.

In the next chapter, we explore the five major methods by which financial statement fraud is committed, but before we delve into the mechanics of these schemes, it is important to consider three general questions that go to the heart of these crimes:

1. Who commits financial statement fraud?
2. Why do people commit financial statement fraud?
3. How do people commit financial statement fraud?

Who Commits Financial Statement Fraud?

Three main groups of people commit financial statement fraud. In descending order of likelihood of involvement, they are:

1. *Senior management.* In 2010, the Committee of Sponsoring Organizations of the Treadway Commission (COSO) released *Fraudulent Financial Reporting: 1998–2007*, a study of 347 alleged financial statement frauds from 1998 to 2007. The Securities and Exchange Commission named the CEO and/or CFO for involvement in 89 percent these fraud cases. And within two years of the completion of the SEC investigation, about 20 percent of the CEOs/CFOs had been indicted. Over 60 percent of those indicted were convicted. Motives for senior managers to commit financial statement fraud are varied and are described later.

2. *Mid- and lower-level employees.* This category of employees may falsify financial statements for their area of responsibility (subsidiary, division, or other unit) to conceal their poor performance or to earn bonuses based on the higher performance.

3. *Organized criminals.* This group may use financial statement schemes to obtain fraudulent loans from a financial institution or to hype a stock they are selling as part of a ''pump-and-dump'' scheme.

Why Do People Commit Financial Statement Fraud?

Senior managers (CEOs, CFOs, etc.) and business owners may cook the books for several key reasons:

- *To conceal true business performance.* This may be to overstate or understate results.
- *To preserve personal status/control.* Senior managers with strong egos may be unwilling to admit that their strategy has failed and that business performance is bad, since doing so may lead to their termination.
- *To maintain personal income/wealth* from salary, bonus, stock, and stock options.

We can better prevent and detect fraud if we first understand the different pressures that senior managers and business owners can face that might drive them to commit fraud. If we understand the motivating factors behind these crimes, it stands to reason that we will be in a better position to recognize circumstances that might motivate or pressure people into committing financial statement fraud. We also will increase our likelihood of detecting these crimes by knowing the most likely places to look for fraud on an organization's financials.

As with other forms of occupational fraud, financial statement schemes generally are tailored to the circumstances that exist in the organization. In other words, the evaluation criteria used by those with power over management will tend to drive management behavior in fraud cases. For example, tight loan covenants might drive managers to misclassify certain liabilities as long term rather than current in order to improve the entity's current ratio (current assets to current liabilities) without affecting reported earnings.

Some of the more common reasons why senior management will *overstate* business performance are to:

- Meet or exceed the earnings or revenue growth expectations of stock market analysts.
- Comply with loan covenants.
- Increase the amount of financing available from asset-based loans.
- Meet a lender's criteria for granting/extending loan facilities.
- Meet corporate performance criteria set by the parent company.
- Meet personal performance criteria.
- Trigger performance-related compensation or earn-out payments.
- Support the stock price in anticipation of a merger, acquisition, or sale of personal stockholding.
- Show a pattern of growth to support a planned securities offering or sale of the business.

Alternatively, senior management may *understate* business performance to:

- Defer "surplus" earnings to the next accounting period. If current period budgets have been met and there is no reward for additional performance, corporate managers may prefer to direct additional earnings into the next period to help meet their new targets.
- Take all possible write-offs in one "big bath" now so future earnings will be consistently higher.
- Reduce expectations now so future growth will be better perceived and rewarded.
- Preserve a trend of consistent growth, avoiding volatile results.
- Reduce the value of an owner-managed business for purposes of a divorce settlement.
- Reduce the value of a corporate unit whose management is planning a buyout.

How Do People Commit Financial Statement Fraud?

The mechanics of the major types of financial statement fraud are discussed in the next chapter. As you review that material, keep in mind that, regardless of method, there are three general ways in which fraudulent financial statements can be produced. By being aware of these three approaches, those who investigate financial statement fraud can be alert for evidence of attempts to manipulate the accounting and financial reporting process or to go outside it. Financial statement frauds may involve more than one of these three methods, although they commonly start with the first method and progressively add the other two methods as the fraud grows. The three general methods are:

1. *Playing the accounting system.* In this approach, fraudsters use the accounting system as a tool to generate the results they want. For example, in order to

increase or decrease earnings to a desired figure, fraudsters might manipulate the assumptions used to calculate depreciation charges, allowances for bad debts, or allowances for excess and obsolete inventory. To avoid recognizing expenses and liabilities, vendor invoices might not be recorded on a timely basis. Genuine sales might be recorded prematurely. Transactions recorded in the accounting system have a basis in fact, even if they are recorded improperly. There is a documentary trail to support the results reported in the financial statements, although the assumptions shown in some of those documents may be questionable.

2. *Beating the accounting system.* In this approach, fraudsters feed false and fictitious information into the accounting system to manipulate reported results by an amount greater than can be achieved simply by playing the accounting system. Fictitious sales may be recorded to legitimate or phony customers. Inventory and receivables figures may be invented, with documents later being forged to support the claimed numbers. Senior financial management might determine allowances for bad debts and for excess and obsolete inventory without regard to the formulas or methods historically used in the entity to determine these amounts. Journal entries might be disguised in an attempt to conceal their fraudulent intent (e.g., splitting big round-sum adjustments into many smaller entries of odd amounts) or transactions may be hidden through use of intercompany accounts to conceal the other side of a transaction. Some transactions recorded in the accounting system may have no basis in fact, and some that do may be improperly recorded. There will be no documentary trail to support certain transactions or balances unless the fraudsters prepare forged or altered documents to help support this fraud.

3. *Going outside the accounting system.* In this approach, fraudsters produce whatever financial statements they wish. These financial statements could be based on the results of an accounting and financial reporting process for an operating entity, with additional manual adjustments to achieve the results desired by the fraudsters. Alternatively, they could just be printed up using phony numbers supplied by fraudsters. In some cases, fraudsters may go back and enter false data in the accounting system to support the phony financial statements. In other cases, they may not bother, or there might be no accounting system. So not all transactions may be recorded in an accounting system, and some or all transactions may have no basis in fact. To catch this type of fraud, it is usually necessary to start by tracing the published financial statements back to the output of the accounting system. As in the previous situation, there is no documentary trail to support certain transactions or balances reported in the financial statements unless the fraudsters prepare forged or altered documents to help support this fraud.

MAJOR GENERALLY ACCEPTED ACCOUNTING PRINCIPLES

Over the years, businesses have found numerous ingenious ways to overstate their true earnings and assets. As a result, a number of accounting conventions, or what are called *generally accepted accounting principles* (GAAP), have developed. Most historic accounting principles have now been codified by the Financial Accounting Standards

Board (FASB), an independent public watchdog organization responsible for standard setting.[1]

Generally accepted accounting principles include these eight major standards:

1. Materiality
2. Matching
3. Conservatism
4. Going concern
5. Cost
6. Objective evidence
7. Consistency
8. Full disclosure

Materiality

Financial statements are not meant to be perfect, only reasonable and fair. There are doubtless many small errors in the books of major and minor corporations, but what does it really mean when considering the big picture? The answer is that it depends on who is looking at the financial statements and making decisions based on them. If a company's estimated earnings are $1 million a year on its financial statements, and it turns out that figure is actually $990,000 (or $1,010,000), who cares? Probably not many people. But suppose that $1 million in earnings on the financial statements is actually $500,000—half what the company showed. Then many people, investors and lenders principally, would care a great deal.

Materiality, then, according to GAAP, is a user-oriented concept. "If there exists a misstatement so significant that reasonable, prudent users of the financial statements would make a different decision than they would if they had been given correct information, then the misstatement is material and requires correction."[2]

A typical issue involving materiality and fraud would be asset misappropriations. Many of them are quite small and not material to the financial statements as a whole. But what of the aggregate? If many steal small amounts, the result could indeed be material.

Matching

The matching concept requires that the books and records and the resultant financial statements match revenue and expense in the proper accounting period. Fraud can occur when purposeful attempts are made to manipulate the matching concept. For example, through controlling the year-end cut-off in financial figures, many companies boost their current net income by counting revenue from the following year early and by delaying the posting of this year's expenses until the following year.

Conservatism

The conservatism constraint requires that when there is any doubt, we should avoid overstating assets and income. The intention of this principle is to provide a reasonable guideline in a questionable situation. If there is no doubt concerning an accurate valuation, this constraint need not be applied. An example of conservatism in accounting is the use of the ''lower of cost or market'' rule as it relates to inventory valuation. If a company's financial statements intentionally violate the conservatism constraint, they could be fraudulent.

Going Concern

In valuing a firm's assets for financial statement purposes, it is assumed that the business is one that will continue into the future. That is because the worth of the business, if it is any good, will always be higher than the value of its hard assets. For example, if you wanted to buy a business that paid you a 10 percent return, then you would pay up to $1 million for an investment that earned $100,000 a year. The value of the actual assets underlying the business, if they were sold at auction, typically would not bring nearly $1 million. This is the *going concern* concept, which assumes the business will go on indefinitely in the future. If there is serious doubt about whether a business can continue, the accountants must disclose this information as a footnote in the financial statements.

Fraud in the going concern concept usually results from attempts by an entity to conceal its terminal business condition. For example, assume a company is in the computer parts manufacturing business. Last year the company earned $100,000 after taxes. This year management is aware that new technology will make the business totally obsolete, and by next year, the business will likely close. This fact might not be known to the company's auditors. And when they prepare the financial statements for their company, management has the duty to inform the accountants of the business's future ability to earn money. They in turn will insist that the financial statements for the current period reflect this future event.

Cost

Generally accepted accounting principles require that most assets be carried on the financial statements at cost, as this is generally the most conservative method. However, if the assets are worth less than what they cost, this lower value is to be carried on the financial statements. Using the lower of cost or market value produces the most conservative asset valuations. The cost figure generated for assets, providing they are worth more than they cost, is called historical or acquisition cost. But there are other cost definitions as well.[3]

Fair Value

The fair value of an asset is the price that the asset would sell at on the open market in a transaction between a willing buyer and a willing seller. It is sometimes referred to as ''current market value.'' To curb overly subjective estimates, fair value accounting relies primarily on quoted market prices and other objectively observable data for use in determining asset value. Under GAAP, this method of valuation is allowed only for certain assets, such as marketable securities.

Price-Level Adjusted Historical Cost

The price-level adjusted historical cost method of pricing would carry an asset's value on the financial statements as what it would currently cost, considering inflation. At present, this method is not an acceptable way to carry costs on the balance sheet.

Net Realizable Value

The net realizable value of an asset is the amount of money that would be realized upon the sale of the asset at some point in the future, less the costs associated with owning, operating, and selling it. Net realizable value differs from fair value in that it is based on a projected future sale while fair value uses the asset's current value. Because this method deals with a projection, it is generally not acceptable for costing assets.

Future Profits

The reason businesses acquire assets is to use them to produce goods and services. This method requires determining an estimate of the future profits the company could earn because it has the asset. This method, like others, is not acceptable for asset costing because of the subjective nature of the information.

Replacement Cost

The replacement cost method is really the opposite of net realizable value. Instead of determining the net value of the item if it is sold, this method assumes the value of the asset if it must be replaced. During inflationary periods, replacement cost would boost assets and equity. Replacement cost is not permitted to determine the value of assets under GAAP.

Objective Evidence

Another generally accepted accounting principle that is often impacted by fraud deals with the subject of objective evidence. Accounting records are designed to be kept on objective, rather than subjective, evidence. That is to say, almost everyone can agree on what the asset costs historically versus what it may be worth at the present time. In valuing assets on the financial statements, the accountant looks for objective evidence of that asset's cost—an invoice, a canceled check, a contract. Built into this assumption of objective evidence, but not specifically stated, is that such evidence can be presented fraudulently; a document can be forged or faked. So the evidence used by the accountant to value assets at their cost does not have to be absolute, only reasonable.

Consistency

In order for financial information to be presented fairly over a period of time, the method of presentation must be consistent, even if it is not the most accurate measure from year to year. For example, one easy way for the value of assets and income to be inflated is through the depreciation methods companies use on their books. Assume a valuable piece of equipment was purchased by a company for $99,000 and was expected to last three years. That means that under *straight-line* depreciation, the write-off in the first year would be $33,000 maximum. Under the *double declining balance* method of depreciation, the write-off would be $66,000 the first year. By switching depreciation methods from one year to the next, a company could influence its net income by as much as $33,000. In reality, this is not income but a way to compare apples and oranges. If a company changes the way it keeps its books from one year to the next, and if these changes have a material impact on the financial statements, the company must disclose the changes in a footnote to the financials. Fraud often occurs when consistency is intentionally avoided to show false profits.

Full Disclosure

The principle behind full disclosure, as in the consistency example, is that any material deviation from GAAP must be explained to the reader of the financial information. In addition, any known event that could have a material impact on future earnings must be explained or disclosed. For example, as discussed earlier, suppose a company is aware that its principal manufacturing method for computer parts is being made obsolete by competitors. Such an event must be disclosed. If the company is being sued and is in danger of a material monetary judgment, that must be disclosed too. In actuality, any potential adverse event of a material nature must be disclosed in the financials. Many major financial frauds have been caused by the purposeful omission of footnote disclosures to the statements.

RESPONSIBILITY FOR FINANCIAL STATEMENTS

Financial statements are the responsibility of company management. Therefore, it is hard to imagine that financial statement fraud can be committed without some knowledge or consent of management, although such fraud can be perpetrated by anyone who has the opportunity and the motive to omit or misstate the data presented in furtherance of his or her purpose.

Financial statement fraud generally is instigated by members of management—at the very least, by persons under the direction and control of management. In the instances where management does not investigate suspected frauds, how can it assure itself that fraud will be prevented and, if fraud does occur, that it will be detected?

A company's board of directors and senior management generally set the code of conduct for the company. This code of conduct is often referred to as the company's "ethic." The ethic is the standard by which all other employees will tend to conduct themselves. It stands to reason, therefore, that if the company's ethic is one of high integrity, the company's employees will tend to operate in a more honest manner. If, however, the ethic is corrupt, the employees will view that as a license to be corrupt also. An unimpeachable company ethic does not, in and of itself, ensure that financial statement fraud will not occur; additional measures are required in order for management to discharge its responsibilities with respect to prevention and detection of fraudulent financial reporting.

USERS OF FINANCIAL STATEMENTS

Financial statement fraud schemes are perpetrated most often by management against potential users of the statements. These users of financial statements include company ownership and management, lending organizations, and investors. Fraudulent statements are used for a number of reasons. The most common is to increase the apparent prosperity of the organization in the eyes of potential and current investors. Doing this not only may induce new investment but can help keep current investors satisfied. Fraudulent financial statements can be used to dispel negative perceptions of an organization in the open market. Company management often uses financial statements to judge employee or management performance. Employees are tempted to manipulate statements to ensure continued employment and additional compensation that may be tied to performance. Certain internal goals, such as satisfying budgets, contribute added pressure to the manager responsible. Exhibit 12.1 displays the role of financial information and statements in the users' decision-making process.

TYPES OF FINANCIAL STATEMENTS

According to Statement on Auditing Standards (SAS) 62 (AU 623), *Special Reports*, published by the AICPA Auditing Standards Board of the American Institute of Certified Public Accountants, financial statements include presentations of financial data and accompanying notes prepared in conformity with either GAAP or some other comprehensive basis of accounting. Such financial statements include:

- Balance sheet
- Statement of income or statement of operations
- Statement of retained earnings
- Statement of cash flows
- Statement of changes in owners' equity

Exhibit 12.1   Role of Financial Information in the Decision-Making Process

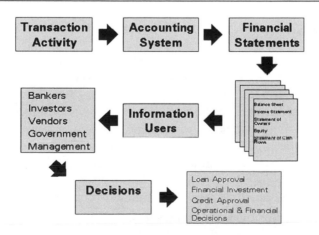

- Statement of assets and liabilities that does not include owners' equity accounts
- Statement of revenue and expenses
- Summary of operations
- Statement of operations by product lines
- Statement of cash receipts and disbursements[4]

Although not specifically noted in SAS 62 (AU 623), financial statements also typically include other financial data presentations, such as:

- Prospective financial information
- Proxy statements
- Interim financial information
- Current value financial representations
- Personal financial statements
- Bankruptcy financial statements
- Registration statement disclosures

Other comprehensive bases of accounting, according to SAS 62 (AU 623), include:

- Government or regulatory agency accounting
- Tax basis accounting
- Cash receipts and disbursements, or modified cash receipts and disbursements
- Any other basis with a definite set of criteria applied to all material items, such as the price-level basis of accounting[5]

As we see from the preceding lists, the term "financial statement" includes almost any financial data presentation prepared according to GAAP or in accord with another comprehensive basis of accounting. Throughout the remainder of this chapter and Chapter 13, the term "financial statements" includes the listed forms of reporting financial data, including the accompanying footnotes and management's discussion.

SARBANES-OXLEY ACT

On July 30, 2002, the Sarbanes-Oxley Act[6] (SOX) was signed into law. This Act, which was triggered in large part by several corporate accounting scandals, significantly changed the laws of corporate governance and the rules and regulations under which accounting firms must operate. The Sarbanes-Oxley Act was designed to restore investor confidence in capital markets and help eliminate financial statement fraud in publicly traded companies while at the same time significantly increasing the penalties for corporate accounting fraud. The most significant changes brought on by the Act include:

- The creation of the Public Company Accounting Oversight Board
- Requirements for senior financial officers to certify SEC filings

- New standards for audit committee independence
- New standards for auditor independence
- Enhanced financial disclosure requirements
- New protections for corporate whistleblowers
- Enhanced penalties for white-collar crime

Public Company Accounting Oversight Board

Title I of SOX establishes the Public Company Accounting Oversight Board (PCAOB), whose purpose is:

> *to oversee the audit of public companies that are subject to the securities laws, and related matters, in order to protect the interests of investors and further the public interest in the preparation of informative, accurate, and independent audit reports for companies the securities of which are sold to, and held by and for, public investors. [Section 101]*

In short, the PCAOB is charged with overseeing public company audits, setting audit standards, and investigating acts of noncompliance by auditors or audit firms. The PCAOB is appointed and overseen by the SEC. It is made up of five persons, two who are or have been certified public accountants and three who have never been CPAs. The Act lists the PCAOB's duties, which include:

- Registering public accounting firms that audit publicly traded companies.
- Establishing or adopting auditing, quality control, ethics, independence, and other standards relating to audits of publicly traded companies.
- Inspecting registered public accounting firms.
- Investigating registered public accounting firms and their employees, conducting disciplinary hearings, and imposing sanctions where justified.
- Performing such other duties as are necessary to promote high professional standards among registered accounting firms, to improve the quality of audit services offered by those firms, and to protect investors.
- Enforcing compliance with SOX, the rules of the PCAOB, professional standards, and securities laws relating to public company audits.

Registration with the Board

Public accounting firms must be registered with the Public Company Accounting Oversight Board in order to legally prepare or issue an audit report on a publicly traded company. In order to become registered, accounting firms must disclose, among other things, the names of all public companies they audited in the preceding year; the names of all public companies they expect to audit in the current year; and the annual fees they received from each of their public audit clients for audit, accounting, and nonaudit services.

Auditing, Quality Control, and Independence Standards and Rules

Section 103 of SOX requires the PCAOB to establish standards for auditing, quality control, ethics, independence, and other issues relating to audits of publicly traded companies. Although SOX places the responsibility on the PCAOB to establish audit standards, it also sets forth certain rules that the PCAOB is required to include in those auditing standards. These rules include:

- Audit work papers must be maintained for at least seven years.
- Auditing firms must include a concurring or second partner review and approval of audit reports and concurring approval in the issuance of the audit report by a qualified person other than the person in charge of the audit.
- All audit reports must describe the scope of testing of the company's internal control structure and must present the auditor's findings from the testing, including an evaluation of whether the internal control structure is acceptable and a description of material weaknesses in internal controls and any material noncompliance with controls.

Inspections of Registered Public Accounting Firms

The Act also authorizes the PCAOB to conduct regular inspections of public accounting firms to assess their degree of compliance with laws, rules, and professional standards regarding audits. Inspections are to be conducted once a year for firms that regularly audit more than 100 public companies and at least once every three years for firms that regularly audit 100 or fewer public companies.

Investigations and Disciplinary Proceedings

The PCAOB has the authority to investigate registered public accounting firms (or their employees) for potential violations of SOX, professional standards, any rules established by the PCAOB, or any securities laws relating to the preparation and issuance of audit reports. During an investigation, the PCAOB has the power to compel testimony and document production.

The PCAOB also has the power to issue sanctions for violations or for noncooperation with an investigation. Sanctions can include temporary or permanent suspension of a firm's registration with the PCAOB (which would mean that firm could no longer legally audit publicly traded companies), temporary or permanent suspension of a person's right to be associated with a registered public accounting firm, prohibition from auditing public companies, and civil monetary penalties of up to $750,000 for an individual and up to $15 million for a firm.

Certification Obligations for CEOs and CFOs

One of the most significant changes effected by the Sarbanes-Oxley Act is the requirement that the chief executive officer and the chief financial officer of public companies personally certify annual and quarterly SEC filings. These certifications essentially require CEOs and CFOs to take responsibility for their companies' financial statements and prevent them from delegating this responsibility to their subordinates and then claiming ignorance when fraud is uncovered in the financial statements. There are two types of officer certifications mandated by SOX: criminal certifications, which are set forth in Section 906 of the Act and codified at 18 United States Code § 1350, and civil certifications, which are set forth in Section 302.

Criminal Certifications (Section 906)

Periodic filings with the SEC must be accompanied by a statement, signed by the CEO and CFO, that certifies that the report fully complies with the SEC's periodic reporting requirements and that the information in the report fairly presents, in all material respects, the financial condition and results of operation of the company. These certifications are known as criminal certifications because the Act imposes criminal penalties on officers who violate the certification requirements.

- Corporate officers who *knowingly* violate the certification requirements are subject to fines of up to $1 million and up to 10 years' imprisonment, or both.
- Corporate officers who *willfully* violate the certification requirements are subject to fines of up to $5 million and up to 20 years' imprisonment, or both.

Civil Certifications (Section 302)

Section 302 of the Act requires the CEO and CFO personally to certify the following in their reports:

1. They have personally reviewed the report.
2. Based on their knowledge, the report does not contain any material misstatement that would render the financials misleading.
3. Based on their knowledge, the financial information in the report fairly presents in all material respects the financial condition, results of operations, and cash flow of the company.
4. They are responsible for designing, maintaining, and evaluating the company's internal controls, they have evaluated the controls within 90 days prior to the report, and they have presented their conclusions about the effectiveness of those controls in the report.
5. They have disclosed to the auditors and the audit committee any material weaknesses in the controls and any fraud, whether material or not, that involves management or other employees who have a significant role in the company's internal controls.
6. They have indicated in their report whether there have been significant changes in the company's internal controls since the filing of the last report.

Note that in items 2 and 3, the CEO and CFO are not required to certify that the financials are accurate or that there is no misstatement. They are simply required to certify that *to their knowledge* the financials are accurate and not misleading. However, this does not mean that senior financial officers can simply plead ignorance about their companies' SEC filings in order to avoid liability. The term "fairly presents" in item 3 is a broader standard than that required by GAAP. In certifying that their SEC filings meet this standard, the CEO and CFO essentially must certify that the company: (1) has selected appropriate accounting policies to ensure the material accuracy of the reports, (2) has properly applied those accounting standards, and (3) has disclosed financial information that reflects the underlying transactions and events of the company. Furthermore, the other new certification rules (see items 1 and 4–6) mandate that CEOs and CFOs take an active role in their companies' public reporting and in the design and maintenance of internal controls.

It is significant that in item 4, the CEO and CFO not only have to certify that they are responsible for their companies' internal controls but also that they have evaluated the controls *within 90 days prior to their quarterly or annual report*. Essentially, this certification requirement mandates that companies actively and continually reevaluate their control structures to prevent fraud.

Item 5 requires the CEO and CFO to certify that they have disclosed to their auditors and their audit committee any material weaknesses in the company's internal controls and also any fraud, *whether material or not*, that involves management or other key employees. The CEO and CFO must report to their auditors and audit committee *any fraud* committed by management. This places significant responsibility on the CEO and CFO to take part in antifraud efforts and to be aware of fraudulent activity within their companies in order to meet this certification requirement. Item 6 is significant because periodic SEC filings must include statements detailing significant changes to the internal controls of publicly traded companies.

Management Assessment of Internal Controls

In conjunction with the Section 302 certification requirements on the responsibility of the CEO and CFO for internal controls, Section 404 of SOX requires all annual reports to contain an internal control report that: (1) states management's responsibility for establishing and maintaining an adequate internal control structure and procedures for financial reporting; and (2) contains an assessment of the effectiveness of the internal control structure and procedures of the company for financial reporting. The filing company's independent auditor will also be required to issue an attestation report on management's assessment of the company's internal control over financial reporting. This attestation report must be filed with the SEC as part of the company's annual report.

New Standards for Audit Committee Independence

Audit Committee Responsibilities

Section 301 of SOX requires that the audit committee for each publicly traded company shall be directly responsible for appointing, compensating, and overseeing the work of the company's outside auditors. The Act also mandates that the auditors must report directly to the audit committee—not to management—and makes it the responsibility of the audit committee to resolve disputes between management and the auditors. Section 301 also requires that the audit committee must have the authority and funding to hire independent counsel and any other advisors it deems necessary to carry out its duties.

Composition of the Audit Committee

SOX mandates that each member of a company's audit committee must be a member of its board of directors and must otherwise be "independent." The term "independent" means that audit committee members can receive compensation from the company only for their service on the board of directors, the audit committee, or another committee of the board of directors. They cannot be paid by the company for any other consulting or advisory work.

Financial Expert

Section 407 of the Act requires every public company to disclose in its periodic reports to the SEC whether the audit committee has at least one member who is a "financial expert" and, if the committee does not, to explain the reasons why. The Act defines a "financial expert" as a person who, through education and experience as a public accountant or auditor, or a comptroller, chief financial officer, or a similar position: (1) has an understanding of generally accepted accounting principles and financial statements; (2) has experience in preparing or auditing financial statements of comparable companies and the application of such principles in accounting for estimates, accruals, and reserves; (3) has experience with internal controls; and (4) has an understanding of audit committee functions.

Establishing a Whistleblowing Structure

The Act makes it the responsibility of the audit committee to establish procedures (e.g., a hotline) for receiving and dealing with complaints and anonymous employee tips regarding irregularities in the company's accounting methods, internal controls, or auditing matters.

New Standards for Auditor Independence

Restrictions on Nonaudit Activity

Perhaps the greatest concern arising out of the public accounting scandals of 2001 and 2002 was the fear that public accounting firms that received multimillion-dollar consulting fees from their public company clients could not maintain an appropriate level of objectivity in conducting audits for those clients. In order to address this concern, Congress, in Section 201 of SOX, established a list of activities that public accounting firms are now prohibited from performing on behalf of their audit clients. The prohibited services are:

- Bookkeeping services
- Financial information systems design and implementation
- Appraisal or valuation services, fairness opinions, or contribution-in-kind reports
- Actuarial services
- Internal audit outsource services
- Management functions or human resources
- Broker or dealer, investment advisor, or investment banking services
- Legal services and expert services unrelated to the audit
- Any other service that the PCAOB proscribes

There are certain other nonaudit services—most notably tax services—that are not expressly prohibited by the Act. However, in order for a public accounting firm to perform these services on behalf of an audit client, that service must be approved in advance by the client's audit committee. Approval of the nonaudit services must be disclosed in the client's periodic SEC reports.

Mandatory Audit Partner Rotation

Section 204 of SOX requires public accounting firms to rotate the lead audit partner or the partner responsible for reviewing the audit every five years.

Conflict of Interest Provisions

Another provision of Sarbanes-Oxley aimed at improving auditor independence is Section 206, which seeks to limit conflicts or potential conflicts that arise when auditors cross over to work for their former clients. The Act makes it unlawful for a public accounting firm to audit a company if, within the prior year, the client's CEO, CFO, controller, or chief accounting officer worked for the accounting firm and participated in the company's audit.

Auditor Reports to Audit Committees

Section 301 requires that auditors report directly to the audit committee, and Section 204 makes certain requirements as to the contents of those reports. In order to help ensure that the audit committee is aware of questionable accounting policies or treatments that were used in the preparation of the company's financial statements, Section 204 states that auditors must make a timely report of these issues to the audit committee:

- All critical accounting policies and practices used
- Alternative GAAP methods that were discussed with management, the ramifications of the use of those alternative treatments, and the treatment preferred by the auditors
- Any other material written communications between the auditors and management

Auditors' Attestation to Internal Controls

As stated previously, Section 404 of the Act requires every annual report to contain an internal control report that states that the company's management is responsible for internal controls and that it also assesses the effectiveness of the internal control structures. Section 404 requires the company's external auditors to attest to and issue a report on management's assessment of internal controls.

Improper Influence on Audits

The Act also makes it unlawful for any officer or director of a public company to take any action to fraudulently influence, coerce, manipulate, or mislead an auditor in the performance of an audit of the company's financial statements. This is yet another attempt by Congress to ensure the independence and objectivity of audits in order to prevent accounting fraud and strengthen investor confidence in the reliability of public company financial statements.

Enhanced Financial Disclosure Requirements

Off-Balance-Sheet Transactions

The Sarbanes-Oxley Act directs the SEC to issue rules that require the disclosure of all material off-balance-sheet transactions by publicly traded companies. As directed by Section 401 of the Act, the rules require disclosure of

> *all material off-balance-sheet transactions, arrangements, obligations (including contingent obligations), and other relationships the company may have with unconsolidated entities or persons that may have a material current or future effect on the company's financial condition, changes in financial condition, liquidity, capital expenditures, capital resources, or significant components of revenues or expenses.*

These disclosures are required in all annual and quarterly SEC reports.

Pro Forma Financial Information

Section 401 also directs the SEC to issue rules on pro forma financial statements. These rules require that pro forma financials must not contain any untrue statements or omissions that would make them misleading, and they require that the pro forma financials be reconciled to GAAP. These rules apply to all pro forma financial statements that are filed with the SEC or that are included in any public disclosure or press release.

Prohibitions on Personal Loans to Executives

Section 402 makes it illegal for public companies to make personal loans or otherwise extend credit, either directly or indirectly, to or for any director or executive officer. There is an exception that applies to consumer lenders if the loans are consumer loans of the type the company normally makes to the public, and on the same terms.

Restrictions on Insider Trading

Section 403 establishes disclosure requirements for stock transactions by directors and officers of public companies, or by persons who own more than 10 percent of a publicly traded company's stock. Reports of changes in beneficial ownership by these persons must be filed with the SEC by the end of the second business day following the transaction.

Under Section 306, directors and officers are also prohibited from trading in the company's securities during any pension fund blackout periods. This restriction applies only to securities that were acquired as a result of their employment or service to the company. A blackout period is defined as any period of more than three consecutive business days in which at least 50 percent of the participants in the company's retirement plan are restricted from trading in the company's securities. If a director or officer violates this provision, he or she can be forced to disgorge to the company all profits received from the sale of securities during the blackout period.

Codes of Ethics for Senior Financial Officers

Pursuant to Section 406 of SOX, the SEC has established rules that require public companies to disclose whether they have adopted a code of ethics for their senior financial officers and, if not, to explain the reasons why. The new rules also require immediate public disclosure any time there is a change of the code of ethics or a waiver of the code of ethics for a senior financial officer.

Enhanced Review of Periodic Filings

Section 408 of the Act requires the SEC to make regular and systematic reviews of disclosures made by public companies in their periodic reports to the SEC. Reviews of a company's disclosures, including its financial statements, must be made at least once every three years. Prior to this enactment, reviews were typically minimal and tended to coincide with registered offerings.

Real-Time Disclosures

Under Section 409, public companies must publicly disclose information concerning material changes in their financial condition or operations. These disclosures must be "in plain English" and must be made "on a rapid and current basis."

Protections for Corporate Whistleblowers under Sarbanes-Oxley

The Sarbanes-Oxley Act establishes broad new protections for corporate whistleblowers. Two sections of the Act address whistleblower protections: Section 806 deals with civil protections and Section 1107 establishes criminal liability for those who retaliate against whistleblowers.

Civil Liability Whistleblower Protection

Section 806 of the Act, which is codified at 18 USC § 1514A, creates civil liability for companies that retaliate against whistleblowers. It should be noted that this provision does not provide universal whistleblower protection; it only protects employees of publicly traded companies. Section 806 makes it unlawful to fire, demote, suspend, threaten, harass, or in any other manner discriminate against an employee for providing information or aiding in an investigation of securities fraud. In order to trigger Section 806 protections, the employee must report the suspected misconduct to a federal regulatory or law enforcement agency, a member of Congress or a committee of Congress, or a supervisor. Employees are also protected against retaliation for filing, testifying in, participating in, or otherwise assisting in a proceeding filed or about to be filed relating to an alleged violation of securities laws or SEC rules.

The whistleblower protections apply even if the company ultimately is found not to have committed securities fraud. As long as the employee reasonably believes she is reporting conduct that constitutes a violation of various federal securities laws, then she is protected. The protections cover retaliatory acts not only by the company but also by any officer, employee, contractor, subcontractor, or agent of the company.

If a public company is found to have violated Section 806, the Act provides for an award of compensatory damages sufficient to "make the employee whole." Penalties include reinstatement; back pay with interest; and compensation for special damages including litigation costs, expert witness fees, and attorneys' fees.

Criminal Sanction Whistleblower Protection

Section 1107 of the Act—codified at 18 USC § 1513—makes it a crime to knowingly, with the intent to retaliate, take any harmful action against a person for providing truthful information relating to the commission or possible commission of any federal offense. This protection is triggered only when information is provided to a law enforcement officer; it does not apply to reports made to supervisors or to members of Congress, as is the case under Section 806.

In general, the coverage of Section 1107 is much broader than the civil liability whistleblower protections of Section 806. While the Section 806 protections apply only to employees of publicly traded companies, Section 1107's criminal whistleblower protections cover all individuals (and organizations) regardless of where they work. Also, Section 806 applies only to violations of securities laws or SEC rules and regulations, whereas Section 1107 protects individuals who provide truthful information about the commission or possible commission of *any federal offense*.

Violations of Section 1107 can be punished by fines of up to $250,000 and up to ten years in prison for individuals. Corporations that violate the Act can be fined up to $500,000.

Enhanced Penalties for White-Collar Crime

As part of Congress's general effort to deter corporate accounting fraud and other forms of white-collar crime, SOX also enhances the criminal penalties for a number of white-collar offenses.

Attempt and Conspiracy

The Act amends the mail fraud provisions of the USC (Chapter 63) to make "attempt" and "conspiracy to commit" offenses subject to the same penalties as the offense itself. This applies to mail fraud, wire fraud, securities fraud, bank fraud, and healthcare fraud.

Mail Fraud and Wire Fraud

Sarbanes-Oxley amends the mail fraud and wire fraud statutes (18 USC §§ 1341, 1343), increasing the maximum jail term from 5 to 20 years.

Securities Fraud

Section 807 of the Act makes securities fraud a crime under 18 USC § 1348, providing for fines up to $250,000 and up to 25 years in prison.

Document Destruction

Section 802 of the Act makes destroying evidence to obstruct an investigation or any other matter within the jurisdiction of any U.S. department illegal and punishable by a fine of up to $250,000 and up to 20 years in prison.

The final rules adopted by the SEC under Section 802 specifically require that accountants who perform audits on publicly traded companies must maintain all audit or review work papers for a period of seven years. Although the original provisions of Section 802 required a retention period of only five years, the SEC extended the requirement to be consistent with the seven-year retention period required under the Auditing Standards promulgated by the PCAOB per Section 103 of the Act. Violations of the final SEC rules may be punished by fines up to $250,000 and up to ten years in jail for individuals or fines up to $500,000 for corporations.

Section 1102 of the Act amends Section 1512 of the USC to make it a criminal offense to corruptly alter, destroy, mutilate, or conceal a record or document with the intent to impair its integrity or use in an official proceeding, or to otherwise obstruct, influence, or impede any official proceeding or attempt to do so. Violations of this section are punishable by fines up to $250,000 and imprisonment for up to 20 years.

Freezing of Assets

During an investigation of possible securities violations by a publicly traded company or any of its officers, directors, partners, agents, controlling persons, or employees, the SEC can petition a federal court to issue a 45-day freeze on "extraordinary payments" to any of the foregoing persons. If granted, the payments will be placed in an interest-bearing escrow account while the investigation commences. This provision was enacted to prevent corporate assets from being improperly distributed while an investigation is under way.

Bankruptcy Loopholes

Section 803 amends the bankruptcy code so that judgments, settlements, damages, fines, penalties, restitution, and disgorgement payments resulting from violations of federal securities laws are nondischargeable. This is intended to prevent corporate wrongdoers from sheltering their assets under bankruptcy protection.

Disgorgement of Bonuses

One of the most noteworthy aspects of the Act is Section 304, which states that if a publicly traded company is required to prepare an accounting restatement due to the company's material noncompliance, as a result of "misconduct," with any financial reporting requirement under securities laws, then the CEO and CFO must reimburse the company for:

- Any bonus or other incentive-based or equity-based compensation received during the 12 months after the initial filing of the report that requires restating.
- Any profits realized from the sale of the company's securities during the same 12-month period.

While the Act requires the CEO and CFO to disgorge their bonuses if the company's financial statements have to be restated because of "misconduct," it makes no mention of *whose* misconduct triggers this provision. There is nothing in the text of Section 304 that limits the disgorgement provision to instances of misconduct by the CEO and CFO. Presumably, then, the CEO and CFO could be required to disgorge their bonuses and profits from the sale of company stock even if they had no knowledge of and took no part in the misconduct that made the restatement necessary.

FINANCIAL STATEMENT FRAUD DATA FROM ACFE *2009 GLOBAL FRAUD SURVEY*

Frequency and Cost

Financial statement frauds were by far the least common method of occupational fraud in our study. Of 1,843 cases in our 2009 survey, less than 5 percent involved financial statement fraud. (The sum of these percentages exceeds 100 percent because some cases involved multiple fraud schemes that fell into more than one category. Various charts in this chapter may reflect percentages that total in excess of 100 percent for similar reasons.) (See Exhibit 12.2.)

Although they were the least frequently reported category of occupational fraud, financial statement schemes were the most costly by far. The median loss associated

347

Exhibit 12.2 *2009 Global Fraud Survey*: **Frequency of Three Major Categories**

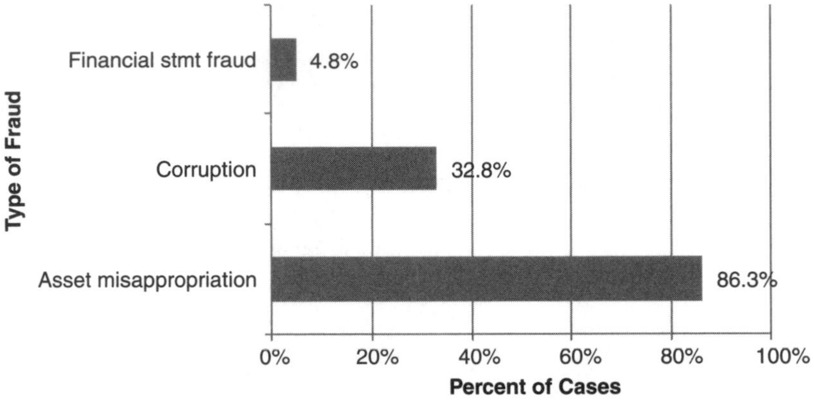

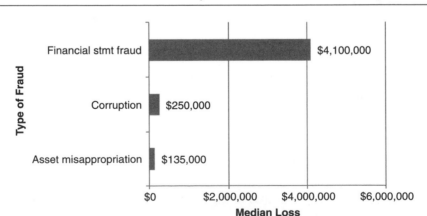

with fraudulent financial statement schemes in our survey was $4.1 million, which was 16 times the median loss caused by corruption schemes and more than 30 times the median loss in asset misappropriations. (See Exhibit 12.3.)

As Exhibit 12.4 shows, financial statement frauds were skewed heavily to the highest dollar ranges. We received 67 financial statement cases in which the dollar loss was reported, and in over two-thirds of these frauds, the victims lost at least $1 million.

Types of Fraudulent Financial Statement Schemes

Financial statement frauds can be broken down into five distinct categories: fictitious revenues, improper asset valuations, concealed liabilities and expenses, timing differences, and improper disclosures. As Exhibit 12.5 shows, the distribution of these scheme types was somewhat uniform, with each of the first three categories occurring in at least 40 percent of the fraudulent financial statement schemes we reviewed.

Exhibit 12.3 *2009 Global Fraud Survey*: **Median Loss of Three Major Categories**

Exhibit 12.4 *2009 Global Fraud Survey*: Dollar Loss Distribution for Fraudulent Financial Statement Schemes

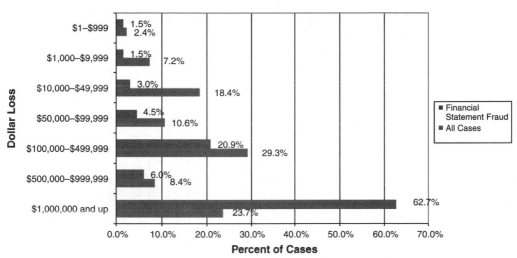

Improper disclosures were the least common scheme among the 89 financial statement frauds we reviewed; they occurred in 25 percent of the cases.

Detection of Fraudulent Financial Statement Schemes

Eighty-two respondents told us how the financial statement fraud cases they investigated were detected initially. The most common methods were tips, management review, internal audit, and by accident. Additionally, there were two notable departures from the results for all cases: external audits, which accounted for only 5 percent of detections overall but led to the detection of more than 10 percent of the financial statement frauds reviewed, and cases uncovered when the perpetrator confessed, which

Exhibit 12.5 *2009 Global Fraud Survey*: Fraudulent Financial Statement Schemes by Category

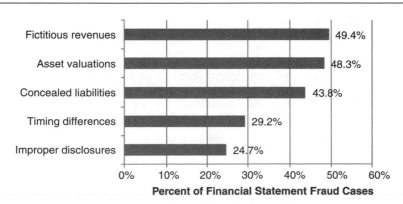

Exhibit 12.6 *2009 Global Fraud Survey*: Detection of Fraudulent Financial Statement Schemes

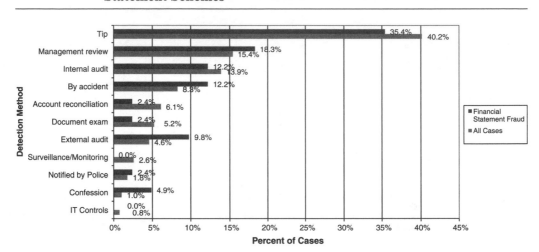

accounted for just 1 percent of all cases but nearly 5 percent of the financial statement manipulations. (See Exhibit 12.6.)

Perpetrators of Fraudulent Financial Statement Schemes

The trend for perpetrators in financial statement fraud cases ran contrary to the general trend among all occupational frauds. The percentage of financial statement frauds increased with the level of authority among perpetrators: The majority of financial statement frauds were committed by owner/executives and managers, each group of which accounted for just under 45 percent of cases reviewed. In contrast, only 10 percent involved employees. This trend was to be expected, since generally only upper-level personnel have access to financial statements or the means to cause material misstatements. (See Exhibit 12.7.)

Exhibit 12.7 *2009 Global Fraud Survey*: Perpetrators of Fraudulent Financial Statement Schemes

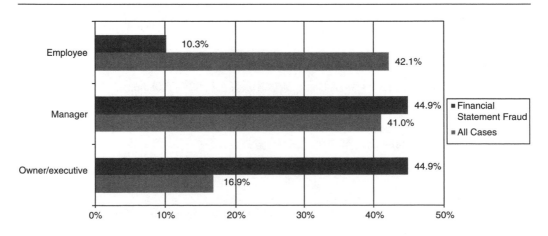

Exhibit 12.8 *2009 Global Fraud Survey*: **Median Loss by Perpetrator of Fraudulent Financial Statement Schemes**

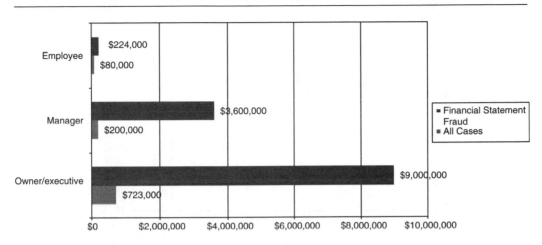

Not surprisingly, the median losses caused by financial statement schemes in each of the three perpetrator categories far exceeded the losses caused by occupational frauds overall. Managers caused a median loss of $3.6 million in financial statement frauds while owner/executives undertaking such schemes caused a median loss of $9 million. (See Exhibit 12.8.)

Victims of Fraudulent Financial Statement Schemes

Exhibit 12.9 shows how the financial statement fraud cases in our survey were distributed based on the size of the victim organization. The distribution was weighted more

Exhibit 12.9 *2009 Global Fraud Survey*: **Size of Victim in Fraudulent Financial Statement Schemes**

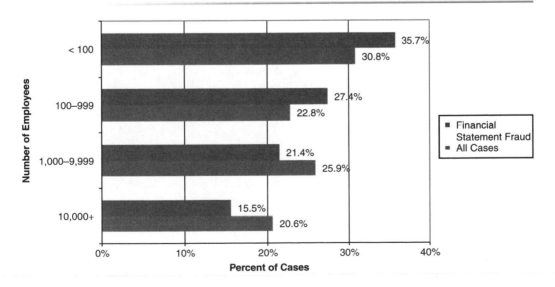

Exhibit 12.10 *2009 Global Fraud Survey*: Median Loss by Size of Victim
in Financial Statement Schemes

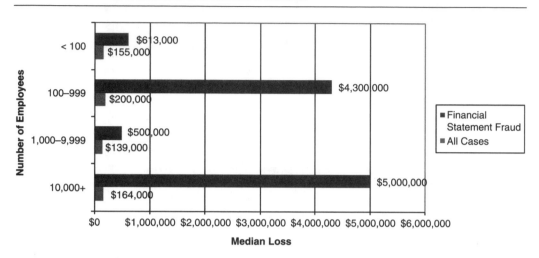

heavily toward victims in the two smallest categories than was the case for all occupational frauds.

In Exhibit 12.10, we see how median losses varied based on the victim's size. The median losses for each size category due to financial statement frauds far exceeded those for all fraud cases.

NOTES

1. Steven A. Finkler, *Finance and Accounting for Nonfinancial Managers* (Englewood Cliffs, NJ: Prentice-Hall, 1996), pp. 32–34.
2. Ibid., p. 34.
3. Ibid., pp. 45–51.
4. American Institute of Certified Public Accountants, Statements on Auditing Standards, ''Special Reports,'' SAS 62 (AU 623).
5. Ibid.
6. Public Law 107–204, 116 Stat. 745 (2002).

CHAPTER 13

Fraudulent Financial Statement Schemes

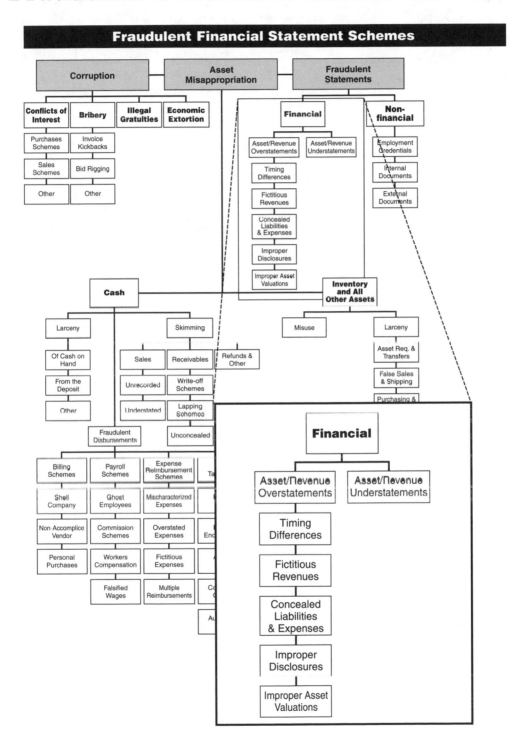

Case Study: That Way Lies Madness

"I'm Crazy Eddie!" a goggle-eyed man screams from the television set, pulling at his face with his hands. "My prices are *in-sane!*" Eddie Antar* got into the electronics business in 1969, with a modest store called Sight and Sound. Less than 20 years later, he had become Crazy Eddie, a millionaire many times over and an international fugitive from justice. He was shrewd, daring, and self-serving; he was obsessive and greedy. But he was hardly *insane.* A U.S. Attorney said, "He was not Crazy Eddie. He was Crooked Eddie."

The man on the screen was not Eddie at all. The face so dutifully watched throughout New Jersey, New York, and Connecticut—that was an actor, hired to do a humiliating but effective characterization. The real Eddie Antar was not the kind of man to yell and rend his clothes. He was busy making money, and he was making a lot of it illegally. By the time his electronics empire folded, Antar and members of his family had distinguished themselves with a fraud of massive proportions, reaping more than $120 million. A senior official at the Securities and Exchange Commission quipped, "This may not be the biggest stock fraud of all time, but for outrageousness it is going to be very hard to beat." The SEC was joined by the FBI, the Postal Inspection Service, and the U.S. Attorney in tracking Eddie down. They were able to show a multipronged fraud in which Antar:

1. Listed smuggled money from foreign banks as sales.
2. Made false entries to accounts payable.
3. Overstated Crazy Eddie, Inc.'s inventory by breaking into and altering audit records.
4. Took credit for merchandise as "returned" while also counting it as inventory.
5. "Shared" inventory from one store to boost other stores' audit counts.
6. Arranged for vendors to ship merchandise and defer the billing, besides claiming discounts and advertising credits.
7. Sold large lots of merchandise to wholesalers, then spread the money to individual stores as retail receipts.

It was a long list, and a profitable one for Eddie Antar and the inner circle of his family. The seven action items were designed to make Crazy Eddie's look like it was booming. In fact, it was. It was the single biggest retailer of stereos and televisions in the New York metropolitan area, with a dominant and seemingly impregnable share of the market. But that was not enough for Eddie. He took the chain public and then made some real money. Shares that initially sold at $8 each later peaked at $80, thanks to the Antar team's masterful tweaking of company accounts.

Inflating Crazy Eddie's stock price was not the first scam Antar had pulled. In the early days, as Sight and Sound grew into Crazy Eddie's and spawned multiple stores, Eddie was actually underreporting his earnings. Eddie's cousin, Sam Antar, remembered learning how the company did business by watching his father during the early

*Several names and details have been changed to preserve anonymity.

days. "The store managers would drop off cash to the house after they closed at ten o'clock, and my father would make one bundle for deposit into the company account, and several bundles for others in the family," Sam Antar said. "Then he would drive over to their houses and drop off their bundles at two in the morning." For every few dollars to the company, the Antars took a dollar for themselves. The cash was secreted away into bank accounts at Bank Leumi of Israel. Eddie smuggled some of the money out of the country himself, by strapping stacks of large bills across his body. The Antars sneaked away with at least $7 million over several years. Skimming the cash meant tax-free profits and one gargantuan nest egg waiting across the sea.

But entering the stock market was another story. Eddie anticipated the initial public offering (IPO) of shares by quietly easing money from Bank Leumi back into the operation. The company really was growing, but injecting the pilfered funds as sales receipts made the growth look even more impressive: Skim the money and beat the tax man, then draw out funds as you need them to boost sales figures. It keeps the ship running smooth and sunny.

But Paul Hayes, a special agent who worked the case with the FBI, pointed out Crazy Eddie's problem. "After building up the books, they set a pattern of double-digit growth, which they had to sustain. When they couldn't sustain it, they started looking for new ways to fake it," Hayes said.

Eddie, his brothers, his cousins, and several family loyalists all owned large chunks of company stock. No matter what actually happened at the stores, they wanted that stock to rise. So the seven-point plan was born. There was the skimmed money waiting overseas, being brought back and disguised as sales. But there were limits to how much cash the family had available and could get back into the country, so they turned to other methods of inflating the company's financials. In the most daring part of the expanded scam, Antar's people broke into auditors' records and boosted the inventory numbers. With the stroke of a pen, 13 microcassette players became 1,327.

Better than that, the Antars figured out how to make their inventory do double work. Debit memos were drawn up showing substantial lots of stereos or video cassette recorders as "returned to manufacturer." Crazy Eddie's was given a credit for the wholesale cost due back from the manufacturer. But the machines were kept at the warehouse to be counted as inventory. In a variation of the inventory scam, at least one wholesaler agreed to ship Crazy Eddie truckloads of merchandise, deferring the billing to a later date. That way Crazy Eddie's had plenty of inventory volume, plus the return credits listed on the account book. And what if auditors got too close and began asking questions? Executives would throw the records away. A "lost" report was a safe report.

Eddie Antar did not stop at simple bookkeeping and warehouse games; he "shared inventory" among his nearly 40 stores. After auditors had finished counting a warehouse's holdings and had gone for the day, workers tossed the merchandise into trucks. The inventory was hauled overnight to an early-morning load-in at another store. When the auditors arrived at that store, they found a full stockroom waiting to be counted. Again, this ruse carried a double payoff. The audit looked strong because of the inventory items counted multiple times, and the bookkeeping looked good because only one set of invoices was entered as payable to Eddie's creditors. Also, the game could be repeated for as long as the audit route demanded.

Eddie's trump card was the supplier network. He had considerable leverage with area wholesalers, because Crazy Eddie's was the biggest and baddest retail outlet in the region. Agent Paul Hayes remembers Eddie as "an aggressive businessman: He'd put the squeeze on a manufacturer and tell them he wasn't going to carry their product. Now, he was king of what is possibly the biggest consolidated retail market in the nation. Japanese manufacturers were fighting each other to get into this market. . . . So when Eddie made a threat, that was a threat with serious potential impact."

Suppliers gave Crazy Eddie's buyers extraordinary discounts and advertising rebates. If they did not, the Antars had another method: They made up the discount. For example, Crazy Eddie's might owe George-Electronics $1 million; by claiming $500,000 in discounts or ad credits, the bill was cut in half. Sometimes there was a real discount, sometimes there was not. (It was not easy, after Eddie's fall, to tell what was a shrewd business deal and what was fraud. "They had legitimate discounts in there," says Hayes, "along with the criminal acts. That's why it was tough to know what was smoke and what was fire.")

Eddie had yet another arrangement with manufacturers. For certain high-demand items—high-end stereo systems, for example—a producing company would agree to sell only to Crazy Eddie. Eddie placed an order big enough for what he needed and then added a little more. The excess he sold to a distributor who had already agreed to send the merchandise outside Crazy Eddie's tristate area. And then came the really good part: By arrangement, the distributor paid for the merchandise in a series of small checks—$100,000 worth of portable stereos would be paid off with 10 checks of $10,000 each. Eddie sprinkled this money into his stores as register sales. He knew that *Wall Street* analysts use comparable store sales as a bedrock indicator. New stores are compared with old stores, and any store open more than a year is compared with its performance during the previous term. The goal is to outperform the previous year. So the $10,000 injections made Eddie's "comps" look fantastic.

As the doctored numbers circulated in enthusiastic financial circles, CRZY stock doubled its earnings per share during its first year on the stock exchange. The stock split two for one in both of its first two fiscal terms as a publicly traded company. As chairman and chief executive, Eddie Antar used his newsletter to trumpet soaring profits, declining overhead costs, and a new 210,000-square-foot corporate headquarters. Plans were under way for a home-shopping arm of the business. Besides the electronics stores, there was now a subsidiary, Crazy Eddie Record and Tape Asylums, in the Antar fold. At its peak, the operation included 43 stores and reported sales of $350 million a year. This was a long way from the Sight and Sound storefront operation where it all began.

It was almost eerie how deliberately the Antar conspirators manipulated investors and how directly their crimes affected brokers' assessments. At the end of Crazy Eddie's second public year, a major brokerage firm issued a gushing recommendation to "buy." The recommendation was explicitly "based on 35 percent EPS [earnings per share] growth" and "comparable store sales growth in the low double-digit range.'' These double-digit expansions were from the "comps" that Eddie and his gang had cooked up with wholesalers' money and by juggling inventories. CRZY stock, the report predicted, would double and then some during the next year. As if following an Antar script, the brokers declared, "Crazy Eddie is the only retailer in our universe that has not reported a disappointing quarter in the last two years. We do not believe that is an accident. . . . We believe Crazy Eddie is becoming the kind of company that can continually produce above-average comparable store sales growth." The brokers could not have known what Herculean efforts were needed to yield just that impression. The report praised Eddie's management skills. "Mr. Antar has created a strong organization beneath him that is close-knit and directed. . . . Despite the boisterous (less charitable commentators would say obnoxious) quality of the commercials, Crazy Eddie management is quite conservative."

Well, yes, in a manner of speaking. They were certainly holding tightly to the money as it flowed through the market. According to federal indictments, the conspiracy inflated the company's value during the first year by about $2 million. By selling off shares of the overvalued stock, the partners pocketed over $28.2 million. The next year they illegally boosted income by $5.5 million and retail sales by $2.2 million. This time the group cashed in their stock for a cool $42.2 million windfall. In the last year before the boom went bust, Eddie and his partners inflated income by $37.5 million and retail by $18 million. They did not have that much stock left, though, so despite the big blowup they cashed in for only about $8.3 million.

Maybe he knew the end was at hand, but with takeovers looming, Eddie kept fighting. He had started his business with one store in Brooklyn almost 20 years before, near the neighborhood where he grew up, populated mainly by Jewish immigrants from Syria. Despite these humble beginnings, he would one day be called "the Darth Vader of capitalism" by a prosecuting attorney, referring not just to his professional inveigling but to his personal life as well. Eddie's affair with another woman broke up his marriage and precipitated a lifelong break with his father. Eventually he divorced his wife and married his lover. Rumors hinted that Eddie had been unhappy because he had five daughters and no sons from his first marriage. Neighbors said the rest of the family sided with the ex-wife. Eddie and his brothers continued in business together, but they had no contact outside the company. Allen Antar, a few years younger, should have been able to sympathize—he had also been estranged from the family when he filed for a divorce and married a woman who was not Jewish. (Allen eventually divorced that woman and remarried his first wife.) Later at trial, the brothers Antar were notably cold to one another. Even Eddie's own lawyer called him a "huckster."

But this Darth Vader had a compassionate side. Eddie was known as a quiet man, and modest. He was seldom photographed and almost never granted interviews. He was said to have waited hours at the bedside of a dying cousin, Mort Gindi, whose brother, also named Eddie, was named as a defendant in the Antars' federal trial. His cousin Sam remembers him as "a leader, someone I looked up to since I was a kid. Eddie was strong, he worked out with weights; when the Italian kids wanted to come into our neighborhood and beat up on the Jewish kids, Eddie would stop them. That was when we were kids. Later, it turned out different.''

Eddie had come a long way. He had realized millions of dollars by selling off company stock at inflated prices. This money was stashed in secret accounts around the world, held under various assumed identities. In fact, Eddie had done so well that he was left vulnerable as leader of the retail empire. When Elias Zinn, a Houston businessman, joined with the Oppenheimer-Palmieri Fund and waged a proxy battle for Crazy Eddie's, the Antars had too little shareholders' power to stave off the bid. They lost. For the first time, Crazy Eddie's was out of Eddie's hands.

The new owners did not have long to celebrate. They discovered that their ship was sinking fast. Stores were alarmingly understocked, shareholders were suing, and suppliers were shutting down credit lines because they were being paid either late or not at all. An initial review showed the company's inventory had been overstated by $65 million—a number later raised to over $80 million. In a desperate maneuver, the new management set up a computerized inventory system and established lines of credit. They made peace with the vendors and cut 150 jobs to reduce overhead. But it was too late. Less than a year after the takeover, Crazy Eddie's was dead.

Eddie Antar, however, was very much alive. But nobody knew where. He had disappeared when it became apparent that the takeover was forcing him out. He had set up dummy companies in Liberia, Gibraltar, and Panama, along with well-supplied bank accounts in Israel and Switzerland. Sensing that his days as Crazy Eddie were numbered, he fled the United States, traveling the world with faked passports, calling himself, at different times, Harry Page Shalom and David Cohen. Shalom was a real person, a longtime friend of Eddie's, another in a string of chagrined and erstwhile companions.

It was as David Cohen that Eddie ended his flight from justice and reality. After 28 months on the run, he stalked into a police station in Bern, Switzerland—but not to turn himself in. ''David Cohen'' was demanding help from the police. He was mad because bank officials refused to let him at the $32 million he had on account there. The bank would not tell Cohen anything—just that he could not access those funds. But officials discreetly informed police that the money had been frozen by the U.S. Department of Justice. Affidavits in the investigation had targeted the account as an Antar line. It did not take long to realize that David Cohen, the irate millionaire in the Bern police station, was Eddie Antar. It was the last public part Crazy Eddie would play for a while. He eventually pled guilty to racketeering and conspiracy charges and was sentenced to 82 months in prison with credit for time served. This left him with about three and a half years of jail time. He was also ordered to repay $121 million to bilked investors. Almost $72 million was recovered from Eddie's personal accounts. ''I don't ask for mercy,'' Eddie told the judge at his trial. ''I ask for balance.''

Eddie's brother Mitchell, was first convicted and given four and a half years, with $3 million in restitution burdens, but his conviction was overturned because of a prejudicial remark by the judge in the first trial. Mitchell later pled guilty to two counts of securities fraud, and the rest of the charges were dropped. Allen

Antar was acquitted at the first trial, but he and his father, Sam, were both later found guilty of insider trading and ordered to pay $11.9 million and $57.5 million, respectively, in disgorgement and interest.

What happened to the Crazy Eddie stores? In 1998, Eddie's nephews attempted to revive the legacy and held a grand opening for a new electronics store in New Jersey. At the beginning of the new millennium, the store's doors closed and Crazy Eddie shifted focus to become a dot-com retailer. But by 2004, the company had once again faltered and closed, this time amid allegations that it had resold unauthorized products online.

METHODS OF FINANCIAL STATEMENT FRAUD

Most financial statement schemes can be classified in one or more of these categories:

- Fictitious revenues
- Timing differences
- Concealed liabilities and expenses
- Improper disclosures
- Improper asset valuation

However, because the maintenance of financial records involves a double-entry system, fraudulent accounting entries always affect at least two accounts and, therefore, at least two categories on the financial statements. While the schemes described in the following pages reflect the major financial statement fraud classifications, keep in mind that the other side of the fraudulent transaction exists elsewhere. It is common for schemes to involve a combination of several methods.

FICTITIOUS REVENUES

Fictitious or fabricated revenues involve the recording of sales of goods or services that did not occur. Fictitious sales most often involve fake or phantom customers but also can involve legitimate customers. For example, a fictitious invoice can be prepared (but not mailed) for a legitimate customer although the goods are not delivered or the services are not rendered. At the beginning of the next accounting period, the sale might be reversed to help conceal the fraud, but this may lead to a revenue shortfall in the new period, creating the need for more fictitious sales. Another method is to use legitimate customers and artificially inflate or alter invoices reflecting higher amounts or quantities than actually sold.

Generally speaking, revenue is recognized when it is (1) realized or realizable and (2) earned. The Securities and Exchange Commission issued Staff Accounting Bulletin (SAB) Topic 13, "Revenue Recognition" (codified in Financial Accounting Standards Board [FASB] Accounting Standards Codification [ASC] 605, "Revenue Recognition"), to provide additional guidance on revenue recognition criteria and to rein in some of the inappropriate practices that had been observed. FASB ASC 605 states that revenue typically is considered realized or realizable, and earned, when all of these criteria are met:

- Persuasive evidence of an arrangement exists.
- Delivery has occurred or services have been rendered.
- The seller's price to the buyer is fixed or determinable.
- Collectibility is reasonably assured.

One particular case details a typical example of fictitious revenue. Interested in inflating their financial standing, a publicly traded company engineered sham transactions for more than seven years. The company's management utilized several shell companies, supposedly making a number of favorable sales. The sales transactions were fictitious, as were the supposed customers. As the amounts of the sales grew, so did the suspicions of internal auditors. The sham transactions included the payment of funds for assets while the same funds were returned to the parent company as receipts on sales. The management scheme went undetected for so long that the company's books eventually were inflated by more than $80 million. The perpetrators finally were discovered and prosecuted in both civil and criminal courts.

An example of a sample entry from this type of case is detailed next. To record a purported purchase of fixed assets, a fictional entry is made by debiting fixed assets and crediting cash for the amount of the alleged purchase:

Date	Description	Reference	Debit	Credit
12/01/Y1	Fixed Assets	104	350,000	
	Cash	101		350,000

A fictitious sales entry is then made for the same amount as the false purchase, debiting accounts receivable and crediting the sales account. The cash outflow that supposedly paid for the fixed assets is "returned" as payment on the receivable account, although in practice the cash might never have moved if the fraudsters had not bothered to falsify that extra documentary support.

Date	Description	Reference	Debit	Credit
12/01/Y1	Accounts Receivable	120	350,000	
	Sales	400		350,000
12/15/Y1	Cash	101	350,000	
	Accounts Receivable	120		350,000

The result of the completely fabricated sequence of events is an increase in both company assets and yearly revenue. Alternatively the debit could be directed to other accounts, such as inventory or accounts payable, or it simply could be left in accounts receivable if the fraud were committed close to year-end and the receivable could be left outstanding without attracting undue attention.

Sales with Conditions

Sales with conditions are a form of fictitious revenue scheme in which a sale is booked even though some terms have not been completed and the rights and risks of ownership have not passed to the purchaser. These transactions do not qualify for recording as revenue, but nevertheless they may be recorded in an effort to boost a company's revenue fraudulently. These types of sales are similar to schemes involving the recognition of revenue in improper periods since the conditions for sale may become satisfied in the future, at which point revenue recognition would become appropriate. Premature recognition schemes are discussed later in this chapter.

Pressures to Boost Revenues

External pressures to succeed that are placed on business owners and managers by bankers, stockholders, families, and even communities often provide the motivation to commit fraud. For example, in addition to other charges, GE was alleged by the SEC to have manipulated earnings for two years in a row (2002 and 2003) in order to meet performance targets by recording $381 million in "sales" of locomotives to financial partners. Since GE had not ceded ownership of the assets and had agreed to maintain and secure them on its property, the transactions were, in reality, more like loans than sales. GE settled the SEC's charges in 2009 for $50 million, neither admitting nor denying guilt. In a different case, the former chairman of Satyam Computer Services, B. Ramalinga Raju, confessed to his board in January of 2009 that he had been falsifying revenue and profits for approximately six years to create a fictitious cash balance of $1 billion and hide poor performance. India's Central Bureau of Investigation, which is investigating the case, estimates the fraud to be significantly higher—at $2.6 billion.

In another example, a real estate investment company arranged for the sale of shares that it held in a nonrelated company. The sale occurred on the last day of the year and accounted for 45 percent of the company's income for that year. A 30 percent down payment was recorded as received, and a corresponding receivable was recorded for the balance. With the intent to show a financially healthier company, the details of the sale were made public in an announcement to the press, but the sale of the stock was completely fabricated. To cover the fraud, off-book loans were made in the amount of the down payment. Other supporting documents also were falsified. The $40 million misstatement ultimately was uncovered, and the real estate company owner faced criminal prosecution.

In a similar case, a publicly traded textile company engaged in a series of false transactions designed to improve its financial image. Receipts from the sale of stock were returned to the company in the form of revenues. The fraudulent management team even went so far as to record a bank loan on the company books as revenue. At the time that the scheme was uncovered, the company books were overstated by some $50,000, a material amount to this particular company.

The pressures to commit financial statement fraud also may come from within a company. Departmental budget requirements including income and profit goals can create situations in which financial statement fraud is committed. In one instance, the accounting manager of a small company misstated financial records to cover its financial shortcomings. The financial statements included a series of entries made by the accounting manager designed to meet budget projections and to cover up losses in the company pension fund. Influenced by dismal financial performance in recent months, the accountant also consistently overstated period revenues. To cover his scheme, he debited liability accounts and credited the equity account. The perpetrator finally resigned, leaving a letter of confession. He was later prosecuted in criminal court.

Red Flags Associated with Fictitious Revenues

- Rapid growth or unusual profitability, especially compared to that of other companies in the same industry
- Recurring negative cash flows from operations or an inability to generate cash flows from operations while reporting earnings and earnings growth
- Significant transactions with related parties or special-purpose entities not in the ordinary course of business or where those entities are not audited or are audited by another firm
- Significant, unusual, or highly complex transactions, especially those close to period-end that pose difficult "substance over form" questions
- Unusual growth in the number of days sales in receivables
- A significant volume of sales to entities whose substance and ownership is not known
- An unusual surge in sales by a minority of units within a company or of sales recorded by corporate headquarters

TIMING DIFFERENCES

As mentioned earlier, financial statement fraud also may involve timing differences—that is, the recording of revenue and/or expenses in improper periods. This can be done to shift revenues or expenses between one period and the next, increasing or decreasing earnings as desired.

Matching Revenues with Expenses

Remember, according to generally accepted accounting principles, revenue and corresponding expenses should be recorded or matched in the same accounting period; failing to do so violates the matching principle of GAAP. For example, suppose a company accurately records sales that occurred in the month of December but fails to fully record expenses incurred as costs associated with those sales until January—in the next accounting period. The effect of this error would be to overstate the net income of the company in the period in which the sales were recorded and also to understate net income in the subsequent period when the expenses are reported.

The next example depicts a sales transaction in which the cost of sales associated with the revenue is not recorded in the same period. A journal entry is made to record the billing of a project that is not complete. Although a contract has been signed for this project, goods and services for it have not been delivered, and the project is not even scheduled to start until January. In order to boost revenues for the current year, this sales transaction is recorded fraudulently before year-end:

Date	Description	Reference	Debit	Credit
12/31/Y1	Accounts Receivable	120	17,000	
	Sales–Project C	401		17,000
	To record sale of product and services–Project C			
	Fiscal Year End–97			

In January, the project is started and completed. The entries below show accurate recording of the $15,500 of costs associated with the sale:

Date	Description	Reference	Debit	Credit
01/31/Y1	Cost of Sales–Project C	702	13,500	
	Inventory	140		13,500
	To record relief of inventory for Project C			
01/31/Y1	Labor Costs–Project C	550	2,000	
	Cash	101		2,000
	To record payroll expense for Project C			

If recorded correctly, the entries for the recognition of revenue and the costs associated, for example, with the sales entry would be recorded in the accounting period in which they actually occur: January. The effect on the income statement for the company is shown in Exhibit 13.1.

This example depicts exactly how nonadherence to GAAP's matching principle can cause material misstatement in yearly income statements. As the income and expenses were stated in error, year YY yielded a net income of $17,000+ while year ZZ produced a loss ($13,400). Correctly stated, revenues and expenses are matched and recorded together within the same accounting period, showing moderate yet accurate net incomes of $0 in year YY and $3,600 in year ZZ.

Exhibit 13.1   Income Statement: Incorrectly Stated versus Correctly Stated

	Incorrectly Stated		Correctly Stated	
	Year YY	Year ZZ	Year YY	Year ZZ
Sales Revenue				
Project B	25,000		25,000	
Project C	17,000			17,000
Project D		26,500		26,500
Total Sales	42,000	26,500	25,000	43,500
Cost of Sales				
Project B	22,500		22,500	
Project C		15,500		15,500
Project D		21,400		21,400
Total Cost of Sales	22,500	36,900	22,500	36,900
Gross Margin	19,500	(10,400)	2,500	6,600
G&A Expenses	2,500	3,000	2,500	3,000
Net Income	17,000	(13,400)	0	3,600

Premature Revenue Recognition

Generally, revenue should be recognized in the accounting records when a sale is complete—that is, when title is passed from the seller to the buyer. This transfer of ownership completes the sale and is usually not final until all obligations surrounding the sale are complete and the four criteria set out in FASB ASC 605 have been satisfied. As mentioned previously, those four criteria are:

1. Persuasive evidence of an arrangement exists.
2. Delivery has occurred or services have been rendered.
3. The seller's price to the buyer is fixed or determinable.
4. Collectibility is reasonably assured.

One case details how early recognition of revenue not only leads to financial statement misrepresentation but also can serve as a catalyst to further fraud. A retail drugstore chain's management got ahead of itself in recording income. In a scheme that was used repeatedly, management enhanced earnings by recording unearned revenue prematurely, resulting in the impression that the drugstores were much more profitable than they actually were. When the situation came to light and was investigated, several embezzlement schemes, false expense report schemes, and instances of credit card fraud also were uncovered.

In another case, the president of a not-for-profit organization was able to illicitly squeeze the maximum amount of private donations by cooking the company books. To enable the organization to receive additional funding that was dependent on the amounts of already received contributions, the organization's president recorded promised donations before they actually were received. By the time the scheme was discovered by the organization's internal auditor, the fraud had been perpetrated for more than four years.

When managers recognize revenues prematurely, one or more of the criteria set forth in FASB ASC 605 is typically not met. Examples of common problems with premature revenue recognition are set out next.

Persuasive Evidence of an Arrangement Does Not Exist

- No written or verbal agreement exists.
- A verbal agreement exists but a written agreement is customary.
- A written order exists but is conditional on sale to end users (i.e., a consignment sale).
- A written order exists but contains a right of return.
- A written order exists, but a side letter alters the terms in ways that eliminate the required elements for an agreement.
- The transaction is with a related party, which fact has not been disclosed.

Delivery Has Not Occurred or Services Have Not Been Rendered

- Shipment has not been made and the criteria for recognizing revenue on ''bill-and-hold'' transactions set out in FASB ASC 605 have not been met.
- Shipment has been made not to the customer but to the seller's agent, an installer, or a public warehouse.

- Some but not all of the components required for operation were shipped.
- Items of the wrong specification were shipped.
- Delivery is not complete until installation and customer testing and acceptance has occurred.
- Services have not been provided at all.
- Services are being performed over an extended period, and only a portion of the service revenues should have been recognized in the current period.
- The mix of goods and services in a contract has been misstated in order to accelerate revenue recognition improperly.

The Seller's Price to the Buyer Is Not Fixed or Determinable

- The price is contingent on some future events.
- A service or membership fee is subject to unpredictable cancellation during the contract period.
- The transaction includes an option to exchange the product for others.
- Payment terms are extended for a substantial period, and additional discounts or upgrades may be required to induce continued use and payment instead of switching to alternative products.

Collectibility Is Not Reasonably Assured

- Collection is contingent on some future events (e.g., resale of the product, receipt of additional funding, or litigation).
- The customer does not have the ability to pay (e.g., it is financially troubled, it has purchased far more than it can afford, or it is a shell company with minimal assets).

Long-term Contracts

Long-term contracts pose special problems for revenue recognition. Long-term construction contracts, for example, use either the completed contract method or the percentage-of-completion method, depending partly on the circumstances. The completed contract method does not record revenue until the project is 100 percent complete. Construction costs are held in an inventory account until completion of the project. The percentage-of-completion method recognizes revenues and expenses as measurable progress on a project is made, but this method is particularly vulnerable to manipulation. Managers can easily manipulate the percentage of completion and the estimated costs to complete a construction project in order to recognize revenues prematurely and conceal contract overruns.

Channel Stuffing

Another difficult area of revenue recognition is channel stuffing, which is also known as trade loading. This refers to the sale of an unusually large quantity of a product to distributors, who are encouraged to overbuy through the use of deep discounts and/or extended payment terms. This practice is especially attractive in industries with high gross margins (cigarettes, pharmaceuticals, perfume, soda concentrate, and branded consumer goods) because it can increase short-term earnings. The downside is that stealing from the next period's sales makes it harder to achieve sales goals in the next period, sometimes leading to increasingly disruptive levels of channel stuffing and ultimately a restatement.

Although orders are received in a channel stuffing scheme, the terms of the order might raise some question about the collectibility of accounts receivable, and there may be side agreements that grant a right of return, effectively making the sales consignment sales. There may be a greater risk of returns for certain products if they cannot be sold before their shelf life expires. This is a particular problem for pharmaceuticals, because retailers will not accept drugs that have a short shelf life remaining. As a result, channel stuffing should be viewed skeptically; in certain circumstances it may constitute fraud.

Recording Expenses in the Wrong Period

The timely recording of expenses often is compromised due to pressures to meet budget projections and goals or due to lack of proper accounting controls. As the expensing of certain costs is pushed into periods other than the ones in which they actually occur, costs are not properly matched against the income that they help produce. Consider one case in which supplies were purchased and applied to the current year budget but actually were used in the following accounting period. A manager at a publicly traded company completed 11 months of operations remarkably under budget when compared to total year estimates. He therefore decided to get a head start on the next year's expenditures. In order to spend all current year budgeted funds allocated to his department, he bought $50,000 in unneeded supplies. The supplies expense transactions were recorded against the current year's budget. Staff auditors noticed the huge leap in expenditures, however, and inquired about the situation. The manager came clean, explaining that he was under pressure to meet budget goals for the following year. Because the manager was not attempting to keep the funds for himself, no legal action was taken.

The correct recording of such transactions would be to debit supplies inventory for the original purchase and subsequently expense the items out of the account as they are used. The example journal entries detail the correct method of expensing the supplies over time.

Date	Description	Reference	Debit	Credit
12/31/YY	Supplies Inventory	109	50,000	
	Accounts Payable	201		50,000
	To record the purchase of supplies			
Record in	Supplies Expense	851	2,000	
Period Used	Supplies Inventory	109		2,000
	To record supplies consumed in the current period			

Similar entries should be made monthly, as the supplies are used, until they are consumed and $50,000 in supplies expense is recorded.

Red Flags Associated with Timing Differences

- Rapid growth or unusual profitability, especially compared to that of other companies in the same industry
- Recurring negative cash flows from operations or an inability to generate cash flows from operations while reporting earnings and earnings growth
- Significant, unusual, or highly complex transactions, especially those close to period end that pose difficult "substance over form" questions
- Unusual increase in gross margin or margin in excess of industry peers
- Unusual growth in the number of days sales in receivables
- Unusual decline in the number of days purchases in accounts payable

Case Study: The Importance of Timing

What about a scheme in which nobody gets any money? One that was never intended to enrich its players or to defraud the company they worked for? It happened in Huntsville, Alabama, on-site at a major aluminum products plant with over $300 million in yearly sales. A few shrewd men cooked the company's books without taking a single dime for themselves.

Terry Isbell* was an internal auditor making a routine review of accounts payable. He was running a computer search to look at any transactions over $50,000 and found among the hits a bill for replacing two furnace liners. The payments went out toward the last of the year, to an approved vendor, with the proper signatures from Steven Leonyrd, a maintenance engineer, and Doggett Stine, the sector's purchasing manager. However, there was nothing else in the file. Maintenance and repair jobs of this sort were supposed to be done on a time-and-material basis so there should have been work reports, vouchers, and inspection sheets in the file along with the paid invoices. But there was nothing.

Isbell talked with Steven Leonyrd, who showed him the furnaces, recently lined and working to perfection. So where was the paperwork? "It'll be in the regular work file for the first quarter," Leonyrd replied.

"The bill was for last year, November and December," Isbell pointed out. That was because the work was paid for in "advance payments," according to Leonyrd. There was not room in the work schedule to have the machines serviced in November, so the work was billed to that year's nonrecurring maintenance budget. Later, sometime after the first of the year, the work was actually done.

Division management okayed Isbell to make an examination. He found $150,000 in repair invoices without proper documentation. The records for materials and supplies, which were paid for in one year and received in the next, totaled $250,000. A check of later records and an inspection showed that everything paid for had in fact been received—just later than promised.

*Several names and details have been changed to preserve anonymity.

So it was back to visit Leonyrd, who said the whole thing was simple. "We had this money in the budget for maintenance and repair, supplies outside the usual scope of things. It was getting late in the year, looked like we were just going to lose those dollars, you know, they'd just revert back to the general fund. So we set up the work orders and made them on last year's budget. Then we got the actual stuff later." Who told Leonyrd to set it up that way? "Nobody. Just made sense, that's all."

Nobody, Isbell suspected, was the purchasing manager who handled Leonyrd's group, Doggett Stine. Stine was known as "a domineering-type guy" among the people who worked for him, a kind of storeroom bully. Isbell asked him about the arrangement with Leonyrd. "That's no big deal," Stine insisted. "Just spent the money while it was there. That's what it was put there for, to keep up the plant. That's what we did." It was not his idea, said Stine, but it was not really Leonyrd's either, just a discussion and an informal decision. The storeroom receiving supervisor agreed it was a grand idea and made out the documents as he was told. Accounting personnel processed the invoices as they were told. A part-time bookkeeper said to Isbell she remembered some discussion about arranging to spend the money, but she did not ask any questions.

Isbell was in a funny position, a little bit like Shakespeare's Malvolio, who spends his time in the play *Twelfth Night* scolding the other characters for having such a good time. Leonyrd had not pocketed anything, and neither had Stine; being a bully was hardly a fraudulent offense. There was about $6,000 in interest lost, supposing the money had stayed in company bank accounts, but that was not exactly the point. More seriously, this effortless cash flow diversion represented a kink in the handling and dispersal of funds. Isbell was not thinking rules for their own sake or standing on ceremony—money this easy to come by just meant the company had gotten a break. The next guys might not be so civic-minded and selfless; they might start juggling zeros and signatures instead of dates.

Under Isbell's recommendation, the receiving department started reporting directly to the plant's general accounting division, and its supervisor was assigned elsewhere. Doggett Stine had subsequently retired. Steven Leonyrd was demoted and transferred to another sector; he was fired a year later for an unrelated scheme. He had approached a contractor to replace the roof on his house, with the bill to be charged against "nonrecurring maintenance" at the plant. But the contractor alerted plant officials to their conniving employee, who was also known to be picking up extra money for "consulting work" with plant-related businesses. *Rats*, Leonyrd must have thought, *foiled again*.

CONCEALED LIABILITIES AND EXPENSES

As previously discussed, understating liabilities and expenses is one of the ways that financial statements can be manipulated to make a company appear more profitable. Because pretax income will increase by the full amount of the expense or liability not recorded, this financial statement fraud method can have a significant impact on reported earnings with relatively little effort by the fraudster. This method is much easier to commit than falsifying many sales transactions. Missing transactions are generally harder for auditors to detect than improperly recorded ones because there is no audit trail.

There are three common methods for concealing liabilities and expenses:

1. Liability/expense omissions
2. Capitalized expenses
3. Failure to disclose warranty costs and liabilities

Liability/Expense Omissions

The preferred and easiest method of concealing liabilities/expenses is to simply fail to record them. Multimillion-dollar judgments against the company from a recent court decision might be conveniently ignored. Vendor invoices might be thrown away (they will send another later) or stuffed into drawers rather than being posted into the accounts payable system, thereby increasing reported earnings by the full amount of the invoices. In a retail environment, debit memos might be created for chargebacks to vendors, supposedly to claim permitted rebates or allowances but sometimes just to create additional income. These items may or may not be properly recorded in a subsequent accounting period, but that does not change the fraudulent nature of the current financial statements.

One of the highest-profile liability omission cases of recent vintage involved Adelphia Communications, which in July 2002 was charged by the SEC with, among other things, fraudulently excluding over $2.3 billion in bank debt from its consolidated financial statements. According to the complaint filed by the SEC, Adelphia's founder and his three sons fraudulently excluded the liabilities from the company's annual and quarterly consolidated financial statements by deliberately shifting those liabilities onto the books of Adelphia's off-balance-sheet, unconsolidated affiliates. Failure to record this debt violated GAAP requirements and precipitated a series of misrepresentations about those liabilities by Adelphia and the defendants, including the creation of sham transactions backed by fictitious documents to give the false appearance that Adelphia actually had repaid debts when, in truth, it had simply shifted them to unconsolidated entities controlled by the founder and to misleading financial statements that, in their footnotes, gave the false impression that liabilities listed in the company's financials included all outstanding bank debt.

Often perpetrators of liability and expense omissions believe they can conceal their fraud in future periods. They often plan to compensate for their omitted liabilities with visions of other income sources, such as profits from future price increases.

Just as they are easy to conceal, omitted liabilities are probably one of the most difficult financial statement schemes to uncover. A thorough review of all post–financial statement date transactions, such as accounts payable increases and decreases, can aid in the discovery of omitted liabilities in financial statements, as can a computerized analysis of expense records. Additionally, if the auditor requested and was granted unrestricted access to the client's files, a physical search could turn up concealed invoices and unposted liabilities. Probing interviews of accounts payable and other personnel can reveal unrecorded or delayed items too.

Capitalized Expenses

Capital expenditures are costs that provide a benefit to a company over more than one accounting period. Manufacturing equipment is an example of this type of expenditure. Revenue expenditures or *expenses* directly correspond to the generation of current revenue and provide benefits only for the current accounting period. An example of expenses is labor costs for one week of service. These costs correspond directly with revenues billed in the current accounting period.

Capitalizing revenue-based expenses is another way to increase income and assets since they are amortized over a period of years rather than expensed immediately. If expenditures are capitalized as assets and not expensed during the current period, income will be overstated. As the assets are depreciated, income in subsequent periods will be understated.

The improper capitalization of expenses was one of the key methods of financial statement fraud alleged to have been used by WorldCom, Inc. in its high-profile fraud that came to light in early 2002. According to a complaint filed by the SEC, WorldCom materially overstated the income it reported on its financial statements by approximately $9 billion, mainly using two methods. First, WorldCom reduced its operating expenses by improperly releasing as a credit to operating expenses certain provisions previously established for line costs and for taxes. Second, it improperly reduced its operating expenses by recharacterizing certain expenses as capital assets. Much of the $9 billion related to improper accounting for "line costs," which were among World-Com's major operating expenses. By improperly reducing provisions held against "line costs" and by transferring certain "line costs" to its capital asset accounts, WorldCom falsely portrayed itself as a profitable business when it was not and concealed large losses. These improper accounting practices were designed to and did inflate income to correspond with estimates by Wall Street analysts and to support the price of WorldCom's stock.

Expensing Capital Expenditures

Just as capitalizing expenses is improper, so is expensing costs that should be capitalized. An organization may want to minimize its net income due to tax considerations, or to increase earnings in future periods. Expensing an item that should be depreciated over a period of time would help accomplish just that—net income is lower and so are taxes.

Returns and Allowances and Warranties

Improper recording of sales returns and allowances occurs when a company fails to properly record or present the expense associated with sales returns and customer allowances stemming from customer dissatisfaction. It is inevitable that a certain percentage of products sold will, for one reason or another, be returned. When this happens, management must record the related expense as a contra sales account, which reduces the amount of net sales presented on the company's income statement.

Likewise, when a company offers a warranty on product sales, it must estimate the amount of warranty expense it reasonably expects to incur over the warranty period and accrue a liability for that amount. In warranty liability fraud, the warranty liability usually is either omitted altogether or substantially understated. Another similar area is the liability resulting from defective products (product liability).

Red Flags Associated with Concealed Liabilities and Expenses

- Recurring negative cash flows from operations or an inability to generate cash flows from operations while reporting earnings and earnings growth
- Assets, liabilities, revenues, or expenses based on significant estimates that involve subjective judgments or uncertainties that are difficult to corroborate
- Nonfinancial management's excessive participation in or preoccupation with the selection of accounting principles or the determination of significant estimates
- Unusual increase in gross margin or margin in excess of industry peers
- Allowances for sales returns, warranty claims, and the like that are shrinking in percentage terms or are otherwise out of line with industry peers
- Unusual reduction in the number of days purchases remain in accounts payable
- Reducing accounts payable while competitors are stretching out payments to vendors

IMPROPER DISCLOSURES

As discussed earlier, accounting principles require that financial statements and notes include all the information necessary to prevent a reasonably discerning user of the financial statements from being misled. The notes should include narrative disclosures, supporting schedules, and any other information required to avoid misleading potential investors, creditors, or any other users of the financial statements.

Management has an obligation to disclose all significant information appropriately in the financial statements and in management's discussion and analysis. In addition, the disclosed information must not be misleading. Improper disclosures relating to financial statement fraud usually involve:

- Liability omissions
- Subsequent events
- Management fraud
- Related party transactions
- Accounting changes

Liability Omissions

Typical omissions include the failure to disclose loan covenants or contingent liabilities. Loan covenants are agreements, in addition to or part of a financing arrangement, that a borrower has promised to keep as long as the financing is in place. The agreements can contain various types of covenants including certain financial ratio limits and restrictions on other major financing arrangements. Contingent liabilities are potential obligations that will materialize only if certain events occur in the future. A corporate guarantee of personal loans taken out by an officer or a private company controlled by an officer is an example of a contingent liability. The company's potential liability, if material, must be disclosed.

Subsequent Events

Events occurring or becoming known after the close of the period may have a significant effect on the financial statements and should be disclosed. Fraudsters typically avoid disclosing court judgments and regulatory decisions that undermine the reported values of assets, indicate unrecorded liabilities, or adversely reflect on management integrity. Public record searches can reveal this information.

Management Fraud

Management has an obligation to disclose to the shareholders significant fraud committed by officers, executives, and others in positions of trust. Withholding such information from auditors likely also would involve lying to auditors, an illegal act in itself.

Related Party Transactions

Related party transactions occur when a company does business with another entity whose management or operating policies can be controlled or significantly influenced by the company or by some other party in common. There is nothing inherently wrong with related party transactions, as long as they are fully disclosed. If the transactions are not conducted on an arm's-length basis, the company may suffer economic harm, injuring stockholders.

The financial interest that a company official might have may not be readily apparent. For example, common directors of two companies that do business with each other, any corporate general partner and the partnerships with which it does business, and any controlling shareholder of the corporation with which he/she/it does business may be related parties. Family relationships also can be considered related parties. These relationships include all lineal descendants and ancestors, without regard to financial interests. Related party transactions sometimes are referred to as self-dealing. While these transactions are sometimes conducted at arm's length, they often are not.

In the highly publicized Tyco fraud case, which broke in 2002, the SEC charged former top executives of the company, including its former chief executive, L. Dennis Kozlowski, with failing to disclose to shareholders hundreds of millions of dollars of low-interest and interest-free loans they took from the company and, in some cases, never repaid. The SEC complaint alleged that three former executives, including Kozlowski, also sold shares of Tyco stock valued at millions of dollars while their self-dealing remained undisclosed. The complaint alleged numerous improper transactions, including Kozlowski's use of $242 million of loans for impermissible and unauthorized purposes, such as funding an extravagant lifestyle. With these un-disclosed loans, Kozlowski allegedly amassed millions of dollars in fine art, yachts, and estate jewelry as well as a $31 million Park Avenue apartment and a palatial estate in Nantucket. Kozlowski also allegedly engaged in undisclosed non–arm's-length real estate transactions with Tyco or its subsidiaries and received undisclosed compensation and perquisites including forgiveness of multimillion-dollar loans, rent-free use of large New York apartments, and use of corporate aircraft for personal purposes at little or no cost.

Accounting Changes

ASC 250, "Accounting Changes and Error Corrections," describes three types of accounting changes that must be disclosed to avoid misleading the user of financial statements: accounting principles, estimates, and reporting entities. Although the required treatment for each type of change is different, they are all susceptible to ma-nipulation by determined fraudster. For example, fraudsters may fail to properly retro-actively restate the financial statements for a change in accounting principle if the change causes the company's financial statements to appear weaker. Likewise, they may fail to disclose significant changes in estimates on the useful lives and estimated salvage values of depreciable assets or the estimates underlying the determination of warranty or other liabilities. They may even secretly change the reporting entity, by adding entities owned privately by management or excluding certain company-owned units, in order to improve reported results.

Red Flags Associated with Improper Disclosures

- Domination of management by a single person or small group (in a non–owner-managed business) without compensating controls
- Ineffective board of directors or audit committee oversight over the financial report-ing process and internal control
- Ineffective communication, implementation, support, or enforcement of the entity's values or ethical standards by management or the communication of inappropriate values or ethical standards
- Rapid growth or unusual profitability, especially compared to that of other compa-nies in the same industry
- Significant, unusual, or highly complex transactions, especially those close to period end that pose difficult substance-over-form questions
- Significant related party transactions not in the ordinary course of business or with related entities not audited or audited by another firm
- Significant bank accounts or subsidiary or branch operations in tax-haven jurisdic-tions for which there appears to be no clear business justification
- Overly complex organizational structure involving unusual legal entities or manage-rial lines of authority

- Known history of violations of securities laws or other laws and regulations, or claims against the entity, its senior management, or board members alleging fraud or violations of laws and regulations
- Recurring attempts by management to justify marginal or inappropriate accounting on the basis of materiality
- Formal or informal restrictions on the auditor that inappropriately limit access to people or information or the ability to communicate effectively with the board of directors or audit committee

IMPROPER ASSET VALUATION

Under the "lower of cost or market value" rule, where an asset's cost exceeds its current market value (as happens often with obsolete technology), it must be written down to market value. With the exception of certain securities, asset values are not increased to reflect current market value. Often it is necessary to use estimates in accounting. For example, estimates are used in determining the residual value and the useful life of a depreciable asset, the uncollectible portion of accounts receivable, or the excess or obsolete portion of inventory. Whenever estimates are used, there is an additional opportunity for fraud by manipulating those estimates.

Many schemes are used to inflate current assets at the expense of long-term assets. The net effect is seen in the current ratio. The misclassification of long-term assets as current assets can be of critical concern to lending institutions that often require the maintenance of certain financial ratios. This is of particular consequence when the loan covenants are on unsecured or undersecured lines of credit and other short-term borrowings. Sometimes these misclassifications are referred to as window dressing.

Most improper asset valuations involve the fraudulent overstatement of inventory or receivables. Other improper asset valuations include manipulation of the allocation of the purchase price of an acquired business in order to inflate future earnings, misclassification of fixed and other assets, or improper capitalization of inventory or start-up costs. Improper asset valuations usually fall into one of these categories:

- Inventory valuation
- Accounts receivable
- Business combinations
- Fixed assets

Inventory Valuation

Since inventory must be valued at the acquisition cost except when the cost is determined to be higher than the current market value, inventory should be written down to its current value or written off altogether if it has no value. Failing to write down inventory results in overstated assets and the mismatching of cost of goods sold with revenues. Inventory also can be stated improperly through the manipulation of the physical inventory count, by inflating the unit costs used to price out inventory, by failing to relieve inventory for costs of goods sold, or by other methods. Fictitious inventory schemes usually involve the creation of fake documents, such as inventory count sheets, receiving reports, and similar items. Companies even have programmed special computer reports of inventory for auditors that incorrectly added up the line item values so as to inflate the overall inventory balance. Computer-assisted audit techniques can help auditors significantly to detect many of these inventory fraud techniques. One case involved an inventory valuation scheme in which the fraud was committed through tampering with the inventory count. During a routine audit of a publicly traded medical supply company, the audit team found a misstatement of the inventory value that could hardly be classified as routine. The client's inventory was measured in metric volumes. Apparently, as the count was taken, an employee arbitrarily moved the decimal unit. This resulted in the inventory being grossly overstated. The discovery forced the company to restate its financial statements, resulting in a write-down of the inventory amount by more than $1.5 million.

One of the most popular methods of overstating inventory is through fictitious (phantom) inventory. For example, in one case, a certified fraud examiner (CFE) conducting a systems control review at a large cannery and product wholesaler in the Southwest observed a forklift driver constructing a large facade of finished product in a remote location of the warehouse. The inventory was cordoned off and a sign indicated that it was earmarked for a national food processor. The cannery was supposedly warehousing the inventory until requested by the customer. When the CFE investigated, he discovered that the inventory held for the food processor was later resold to a national fast food supplier.

A review of the accounts receivable aging report indicated sales of approximately $1.2 million to this particular customer in prior months, and the aging also showed that cash receipts had been applied against those receivables. An analysis of ending inventory above failed to reveal any improprieties because the relief of inventory had been properly recorded with cost of sales. Copies of all sales documents to this particular customer were then requested. The product was repeatedly sold free on board (FOB) shipping point and title had passed. But bills of lading indicated that only $200,000 of inventory had been shipped to the original purchaser. There should have been $1 million of finished product on hand for the food processor. However, there was nothing behind the facade of finished products. An additional comparison of bin numbers on the bill of lading with the sales documents revealed that the same product had been sold twice.

The corporate controller was notified and the plant manager questioned. He explained that "he was doing as he was told." The vice president of marketing and the vice president of operations both knew of the situation but felt there was "no impropriety." The chief financial officer (CFO) and president of the company felt differently and fired the vice presidents. The company eventually was forced into bankruptcy.

Accounts Receivable

Accounts receivable are subject to manipulation in the same manner as sales and inventory, and in many cases, the schemes are conducted together. The two most common schemes involving accounts receivable are fictitious receivables and failure to write off accounts receivable as bad debts (or failure to establish an adequate allowance for bad debts). Fictitious receivables commonly arise from fictitious revenues, discussed earlier. Accounts receivable should be reported at net realizable value—that is, the amount of the receivable less amounts expected not to be collected.

Fictitious Accounts Receivable

Fictitious accounts receivable are common among companies with financial problems as well as with managers who receive a commission based on sales. The typical entry under fictitious accounts receivable is to debit (increase) accounts receivable and credit (increase) sales. Of course, these schemes are more common around the end of the accounting period, since accounts receivable are expected to be paid in cash within a reasonable time. Fraudsters commonly attempt to conceal fictitious accounts receivable by providing false confirmations of balances to auditors. They get the audit confirmations because the mailing address they provide for the phony customers is typically a mailbox under their control, a home address, or the business address of a co-conspirator. Such schemes can be detected by using satellite imaging software, business credit reports, public records, or even the telephone book to identify significant customers who have no physical existence or no apparent business need for the product sold to them.

Failure to Write Down

Companies are required to accrue losses on uncollectible receivables when the criteria in FASB ASC 450, "Contingencies," are met and to record impairment of long-lived assets and goodwill under FASB ASC 350, "Intangibles–Goodwill and Other." Companies struggling for profits and income may be tempted to omit the recognition of such losses because of the negative impact on income.

Business Combinations

Companies are required to allocate the purchase price they have paid to acquire another business to the tangible and intangible assets of that business. Any excess of the purchase price over the value of the acquired assets is treated as goodwill. Changes in goodwill accounting have decreased the incentive for companies to allocate an excessive amount to purchased assets to minimize the amount allocated to goodwill that previously was required to be amortized and that reduced future earnings. However, companies still may be tempted to overallocate the purchase price to in-process research and development assets, in order to write them off immediately. Or they may establish excessive reserves for various expenses at the time of acquisition, intending to release those excess reserves quietly into earnings at a future date.

Fixed Assets

Fixed assets are subject to manipulation through several different schemes. Some of the more common schemes are:

- Booking fictitious assets
- Misrepresenting asset valuation
- Improperly capitalizing inventory and start-up costs

Booking Fictitious Assets

One of the easiest methods of asset misrepresentation is in the recording of fictitious assets. This false creation of assets affects account totals on a company's balance sheet. The corresponding account commonly used is the owners' equity account. Because company assets often are physically found in many different locations, this fraud sometimes is easy to overlook. One of the most common fictitious asset schemes is simply to create fictitious documents. In one example, a real estate development and mortgage financing company produced fraudulent statements that included fictitious and inflated asset amounts and illegitimate receivables. The company also recorded expenses that actually were for personal, instead of business, use. To cover the fraud, the company raised cash through various illegal securities offerings, guaranteeing over $110 million with real estate projects. The company subsequently defaulted on those loans. The company declared bankruptcy shortly before the owner passed away.

In other instances, equipment is leased, not owned, yet that the fact is not disclosed during the audit of fixed assets. Bogus fixed assets sometimes can be detected because the fixed asset addition makes no business sense.

Misrepresenting Asset Valuation

Fixed assets should be recorded at cost. Although assets may appreciate in value, this increase in value should not be recognized on company financial statements. Many financial statement frauds have involved the reporting of fixed assets at market values instead of the lower acquisition costs or at even higher inflated values with phony valuations to support them. Further, companies may falsely inflate the value of fixed assets by failing to record impairments of long-lived assets and of goodwill as required by FASB ASC 350, "Intangibles—Goodwill and Other." Misrepresentation of asset values frequently goes hand in hand with other schemes.

One of the highest-profile asset valuation fraud cases of recent years involved former Enron CFO Andrew S. Fastow. In October 2002, the SEC filed a civil enforcement action against Fastow, who also faced criminal charges relating to an alleged self-enriching scheme to defraud Enron's security holders through use of certain off-balance-sheet entities. One of the six transactions in the SEC's complaint against Fastow was Raptor I/Avici. According to the complaint, Enron and the Fastow-controlled partnership LJM2 engaged in complex transactions with an entity called Raptor I.

Raptor I was used to manipulate Enron's balance sheet and income statement and to generate profits for LJM2 and Fastow at Enron's expense. In September 2000, Fastow and others used Raptor I to effectuate a fraudulent hedging transaction and thus avoid a decrease in the value of Enron's investment in the stock of a public company called Avici Systems Inc. Specifically, Fastow and others backdated documents to make it appear that Enron locked in the value of its investment in Avici in August 2000, when Avici's stock was trading at its all-time high price.

Understating Assets

In some cases, as with some government-related or government-regulated companies in which additional funding often is based on asset amounts, it may be advantageous to understate assets. This understatement can be done directly or through improper depreciation. In one case, for example, the management of the company falsified its financial statements by manipulating the depreciation of the fixed assets. The depreciation reserve was accelerated by the amount of $2.9 million over a six-month period. The purpose of the scheme was to avoid cash contributions to a central government capital asset acquisition account.

Capitalizing Nonasset Costs

Excluded from the cost of a purchased asset are interest and finance charges incurred in the purchase. For example, as a company finances a capital equipment purchase, monthly payments include both principal liability reduction and interest payments. On initial purchase, only the original cost of the asset should be capitalized. The subsequent interest payments should be charged to interest expense and not to the asset. Without reason for intensive review, fraud of this type can go unchecked. In one case, a new investor in a closely held corporation sued for rescission of purchase of stock, alleging that the company compiled financial information that misrepresented the financial history of the business. A fraud examination uncovered assets that were overvalued due to capitalization of interest expenses and other finance charges. Also discovered was the fact that one of the owners was understating revenue by $150,000 and embezzling the funds. The parties subsequently settled out of court.

Misclassifying Assets

In order to meet budget requirements, and for various other reasons, assets sometimes are misclassified into general ledger accounts in which they do not belong. The manipulation can skew financial ratios and help comply with loan covenants or other borrowing requirements. In one example, a purchasing employee at a retail jewelry firm feared being called to the carpet on some bad jewelry purchases. Instead of taking the blame for bad margins on many items, the employee arbitrarily redistributed costs of shipments to individual inventory accounts. The cover-up did not take; the company's CFO detected the fraud after he initiated changes to control procedures. When the CFO created a separation of duties between the buying function and the costing activities, the dishonest employee was discovered and terminated.

Red Flags Associated with Improper Asset Valuation

- Recurring negative cash flows from operations or an inability to generate cash flows from operations while reporting earnings and earnings growth
- Significant declines in customer demand and increasing business failures in either the industry or the overall economy
- Assets, liabilities, revenues, or expenses based on significant estimates that involve subjective judgments or uncertainties that are difficult to corroborate
- Nonfinancial management's excessive participation in or preoccupation with the selection of accounting principles or the determination of significant estimates
- Unusual increase in gross margin or margin in excess of industry peers
- Unusual growth in the number of days sales in receivables
- Unusual growth in the number of days purchases in inventory
- Allowances for bad debts, excess and obsolete inventory, and so on that are shrinking in percentage terms or that are otherwise out of line with those of industry peers
- Unusual change in the relationship between fixed assets and depreciation
- Adding to assets while competitors are reducing capital tied up in assets

DETECTION OF FRAUDULENT FINANCIAL STATEMENT SCHEMES

SAS 99 (AU 316)—"Consideration of Fraud in a Financial Statement Audit"

In response to the high-profile financial frauds that occurred in 2001 and 2002, the Auditing Standards Board of the American Institute of Certified Public Accountants replaced the existing fraud audit standard—Statement on Auditing Standards (SAS) No. 82—with SAS 99 (AU 316), "Consideration of Fraud in a Financial Statement Audit" to give expanded guidance to auditors for detecting material fraud. SAS 99 was an attempt to restore investor confidence in U.S. capital markets and audited financial statements.

SAS No. 1 (AU 110), "Responsibilities and Functions of the Independent Auditor," states: "The auditor has a responsibility to plan and perform the audit to obtain reasonable assurance about whether the financial statements are free of material misstatement, whether caused by error or fraud." The purpose of SAS No. 99 (AU 316) is to "establish standards and provide guidance to auditors in fulfilling that responsibility." It is divided into ten main sections:

1. Description and characteristics of fraud
2. Importance of exercising professional skepticism
3. Discussion among engagement personnel regarding risk of material misstatement due to fraud
4. Obtaining information needed to identify risks of material misstatements due to fraud
5. Identifying risks that may result in material misstatements due to fraud

6. Assessing the identified risks after evaluating the entity's programs and controls
7. Responding to the results of the assessment
8. Evaluating audit evidence
9. Communicating about fraud to management, the audit committee, and others
10. Documenting the auditor's consideration of fraud

A brief description of each of these sections is presented next.

Description and Characteristics of Fraud

This section emphasizes that the auditor should be interested in acts that result in a material misstatement of the financial statements. Misstatements can be the result of fraud or error, depending on whether the misstatement was intentional or unintentional.

Two types of misstatements are considered relevant for audit purposes:

1. Misstatements arising from fraudulent financial reporting
2. Misstatements arising from misappropriation of assets

Misstatements Arising from Fraudulent Financial Reporting

This category is defined as intentional misstatements or omissions of amounts or disclosures in financial statements that are "designed to deceive financial statement users." Fraudulent financial reporting may be accomplished by:

- Manipulation, falsification, or alteration of accounting records or supporting documents
- Misrepresentation or intentional omission of events, transactions, or other significant information
- Intentional misapplication of accounting principles relating to amounts, classification, manner of presentation, or disclosure

Misstatements Arising from Misappropriation of Assets

Also referred to as theft or defalcation, this category includes the theft of an entity's assets such that the effect of the theft causes the financial statements, in all material respects, not to be in conformity with GAAP.

This section goes on to remind the auditor that, by definition, fraud often is concealed, and managers are in a position to perpetrate fraud more easily because they are in the position of being able to manipulate accounting records directly or indirectly. Auditors cannot obtain absolute assurance that material misstatements are not present, but they should be aware of the possibility that fraud may be concealed and that employees may be in collusion with each other or with outside vendors. If the auditors notice records or activity that seem unusual, they should at least consider the possibility that fraud may have occurred.

Importance of Exercising Professional Skepticism

SAS 1 (AU 110) states that due professional care requires the auditor to exercise professional skepticism. Because of the characteristics of fraud, the auditor should conduct the engagement "with a mind-set that recognizes the possibility that a material misstatement due to fraud could be present." An "ongoing questioning" of whether information the auditor obtains could suggest a material misstatement due to fraud also is required.

Discussion among Engagement Personnel Regarding Risk of Material Misstatement Due to Fraud

Prior to or in conjunction with the information-gathering procedures to be discussed, the members of the audit team should discuss the potential for material misstatements due to fraud. The discussion should include "brainstorming" among the audit team members about:

- How and where they believe the entity's financial statement might be susceptible to fraud
- How management could perpetrate or conceal fraud
- How assets of the entity could be misappropriated

This discussion also should include a consideration of known external and internal factors affecting the entity that might:

- Create incentives/pressures for management and others to commit fraud
- Provide the opportunity for fraud to be perpetrated
- Indicate a culture or environment that enables management and others to rationalize committing fraud

The discussion also should emphasize the need to maintain "a questioning mind" in gathering and evaluating evidence throughout the audit and to obtain additional information if necessary.

Obtaining Information Needed to Identify Risks of Material Misstatements Due to Fraud

SAS No. 108 (AU 311), "Communications between Predecessor and Successor Auditors," provides guidance on how the auditor obtains knowledge about the entity's business and industry. As part of that process, auditors should perform four procedures to obtain information to use in identifying the risks of material misstatement due to fraud:

1. Make inquiries of management and others within the entity to obtain their views about the risks of fraud and how they are addressed.

2. Consider any unusual or unexpected relationships that have been identified in performing analytical procedures in planning the audit.

3. Consider whether one or more fraud risk factors exist.

4. Consider other information that may be helpful in the identification of risks of material misstatement due to fraud.

Obtaining the Views of Management and Others within the Entity about the Risks of Fraud and How They Are Addressed

This step involves asking management about a number of issues, including:

- Whether management has knowledge of fraud or suspected fraud
- Management's understanding of the risk of fraud
- Programs and controls the entity has established to help prevent, deter, or detect fraud
- Whether and how management communicates to employees its views on business practices and ethical behavior

Auditors also should question the audit committee directly about its views concerning the risk of fraud and whether the committee has knowledge of fraud or suspected fraud. Auditors should do the same with the company's internal audit department.

Additionally, auditors may need to conduct similar inquiries of the entity's other personnel if they believe others may have additional information about the risks of fraud.

Considering the Results of Analytical Procedures Performed in Planning the Audit

SAS 99 (AU 316) requires that analytical procedures be performed in planning the audit with an objective of identifying the existence of unusual transactions or events, and amounts, ratios, and trends that might indicate matters "that have financial statement and audit planning implications." If the results of these procedures yield unusual or unexpected relationships, the auditor should consider the results in identifying the risks of material misstatement due to fraud.

Considering Fraud Risk Factors

As discussed, even though fraud is concealed, auditors may identify events or conditions that indicate incentives or pressures to commit fraud, opportunities to carry out fraud, or attitudes and rationalizations to justify fraudulent conduct. These events and conditions are referred to as fraud risk factors. Auditors should determine whether one or more of the fraud risk factors are present and should be considered in identifying and assessing the risks of material misstatement due to fraud. The appendix to SAS 99 (AU 316) contains a list of examples of fraud risk factors.

Considering Other Information

Finally, auditors also should consider any other information that they feel may be helpful in identifying the risks of material misstatement.

Identifying Risks that May Result in Material Misstatements Due to Fraud

After gathering the information as discussed previously, auditors should consider the information in the context of the three conditions present when fraud occurs—incentives/pressures, opportunities, and attitudes/rationalizations. Auditors should consider:

- The *type* of risk that may exist, that is, whether it involves fraudulent financial reporting or misappropriation of assets
- The *significance* of the risk, that is, whether it is of a magnitude that could result in a possible material misstatement
- The *likelihood* of the risk, that is, the likelihood that it will result in a material misstatement
- The *pervasiveness* of the risk, that is, whether the potential risk is pervasive to the financial statement as a whole or is specifically related to a particular assertion, account, or class of transactions

Assessing the Identified Risks after Evaluating the Entity's Programs and Controls

Auditors must obtain an understanding of each of the components of internal control sufficient to plan the audit. As part of this step, auditors should evaluate whether the entity's programs and controls that address identified risks of fraud have been suitably designed and placed in operation. These programs and controls may involve:

- Specific controls designed to mitigate specific risks of fraud (e.g., controls to prevent misappropriation of particular, susceptible assets)
- Broader programs designed to prevent, deter, and detect fraud (e.g., ethics policies)

Exhibit I of SAS 99 (AU 316) provides examples of programs and controls an entity might implement to create a culture of honesty and to prevent fraud.

Responding to the Results of the Assessment

Once auditors have gathered the information and assessed the risk of fraud, they must determine what impact the assessment will have on how the audit is conducted. For example, auditors may need to design additional or different auditing procedures to obtain more reliable evidence in support of account balances or transactions, or obtain additional corroboration of management's explanations and representations concerning material matters (such as third-party confirmation, documentation from independent sources, use of a specialist, analytical procedures, etc.).

Overall Responses to the Risk of Material Misstatement

Judgments about the risk of material misstatement due to fraud have an overall effect on how the audit is conducted in several ways:

- *Assignment of personnel and supervision.* Auditors may need to consult with specialists in a particular field.
- *Accounting principles.* Auditors should consider management's selection and application of significant accounting principles, particularly those related to subjective measurements and complex transactions.
- *Predictability of auditing procedures.* Auditors should incorporate an "element of unpredictability" in the selection of auditing procedures to be performed, such as using differing sampling methods at different locations or at locations on an unannounced basis.

Responses Involving Procedures Performed to Address the Identified Risks

This section notes that the auditing procedures performed in response to identified risks will vary depending on the type of risks identified. Such procedures may involve both substantive tests and tests of the operating effectiveness of the entity's programs and controls. However, because management may have the ability to override controls that otherwise may appear to be operating effectively, it is unlikely that the audit risk can be reduced appropriately by performing only tests of controls.

Therefore, auditors' responses to specifically identified risks of fraud should include:

- Changing the *nature* of the auditing procedures to obtain more reliable or additional corroborative information (i.e., through independent sources or physical inspection)
- Changing the *timing* of substantive tests (e.g., an auditor may conduct substantive tests at or near the end of the reporting period)
- Making the *extent* of the procedures reflect the assessment of the risk of fraud (i.e., increasing the sample sizes or performing analytical procedures at a more detailed level)

SAS 99 (AU 316) provides a number of examples of responses auditors may take in regard to risks of misstatements arising from both fraudulent financial reporting and asset misappropriation. Some of the examples concerning fraudulent financial reporting include:

- *Revenue recognition*—performing substantive analytical procedures relating to revenue using disaggregated data (e.g., comparing revenue reported by month and by product line during the current reporting period with comparable prior periods), confirming with customers relevant contract terms, or questioning staff about shipments near the end of a period
- *Inventory quantities*—examining inventory records to identify locations or items that require specific attention during or after the physical inventory count, more

rigorous examination of the count such as by examining contents of boxed items, or additional testing of count sheets, tags, or other records

- *Management estimates*— depending on the situation, engaging a specialist or developing an independent estimate for comparison to management's estimate; gathering further information may help the auditor evaluate the reasonableness of management's estimates and underlying assumptions

If auditors identify a risk of material misstatement due to fraud relating to misappropriation of assets, they may wish to include additional procedures. For example, if a particular asset is highly susceptible to misappropriation, they may wish to conduct further testing of the controls to prevent and detect such misappropriation.

Responses to Further Address Risk of Management Override of Controls

Because management is in a unique position to override existing controls, if such a risk is identified, auditors may need to perform further procedures to address the risk of management override of controls.

Examining Journal Entries and Other Adjustments for Evidence of Possible Material Misstatement Due to Fraud

Material misstatements of financial statements often involve recording inappropriate or unauthorized journal entries or making adjustments to amounts reported in the financial statements that are not reflected in journal entries (i.e., consolidating adjustments or reclassifications). Therefore, auditors should design procedures to test the appropriateness of journal entries recorded in the general ledger and other adjustments (i.e., entries posted directly to financial statement drafts).

Reviewing Accounting Estimates for Biases that Could Result in Material Misstatement Due to Fraud

In preparing financial statements, management is responsible for making a number of judgments or assumptions that affect significant accounting estimates. Fraudulent financial reporting often is accomplished through intentional misstatement of these estimates. In performing the audit, auditors should consider whether the differences between estimates supported by the audit evidence and the estimates included in the financial statements indicate a possible bias on the part of management. If so, auditors should perform a retrospective review of significant accounting estimates of the prior year. This review should provide auditors with additional information about whether management may have a bias in presenting the current-year estimates.

Evaluating the Business Rationale for Significant Unusual Transactions

During the course of an audit, auditors may become aware of significant transactions that are outside the normal course of the entity's business or appear unusual, given their understanding of the entity's operations. Auditors should gain an understanding of the business rationale for these transactions and whether the rationale (or lack thereof) suggests that the transactions may have been entered into to engage in fraudulent financial reporting or to conceal misappropriation of assets. Some factors to be considered include:

- Are the transactions overly complex?
- Has management discussed the transactions with the board of directors and audit committee?
- Has management placed more emphasis on the need for a particular accounting treatment than on the underlying economics of the particular transaction?
- Do the transactions involve unconsolidated, unrelated parties (including special-purpose entities) or parties that do not have the substance or the financial strength to support the transaction?

Evaluating Audit Evidence

Assessing Risks of Material Misstatement Due to Fraud throughout the Audit

During the performance of the audit, auditors may identify conditions that either change or support a judgment regarding the assessment of risks. Examples include:

- Discrepancies in the accounting records (i.e., transactions that are not recorded, un-supported or unauthorized balances or transactions, or last-minute adjustments)
- Conflicting or missing evidential matter (i.e., missing or altered documents/records, unexplained items or reconciliations, or missing inventory)
- Problematic or unusual relationships between the auditor and management (i.e., denial of access to records, facilities, employees, or customers; complaints by management about the conduct of the audit team; unusual delays in providing information; or unwillingness to add or revise disclosures)

Evaluating Whether Analytical Procedures Performed Indicate
a Previously Unrecognized Risk of Fraud

Analytical procedures performed during the audit may result in identifying unusual or unexpected relationships that should be considered in assessing the risk of material misstatement due to fraud. Determining whether a particular trend or relationship is a risk of fraud requires professional judgment. Unusual relationships involving year-end revenue and income often are particularly relevant and might include uncharacteristically large amounts of income reported in the last week or two of the reporting period from unusual transactions and income that is inconsistent with trends in cash flow from operations.

Analytical procedures are useful because management or employees generally are unable to manipulate all the information necessary to produce normal or expected relationships. SAS 99 (AU 316) provides several examples, including:

- The relationship of net income to cash flows from operations may appear unusual because management recorded fictitious revenues and receivables but was unable to manipulate cash.
- Changes in inventory, accounts payable, sales, or costs of sales from the prior period to the current period may be inconsistent, indicating a possible theft of inventory because the employee was unable to manipulate all of the related accounts.
- An unexpected or unexplained relationship between sales volume as determined from the accounting records and production statistics maintained by operations personnel (which is more difficult for management to manipulate) may indicate a possible misstatement of sales.

Evaluating Risks of Material Misstatement at or near the Completion of Fieldwork

At or near the completion of fieldwork, auditors should evaluate whether the accumulated results of auditing procedures and other observations affect the assessment of risk of material misstatements due to fraud made earlier. Such an evaluation may identify whether there is a need to perform further audit procedures.

Responding to Misstatements that May Be the Result of Fraud

If auditors believe that misstatements are or may be the result of fraud but the effect of the misstatements is not material to the financial statements, they nevertheless should evaluate the implications, especially those dealing with the ''organizational position'' of the person involved, which may require a reevaluation of the assessment of the risk of material misstatement. An example is theft of cash from a small petty cash fund. The amount of the theft generally would not be of significance to auditors, but if the theft was perpetrated by higher-level management, it may be indicative of a more pervasive problem, such as management integrity.

If auditors believe that a misstatement is or may be the result of fraud, and either have determined that the effect of the misstatement is material to the financial statements or have been unable to evaluate whether the effect is material, they should:

- Attempt to obtain additional evidence to determine whether material fraud occurred and its effect on the financial statements.
- Consider the implications for other aspects of the audit.
- Discuss the matter and the approach for further investigation with an appropriate level of management that is at least one level above those involved, and with senior management and the audit committee.
- If appropriate, suggest the client consult with legal counsel.

Communicating about Fraud to Management, the Audit Committee, and Others

SAS 99 (AU 316) states: "Whenever an auditor has determined that there is evidence that fraud may exist, the matter should be brought to the attention of an appropriate level of management." It is considered appropriate to do so even if the matter might be considered inconsequential. Fraud involving senior management and fraud (by anyone) that causes a material misstatement should be reported directly to the audit committee.

If auditors have identified risks of material misstatement due to fraud that have continuing control implications, they also should consider whether these risks should be communicated to senior management and the audit committee. Conversely, auditors also should consider whether the absence of controls to deter, detect, or prevent fraud should be reported.

The disclosure of possible fraud to parties other than the client's senior management and its audit committee is ordinarily not part of an auditor's responsibility and may be precluded by the auditor's legal or ethical obligations of confidentiality, unless the matter is reflected in the auditor's report.

However, SAS 99 (AU 316) points out that there may be a duty to disclose the information to outside parties in these circumstances:

- To comply with certain legal and regulatory requirements (such as SEC rules)
- To a successor auditor pursuant to SAS 84 (AU 315), "Communications Between Predecessor and Successor Auditors"
- In response to a subpoena
- To a funding agency or other specified agency in accordance with the requirements for audits of entities that receive governmental financial assistance

Documenting the Auditor's Consideration of Fraud

SAS 99 (AU 316) concludes by requiring that auditors document:

- Discussion among engagement personnel regarding the susceptibility of the entity's financial statements to material misstatement due to fraud (including how and when the discussion occurred, the team members who participated, and the subject matter discussed)
- Procedures performed to obtain information necessary to identify and assess the risks of material misstatement due to fraud
- Specific risks of material misstatement due to fraud that were identified
- If the auditor has not identified improper revenue recognition as a risk, the reasons supporting the auditor's conclusion
- The results of the procedures performed to further address the risk of management override of controls
- Other conditions and analytical relationships that caused the auditor to believe that additional auditing procedures or other responses were required to address such risks
- The nature of the communication about fraud made to management or the audit committee

Financial Statement Analysis

Comparative financial statements provide information for current and past accounting periods. Accounts expressed in whole-dollar amounts yield a limited amount of information. The conversion of these numbers into ratios or percentages allows statement readers to analyze them based on their relationship to each other as well as to major changes in historical totals. In fraud detection and investigation, the determination of the reasons for relationships and changes in amounts can be important. These determinations are the red flags that point an examiner in the direction of possible fraud. If large enough, a fraudulent misstatement will affect the financial statements in such a way that relationships between the numbers become questionable. Many schemes are detected because the financial statements, when analyzed closely, do not make sense. Financial statement analysis includes:

- Vertical analysis
- Horizontal analysis
- Ratio analysis

Percentage Analysis: Vertical and Horizontal

Traditionally, there are two methods of percentage analysis of financial statements. *Vertical analysis* is a technique for analyzing the relationships between the items on an income statement, balance sheet, or statement of cash flows by expressing components as percentages. This method often is referred to as common sizing financial statements. In the vertical analysis of an income statement, net sales is assigned 100 percent; for a balance sheet, total assets are assigned 100 percent on the asset side and total liabilities and equity are expressed as 100 percent. All other items in each of the sections are expressed as a percentage of these numbers.

Horizontal analysis is a technique for analyzing the percentage change in individual financial statement items from one year to the next. The first period in the analysis is considered the base, and the changes in the subsequent periods are computed as a percentage of the base period. If more than two periods are presented, each period's changes are computed as a percentage of the preceding period. Like vertical analysis, this technique will not work for small, immaterial frauds.

Exhibit 13.2 is an example of financial statements that are analyzed by both horizontal and vertical analysis.

Vertical Analysis Discussion

Vertical analysis is the expression of the relationship or percentage of an item on a financial statement to a specific base item. In the example in Exhibit 13.2, vertical analysis of the income statement includes net sales as the base amount. All other items then are analyzed as a percentage of that total. Vertical analysis emphasizes the relationship of statement items within each accounting period. These relationships can be used with historical averages to determine statement anomalies.

In the example, we can observe that accounts payable is 29 percent of total liabilities. Historically we may find that this account averages slightly over 25 percent. In

Exhibit 13.2   Horizontal and Vertical Analysis

Balance Sheet	Vertical Analysis				Horizontal Analysis	
	Year One		Year Two		Change	%Change
Assets						
Current Assets						
Cash	45,000	14%	15,000	4%	(30,000)	−67%
Accts Receivable	150,000	45%	200,000	47%	50,000	33%
Inventory	75,000	23%	150,000	35%	75,000	100%
Fixed Assets (net)	60,000	18%	60,000	14%	—	0%
Total	330,000	100%	425,000	100%	95,000	29%
Accts Payable	95,000	29%	215,000	51%	120,000	126%
Long-term Debt	60,000	18%	60,000	14%	—	0%
Stockholder's Equity					—	
Common Stock	25,000	8%	25,000	6%	—	0%
Paid-in Capital	75,000	23%	75,000	18%	—	0%
Retained Earnings	75,000	23%	50,000	12%	(25,000)	−33%
Total	330,000	100%	425,000	100%	95,000	29%

Income Statement	Vertical Analysis				Horizontal Analysis	
	Year One		Year Two		Change	%Change
Net Sales	250,000	100%	450,000	100%	200,000	80%
Cost of Goods Sold	125,000	50%	300,000	67%	175,000	140%
Gross Margin	125,000	50%	150,000	33%	25,000	20%
Operating Expenses						
Selling Expenses	50,000	20%	75,000	17%	25,000	50%
Administrative Expenses	60,000	24%	100,000	22%	40,000	67%
Net Income	15,000	6%	(25,000)	−6%	(40,000)	−267%

Additional Information		
Average Net Receivables	155,000	210,000
Average Inventory	65,000	130,000
Average Assets	330,000	425,000

year 2, accounts payable increased to 51 percent. Although the change in the account total may be explainable through a correlation with a rise in sales, this significant rise might be a starting point in a fraud examination. Source documents should be examined to determine the cause of this percentage increase. With this type of examination, fraudulent activity may be detected. The same type of change can be seen as selling expenses decline as a part of sales in year 2 from 20 to 17 percent. Again, this change may be due to higher-volume sales or another bona fide situation. But close examination may point a fraud examiner to uncover fictitious sales, since accounts payable rose significantly without a corresponding increase in selling expenses.

Horizontal Analysis Discussion

Horizontal statement analysis uses percentage comparison from one accounting period to the next. The percentage change is calculated by dividing the amount of increase or decrease for each item by the base period amount. It is important to consider the amount of change as well as the percentage in horizontal comparisons. A 5 percent change in an account with a very large dollar amount actually may be much more of a change than a 50 percent change in an account with much less activity.

In the last example, it is very obvious that the 80 percent increase in sales has a much greater corresponding increase in cost of goods sold, which rose 140 percent. These accounts often are used to hide fraudulent expenses, withdrawals, or other illegal transactions.

Ratio Analysis

Ratio analysis is a means of measuring the relationship between two different financial statement amounts. The relationship and comparison are the keys to the analysis, which allows for internal evaluations using financial statement data. Traditionally, financial statement ratios are used in comparisons to an entity's industry average. They can be very useful in detecting red flags for a fraud examination. Because the financial ratios highlight a significant change in key areas of an organization from one year to the next, or over a period of years, it becomes obvious that there may be a problem. As in all other analyses, specific changes often can be explained by changes in the business operations. Changes in key ratios are not, in and of themselves, proof of any wrongdoing. Whenever a change in specific ratios is detected, the appropriate source accounts should be researched and examined in detail to determine whether fraud has occurred. For instance, a significant decrease in a company's current ratio may have resulted from an increase in current liabilities or a reduction in assets, both of which could be used to conceal fraud. Like the statement analysis discussed previously, the analysis of ratios is limited by its inability to detect fraud on a smaller, immaterial scale. Some key financial ratios include:

- Current ratio
- Quick ratio
- Receivable turnover
- Collection ratio
- Inventory turnover
- Average days inventory in stock
- Debt-to-equity ratio
- Profit margin
- Asset turnover

Many other kinds of financial ratios are analyzed in industry-specific situations, but the ratios just listed are ones that may lead to discovery of fraud. The calculations in Exhibit 13.3 are based on the sample financial statements presented earlier.

Interpretation of Financial Ratios

$$\text{Current Ratio} = \frac{\text{Current Assets}}{\text{Current Liabilities}}$$

Exhibit 13.3   Ratio Analysis

Ratio Analysis

Ratio	Calculation	Year 1	Year 2
Current Ratio	$\dfrac{\text{Current Assets}}{\text{Current Liabilities}}$	$\dfrac{270,000}{95,000} = 2.84$	$\dfrac{365,000}{215,000} = 1.70$
Quick Ratio	$\dfrac{\text{Cash} + \text{Securities} + \text{Receivables}}{\text{Current Liabilities}}$	$\dfrac{195,000}{95,000} = 2.05$	$\dfrac{215,000}{215,000} = 1.00$
Receivable Turnover	$\dfrac{\text{Net Sales on Account}}{\text{Average Net Receivables}}$	$\dfrac{250,000}{155,000} = 1.61$	$\dfrac{450,000}{210,000} = 2.14$
Collection Ratio	$\dfrac{365}{\text{Receivable Turnover}}$	$\dfrac{365}{1.61} = 226.30$	$\dfrac{365}{2.14} = 170.33$
Inventory Turnover	$\dfrac{\text{Cost of Goods Sold}}{\text{Average Inventory}}$	$\dfrac{125,000}{65,000} = 1.92$	$\dfrac{300,000}{130,000} = 2.31$
Average Number of Days Inventory in Stock	$\dfrac{365}{\text{Inventory Turnover}}$	$\dfrac{365}{1.92} = 189.80$	$\dfrac{365}{2.31} = 158.17$
Debt to Equity	$\dfrac{\text{Total Liabilities}}{\text{Total Equity}}$	$\dfrac{155,000}{175,000} = 0.89$	$\dfrac{275,000}{150,000} = 1.83$
Profit Margin	$\dfrac{\text{Net Income}}{\text{Net Sales}}$	$\dfrac{15,000}{250,000} = 0.06$	$\dfrac{(25,000)}{450,000} = (0.06)$
Asset Turnover	$\dfrac{\text{Net Sales}}{\text{Average Assets}}$	$\dfrac{250,000}{330,000} = 0.76$	$\dfrac{450,000}{425,000} = 1.06$

The current ratio—current assets divided by current liabilities—is probably the most used ratio in financial statement analysis. This comparison measures a company's ability to meet present obligations from its liquid assets. The number of times that current assets exceeds current liabilities has long been a quick measure of financial strength.

In detecting fraud, this ratio can be a prime indicator of manipulation of accounts. Embezzlement will cause the ratio to decrease. Liability concealment will cause a more favorable ratio.

In the case example, the drastic change in the current ratio from year 1 (2.84) to year 2 (1.70) should cause an examiner to look at these accounts in more detail. For instance, a billing scheme usually will result in a decrease in current assets—cash—which will in turn decrease the ratio.

$$\text{Quick Ratio} = \frac{\text{Cash} + \text{Securities} + \text{Receivables}}{\text{Current Liabilities}}$$

The quick ratio, often referred to as the acid test ratio, compares assets that can be liquidated immediately. In this calculation, the total of cash, securities, and receivables is divided by current liabilities. This ratio is a measure of a company's ability to meet sudden cash requirements. In turbulent economic times, it is used more often, giving the analyst a worst-case look at the company's working capital situation.

An examiner will analyze this ratio for fraud indicators. In year 1 of the example, the company balance sheet reflects a quick ratio of 2.05. This ratio drops in year 2 to 1.00. In this situation, a fraud affecting the quick ratio might be fictitious accounts receivable that have been added to inflate sales in one year. The ratio calculation will be abnormally high, and there will not be an offsetting current liability.

$$\text{Receivable Turnover} = \frac{\text{Net Sales on Account}}{\text{Average Net Receivables}}$$

"Receivable turnover" is defined as net sales divided by average net receivables. It measures the number of times accounts receivable is turned over during the accounting period. In other words, it measures the time between on-account sales and collection of funds. This ratio uses both income statement and balance sheet accounts in its analysis. If the fraud involves fictitious sales, this bogus income will never be collected. As a result, the turnover of receivables will decrease.

$$\text{Collection Ratio} = \frac{365}{\text{Receivable Turnover}}$$

Accounts receivable aging is measured by the collection ratio. This ratio divides 365 days by the receivable turnover ratio to arrive at the average number of days to collect receivables. In general, the lower the collection ratio, the faster receivables are collected. A fraud examiner may use this ratio as a first step in detecting fictitious receivables or larceny and skimming schemes. Normally, this ratio will stay fairly consistent from year to year, but changes in billing policies or collection efforts may cause a fluctuation. The example shows a favorable reduction in the collection ratio from 226.3 in year 1 to 170.33 in year 2. This means that the company is collecting its receivables more quickly in year 2 than in year 1.

$$\text{Inventory Turnover} = \frac{\text{Cost of Goods Sold}}{\text{Average Inventory}}$$

The relationship between a company's cost of goods sold and average inventory is shown through the inventory turnover ratio. This ratio measures the number of times inventory is sold during the period and is a good determinant of purchasing, production, and sales efficiency. In general, a higher inventory turnover ratio is considered more favorable. For example, if cost of goods sold has increased due to theft of inventory (ending inventory has declined, but not through sales), then this ratio will be abnormally high. In the case example, inventory turnover increases in year 2, signaling the possibility that an embezzlement is buried in the inventory account. An examiner should look at the changes in the components of the ratio to determine a direction in which to discover possible fraud.

$$\text{Average Number of Days Inventory Is in Stock} = \frac{365}{\text{Inventory Turnover}}$$

The ratio of the average number of days inventory is in stock is a restatement of the inventory turnover, expressed in days. This rate is important for several reasons. An increase in the number of days inventory stays in stock causes additional expenses, including storage costs, risk of inventory obsolescence, and market price reductions as well as interest and other expenses incurred due to tying up funds in inventory stock. Inconsistency or significant variance in this ratio is a red flag for fraud investigators. Examiners may use this ratio to examine inventory accounts for possible larceny schemes. Purchasing and receiving inventory schemes also can affect the ratio, and false debits to cost of goods sold will result in an increase in the ratio. Significant changes in the inventory turnover ratio are good indicators of possible fraudulent inventory activity.

$$\text{Debt-to-Equity Ratio} = \frac{\text{Total Liabilities}}{\text{Total Equity}}$$

The debt-to-equity ratio is computed by dividing total liabilities by total equity. This ratio is heavily considered by lending institutions. It provides a clear picture of the comparison between the long-term and short-term debt of the company and the owner's financial injection plus earnings to date. This balance of resources provided by creditors and what is provided by the owners is crucial when analyzing the financial status of a company. Debt-to-equity requirements often are included as borrowing covenants in corporate lending agreements. The example displays a year 1 ratio of 0.89 and a year 2 ratio of 1.83. The increase in the ratio corresponds with the rise in accounts payable. Sudden changes in this ratio may signal an examiner to look for fraud.

$$\text{Profit Margin} = \frac{\text{Net Income}}{\text{Net Sales}}$$

''Profit margin ratio'' is defined as net income divided by net sales. This ratio often is referred to as the efficiency ratio because it reveals profits earned per dollar of sales. The ratio of net income to sales relates not only to the effects of gross margin changes but also to charges to sales and administrative expenses. As fraud is committed, artificially inflated sales will not have a corresponding increase to cost of goods sold, net income will be overstated, and the profit margin ratio will be abnormally high. False expenses and fraudulent disbursements will cause an increase in expenses and a decrease in the profit margin ratio. Over time, this ratio should be fairly consistent.

$$\text{Asset Turnover} = \frac{\text{Net Sales}}{\text{Average Assets}}$$

Net sales divided by average operating assets is the calculation used to determine the asset turnover ratio. This ratio is used to determine the efficiency with which asset resources are utilized. The case example reflects a greater use of assets in year 2 than in year 1.

PREVENTION OF FINANCIAL STATEMENT FRAUD

Preventing financial statement fraud is more complex than preventing asset misappropriation and other frauds. Adding traditional internal controls is unlikely to be effective. As we saw earlier, the 1999 study by the Committee of Sponsoring Organizations of the Treadway Commission (COSO) indicated that either the CEO or the CFO was involved in 89 percent of the financial statement frauds studied. People at this high level can use their authority to override most internal controls, so those controls often will be of limited value in preventing financial statement fraud. A different approach is needed.

Following the principles of the fraud triangle, introduced in Chapter 1 of this book, a general approach to reducing financial statement fraud is to:

- Reduce pressures to commit financial statement fraud.
- Reduce the opportunity to commit financial statement fraud.
- Reduce rationalization of financial statement fraud.

Reduce Pressures to Commit Financial Statement Fraud

- Establish effective board oversight of the "tone at the top" created by management.
- Avoid setting unachievable financial goals.
- Avoid applying excessive pressure on employees to achieve goals.
- Change goals if changed market conditions require it.
- Ensure that compensation systems are fair and do not create too much incentive to commit fraud.
- Discourage excessive external expectations of future corporate performance.
- Remove operational obstacles blocking effective performance.

Reduce the Opportunity to Commit Financial Statement Fraud

- Maintain accurate and complete internal accounting records.
- Carefully monitor the business transactions and interpersonal relationships of suppliers, buyers, purchasing agents, sales representatives, and others who interface in the transactions between financial units.
- Establish a physical security system to secure company assets, including finished goods, cash, capital equipment, tools, and other valuable items.
- Divide important functions among employees, separating total control of one area.
- Maintain accurate personnel records including background checks on new employees.

- Encourage strong supervisory and leadership relationships within groups to ensure enforcement of accounting procedures.
- Establish clear and uniform accounting procedures with no exception clauses.

Reduce Rationalization of Financial Statement Fraud

- Promote strong values, based on integrity, throughout the organization.
- Have policies that clearly define prohibited behavior with respect to accounting and financial statement fraud.
- Provide regular training to all employees that explains prohibited behavior.
- Have confidential advice and reporting mechanisms to communicate inappropriate behavior.
- Have senior executives communicate to employees that integrity takes priority and that goals must never be achieved through fraud.
- Ensure management practices what it preaches and sets an example by promoting honesty in the accounting area. Dishonest acts by management, even if they are directed at someone outside the organization, create a dishonest environment that can spread to other business activities and other employees, internal and external.
- Clearly communicate the consequences of violating the rules and the punishment of violators.

Case Study: All on the Surface

Michael Weinstein* chuckled a lot. He smoked big cigars and laughed at the people who used to think he was just a chubby schmo. *Forbes* and *Business Week* stoked the fire with adoring articles. *Business Week* called Weinstein's Coated Sales, Inc., "the fourth fastest growing company in the country" and predicted greater returns to come. Of Coated Sales' 20 competitors, 11 were either defunct or absorbed. "The survivors," observed a writer in *Forbes*, "are more likely to cower than laugh when they see Weinstein." In a few years' time, revenues at Coated had jumped from $10 to $90 million per annum. The stock was peaking at eight times its opening price. "One of my goals," Weinstein stated dramatically, "is to see us be almost alone."

Which didn't take long. Weinstein's auditors walked out on him. The Big Six firm resigned and announced publicly it had no trust in the management of Coated Sales. Senior management scrambled en masse to get out of the way. Weinstein was suspended. New people started looking at the books. In two months, Coated Sales was filing for bankruptcy. The last laugh fell hollow down the empty hallways.

Michael Weinstein was once the all-American businessman. At 19, he borrowed $1,000 from his father and bought into a drugstore. At 31, he had a chain of stores,

*Several names and details have been changed to preserve anonymity.

which he sold and reaped several million dollars in take-home pay. Weinstein remembered thinking, ''I have a problem.'' Just when all his contemporaries were reaching their 30-something years, starting careers, raising their families, he was retiring. What to do with all that time?

His buddy Dick Bober talked him into the coated fabrics business. Weinstein did not know anything about coated fabrics. But he was not a pharmacist either, and that venture had proved fortunate. Coating fabrics, he learned, was a crucial step in making lots of products, from conveyer belts to bulletproof vests. Things like parachutes, helmet liners, and camouflage suits all use coated fabrics. So there were some large government contracts waiting to be served. Uniforms and equipment have to be stainproofed, fungus-proofed, waterproofed, and dyed. According to one estimate, coating adds from 10 to 50 percent to the base value of raw material, lending the luster of money to an otherwise workaday industry.

Weinstein threw himself into the business and eventually into the manufacturing process. As a pilot, he hated the life vests stowed on commercial airliners. ''They had always bugged me,'' he said. ''They [are] heavy and expensive to make,'' he told Coated researchers. The company designed a prototype using coated nylon, which was 60 percent lighter than the standard, and 70 percent cheaper to make. Before his company's untimely demise, Weinstein could boast that every Western airline carried life vests manufactured with materials made by Coated Sales.

The Coated Sales laboratory helped develop a super-proofed denim to protect oil rig workers, firemen, and people handling hazardous materials. Coated Sales employees worked on aircraft emergency slides, radiator hoses, telephone earpieces, a sewage filtration fabric, marine dive suits, backpacks, and, just for the flair of it, made some of the sailcloth for *Stars & Stripes*, the schooner piloted by Dennis Conner to win the America's Cup. Just two years before the crash, Weinstein became the first coated fabrics operator to own a large-scale finishing plant, a $27 million facility without rival in the industry.

At the same time, Weinstein's darling was digging its own grave. Expanding into new markets, developing cutting-edge product lines, herding new companies into the fold—all this takes money. Especially when the CEO and senior management like to live large and let people know about it. There is a constant cash crunch. Larger scale means larger crunch. Inside the workings of Coated Sales, shipments of fabric and equipment were being bought and sold quickly, often at a loss, just to get to the short-term money.

For years, Coated had used Main Hurdman for auditing, with no sign of trouble. But when Main Hurdman was acquired by Peat-Marwick, the new auditors saw a very different picture. One associate called a luggage manufacturer to ask about 750,000 pieces of merchandise purchased from Coated. The luggage company said it never placed an order like that. No idea. When audit team members spoke about their concerns, Coated sent in its legal counsel to talk with the auditors. Its lead counsel, Philip Kagan, tried to get them to make a deal, to go ahead and let the financial statement slide; there were some problems, he admitted, but nothing beyond repair. The matter was being taken care of. No way, said the auditors, and walked out.

In two months' time, the company that flew higher than the rest had fallen into bankruptcy. Early estimates put shareholder losses at more than $160 million. Coated's top 20 creditors claimed they were out at least $17 million. The bankruptcy court appointed Coopers & Lybrand's insolvency and litigation practice to work with the debtor in possession. Besides the usual assessments, the group was to determine what went wrong, and just how wrong—in dollar amounts—it had gone. CFE Harvey Creem says, "We knew there was something of concern with a loan and how the money was used. Once we started poking around, the iceberg got larger." Creem worked with the debtor's lawyers, who determined that the proceeds of a bank loan had been transferred to a brokerage account, one no longer carried in the ledgers. It was a supposedly dormant account from the company's first public offering, used for temporary investments until it was zeroed out. During the most recent fiscal year, there had been some activity on the account. Proceeds from a loan had been deposited into the brokerage account, transferred out to a cash account, and listed as if they were payments from customers against their accounts receivable. Coated Sales was due a lot of money, its receivables growing by $20 million a year. But a lot of the payments on those receivables were being made with Coated's own money, part of which originated from bank loans. The broad outline of the fraud was clear. "When you find a single check for, say, $2 million, used to pay off several different accounts, you know something's up. . . . Usually each customer sends their own check to pay off their own debt. In this case, a check listed under one name was used to pay off debts for several different people. Now, a company that not only pays its own debts but the debts of other companies too—that's not impossible, but it's not likely. The basics of the operation took two or three hours to break," says Creem. "Then it was tracking the scope of what happened."

Creem describes how he and his colleagues started at the bankruptcy filing date and "went in and analyzed the receivables in-depth. . . . Large chunks of them were totally fallacious; they had nothing supporting them." The tracking effort was helped along by a number of lower-level employees: "Some of them didn't really know what was happening and they were willing to help. Some may have known, but they were repentant, so they were willing to talk." In about three years of scamming, Weinstein and his management had inflated their sales and profits, resulting in overstated equity by $55 million. They used these phony numbers to get loans from several banks, including a $52 million line of credit from BancBoston and a $15 million line from First Fidelity in Newark, New Jersey.

The rigged loans solved the cash flow problem and brought very pleasant side effects. Stock in Coated Sales—traded under the ticker symbol RAGS—had been headed through the roof. Huge leaps in revenue and a monstrous control of the market had propelled the stock to $12 a share, eight times more than what it opened for. The company's upper echelon, including president Ernest Glantz and Weinstein's longtime partner vice president Dick Bober, was cashing in in a big way. By himself, Weinstein made more than $10 million in a short-term selling spree. Additionally, one of the myriad lawsuits against him accused Weinstein of departing with $968,000 in company cash.

Creem followed the trail of rigged profits into several intriguing corners. "To float this past the auditors for as long as they did, they found several ways to create the fiction that customers were actually paying the fake receivables. They would create a fake receivable, say, $10,000 due from a company. They'd hold it as long as they could, sometimes doctoring the dates on the aging, so it looked more recent than it was." Creem says the next step was "rigging a way to pay the account off: They'd transmit their own cash to a vendor. The vendor presumably was in on the scheme too, since they had submitted a fake invoice for the $10,000. This vendor keeps one to two percent for their trouble, and sends the rest back to Coated. That money would be reflected as a payment against the phony receivable."

Guys like Bernard Korostoff made the vendor trick work. Korostoff used his Kaye Mills International Corporation to create false invoices for several big Coated orders. Weinstein's team, having used their phony financials to get loans, sent out the money to Korostoff as if they were paying off a debt. Korostoff kept 1.5 percent for making the transaction possible, turning the rest back to Coated to pay off the falsified receivables. "I never really understood that," says Creem. "These guys are doing this for a measly little percentage. Why would they bother for no more than that? Maybe it was connected in other ways to the business."

The business, as it was being run, was a labyrinth of finagling and deception. Weinstein was faking how much he owed people in order to pay off receivables, which were also being faked. He was using receivables to get million-dollar loans and plowing chunks of the proceeds back into the system to keep suspicious eyes unaware. The false sales not only brought in loan dollars, they created portfolio dollars by driving RAGS stock higher and higher. To support the scam, Weinstein had three ways to keep his circle of money in motion: (1) he could move loan money from the hidden brokerage account to wherever it was needed; (2) he could use fake vendor invoices to launder funds back into the company; or (3) he and his associates could sell off their own stock in the company and apply some of the proceeds to the delinquent receivables.

Four years of this action and Weinstein had demolished Coated Sales. The company exaggerated its accounts receivable by millions, fictionalizing half or more of sales at any given point. At the time, it was the largest stock fraud ever in the state of New Jersey. Weinstein and nine other senior managers were charged with planning, executing, and profiting from the scheme. Weinstein—called "a tall, plump man with a domineering personality" by *Forbes*—owned more than ten airplanes and several helicopters. He had two Rolls-Royces, one at each of his two residences, plus five other luxury automobiles scattered about. He and the other conspirators had used some of the proceeds to buy themselves smaller companies. For flamboyance, he had no better, and for gall, he was unrivaled. After Coated went belly up and federal charges joined the pile of lawsuits against him, Weinstein bought a 13,000-square-foot house in Boca Raton, Florida, valued at $2 million, sitting on a $1 million property. Three different yachts were docked along the Florida coast in case Weinstein needed to get away from all the hassle.

But Weinstein would not slip past this one. He and his inner circle were presented with a 46-page indictment. Bruce Bloom, Coated's CFO, pled guilty and pointed at his cohorts. Coated's lead counsel, Philip Kagan, first declared himself "totally innocent of any wrongdoing" but later decided to plead guilty to the racketeering and conspiracy charges against him. Kagan confessed to helping dupe company auditors and described trying to entice them into ignoring the facts of their ledgers. He also admitted that he had once accepted $115,000 in legal fees from Coated Sales without reporting the money to the SEC as required. Kagan was sentenced to 18 months in prison. Jail terms for other low-level players ranged from one year to 24 months.

Coated president Ernest Glanz was given a year's sentence—part of a deal he made to cooperate with the government. Richard Bober, Weinstein's longtime friend, drew 20 months in prison and a $3 million fine, besides the $55.9 million civil judgment he shared with Weinstein. Creem remembers that when Bober testified in bankruptcy court, "The judge appeared shocked. He started asking Bober questions himself. I don't believe he had ever heard anything quite like this in his courtroom before."

Michael Weinstein struck a plea bargain, which nevertheless carried a pretty stout penalty. He forfeited virtually all of the properties, cars, and boats he had amassed, along with several businesses and numerous bank accounts worth several hundred thousand dollars each. He was given 57 months in federal prison and charged to make restitution for any outstanding stockholder losses.

U.S. Attorney Michael Chertoff saw this as a decisive case, part of what he called "a new genre of corporate boardroom prosecutions." Fed up with the megascams of the megalomaniac executive, legal agencies began using the tough Securities Law Enforcement Remedies Act to go after the big players. "Major financial fraud," Chertoff told a press conference after Weinstein's guilty plea, "not only harms banking institutions but also infects the securities market, victimizing the thousands of persons who invest in stock. When dishonesty roams the boardroom, it is the creditors and investors who suffer."

CHAPTER 14

Occupational Fraud and Abuse:
The Big Picture

DEFINING "ABUSIVE CONDUCT"

The cases we have seen on the preceding pages were, by and large, on the extreme edge of abusive conduct by employees. In short, this data is merely the tip of the iceberg. How deep and massive that iceberg is varies from one organization to another, depending on a complex set of business and human factors.

The depth of the iceberg is also measured by what is defined as abusive conduct. Obviously, the more rules within the organization, the more likely employees are to run afoul of them. Remember, Hollinger and Clark's study revealed that almost *nine out of ten employees* admitted to abusive conduct at some level. Part of that abuse is owing to the diverse nature of individuals. Tom R. Tyler, in his book *Why People Obey the Law*, concluded that individuals obey only those laws that they believe in. If a rule makes no sense to the employees, they will make their own rule.[1]

Let me illustrate the point with another personal experience from the FBI. The FBI did a thorough background investigation before hiring me, notwithstanding the Mr. Zac debacle. They investigate each and every agent prospect. When you are hired, it does not mean you are perfect—just that the bureau has put you through every wringer it can think of, looking for any imperfection that may surface to disqualify you.

Of those who survive that process, only a tiny percentage actually are hired and put through training school—as I was. From day 1, the agents are held to impossibly high standards. To illustrate the mentality at the time, consider what our esteemed instructor told his class of 35 eager, bright-eyed trainees. "The FBI doesn't have any ordinary agents. Every single one of them is above average or better," the instructor bragged. One of the trainees sitting toward the back of the class—a mathematical type of guy—raised his hand. "Excuse me," the trainee said, "I don't think it is possible for every FBI agent to be above average. By definition, to be above average, there must be an average and a below average. So not every agent can be above average; it's statistically impossible." The trainee spoke to the instructor with respect but conviction.

The classroom was silent, and every eye went to the front of the room, where the instructor was carefully formulating his response. "Look, Mister," said the instructor, "if J. Edgar Hoover himself said every agent is above average, that's statistical enough for me." And he meant it.

When we graduated from training class and went into the field, the rookie agents had to join the real world. In the real world, we were paid 25 percent extra for all the overtime we typically incurred. But the record-keeping requirements were so ridiculous that no one—outside the clerks in Washington—paid any attention to the myriad forms we had to fill out every month to receive our overtime pay.

The ridiculous part of the record keeping, as far as the rank-and-file agent was concerned, was that there was no carryover for overtime accumulated from one period to the next. For example, if you put in 50 percent overtime in pay period 14, you still got paid 25 percent. But if you put in only 10 percent overtime in pay period 15, your overtime would be cut to 10 percent because you could not use the overtime you burned in period 14. The kicker was that during the course of the year, all the agents would put in at least 25 percent overtime, and many ran much higher.

As a result, virtually everyone I knew in the field at that time simply claimed 25 percent each pay period, regardless of the actual time they put in. We had to certify, under oath, that we had worked that specific amount of overtime—no more, no less. Our agency could not pay us more than 25 percent, so it "officially" did not want us to put in more time, because government regulations would have required it to pay compensatory time off. So none of us took seriously the certification that bore our signatures. A sworn false statement under oath to the government—which we regularly signed on our forms—warned us all of the criminal penalties involved. Each and every one of us would sign such a form 26 times a year—just to get our paychecks. I commented on the irony of it to a salty old FBI agent one day when both of us were at the sign-in register. "Joe," he said, "welcome to the real world. Here is the way it works: If you've told many lies, you can't get in the FBI. But once you're hired, you have to tell a few just to stay in. And that's all because of these ridiculous regulations."

Other than my admitting that during my professional career I have had my own personal experiences with occupational fraud and abuse, what is the moral to this story? There are two morals, in my view. The first is that we cannot eliminate this problem in the workforce without eliminating people. The human race is notoriously subject to periodic fits of bad judgment. Those in fraud detection or deterrence who are aiming for perfection from the workforce will not only be disappointed, they will find that such attitudes invariably increase the problem.

That paradox is the second moral to the story: To quote my longtime colleague, Dr. Steve Albrecht, "If you set standards too high, you may be inadvertently giving an employee two choices in his mind—to fail or to lie." Your job in establishing antifraud standards, then, is to make them clear and reasonable. More on that later.

MEASURING THE LEVEL OF OCCUPATIONAL FRAUD AND ABUSE

Since the goal of the antifraud professional is to reduce the losses from these offenses, measuring progress in the traditional sense might be difficult. We have clearly established the reasons for this: We know only about the frauds that are discovered.

As we discussed in the introduction to this book, the certified fraud examiners who participated in the *2009 Global Fraud Survey* estimated that the typical organization loses about 5 percent of its gross revenues to all forms of fraud and abuse in the workplace. Considering everything we know, it may be the best number we can use for the present, and at least it gives organizations a rough measure of their potential exposure. Whether that exposure is ever discovered is a different matter. We have seen examples of occupational frauds in this book that have gone undetected for years. Except for a fluke of circumstance, many of them still could be thriving today. That, of course, is the most troublesome aspect of many occupational frauds: The longer they go undetected, the more expensive they become. People who start committing fraud generally will continue unless there is a compelling reason to quit.

On an organizational basis, one good indicator of the real risks of fraud is what has happened in the past. Surprisingly few organizations—especially the smaller ones—make any effort to gather historical, fraud-related data: how many offenses occur, what the losses are from each, and what patterns emerge, if any. But remember, this data will not tell you the size of the iceberg, only the size of the tip. Most important, though, gathering historical fraud information will tell you whether the iceberg is growing or melting.

The Human Factor

The diverse case studies in this book have one common element: the human failings that led trusted people to violate that trust. Were these employees, from those in the mailroom to those in the boardroom, all simply greedy? Were they all simply liars? Did they always have defective morals, which surfaced only when their honesty was tested? Or were they mistreated, underpaid, and only taking what they considered to be "rightfully" theirs? The answer, of course, is that it depends.

Crime is a complex tapestry of motive and opportunity. The sultan of Brunei, reputedly one of the world's richest men, may have unlimited opportunity to defraud people. But does he have the motive? Conversely, minimum-wage cashiers may be very motivated to steal in order to keep their lights turned on. But if they are constantly aware that their cash drawer may be counted by surprise, they may not perceive the opportunity to do so. In any antifraud effort, we always must keep in mind that no one factor alone will deter occupational fraud; we must attack the problem on several fronts.

Greed

Michael Douglas uttered the now-famous line from the movie *Wall Street*: "Greed is good." While some may debate whether that is true, there is little debate that greed is certainly a factor in occupational fraud. Indeed, students of this subject are most likely to describe embezzlers and their ilk by that single word: *greedy*.

The problem with that definition of a fraud motivator is that it is subjective and begs for the response "Greedy? Compared to what?" Most of us consider ourselves greedy to some extent; it is, after all, a very human trait. But there are many greedy people who do not steal, lie, and cheat to get what they want. And how can we measure the amount of greed in a way that will predict behavior? In sum, there is little we can say about greed as a motive that will help us detect or deter occupational fraud.

In-Kind Wages

In nearly all the case studies in this book, one common thread prevails: Those who chose to commit fraud against their employers felt justified in doing so. A perfect example is the case of Bob Walker, the cashier who began stealing to get even with his employer. Walker had been demoted from a management position to head cashier at his store, a move that included a $300 cut to his monthly pay. Feeling morally justified in his theft, Walker went on to process over $10,000 in false refunds—much more than what his demotion cost him in lost wages.

For the purpose of detecting and deterring occupational fraud, it does not matter whether employees are *actually* justified but simply whether they *perceive* that they are. Prevention efforts must begin with education of employees and staff, attacking this misperception on all fronts—the immorality, illegality, and negative consequences of committing occupational fraud and abuse.

Employers also must understand the concept of in-kind wages. I can remember a perfect illustration from my days as an antifraud consultant in the 1980s. A local banker heard me give a speech on fraud prevention, and he later called me. ''We have a hell of a time with teller thefts,'' he confidentially admitted. ''I would like to hire you to evaluate the problem and give us some solutions.''

I spent several days in the bank, going over the accounting procedures, the history of teller thefts, the personnel policies, and the internal controls. I also interviewed bank supervisors, head tellers, and the rank-and-file. The interviews were particularly revealing.

When it came time to give my report, the banker requested that I meet with his entire board to deliver my conclusions orally and respond to questions. I tried to be diplomatic, but when the veneer was stripped away, it was not a pretty picture. The bank was having problems with teller thefts because it: (1) had inadequate personnel screening procedures; (2) had no antifraud training whatsoever; (3) paid inadequate wages to those entrusted with a drawerful of money; and (4) was perceived by the employees as cheap and condescending. When I finished my presentation to the board, I asked for questions. The silence was deafening. After I stood there for what seemed like eternity, my banker colleague meekly thanked me for my suggestions and told me they would call. They did not.

Three basics are absolutely necessary to minimize (not eliminate) occupational fraud and abuse.

1. Hire the right people.
2. Treat them well.
3. Do not subject them to unreasonable expectations.

Unreasonable Expectations

If you have evaluated the case studies in this book carefully, you should have empathy with at least some of the situations that led employees to commit fraud. Ernie Philips's situation, for example, reads like the scenario for a *Movie of the Week*. While trying to support a wife and six adopted children, Philips was forced to undergo several back operations, which kept him home from work. He then became addicted to the pills he was given to alleviate the pain from those operations. His CPA practice was on the verge of folding, and he suffered from depression as well as from chronic anxiety. Under such dire circumstances, how many of us might resort to forging checks in order to get by?

In my view, employers sometimes have unreasonable expectations of their employees that may contribute to occupational fraud and abuse. First, employers frequently expect their employees to be honest in all situations. That belies normal human behavior. According to Patterson and Kim in *The Day America Told the Truth*, fully 91 percent of people surveyed admitted to lying on a regular basis. Thankfully, most of these lies have nothing to do with fraud. But it must be remembered that although not all liars are fraudsters, all fraudsters are liars. The most effective approach to deterrence, therefore, is not to eliminate lying (something that cannot be done) but to keep lies from turning into frauds.

It is easy to see how anyone can confuse the two concepts of lying and fraud. Lies to our family, our coworkers, our superiors, and our customers are typically deceptions motivated by the human desire to tell people what they want to hear—''My, you look nice today!'' So keep your eye on the ball: We want to deter fraud specifically; we do not have the time to reform humanity, no matter how lofty a goal that is. And deterring fraud requires some understanding.

UNDERSTANDING FRAUD DETERRENCE

Deterrence and prevention are not the same thing, although we frequently use the terms interchangeably. *Prevention*, in the sense of crime, involves removing the root causes of the problem. In this case, to prevent fraud, we would have to eliminate the motivation to commit it, such as the societal injustices that lead to crime. As fraud examiners, we must leave that task to the social scientists. Instead, we concentrate on *deterrence*, the modification of behavior through the perception of negative sanctions.

Fraud offenders are much easier to deter than run-of-the-mill street criminals. Much violent crime is committed in the heat of the moment, and criminologists agree that such crimes are very difficult to stop in advance. But fraud offenders are very deliberate people, as you have seen in this book. At each stage of the offense, they carefully weigh—consciously or subconsciously—the individual risks and rewards of their behaviors. For that reason, their conduct is easier to modify.

Impact of Controls

Throughout this book, you have witnessed situations that could have been prevented by the most basic control procedure: separating the money from the record-keeping function. Having said that, it is likely that we accountants and auditors ask controls to do too much. After all, many internal controls have nothing to do with fraud. And still others are related only indirectly. My view is that internal controls are only part of the answer to fraud deterrence. However, some do not share that view. They argue that if the proper controls are in place, occupational fraud is almost impossible to commit without being detected.

Perception of Detection

As alluded to throughout these pages, the deterrence of occupational fraud and abuse begins in the employee's mind. The perception-of-detection axiom is:

> *Employees who perceive that they will be caught engaging in occupational fraud and abuse are less likely to commit it.*

The logic is hard to dispute. Exactly how much deterrent effect this concept provides depends on a number of factors, both internal and external. But as you can see, internal controls can have a deterrent effect only when the employee perceives that such a control exists and is for the purpose of uncovering fraud. Hidden controls have no deterrent effect. Conversely, controls that are not even in place—but are perceived to be—will have the same deterrent value.

How does an entity raise the perception of detection? That, of course, varies from organization to organization. The first step is to bring occupational fraud and abuse out of the closet and deal with the issue in an open forum. Companies and agencies must be cautioned that increasing the perception of detection, if not handled correctly, will smack of Big Brother and can cause more problems than it solves. But organizations can take at least six positive steps to increase the perception of detection:

1. Employee education
2. Proactive fraud policies
3. A higher stance
4. Increased use of analytical review
5. Surprise audits where feasible
6. Adequate reporting programs

Employee Education

Unless the vast majority of employees are in favor of reducing occupational fraud and abuse, any proactive fraud deterrence program is destined for failure. It is therefore necessary to enlist the entire workforce in this effort. Organizations should provide at least some basic antifraud training at the time workers are hired. In this fashion, employees become the eyes and ears of the organization and are more likely to report possible fraudulent activity.

Education of employees should be factual rather than accusatory. Point out that fraud—in any form—is eventually very unhealthy for the organization and the people who work there. Fraud and abuse impact raises, jobs, benefits, morale, and profits as well as the integrity of those who perpetrate them. The fraud-educated workforce is the fraud examiner's best weapon—by far.

Proactive Fraud Policies

When I ask most people how to deter fraud, they typically say something like this: "In order to prevent fraud, we must prosecute more people. That will send a message." There are at least three flaws in this well-meaning argument. First, there is nothing proactive about prosecuting people. As some would say, it is like closing the barn door after the cows have escaped. Second, whether it really sends much of a message is debatable. This concept is called *general deterrence* by criminologists. As logical as the idea sounds on its face, there is no data—out of scores of studies—that shows it actually works.

Without getting into the intricacies of criminological thought, many experts believe punishment to be of little value in deterring crime because the possibilities of being punished are too remote in the minds of potential perpetrators. Think about it for a second. If you are debating whether to commit a crime (of any kind), the first question that comes into your mind is: "Will I be caught?" not "What is the punishment if I am caught?" If you answer yes to the first question, you are very unlikely to commit the offense. That makes the punishment moot, no matter how severe it is.

The foregoing is not to say that crime should not be punished. Quite the opposite—it *must* be done in a civilized society. But remember that the primary benefit of any type of punishment is society's retribution for the act, not that punishment will deter others.

A Higher Stance

Proactive fraud policies begin with management, auditors, and fraud examiners taking a higher stance. As previously stated, that means bringing fraud out of the closet. At every phase of a routine audit or management review, the subject of fraud and abuse should be brought up in a nonaccusatory manner. People should be asked to share their knowledge and suspicions, if any. They should be asked about possible control and administrative weaknesses that might contribute to fraud. What we are trying to accomplish through this method is to make people subtly aware that if they commit illegal acts, others will be looking over their shoulders.

A higher stance also means making sure that hidden controls do not remain hidden. Auditors may have a peculiar image to the uninformed. Employees know auditors are there, but they are not quite sure what the auditors actually do. While this attitude can bring obvious benefits if you are trying to conduct your activities in secret, it is counterproductive in proactive fraud deterrence. You must let employees know that you are looking.

Increased Use of Analytical Review

If an employee embezzles $100,000 from a Fortune 500 corporation, it will not cause even a blip in the financial statements. In large audits, the chances of discovering a bogus invoice are remote at best. That is because of the sampling techniques used by auditors: They look at a relatively small number of transactions in total.

But as you can see from the cases in this book, the real risks are in asset misappropriations in small businesses. These, of course, can be—and frequently are—very material to the bottom line. And the smaller businesses are those that benefit the most from the increased use of analytical review—most specifically, from vertical and horizontal analysis. As a reminder, proactive fraud examiners and auditors should be especially mindful of historical trends that reflect these increases: expenses, cost of sales, receivables with decreasing cash, inventory, sales with decreasing cash, returns and allowances, and sales discounts.

As a part of the analytical review process, it is a good idea to determine the organization's policy on job rotation and enforced vacations. Because many occupational frauds require continuous manual intervention by the perpetrator, a large proportion of these offenses seem to be uncovered when the perpetrator leaves—for vacation, sick time, and job rotation. It stands to reason that the longer a person is in one position, largely unsupervised, the greater the risks of occupational fraud.

Surprise Audits Where Feasible

The story of Bill Gurado best illustrates the concept of the perception of detection in audits. As you recall, Barry Ecker, the auditor, was simply joking when he told Gurado that an audit was imminent. Based on that false information, Gurado confessed that he had been stealing from his branch. The reason? Gurado was convinced that his unlawful conduct was about to be discovered.

The threat of surprise audits, especially in currency-intensive businesses, may be a powerful deterrent to occupational fraud and abuse. In case after case, fraud perpetrators who were aware that audits were coming had time to alter, destroy, and misplace records and other evidence of their offenses. Obviously, surprise audits are more difficult to plan and execute than a normal audit, which is announced in advance. But considering the impact of the perception of detection, surprise audits may certainly be worth the trouble.

Adequate Reporting Programs

As many of the cases in this book illustrate, adequate reporting programs are vital to serious efforts to detect and deter occupational fraud and abuse. In situation after situation that we encountered, employees suspected that illegal activity was taking place, but they had no way to report this information without the fear of being dragged into the investigation.

Reporting programs should emphasize at least six points:

1. Fraud, waste, and abuse occur at some level in nearly every organization.
2. This conduct negatively impacts jobs, raises, and profits.
3. The organization actively encourages employees to come forward with information.
4. There are no penalties for furnishing good-faith information.
5. There is an exact method for reporting, such as a telephone number or address.
6. Reports of suspicious activity do not have to be reported by employees to their immediate supervisors.

Most professionals consider a hotline to be the cornerstone of an employee reporting program. According to some studies, about 5 percent of hotline calls are actually developed into solid cases. In many instances, these schemes would not have been discovered by any other method. As near as we can tell, reports from employees outstrip all other methods of fraud detection combined.

There are three basic kinds of hotlines. The first is a part-time, in-house hotline staffed by an employee with other duties. When the employee is out, a recorder takes the call. These hotlines have the advantage of low cost, but the disadvantages are twofold: (1) some calls might be missed, and (2) some employees are reluctant to report fraud to organizational personnel.

The second type of hotline is a full-time, in-house one. Its advantage is that employees can make calls anytime, day or night, and talk to an actual person. These kinds of hotlines are expensive, and they usually are found only in the largest corporations and governmental agencies.

The last type is called a third-party hotline. It is staffed by an outside company, usually 24 hours a day, and is priced to subscribers based on the number of employees. Third-party hotlines offer three distinct advantages: cost, efficiency, and anonymity.

Hotlines, regardless of their type, work to increase the perception of detection. Employees who are aware that nefarious activities might be reported by a coworker will be less likely to engage in such conduct. One final advantage of a hotline is that it helps comply in part with the federal Corporate Sentencing Guidelines for corporations.

CORPORATE SENTENCING GUIDELINES

Responding to concerns over the wide disparity in federal sentencing, Congress passed the Sentencing Reform Act in 1984. As part of the broader Comprehensive Crime Control Act of 1984, the Sentencing Report Act established the United States Sentencing Commission (USSC), which was charged with promulgating guidelines governing criminal sentencing in federal courts. Once established, the USSC began studying sentences for individuals, and after three years of study, the USSC submitted the draft guidelines for comment and congressional approval. The Federal Sentencing Guidelines for individuals became effective on November 1, 1987. These guidelines were one of the most dramatic changes in criminal law in the history of this country.

Shortly after the Federal Sentencing Guidelines became effective, the USSC began studying sanctions for organizations, even though it had no clear direction to do so. Four years later, the USSC submitted its Proposed Guidelines for Sentencing Organizations for congressional approval, and on November 1, 1991, these guidelines (hereinafter referred to as "Corporate Sentencing Guidelines") became effective. The underlying philosophy of the Corporate Sentencing Guidelines has been characterized as a carrot-and-stick approach to criminal sentencing. That is, if the organization prevents or discloses certain conduct, its punishment will be reduced.

The purpose of the Corporate Sentencing Guidelines is to establish uniform, mandatory punishments for organizational crimes. Not only do the guidelines seek to make punishments more uniform, but they also dramatically increase the severity with which convicted defendants are punished. Additionally, the Corporate Sentencing Guidelines can mitigate potentially devastating penalties for any entity convicted of a crime that has an effective compliance program in place.

Specifically, the Corporate Sentencing Guidelines offer a reduced sentence to a convicted organization if it had an effective compliance program in place at the time of the offense. Thus, if an organization had implemented and maintained such a program, the judge overseeing the case would consider the organization's acts of due diligence in trying to prevent the illegal conduct when deciding whether to mitigate the entity's punishment.

Initially, the Corporate Sentencing Guidelines were mandatory in application; however, as a result of the Supreme Court's 2005 decision in *United States v. Booker* (543 U.S. 220 (2005)) the guidelines are now considered advisory only. Thus, judges must consider the Corporate Sentencing Guidelines when sentencing convicted organizations, but they are not required to issue sentences within the range set forth by the guidelines. However, sentencing judges still are required to examine the adequacy of the entity's compliance program according to the guidelines.

Vicarious or Imputed Liability

Unlike individuals, corporations can be held legally responsible for the criminal acts of their employees if those acts are done in the course and scope of their employment and for the ostensible purpose of benefiting the corporation.[2]

The corporation will be held criminally responsible even if those in management had no knowledge or participation in the underlying criminal events and even if there were specific policies or instructions prohibiting the activity undertaken by the employees.

In fact, a corporation can be held criminally responsible for the collective knowledge of several of its employees even if no single employee intended to commit an offense.[3] Thus, the combination of vicarious or imputed corporate criminal liability and the Corporate Sentencing Guidelines creates an extraordinary risk for corporations today.

Requirements

The Corporate Sentencing Guidelines encourage organizations to adopt effective compliance programs designed to reduce criminal conduct by their officers, directors, employees, and agents and exercise due diligence in seeking to prevent and detect such conduct. At a minimum, seven steps are required by the guidelines for due diligence:

1. Have policies defining standards and procedures to be followed by the organization's agents and employees.
2. Assign specific high-level personnel who have ultimate responsibility to ensure compliance.
3. Use due care not to delegate significant discretionary authority to people whom the organization knew or should have known had a propensity to engage in illegal activities.
4. Communicate standards and procedures to all agents and employees, and require participation in training programs.

5. Take reasonable steps to achieve compliance—for example, use monitoring and auditing systems and have, and publicize, a reporting system by which employees can report criminal conduct without fear of retribution (hotline or ombudsman program).

6. Consistently enforce standards through appropriate discipline, ranging from dismissal to reprimand.

7. After detection of an offense, take all reasonable steps to respond appropriately to this offense and to prevent further similar offenses—including modifying its programs and appropriately disciplining those who were responsible for the offense and those who failed to detect it.

The Corporate Sentencing Guidelines provide for both criminal and civil sanctions. The maximum fines may reach up to $290 million, and the corporation can be placed on probation for up to five years.

ETHICAL CONNECTION

Phillip Wheelwright defined ethics as:

that branch of philosophy which is the systematic study of reflective choice, of the standards of right and wrong by which a person is to be guided, and of the goods toward which it may ultimately be directed.[4]

More generally, moralists believe that ethical behavior is that which produces the greatest good and that which conforms to moral rules and principles. Although the term ''ethics'' often is used interchangeably with ''morality'' and ''legality,'' the terms are not precisely the same. Ethics is much more of a personal decision. In theory, ethics is how you react to temptation when no one is looking.

There are fundamentally two schools of ethical thought. The first, called the *imperative principle*, advocates that there are concrete ethical principles that cannot be violated. The second, called *situational ethics* or the *utilitarian principle,* generally advocates that each situation must be evaluated on its own; in essence, the end can justify the means. Probably the majority of people in modern-day society follow situational ethics. But regardless of one's particular ethical philosophy, the sticky problems exist in defining what constitutes the ''greatest good.'' It is certainly easy to see how the chief executive of a corporation that employs thousands of individuals would rationalize that committing financial statement fraud will help save jobs, thus justifying his conduct to himself, as the ''greatest good.''

Similarly, an employee can perceive that a major corporation having lots of money would never miss the amount she so desperately needs to keep afloat financially. This was demonstrated in the story of Larry Gunter and Larry Spelber, two employees who saw the opportunity to finance their entire educations by taking six small boxes of computer chips from their employer's warehouse. In a building filled to the brim with computer chips, who would miss six boxes?

It is no surprise that some of the biggest crooks view themselves inwardly as very ethical; to this day, it is doubtful that Charles Keating views himself as more than a victim of circumstance, regardless of the fact that many unsuspecting retirees across America lost every dime they owned because of his actions.

The reality is that, for most, the ''greatest good'' invariably turns out to be what is good for the individual making the ethical decision. Coincidence? Probably not. Ancient and modern philosophers usually subscribe to one of three schools of thought about the essence of people: (1) humans as good, (2) humans as evil, or (3) humans as calculating. In the latter situation, people will *always consistently* seek pleasure and/or avoid pain. This is a lesson most of us learn at a very young age.

Behaviorists tell us that the vast majority of our personalities have been formed by the age of three. A large part of our personalities relates to the values we have, which are instilled in us by our parents and mentors. Even though I am a cynic, I recognize that it is highly unlikely that ethical policies—no matter how strong—will seriously deter those sufficiently motivated to engage in occupational fraud and abuse.

There is no ethical policy stronger than the leadership provided by the head of the organization. Modeling of behavior occurs with strong influences such as the boss. Indeed, the Treadway Commission specifically commented on the importance of the ''tone at the top.'' Unfortunately, the formal ethics policies in place right now are thought to exist mostly in large organizations. In small businesses—which are much more vulnerable to going broke from asset misappropriations—few of the bosses victimized seem to realize the importance of their own personal example.

When employees hear their leaders telling customers what they want to hear, when small-business owners fudge on the myriad taxes they owe, and when CEOs lie to vendors about when they will be paid, nothing good can possibly result. Setting an example is the *real* ethical connection.

Having said that, formal ethics policies are recommended for all organizations, regardless of their size. They certainly do not do any harm, and they may provide some deterrence, but almost as important is that having an ethics policy makes enforcement of conduct generally easier to legally justify. A sample Code of Business Ethics and Conduct from the ACFE *Fraud Examiner's Manual* is in the appendix to this book. Feel free to use the example to develop your own ethics policy. Three things are important regardless of what form your policy finally takes:

1. Set out specific conduct that violates the policy.
2. State that dishonest acts will be punished.
3. Provide information on your organization's mechanism for reporting unethical conduct.

Although some professionals will disagree, I think it is a terrible idea to lace an ethics policy with draconian statements such as ''all violators will be prosecuted to the maximum extent allowed by law.'' First, even to many honest people, such a statement smacks of a veiled threat. Second, the victim of fraud does not decide criminal prosecution; this decision is made by the state. As a practical matter, your organization has little control, and it is unlikely that many first-time offenders will get more than a probated sentence.

Finally, your organization's ethical policy, whatever it is, can be only as good as the reinforcement it gets. A company that provides only one training program on ethics and does not mention the subject again cannot expect results, however marginal. Training must be continuous, and must be positive in tone. Do not preach; instead, keep emphasizing the simple message: Fraud, waste, and abuse are eventually bad for the organization as well as for everyone in it.

CONCLUDING THOUGHTS

Within the pages of this book, many details of occupational fraud and abuse have been revealed, but those searching for a magic bullet to detect these offenses are doubtless still looking. Indeed, the dream of many in the accounting community is to develop new audit techniques that will quickly and easily point the finger of suspicion. To those innocent souls, I wish good luck. Regardless of the ability of computers to automate a great deal of drudgery, there are no new audit techniques, and there have not been any for the last several centuries.

Another factor makes the detection of occupational fraud and abuse difficult. Fraud is one of the few crimes whose clues are not unique to the commission of the offense. For example, clues in a bank robbery case would be the witnesses who saw the robber, the records reflecting the loss, the security cameras, and so on. By contrast, the indicators of a bank embezzlement can be internal control weaknesses, missing or incomplete documents, and figures that do not add up. The problem, of course, is that these latter clues are not conclusive evidence of fraud; the red flags could just as easily turn out to be red herrings.

I am confident that this book will help you detect and deter fraud. But detection can be almost impossible when committed by people clever and motivated enough to hide their tracks. For those of us who are fraud examiners, that fact is sometimes hard to swallow. If you are the best fraud examiner in the world, you will detect some cases and resolve them, but you will never get them all, no matter how hard you try.

In putting forward your best efforts to detect fraud, you will sometimes be tempted to try too hard. You will weigh in your mind whether you should take an unauthorized look at the suspect's bank account; you will wrestle with the dilemma of whether to check the fraudster's credit records secretly. Do not do it.

Overreaching an investigation or fraud examination is the quickest way to ruin it. Not only will you be unsuccessful in proving your case, you will subject yourself to possible criminal and civil penalties. If you get to a point in a fraud examination when you do not know what to do, *stop*. Resolve all doubt in favor of your suspect, or check with counsel on the next step.

In a perfect world, we probably would abandon our efforts to detect fraud and concentrate exclusively on deterrence. As we all know, prevention of any problem—from cancer to crime—is usually cheaper and more effective than the aftermath. In the area of occupational fraud, for reasons we have discussed extensively in this book, deterrence can work better than for nearly every other type of crime.

Deterrence, as we have explicitly stated, is much more than internal control. And we accountants concentrate primarily on those controls to deter fraud. As history has witnessed, it is an inadequate effort. For a number of years I have advocated the concept of the Model Organizational Fraud Deterrence Program. Under the program, we in the audit community would invest the resources to find out what works in organizations that do not have much of a problem with occupational fraud and abuse. What works will be a combination of both accounting and nonaccounting factors. We know some of the factors already, but we need to know more. From new research, we would then develop a complete checklist of the model organization and use that checklist to audit against. Then the external auditor would attest to the organization's compliance to the model, not to whether the auditor has uncovered material fraud. The latter approach, adopted by the accounting community, is bound to drive up the cost of the audit and the price of litigation.

The bad news is that we cannot audit ourselves out of the occupational fraud and abuse problem. But the good news is that there are a multitude of new approaches we can try. Some of them are in this book, which is but a beginning. New approaches combine both audit and investigative skills—the precise attributes of tomorrow's corporate cop, the fraud examiner. Most people do not start their careers to become liars, cheats, and thieves, and it is the fraud examiner's job to ensure they do not end up that way.

NOTES

1. Tom R. Tyler, *Why People Obey the Law* (New Haven, CT: Yale University Press, 1990).
2. See *New York Central and Hudson River Railroad v. United States*, 212 U.S. 481 (1909); *Standard Oil Co. of Texas v. United States*, 307 F.2d 120 (5th Cir. 1962).
3. See *U.S. v. Bank of New England, W.A.*, 921 F.2d 844, 856 (1st Cir.), *cert. denied*, 484 U.S. 943 (1987).
4. Association of Certified Fraud Examiners, *Fraud Examiners' Manual* (Austin, TX: Author, 2011), p. 4.901.

Sample Code of Business Ethics and Conduct

INTRODUCTION

This code of ethics reaffirms the importance of high standards of business conduct. Adherence to this code by all employees is the only sure way we can merit the confidence and support of the public.

Many of us came from a culture that provided answers or direction for almost every situation possible. Managing our business was not so complex, the dilemmas we faced were—for the most part—simple, making our choices relatively easy. We probably would all agree that managing in today's environment is not so simple.

This code has been prepared as a working guide and not as a technical legal document. Thus, emphasis is on brevity and readability rather than providing an all-inclusive answer to specific questions. For example, the term "employee" is used in its broadest sense and refers to every officer and employee of the company and its subsidiaries. The word "law" refers to laws, regulations, orders, and the like.

In observance of this code, as in other business conduct, there is no substitute for common sense. Each employee should apply this code with common sense and the attitude of seeking full compliance with the letter and spirit of the rules presented.

It is incumbent on you, as an employee of the company, to perform satisfactorily and to follow our policies and comply with our rules as they are issued or modified from time to time.

These policies and rules are necessary to effectively manage the business and meet the ever-changing needs of the marketplace. Good performance and compliance with business rules lead to success. Both are crucial since our ability to provide you with career opportunities depends totally on our success in the marketplace. Nonetheless, changes in our economy, our markets, and our technology are inevitable. Indeed, career opportunities will vary between the individual companies. For these reasons, we cannot contract or even imply that your employment will continue for any particular period of time. While you may terminate your employment at any time, with or without cause, we reserve that same right. This relationship may not be modified, except in writing signed by an appropriate representative of the company.

This Code of Business Ethics and Conduct is a general guide to acceptable and appropriate behavior at the company, and you are expected to comply with its contents; however, it does not contain all of the detailed information you will need during the course of your employment. Nothing contained in this code or in other communications creates or implies an employment contract or term of employment. We are committed to reviewing our policies continually. Thus, this code might be modified or revised from time to time.

You should familiarize yourself with this code so that you might readily distinguish any proposal or act that would constitute a violation. Each employee is responsible for his or her actions. Violations can result in disciplinary action, including dismissal and criminal prosecution. There will be no reprisal against an employee who in good faith reported a violation or suspected violation.

The absence of a specific guideline practice or instruction covering a particular situation does not relieve an employee from exercising the highest ethical standards applicable to the circumstances.

If any employee has doubts regarding a questionable situation that might arise, that employee should immediately consult his or her supervisor or higher level.

Competition and Antitrust

Fair Competition

The company supports competition based on quality, service, and price. We will conduct our affairs honestly, directly, and fairly. To comply with the antitrust laws and our policy of fair competition, employees:

- Must never discuss with competitors any matter directly involved in competition between ourselves and the competitor (e.g., sales price, marketing strategies, market shares, and sales policies).
- Must never agree with a competitor to restrict competition by fixing prices, allocating markets, or other means.
- Must not arbitrarily refuse to deal with or purchase goods and services from others simply because they are competitors in other respects.
- Must not require others to buy from us before we will buy from them.
- Must not require customers to take from us a service they do not want just so they can get one they do want.
- Must never engage in industrial espionage or commercial bribery.
- Must be accurate and truthful in all dealings with customers and be careful to accurately represent the quality, features, and availability of company products and services.

Compliance with Laws and Regulatory Orders

The applicable laws and regulatory orders of every jurisdiction in which the company operates must be followed. Each employee is charged with the responsibility of acquiring sufficient knowledge of the laws and orders relating to his or her duties in order to recognize potential dangers and to know when to seek legal advice.

In particular, when dealing with public officials, employees must adhere to the highest ethical standards of business conduct. When we seek the resolution of regulatory or political issues affecting the company's interests, we must do so solely on the basis of the merits and pursuant to proper procedures in dealing with such officials. Employees may not offer, provide, or solicit, directly or indirectly, any special treatment or favor in return for anything of economic value or the promise or expectation of future value or gain. In addition, there shall be no entertaining of employees of the U.S. government.

Foreign Corrupt Practices Act

No employee will engage in activity that might involve the employee or the company in a violation of the Foreign Corrupt Practices Act of 1977. The Foreign Corrupt Practices Act requires that the company's books and records accurately and fairly reflect all transactions and that we maintain a system of internal controls, transactions conform to management's authorizations, and the accounting records are accurate. No employee will falsely report transactions or fail to report the existence of false transactions in the accounting records. Employees certifying the correctness of records, including vouchers or bills, should have reasonable knowledge that the information is correct and proper.

Under the act it is also a federal crime for any U.S. business enterprise to offer a gift, payment, or bribe, or anything else of value, whether directly or indirectly, to any foreign official, foreign political party or party official, or candidate for foreign political office for the purpose of influencing an official act or decision or seeking influence with a foreign government in order to obtain, retain, or direct business to the company or to any person. Even if the payment is legal in the host country, it is forbidden by the act and violates U.S. law.

CONFLICTS OF INTEREST

There are several situations that could give rise to a conflict of interest. The most common are accepting gifts from suppliers, employment by another company, ownership of a significant part of another company or business, close or family relationships with outside suppliers, and communications with competitors. A potential conflict of interest exists for employees who make decisions in their jobs that would allow them to give preference or favor to a customer in exchange for anything of personal benefit to themselves or their friends and families.

Such situations could interfere with an employee's ability to make judgments solely in the company's best interest.

Gifts and Entertainment

Definition of "Gifts"

"Gifts" are items and services of value that are given to any outside parties but do not include items described under items 1, 2, 3, and 4 below.

1. Normal business entertainment items, such as meals and beverages, are not to be considered "gifts."

2. Items of minimal value, given in connection with sales campaigns and promotions or employee services, safety, or retirement awards, are not to be considered "gifts" for purposes of this code.

3. Contributions or donations to recognized charitable and nonprofit organizations are not considered gifts.

4. Items or services with a total value under $100 per year are excluded.

Definition of "Supplier"

"Supplier" includes not only vendors providing services and material to the company but also consultants, financial institutions, advisors, and any person or institution that does business with the company.

Gifts

No employee or member of his or her immediate family shall solicit or accept from an actual or prospective customer or supplier any compensation, advance loans (except from established financial institutions on the same basis as other customers), gifts, entertainment, or other favors that are of more than token value or that the employee would not normally be in a position to reciprocate under normal expense account procedures.

Under no circumstances should a gift or entertainment be accepted that would influence the employee's judgment. In particular, employees must avoid any interest in or benefit from any supplier that could reasonably cause them to favor that supplier over others. It is a violation of the code for any employee to solicit or encourage a supplier to give any item or service to the employee regardless of its value, no matter how small. Our suppliers will retain their confidence in the objectivity and integrity of our company only if each employee strictly observes this guideline.

Reporting Gifts

An employee who receives, or whose family member receives, an unsolicited gift prohibited by these guidelines should report it to his or her supervisor and either return it to the person making the gift or, in the case of perishable gift, give it to a nonprofit charitable organization.

Discounts

An employee may accept discounts on a personal purchase of the supplier's or customer's products only if such discounts do not affect the company's purchase price and generally are offered to others having a similar business relationship with the supplier or customer.

Business Meetings

Entertainment and services offered by a supplier or customer may be accepted by an employee when they are associated with a business meeting and the supplier or customer provides them to others as a normal part of its business. Examples of such entertainment and services are transportation to and from the supplier's or customer's place of business, hospitality suites, golf outings, lodging at the supplier's or customer's place of business, and business lunches and dinners for business visitors to the supplier's or customer's location. The services generally should be of the type normally used by the company's employees and allowable under the applicable company's expense account.

Outside Employment

Employees must not be employed outside the company (1) in any business that competes with or provides services to the company or its subsidiaries, and/or (2) in a manner that would affect their objectivity in carrying out their company responsibilities, and/or (3) where the outside employment would conflict with scheduled hours, including overtime, or the performance of the company assignments. Employees must not use company time, materials, information, or other assets in connection with outside employment.

Relationships with Suppliers and Customers

Business transactions must be entered into solely for the best interests of the company. No employee can, directly or indirectly, benefit from his or her position as an employee or from any sale, purchase, or other activity of the company. Employees should avoid situations involving a conflict or the appearance of conflict between duty to the company and self-interest.

No employee who deals with individuals or organizations doing or seeking to do business with the company, or who makes recommendations with respect to such dealings, should:

- Serve as an officer, director, employee, or consultant.
- Own a substantial interest in any competitor of the company, or any organization doing or seeking to do business with the company. "Substantial interest" means an economic interest that might influence or reasonably be thought to influence judgment or action but shall not include an investment representing less than 1 percent of a class of outstanding securities of a publicly held corporation. The Conflict of Interest Questionnaire included with this book must be completed by every employee.

In addition, no employee who deals with individuals or organizations doing or seeking to do business with the company, or who makes recommendations with respect to such dealings, may:

- Have any other direct or indirect personal interest in any business transactions with the company (other than customary employee purchases of company products and services as consumers and transactions where the interest arises solely by reason of the employee relationship or that of a holder of securities).

- Provide telecommunications or information service or equipment, either directly or as a resaler in a manner that would place the objectivity or integrity of the company in question.

Our policy is that employees will not do business on behalf of the company with a close personal friend or relative; however, recognizing that these transactions do occur, they must be reported on the Conflict of Interest Questionnaire.

This policy is applicable equally to the members of the immediate family of each employee, which normally includes your spouse, children and their spouses, and the father, mother, sisters, and brothers of yourself and your household.

Employment of Relatives

Relatives of employees will not be employed on a permanent or temporary basis by the company where the relative directly reports to the employee or the employee exercises any direct influence with respect to the relative's hiring, placement, promotions, evaluations, or pay.

Confidential Information and Privacy of Communications

Confidential Information

Confidential information includes all information, whether technical, business, financial, or otherwise concerning the company, that the company treats as confidential or secret and/or that is not available or is not made available publicly. It also includes any private information of or relating to customer records, fellow employees, other persons or other companies, and national security information obtained by virtue of the employee's position.

Company policy and various laws protect the integrity of the company's confidential information that must not be divulged except in strict accordance with established company policies and procedures. The obligation not to divulge confidential company information is in effect even though material might not be specifically identified as confidential, and the obligation exists during and continues after employment with the company.

A few examples of prohibited conduct are: (a) selling or otherwise using, divulging, or transmitting confidential company information; (b) using confidential company information to knowingly convert a company business opportunity for personal use; (c) using confidential company information to acquire real estate that the employee knows is of interest to the company; (d) using, divulging, or transmitting confidential company information in the course of outside employment or other relationship or any succeeding employment or other relationship at any time; (e) trading in the company stocks, or the stocks of any company, based on information that has not been disclosed to the public or divulging such information to others so that they might trade in such stock. Insider trading is prohibited by company policy and federal and state law.

Employees shall not seek out, accept, or use any confidential company information of or from a competitor of the company. In particular, should we hire an employee who previously worked for a competitor, we must neither accept not solicit confidential information concerning that competitor from our employee.

Classified National Security Information

Only employees with proper government clearance and a need to know have access to classified national security information. Government regulations outlined in company instructions for safeguarding information must be followed. Disclosing such information, without authorization, even after leaving employment, is a violation of law and this code.

Adverse information about employees having government clearance must be reported to the security or law department's representatives having responsibility for clearances.

COMPANY ASSETS

Cash and Bank Accounts

All cash and bank account transactions must be handled so as to avoid any question or suspicion of impropriety. All cash transactions must be recorded in the company's books of account.

All accounts of company funds, except authorized imprest funds, shall be established and maintained in the name of the company or one of its subsidiaries and may be opened or closed only on the authority of the company's board of directors. Imprest funds must be maintained in the name of the custodian and the custodian is wholly responsible for these funds. All cash received shall be promptly recorded and deposited in a company or subsidiary bank account. No funds shall be maintained in the form of cash, except authorized petty cash, and no company shall maintain an anonymous (numbered) account at any bank. Payments into numbered bank accounts by the company might leave that company open to suspicion of participation in a possibly improper transaction. Therefore, no disbursements of any nature may be made into numbered bank accounts or other accounts not clearly identified to the company as to their ownership.

No payments can be made in cash (currency) other than regular, approved cash payrolls and normal disbursements from petty cash supported by signed receipts or other appropriate documentation. Further, corporate checks shall not be written to "cash," "bearer," or similar designations.

Company Assets and Transactions

Compliance with prescribed accounting procedures is required at all times. Employees having control over company assets and transactions are expected to handle them with the strictest integrity and to ensure that all transactions are executed in accordance with management's authorization. All transactions shall be accurately and fairly recorded in reasonable detail in the company's accounting records.

Employees are personally accountable for company funds over which they have control. Employees who spend company funds should ensure that the company receives good value in return and must maintain accurate records of such expenditures. Employees who approve or certify the correctness of a bill or voucher should know that the purchase and amount are proper and correct. Obtaining or creating "false" invoices or other misleading documentation or the invention or use of fictitious sales, purchases, services, loans entities, or other financial arrangements is prohibited.

Employees must pay for personal telephone calls and use, except to the extent that specifically defined benefit programs or allowances provide otherwise.

Expense Reimbursement

Expenses actually incurred by an employee in performing company business must be documented on expense reports in accordance with company procedures. In preparing expense reports, employees should review these procedures for the documentation that must be submitted in order to be reimbursed for business expenses.

Company Credit Cards

Company credit cards are provided to employees for convenience in conducting company business. No personal expenses can be charged on company credit cards except as specifically authorized by company procedures. Any charged personal expenses must be paid promptly by the employee. Company credit cards should not be used to avoid preparing documentation for direct payment to vendors. Where allowed by local law, charges on company credit cards for which a properly approved expense report has not been received at the time of an employee's termination of employment may be deducted from the employee's last paycheck. The company will pursue repayment by the employee of any amounts it has to pay on the employee's behalf.

Software and Computers

Computerized information and computer software appear intangible, but they are valuable assets of the company and must be protected from misuse, theft, fraud, loss, and unauthorized use or disposal, just as any other company property.

Use of computers must be customer service or job related. Employees cannot access company records of any kind for their personal use. Misappropriation of computer space, time, or software includes, but is not limited to, using a computer to create or run unauthorized jobs, operating a computer in an unauthorized mode, or intentionally causing any kind of operational failure.

Personal computers can be used for company-sanctioned education programs as well as personal use incidental to company business use with the permission of your supervisor. However, personal use cannot be allowed for personal financial gain.

It is also understood that personal computers occasionally will be used at home with the permission of your supervisor.

POLITICAL CONTRIBUTIONS

Federal law and many state laws prohibit contributions by corporations to political parties or candidates. The term "political contributions" includes, in addition to direct cash contributions, the donation of property or services and the purchases of tickets to fund-raising events. Employees can make direct contributions of their own money, but such contributions are not reimbursable. In addition, employees can make contributions to a company-sponsored political action committee (PAC).

Where corporate political contributions are legal in connection with state, local, or foreign elections, such contribution shall be made only from funds allocated for that purpose and with the written approval of the president of the company making the contribution. The amounts of contributions made shall be subject to intercompany allocation.

It is improper for an employee to use his or her position within the company to solicit political contributions from another employee for the purpose of supporting a political candidate or influencing legislation. It is also improper for an employee to make a political contribution in the name of the company.

EMPLOYEE CONDUCT

Conduct on Company Business

Dishonest or illegal activities on company premises or while on company business will not be condoned and can result in disciplinary action, including dismissal and criminal prosecution. The next list illustrates activities that are against company policy and that will not be tolerated on company premises, in company vehicles, or while engaged in company business:

1. Consumption and storage of alcoholic beverages, except where legally licensed or authorized by an officer of the company.
2. The use of controlled substances, such as drugs or alcohol. The unlawful manufacture, distribution, dispensation, possession, transfer, sale, purchase, or use of a controlled substance.
3. Driving vehicles or operating company equipment while under the influence of alcohol or controlled substances.
4. Illegal betting or gambling.
5. Carrying weapons of any sort on company premises, in company vehicles, or while on company business. Even employees with permits or licenses cannot carry weapons on company property or while on company business.

The company reserves the right to inspect any property that might be used by employees for the storage of their personal effects. This includes desks, lockers, and vehicles owned by the company. It is a violation of company policy to store any contraband, illegal drugs, toxic materials, or weapons on company property.

Reporting Violations

All employees are responsible for compliance with these rules, standards, and principles. In the area of ethics, legality, and propriety, each employee has an obligation to the company that transcends normal reporting relationships. Employees should be alert to possible violations of the code anywhere in the company and are encouraged to report such violations promptly. Reports should be made to the employee's supervisor; the appropriate security, audit, or legal department personnel; or elsewhere as the circumstances dictate. Employees also will be expected to cooperate in an investigation of violations.

All cases of questionable activity involving the code or other potentially improper actions will be reviewed for appropriate action, discipline, or corrective steps. Whenever possible, the company will keep confidential the identity of employees about or against whom allegations of violations are brought, unless or until it has been determined that a violation has occurred. Similarly, whenever possible, the company will keep confidential the identity of anyone reporting a possible violation. Reprisal against any employee who has, in good faith, reported a violation or suspected violation is strictly prohibited.

All employees are required to notify the company within five (5) days of any conviction of any criminal statute violation occurring on the job. In addition, any employee who is convicted of a felony, whether related to these rules or not, should report that fact.

Discipline

Violation of this code can result in serious consequences for the company, its image, credibility, and confidence of its customers, and can include substantial fines and restrictions on future operations as well as the possibility of fines and prison sentences for individual employees. Therefore, it is necessary that the company ensure that there will be no violations. Employees should recognize that it is in their best interest, as well as the company's, to follow this code carefully.

The amount of any money involved in a violation might be immaterial in assessing the seriousness of a violation since, in some cases, heavy penalties might be assessed against the company for a violation involving a relatively small amount of money or no money.

Disciplinary action should be coordinated with the appropriate Human Resources representatives. The overall seriousness of the matter will be considered in setting the disciplinary action to be taken against an individual employee. Such action, which might be reviewed with the appropriate Human Resources organization, might include:

- Reprimand
- Probation
- Suspension
- Reduction in salary
- Demotion

- A combination of the above
- Dismissal

In addition, individual cases might involve:

- Reimbursement of losses or damages
- Referral for criminal prosecution or civil action
- A combination of the above

Disciplinary action also might be taken against supervisors or executives who condone, permit, or have knowledge of illegal or unethical conduct by those reporting to them and do not take corrective action. Disciplinary action also might be taken against employees who make false statements in connection with investigations of violations of this code.

The disciplinary action appropriate to a given matter will be determined by the company in its sole discretion. The listing of possible actions is informative only and does not bind the company to follow any particular disciplinary steps, process, or procedure.

The company's rules and regulations regarding proper employee conduct will not be waived in any respect. Violation is cause for disciplinary action, including dismissal. All employees will be held to the standards of conduct described in this booklet.

The company never has and never will authorize any employee to commit an act that violates this code or to direct a subordinate to do so. With that understood, it is not possible to justify commission of such an act by saying it was directed by someone in higher management.

COMPLIANCE LETTER AND CONFLICT OF INTEREST QUESTIONNAIRE

Annually, all officers of the company will represent in writing that there are no violations of this code known to the officer, after the exercise of reasonable diligence, or if such violations have been committed, to disclose such violations in a format to be specified.

Annually, each employee will review the Code of Business Ethics and Conduct, sign the code's Acknowledgment form, and complete and sign the Conflict of Interest Questionnaire. If the employee's circumstances change at any time, a new Conflict of Interest Questionnaire or letter of explanation must be completed.

The Code of Business Ethics and Conduct Acknowledgment form should be signed and given to your supervisor for inclusion in your personnel file.

Albrecht, W. Steve, Conan C. Albrecht, Chad O. Albrecht, and Mark F. Zimbelman. *Fraud Examination*, 3rd ed. Mason, OH: South-Western, 2009.

Albrecht, W. Steve, Keith R. Howe, and Marshall B. Romney. *Deterring Fraud: The Internal Auditor's Perspective*. Altamonte Springs, FL: Institute of Internal Auditors Research Foundation, 1984.

Albrecht, W. Steve, Gerald W. Wernz, and Timothy L. Williams. *Fraud: Bringing Light to the Dark Side of Business*. New York: Irwin Professional, 1995.

Albrecht, W. Steve, Marshal B. Romney, David J. Cherrington, I. Reed Payne, and Allan J. Roe. *How to Detect and Prevent Business Fraud*. Englewood Cliffs, NJ: Prentice-Hall, 1982.

American Accounting Association. *Accounting Education*, 18, no. 2. Sarasota, FL: Author, 2003.

American Accounting Association. *Accounting Horizons*, 7, no. 4. Sarasota, FL: Author, 2003.

American Accounting Association. *Auditing: A Journal of Practice & Theory*, 22, no. 2. Sarasota, FL: Author, 2003.

American Institute of Certified Public Accountants,

Statements on Auditing Standards. "Responsibilities and Functions of the Independent Auditor," SAS 1 (AU 110).

———. "Illegal Acts by Clients," SAS 54 (AU 317).

———. "Auditing Accounting Estimates," SAS 57 (AU 342).

———. "Special Reports," SAS 62 (AU 623).

———. "Compliance Auditing Considerations in Audits of Governmental Entities and Recipients of Governmental Financial Assistance," SAS 74 (AU 801).

———. "Communications Between Predecessor and Successor Auditors," SAS 84 (AU 315).

———. "Consideration of Fraud in a Financial Statement Audit," SAS 99 (AU 316).

———. "Planning and Supervision," SAS 108 (AU 311).

———. "The Auditor's Communication with Those Charged With Governance," SAS 114 (AU 380).

Androphy, Joel M. *White Collar Crime*. New York: McGraw-Hill, 1992.

Antle, Rick, and Stanley J. Garstka. *Financial Accounting*. Cincinnati, OH: South-Western, 2002.

Arens, Alvin A., Randal J. Elder, and Mark S. Beasley. *Essential Auditing and Assurance Services: An Integrated Approach*. Upper Saddle River, NJ: Prentice Hall, 2003.

Associated Press. "Software Executive Pleads Guilty to Stock Fraud." *USA Today*, January 31, 1997.

Association of Certified Fraud Examiners. *2010 ACFE Report to the Nations on Occupational Fraud and Abuse*. Austin, TX: ACFE, 2010.

———. *Fraud Examiners' Manual*. Austin, TX: ACFE, 2011.

———. Report to the Nation on Occupational Fraud and Abuse. Austin, TX: ACFE, 1996.

Banks, David G. "Vendor Fraud: Finding Deals Gone Awry," *White Paper* 16, no. 5 (September/October 2002).

Beasley, M. S., J. V. Carcello, and D. R. Hermanson. *Fraudulent Financial Reporting 1987-1997: An Analysis of U.S. Public Companies*. Committee of Sponsoring Organizations, 1999.

Beasley, M. S., J. V. Carcello, D. R. Hermanson, and T. L. Neal. *Fraudulent Financial Reporting 1998-2007: An Analysis of U.S. Public Companies*. Committee of Sponsoring Organizations of the Treadway Commission, 2010.

Beckett, Paul. "SEC, Publisher of On-Line Newsletter Settle Fraud Case Involving the Internet," *Wall Street Journal*, February 26, 1997.

Bintliff, Russell L. *White Collar Crime Detection and Prevention*. Englewood Cliffs, NJ: Prentice Hall, 1993.

Binstein, Michael, and Charles Bowden. *Trust Me: Charles Keating and the Missing Millions*. New York: Random House, 1993.

Biegelman, Martin T. "Designing a Robust Fraud Prevention Program, Part One," *White Paper* 18, no. 1 (January/February 2004).

———. "Sarbanes-Oxley Act: Stopping U.S. Corporate Crooks from Cooking the Books," *White Paper* 17, no. 2 (March/April 2003).

Bishop, Toby J. F., and Joseph T. Wells. "Breaking Tradition in the Auditing Profession," *White Paper* 17, no. 5 (September/October 2003).

Black, Henry Campbell. *Black's Law Dictionary*, 5th ed. St. Paul, MN: West, 1979.

Bliven, Bruce. "The Tempest over Teapot," *American Heritage* (September/October 1995).

Blount, Ernest C. *Occupational Crime: Deterrence, Investigation, and Reporting; in Compliance with Federal Guidelines*. Boca Raton, FL: CRC Press, 2003.

Bologna, Jack. *Corporate Fraud: The Basics of Prevention and Detection*. Boston: Butterworth-Heinemann, 1984.

Bologna, Jack. *Handbook on Corporate Fraud*. Boston: Butterworth-Heinemann, 1993.

Bologna, Jack, and Robert J. Lindquist. *Fraud Auditing and Forensic Accounting*. New York: John Wiley & Sons, 1987.

Bonner, S. E., Z. V. Palmrose, and S. M. Young. "Fraud Type and Auditor Litigation: An Analysis of SEC Accounting and Auditing Enforcement Releases," *Accounting Review*, no. 73 (October 1998).

Brian, Brad D., and Barry F. McNeil. *Internal Corporate Investigations*, 2nd Ed. Chicago: ABA, 2003.

Brickner, Daniel R. "SAS 99: Another Implement for the Fraud Examiner's Toolbox," *White Paper* 17, no. 3 (May/June 2003).

Caplan, Gerald M. *ABSCAM Ethics: Moral Issues & Deception in Law Enforcement.* Cambridge, MA: Ballinger, 1983.

Carozza, Dick. "Accounting Students Must Have Armor of Fraud Examination," *White Paper* 16, no. 1 (January/February 2002).

Clarke, Michael. *Business Crime: Its Nature and Control.* New York: St. Martin's Press, 1990.

Clarkson, Kenneth W., Roger LeRoy Miller, and Gaylord A. Jentz. *West's Business Law: Text & Cases*, 3rd ed. St. Paul, MN: West, 1986.

Clinard, Marshall B., and Peter C. Yeager. *Corporate Crime.* New York: Macmillan, 1980.

Coderre, David G. *Computer-Aided Fraud Prevention & Detection: A Step-by-Step Guide.* Hoboken, NJ: John Wiley & Sons, 2009.

Comer, Michael J. *Corporate Fraud.* Aldershot, UK: Network Security Management, 1998.

Comer, Michael J. *Investigating Corporate Fraud.* Aldershot, UK: Gower, 2003.

Cook, Larry E. "Risky Business: Conducting the Internal Fraud Risk Assessment," *Fraud Magazine* (March/April 2005).

Cressey, Donald R. *Other People's Money.* Montclair, NJ: Patterson Smith, 1953.

Davia, Howard R., Patrick C. Coggins, John C. Wideman, and Joseph T. Kastantin. *Accountant's Guide to Fraud Detection and Control*, 2nd ed. New York: John Wiley & Sons, 2000.

Davis, Robert C., Arthur J. Lurigio, and Wesley G. Skogan, eds. *Victims of Crime*, 2nd ed. Thousand Oaks, CA: Sage Publications, 1997.

Dean, Bruce A. "Wrap It Up: Packing Your Case for Prosecution." The *White Paper* 16, no. 1 (January/February 2002).

Department of the Treasury, Internal Revenue Service. *Financial Investigations: A Financial Approach to Detecting and Resolving Crimes.* Washington, DC: U.S. Government Printing Office, 1993.

Dirks, Raymond L., and Leonard Gross. *The Great Wall Street Scandal.* New York: McGraw-Hill, 1974.

Drake, John D. *The Effective Interviewer: A Guide for Managers.* New York: AMACOM, 1989.

Ermann, M. David, and Richard J. Lundman. *Corporate Deviance.* New York: Holt Rinehart and Winston, 1982.

Financial Accounting Standards Board. *Accounting Standards Codification* (ASC). Norwalk, CT: Financial Accounting Foundation.

———. ASC Topic 225, "Income Statement."

———. ASC Topic 250, "Accounting Changes and Error Corrections."

———. ASC Topic 350, "Intangibles—Goodwill and Other."

———. ASC Topic 450, "Contingencies."

———. ASC Topic 605, "Revenue Recognition."

———. ASC Topic 730, "Research and Development."

———. ASC Topic 820, "Fair Value Measurements and Disclosures."

Financial Accounting Standards Board. *Concepts Statements.* Norwalk, CT: Financial Accounting Foundation.

———. "Qualitative Characteristics of Accounting Information," Concepts Statement no. 2.

———. "Recognition and Measurement in Financial Statements of Business Enterprises," Concepts Statement no. 5.

———. "Elements of Financial Statements," Concepts Statement no. 6.

Flesher, Dale L., Paul J. Miranti, and Gary John Previts. "The First Century of the CPA," *Journal of Accountancy* (October 1996).

Fusaro, Peter C., and Ross M. Miller. *What Went Wrong at Enron.* Hoboken, NJ: John Wiley & Sons, 2002.

Fridson, Martin S. *Financial Statement Analysis.* New York: John Wiley & Sons, 1991.

Gardner, Dale R. "Teapot Dome: Civil Legal Cases that Closed the Scandal," *Journal of the West* (October 1989).

Gaughan, Patrick A. *Measuring Business Interruption Losses and Other Commercial Damages.* Hoboken, NJ: John Wiley & Sons, 2004.

Geis, Gilbert. *On White-Collar Crime.* Lexington, MA: Lexington Books, 1982.

Geis, Gilbert, and Robert F. Meier. *White-Collar Crime: Offenses in Business, Politics, and the Professions.* Rev. ed. New York: Free Press, 1977.

Georgiades, George. *Audit Procedures.* New York: Harcourt Brace Professional Publishing, 1995.

Green, Scott. *Manager's Guide to the Sarbanes-Oxley Act: Improving Internal Controls to Prevent Fraud.* Hoboken, NJ: John Wiley & Sons, 2004.

Greene, Craig L. "Audit Those Vendors," *White Paper* 17, no. 3 (May/June 2003).

———. "When Employees Count Too Much," *White Paper* 16, no. 6 (November/December 2002).

Hall, Jerome. *Theft, Law and Society*, 2nd ed. 1960.

Hayes, Read. *Retail Security and Loss Prevention.* Stoneham, MA: Butterworth-Heinemann, 1991.

Hubbard, Thomas D., and Johnny R. Johnson. *Auditing*, 4th ed. Houston: Dame Publications, 1991.

Hylas, R. E., and R. H. Ashton. "Audit Detection of Financial Statement Errors," *Accounting Review* 57, no. 4.

Inbau, Fred E., John E. Reid, and Joseph P. Buckley. *Criminal Interrogation and Confessions.* Baltimore: Wilkins, 1986.

Ingram, Donna. "Revenue Inflation and Deflation," *White Paper* 16, no. 6 (November/December 2002).

Inkeles, Alex. *National Character: A Psycho-Social Perspective*. New Brunswick, NJ: Transaction Publishers, 1997.

Institute of Internal Auditors. *Standards for the Professional Practices of Internal Auditing*. Altamonte Springs, FL: Author, 1978.

Kant, Immanuel. *Lectures on Ethics*. New York: Harper & Row, 1963.

Ketz, J. Edward. *Hidden Financial Risks: Understanding Off-Balance-Sheet Accounting*. Hoboken, NJ: John Wiley & Sons, 2003.

Kimmel, Paul D., Jerry J. Weygandt, and Donald E. Kieso. *Financial Accounting: Tools for Business Decision Making*, 3rd ed. Hoboken, NJ: John Wiley & Sons, 2004.

Koletar, Joseph W. *Fraud Exposed: What You Don't Know Could Cost Your Company Millions*. Hoboken, NJ: John Wiley & Sons, 2003.

Langsted, Lars B., Peter Garde, and Vagn Greve, *Criminal Law Denmark*, 2nd ed. Copenhagen: DJOF, 2004.

Lanza, Richard B. *Proactively Detecting Occupational Fraud Using Computer Audit Reports*. IIA Research Foundation, 2003.

Lundelius, Charles R. Jr. *Financial Reporting Fraud: A Practical Guide to Detection and Internal Control*. New York: AICPA, 2003.

Mancino, Jane. "The Auditor and Fraud," *Journal of Accountancy* (April 1997).

Marcella, Albert J., William J. Samplas, and James K. Kincaid. *The Hunt for Fraud: Prevention and Detection Techniques*. Altamonte Springs, FL: Institute of Internal Auditors, 1994.

Marshall, David H., and Wayne W. McManus. *Accounting: What the Numbers Mean*, 3rd ed. Chicago: Irwin, 1996.

Mee, Charles L. Jr. *The Ohio Gang: The World of Warren G. Harding*. New York: M. Evans, 1981.

Merriam-Webster's Collegiate Dictionary, 11th ed. Springfield, MA: Merriam-Webster, 2008.

Mill, John Stuart. *Utilitarianism*. Indianapolis: Bobbs-Merrill, 1957.

Miller, Norman C. *The Great Salad Oil Swindle*. Baltimore: Penguin Books, 1965.

Moritz, Scott. "Don't Get Burned by Smiling CEO Candidates," *White Paper* 16, no. 5 (September/October 2002).

Nash, Jay Robert. *Hustlers and Con Men: An Anecdotal History of the Confidence Man and His Games*. New York: Lippincott, 1976.

National Commission on Fraudulent Financial Reporting. *Report of the National Commission on Fraudulent Financial Reporting*. New York: American Institute of Certified Public Accountants, 1987.

Noonan, John T. Jr. *Bribes*. New York: Macmillan, 1984.

O'Brian, Keith. *Cut Your Losses!* Bellingham, WA: International Self-Press, 1996.

O'Gara, John D. *Corporate Fraud: Case Studies in Detection and Prevention*. Hoboken, NJ: John Wiley & Sons, Inc., 2004.

Patterson, James, and Peter Kim. *The Day America Told the Truth*. New York: Prentice Hall, 1991.

Rabon, Don. *Investigative Discourse Analysis*. Durham: Carolina Academic Press, 1994.

Rakoff, Jed S., Linda R. Blumkin, and Richard A. Sauber. *Corporate Sentencing Guidelines: Compliance and Mitigation*. New York: Law Journal Press, 2002.

Ramos, Michael J. *Consideration of Fraud in a Financial Statement Audit: The Auditor's Responsibilities Under New SAS No. 82*. New York: American Institute of Certified Public Accountants, 1997.

———. *How to Comply with Sarbanes-Oxley Section 404: Assessing the Effectiveness of Internal Control*. Hoboken, NJ: John Wiley & Sons, 2004.

Rezaee, Zabiollah. *Financial Statement Fraud: Prevention and Detection*. Hoboken, NJ: John Wiley & Sons, 2002.

Robertson, Jack C. *Auditing*, 7th ed. Boston: BPI Irwin, 1991.

———. *Fraud Examination for Managers and Auditors*. Austin, TX: Association of Certified Fraud Examiners, 1996.

Romney, Marshall B., W. Steve Albrecht, and D. J. Cherrington. "Red-Flagging the White-Collar Criminal," *Management Accounting* (March 1980).

Sarnoff, Susan K. *Paying for Crime*. Westport, CT: Praeger, 1996.

Securities and Exchange Commission. "Staff Accounting Bulletin No. 104: Revenue Recognition, Corrected Copy," 2003.

Seidler, Lee J., Fredrick Andrews, and Marc J. Epstein. *The Equity Funding Papers: The Anatomy of a Fraud*. New York: John Wiley & Sons, 1997.

Sharp, Kathleen. *In Good Faith*. New York: St. Martin's Press, 1995.

Siegel, Larry J. *Criminology*, 4th ed. New York: West, 1992.

Silverstone, Howard, and Michael Sheetz. *Forensic Accounting and Fraud Investigation for Non-Experts*. Hoboken, NJ: John Wiley & Sons, 2004.

Snyder, Neil H., O. Whitfield, William J. Kehoe, James T. McIntyre, Jr., and Karen E. Blair. *Reducing Employee Theft: A Guide to Financial and Organizational Controls*. New York: Quorum Books, 1991.

Summerford, Ralph Q., and Robin E. Taylor. "Avoiding Embezzlement Embarrassment (and Worse)," *White Paper* 17, no. 6 (November/December 2003).

Sutherland, Edwin H. *White-Collar Crime*. New York: Dryden Press, 1949.

Thomas, William C. "The Rise and Fall of Enron," *Journal of Accountancy* (April 2002).

Thornhill, William T. *Forensic Accounting: How to Investigate Financial Fraud*. Burr Ridge, IL: Irwin Professional, 1995.

Tyler, Tom R. *Why People Obey the Law*. New Haven, CT: Yale University Press, 1990.

United States Central Intelligence Agency. *The World Factbook*.www.cia.gov/library/publications/the-world-factbook/.

United States General Accounting Office. *Financial Statement Restatements: Trends, Market Impacts, Regulatory Responses, and Remaining Challenges*, GAO-03-138, 2002.

Van Drunen, Guido. "Traveling the World in Style on the Company's Nickel," *White Paper* 16, no. 1 (January/February 2002).

Vaughan, Diane. *Controlling Unlawful Organizational Behavior*. Chicago: University of Chicago Press, 1983.

Watson, Douglas M. "Whom Do You Trust? Doing Business and Deterring Fraud; in a Global e-Marketplace," *White Paper* 16, no. 2 (March/April 2002).

Wells, Joseph T. " . . . And Nothing But the Truth: Uncovering Fraudulent Disclosures," *Journal of Accountancy* (July 2001).

————— " . . . And One for Me," *Journal of Accountancy* (January 2002).

————— "Accountancy and White-Collar Crime," *Annals of the American Academy of Political and Social Science* (January 1993).

————— "Billing Schemes, Part 1: Shell Companies that Don't Deliver," *Journal of Accountancy* (July 2002).

————— "Billing Schemes, Part 2: Pass-Throughs," *Journal of Accountancy* (August 2002).

————— "Billing Schemes, Part 3: Pay- and-Return Invoicing," *Journal of Accountancy* (September 2002).

—————. "Billing Schemes, Part 4: Personal Purchases," *Journal of Accountancy* (October 2002).

—————. "The Billion Dollar Paper Clip," *Internal Auditor* (October 1994).

—————. "Collaring Crime at Work," *Certified Accountant* (August 1996).

—————. *Computer Fraud Casebook: The Bytes that Bite*. Hoboken, NJ: John Wiley & Sons, 2009.

—————. "Control Cash-Register Thievery," *Journal of Accountancy* (June 2002).

—————. *Corporate Fraud Handbook*, 2nd ed. Hoboken, NJ: John Wiley & Sons, 2007.

—————. "Corruption: Causes and Cures," *Journal of Accountancy* (April 2003).

—————. *The Encyclopedia of Fraud*. Austin, TX: Obsidian, 2002.

—————. "Enemies Within," *Journal of Accountancy* (December 2001).

—————. "A Fish Story—or Not?" *Journal of Accountancy* (November 2001).

—————. "Follow Fraud to the Likely Perp," *Journal of Accountancy* (March 2001).

—————. "Follow the Greenback Road," *Journal of Accountancy* (November 2003).

—————. "Fraud Assessment Questioning," *Internal Auditor* (August 1992).

—————. "The Fraud Examiners," *Journal of Accountancy* (October 2003).

—————. *Fraud Casebook: Lessons from the Bad Side of Business*. Hoboken, NJ: John Wiley & Sons, 2007.

—————. *Fraud Examination: Investigative and Audit Procedures*. New York: Quorum Books, 1992.

—————. "Getting a Handle on a Hostile Interview," *Security Management* (July 1992).

————. "Ghost Goods: How to Spot Phantom Inventory," *Journal of Accountancy* (June 2001).

————. " . . . Irrational Ratios," *Journal of Accountancy* (August 2001).

————. "Keep Ghosts Off the Payroll," *Journal of Accountancy* (December 2002).

————. "Lambs to Slaughter," *Internal Auditor* (June 2003).

————. "Lapping It Up," *Journal of Accountancy* (February 2002).

————. "Let Them Know Someone's Watching," *Journal of Accountancy* (May 2002).

————. "Money Laundering: Ring Around the Collar," *Journal of Accountancy* (June 2003).

————. "Occupational Fraud: The Audit as Deterrent," *Journal of Accountancy* (April 2002).

————. *Occupational Fraud and Abuse.* Austin, TX: Obsidian, 1997.

————. "The Padding that Hurts," *Journal of Accountancy* (February 2003).

————. "Protect Small Business," *Journal of Accountancy* (March 2003).

————. "The Rewards of Dishonesty," *White Paper* 17, no. 2 (March/April 2003).

————. "Rules for the Written Record," *Journal of Accountancy* (December 2003).

————. "Sherlock Holmes, CPA, Part 1," *Journal of Accountancy* (August 2003).

————. "Sherlock Holmes, CPA, Part 2," *Journal of Accountancy* (September 2003).

————. "Six Common Myths about Fraud," *Journal of Accountancy* (February 1990).

————. "So, You Want to be a Fraud Examiner," *Accounting Today*, December 16, 2002.

————. "Sons of Enron," *MWorld* 2, no. 1 (Spring 2003).

————. "Ten Steps Into a Top-Notch Interview," *Journal of Accountancy* (November 2002).

————. "Timing is of the Essence," *Journal of Accountancy* (May 2001).

————. "Why Ask? You Ask," *Journal of Accountancy* (September 2001).

————. "Why Employees Commit Fraud," *Journal of Accountancy* (February 2001).

————. "The World's Dumbest Fraudsters," *Journal of Accountancy* (May 2003).

Wells, Joseph T., Tedd A. Avey, G. Jack Bologna, and Robert J. Lindquist. *The Accountant's Handbook of Fraud and Commercial Crime.* Toronto: Canadian Institute of Chartered Accountants, 1992.

Welsch, Glenn A., D. Paul Newman, and Charles T. Zlatkovich. *Intermediate Accounting*, 7th ed. Homewood, IL: Irwin, 1986.

Wojcik, Lawrence A. "Sensational Cases and the Mundane—Lessons to Be Learned," First Annual Conference on Fraud, The American Institute of Certified Public Accountants, 1996.

Zack, Gerard M. *Fraud and Abuse in Nonprofit Organizations: A Guide to Prevention and Detection.* Hoboken, NJ: John Wiley & Sons, 2003.